THE NEW NATURALIST LIBRARY

A SURVEY OF BRITISH NATURAL HISTORY

OWLS

EDITORS
SARAH A. CORBET, ScD
DAVID STREETER, MBE, FIBiol
JIM FLEGG, OBE, FIHort
Prof. JONATHAN SILVERTOWN

*

The aim of this series is to interest the general
reader in the wildlife of Britain by recapturing
the enquiring spirit of the old naturalists.
The editors believe that the natural pride of
the British public in the native flora and fauna,
to which must be added concern for their
conservation, is best fostered by maintaining
a high standard of accuracy combined with
clarity of exposition in presenting the results
of modern scientific research.

THE NEW NATURALIST LIBRARY

OWLS

A Natural History of the British and Irish Species

MIKE TOMS

WILLIAM
COLLINS

This edition published in 2014 by William Collins,
An imprint of HarperCollins Publishers

HarperCollins Publishers
77–85 Fulham Palace Road
London W6 8JB
WilliamCollinsBooks.com

First published 2014

© Mike Toms, 2014

A CIP catalogue record for this book is available
from the British Library.

Set in FF Nexus, designed and produced by
Tom Cabot/ketchup

All photos by the author unless otherwise credited.

Printed in Hong Kong by Printing Express

Hardback
ISBN 978-0-00-742555-6
Paperback
ISBN 978-0-00-742557-0

Contents

Editors' Preface

AT THE TIME OF THE FOUNDATION of the New Naturalist Series in 1943, the then Editorial Board drew up a list of possible titles, about 30 in all. Of those 30, only *Owls* has escaped publication until now, 71 years overdue. Over the years, several potential authors were approached, including the late Eric Hosking, doyen of bird photographers, who was Photographic Editor on that first Board and for many subsequent New Naturalists. Eric himself was long associated with owls, and indeed famously lost an eye to a particularly bad-tempered, camera-shy Tawny Owl, but sadly his intended co-author died unexpectedly and this proposal joined other non-deliveries. But all is well – Mike Toms has produced a brilliant volume to fulfill this long-felt need.

For a relatively small family of birds, owls command more than their share of attention. We are all familiar with them from earliest childhood, for example in Edward Lear's 'The Owl and the Pussycat': Lear himself was also an expert ornithological artist. Perhaps surprisingly, we admire and enjoy owls, unlike the myriad small birds that fly into a mobbing frenzy when they discover a roosting owl. On the face of it, owls could well be quite frightening, especially to youngsters. Large boldly-staring, rarely-blinking eyes never leave you, and they can rotate their heads without strangling themselves to follow your movement should you walk behind them. They do have the predators' hooked beak but not as prominent in profile as a hawk and they have sharply competent and muscular talons, as any bird ringer will testify.

Historically, and all over the world, owls have been held to be creatures of magic, associates of witches (no potion would be effective without a portion of owl in its contents, as in Shakespeare's *Macbeth*). This mystic association continues for today's youngsters in the elegant Snowy Owl Hedwig that features in the *Harry Potter* saga. The ghostly appearance and shrieking call of the Barn Owl, which has an almost worldwide distribution, may account for much of this association, but perhaps the Tawny is the owl at the centre of beliefs that owls are creatures of wisdom – the 'wise old owl' – typified by 'Wol' in A. A. Milne's Pooh stories and 'Old Brown' in Beatrix Potter's *Squirrel Nutkin*. Elsewhere, the scientific name of the Little Owl *Athene noctua* (introduced to England from southern Europe) is derived from Pallas Athene, the Greek goddess of wisdom. Anatomically, how an owl's skull can contain its huge eyes and ears, whose highly acute functions Mike Toms details so fascinatingly as vital to their life style, can also find space for the necessary brain-power for all this wisdom remains an unsolved mystery.

Mike Toms is in the fortunate position of being an enthusiastic naturalist and also an ornithological professional, working for the British Trust for Ornithology at its headquarters at Thetford in Breckland. The BTO is world-famous for its blend of a professional scientific staff with the teamwork of thousands of expert volunteer birdwatchers who together investigate changes in bird populations, ecology, distribution and migration, both to derive scientific knowledge and to the general benefit of bird conservation. Mike notes in his introduction the role that a Barn Owl played in firing his enthusiasm when as a young paperboy on a bike he was entranced by his first sighting, which led to a life-long enthusiasm for owls culminating in this excellent volume.

Through his fluent and fascinating text, Mike Toms explores the astonishing range of differences within this small family, some of them nocturnal, some crepuscular, some diurnal, in their food and feeding, breeding biology, and migrations. For example, the Tawny Owl strangely seems to have been included in St Patrick's ban on snakes, and has not colonized Ireland! The volume concludes with a chapter giving detailed accounts of each of our owl species, with mention of the various Continental and Transatlantic vagrants that have reached our shores. At long last we welcome the New Naturalist *Owls* by Mike Toms as it secures its rightful and valued place in our series.

Author's Foreword and Acknowledgements

I STILL REMEMBER MY FIRST close encounter with an owl. It was early one week-day morning and I was a young boy on my paper round, following a route that took me out of our small market town and into the Sussex countryside with its small woodlots and narrow fields. Free-wheeling down a shallow incline, bordered by thick hedgerows, I was surprised by a ghostly white shape that drifted through a gap in the hedge to cross the road just a few feet ahead of me. Abandoning my bicycle and my bright orange bag full of papers, I raced to the hedgerow to scramble through and catch the bird again, now quartering the field. This was my first Barn Owl, seen or heard, and I sat spellbound, enthralled by the way in which the owl appeared to float on buoyant, elegant wings. My fascination with owls began that day and continues still.

While I have been fortunate enough to be able to study owls and to document their populations through my work, it is as a naturalist that I enjoy them the most. They add character to our landscapes with their haunting calls and ghostly appearances, shape our literature and sharpen our experiences of the natural world. Very many other people share my interest in owls and, perhaps more than any other group of birds, they have a hold on us that makes them endlessly fascinating and full of character. Despite their nocturnal habits owls remain an accessible group, just difficult enough to ensure that they never bore you and that there is always something left to surprise. Birdwatchers and landowners alike delight in them, a real boon for the would-be student of owl ecology.

My interest in owls has also given me the opportunity to spend time with other researchers, many of them volunteers, who work to increase our understanding of these magnificent birds. To spend a day in the field with such people is always a pleasure and I am indebted to those who have shared their time, efforts and experience with me over the years. In particular, I owe a great deal to Adrian and Jez Blackburn, David Ramsden, Colin Shawyer, the late Paul Johnson and the much-missed Chris Mead, from all of whom I have learned a great deal, enjoyed many wonderful hours and shared the occasional 'flat-fly'. Of course, this book would not have been possible without the efforts of other researchers, many of whom I have not met but all of whom deserve recognition for work that has increased our understanding of owls and their ecology.

The generosity of the photographers who have allowed me to reproduce their stunning work in these pages deserves special mention. To be able to use such images lifts and enhances this book and I am incredibly grateful to them all: Mohamed Bin Azzan Almazrouei, Tim Birkhead, James Bray, Richard Castell, Michael Demain, Edmund Fellowes, Paul Gale, Katrina van Grouw, Mark Hancox, John Harding, Hugh Harrop, Jo Lashwood, Dave Leech, Amy Lewis, Shay Ohayon, Jill Pakenham, Vincenzo Penteriani, Emma Perry, Gordon Plumb, Steve Round, Paul Stancliffe and Matthew Pope of the Boxgrove Project team at UCL.

I would also like to thank the many people who helped by sending papers, allowed reproduction of their figures, collated datasets and provided advice and encouragement: Thomas Bachmann, Dawn Balmer, Richard Burton, Greg Conway, Chris du-Feu, Simon Gillings, Sofi Hindmarch, Chris Klok, Peter Lack, Dave Leech, Graham Martin, Andy Musgrove, Robert Matics, Ian Newton and Roger Riddington.

I am most grateful for the support of Julia Koppitz, Myles Archibald and the staff at William Collins; to Jim Flegg and the New Naturalist Editorial Board, and Tom Cabot for his work on design and layout. Robert Gillmor has produced a stunning cover, once again showing his deep knowledge of Britain's wildlife and his creative talents.

My interest in owls owes a huge amount to the encouragement and support that I have received from my parents throughout my life and to that which I receive from my wife, Lyn, who, along with my parents, additionally provided support of a practical nature through proof reading. Needless to say, any mistakes that remain are purely of my own doing.

CHAPTER 1

Introducing Owls

O WLS ARE SO FAMILIAR and so different from other birds as to be instantly recognisable. The late Chris Mead once noted that 'O' is for 'Owl', reminding us that our knowledge of what is an owl is something that is often learned at a very early age. They feature in many childhood stories, poems, films and even computer games. Owls have a distinctive appearance which sets them apart from other birds. The round and rather oversized head, with its large forward-facing eyes, is perhaps the most 'owl-like' characteristic but the 240-plus recognised species share other features which, in combination, make an

FIG 1. With their large, forward-facing eyes, strong facial disc and somewhat oversized head, owls have a distinctive appearance that sets them apart from other birds. (Emma Perry)

owl an 'owl'. These include cryptically coloured plumage that is soft to the touch and often somewhat fluffy, a down-curved bill with a pointed tip for tearing flesh, powerful talons with sharp curving claws and a tendency to be chiefly nocturnal in habits. Present a birdwatcher with a species of owl they have never seen before and they will be able to say with confidence that it is an owl, something that would not necessarily be the case had the mystery bird been a thrush, warbler or finch.

Later in this chapter we will explore each of the features that characterise an owl in more detail, seeking to examine how they are used and how they might differ from the features seen in other bird families. In particular, we will examine how owl vision, hearing and plumage structure support the largely nocturnal and predatory habits of these birds. Our examples will be drawn from the British owls but, where appropriate, other species will be used to illustrate important points. Before we can do this, however, we first need to examine the taxonomic relationships that exist between owls and other bird families. We also need to look at the evolutionary history of owls, explaining how we arrived at the owl communities seen in Britain today.

TAXONOMY

Writing in 1857, Charles Darwin predicted that a day would come when we would have 'fairly true genealogical trees of each kingdom of nature'. Today we are at a stage where these trees – which we now call 'phylogenetic trees' – are fairly well established for nearly all groups of organisms. Even so, gaps remain in our knowledge and there has been much debate along the way about taxonomic relationships, particularly in relation to the exact placement of owls alongside other avian orders. An understanding of the relationships that exist between owls and other birds, and indeed within the owls themselves, is a necessary starting point for any research into owl ecology and behaviour. It is also essential for successful conservation action, providing a framework from which the importance of individual populations can be determined.

The naming of parts
From the very beginnings of scientific study, attempts have been made to classify living organisms into groups of related or similar species. The earliest classifications were highly simplistic. Aristotle, for example, separated birds into those that lived on land, those that lived on water and those that lived alongside water and it was not until the 17th century that a truly useful and recognisable avian classification was developed. This system, published by Frances Willughby

FIG 2. Nightjars share large eyes, soft plumage and nocturnal habits with owls and were once thought to be their closest relatives, something now proved incorrect. (Joanne Lashwood)

and John Ray under the title *Ornithologia*, delivered a classification based predominantly on form (e.g. bill shape), an approach that we also see when, 60 or so years later, Linnaeus placed the owls within the order Accipitres alongside the falcons, eagles and vultures. The strong feet, sharp talons and hooked bill are characters shared by both owls and diurnal raptors and were taken to support common ancestry. Certain other features of owls, notably the large eyes, soft plumage and nocturnal habits, were believed by other scientists to suggest that the owls were actually more closely related to the nightjars (Caprimulgiformes). As recently as the early 1990s, a study using DNA-DNA hybridisation supported the placement of owls as nearest neighbours to the nightjars but, as we shall see below, this work has since been challenged and the position of the owls seems to have been finally resolved.

The use of morphological characteristics to establish the degree of relatedness between species can run into problems, particularly where two unrelated species show similarities in appearance simply because the shared characters happen to be similar solutions to the same evolutionary pressures. Convergent characters, such as the similarities in appearance seen in old and new world vultures, for example, are unrelated to the underlying phylogeny. A real breakthrough in resolving this problem has been the advent of affordable molecular and biochemical methods, for example the use of Polymerase Chain Reaction (PCR) amplification of marker genes to allow the sequencing of DNA. The linear DNA molecule carries the all-important genetic information; during the process of cell division its double-stranded nature allows precise replication of the genetic material. Very occasionally, however, a replication error creeps in. If the error happens within a section of DNA molecule that acts as a gene associated with an important process then it may prove deleterious but if it happens elsewhere it may have little or no impact on the individual. Over time, after two evolutionary lines have diverged from their common ancestor, we would expect to see differences emerge within the genetic code because of these replication errors. If we can determine how often the replication errors tend to occur, then we can establish a measure of the genetic distance between the two organisms and, ultimately, construct an evolutionary tree (a phylogeny). Crude estimates from the work carried out to date, suggest that a 2 per cent level of nucleotide substitution equates to roughly 1 million years of divergence, providing the measure by which we can resolve the structure of our phylogeny.

Two kinds of DNA have been the focus for these molecular studies. The first, known as mitochondrial DNA, is transmitted from the mother to her offspring in the cytoplasm of her eggs. Mitochondrial DNA evolves much faster than nuclear DNA (the second type of DNA used in these studies), in part because the mitochondria lack the mechanisms found in the nucleus for repairing mutations (it should be noted though that the latter are not infallible). Various mitochondrial genes have been used but the most widely favoured is the cytochrome b gene, which has proved to be a good marker at the species and genus level. It does, unfortunately, lose resolution for divergence events that happened more than 20 million years ago and this is where the more slowly-evolving nuclear genes have an important role to play. The inclusion of nuclear genes in studies also helps to tackle problems associated with inbreeding events and introgression (where the genes of one species enter the gene pool of another through hybridisation). The resulting phylogenetic tree represents a hypothesis of the relationships between individuals and does not necessarily present the true evolutionary history behind the tree. Recent and more sophisticated methods may provide an opportunity to reconstruct the route by which one sequence evolved into another.

The relationship between owls and other birds

The molecular phylogeny and systematics of owls have been the subject of detailed study by Professor Michael Wink and colleagues (Wink *et al.*, 2008) who have, to date, examined roughly two-thirds of all recognised owl species. The results of

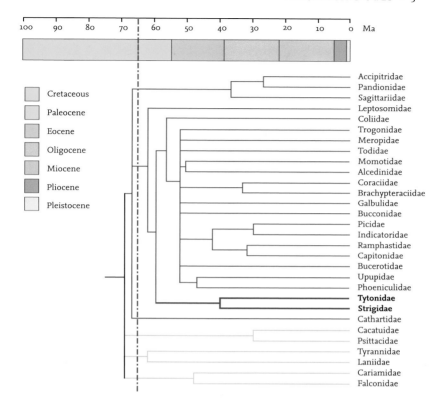

FIG 3. The evolution of owls. Redrawn from Ericson *et al.*, 2006.

this work have highlighted that, while most of our recent understanding of the relationships within the owls is correct, there are some inconsistencies.

The placement of the owls in relation to other birds is something that has attracted considerable debate, particularly with respect to resolving which birds can be regarded as being their closest relatives. A recent study, using five different nuclear genes, now provides good evidence that the owls are members of the Coronaves, where they fall into a clade with the diurnal raptors (excluding falcons), the latter clustering instead alongside the parrots and shrikes (Fain & Houde, 2004; Ericson *et al.*, 2006). The nightjars (Caprimulgiformes), thought by some authors to be the owl's nearest neighbours, are part of the Metaves, apparently resolving the debate over the distance between these two groups and it would seem that the similarities between owls and nightjars are the result of convergence (see Figure 3).

Phylogeny and the British owls

Molecular studies support the separation of the owls into two families: the Tytonidae (which includes the Barn Owl) and the Strigidae (which holds all the other British species). This treatment was initially proposed by Nitzsch who, working in the 1820s, also proposed that owls should be treated as a separate order (Strigiformes) distinct from the diurnal raptors. The Tytonidae are characterised by having a large head in relation to body size, long legs and a heart-shaped facial disc. Two genera are recognised within the Tytonidae: *Tyto*, which includes the typical barn owls, the grass owls, the sooty owls and the masked owls and *Phodilus*, the bay owls. It is thought that *Tyto* and *Phodilus* shared a common ancestor more than 10 million years ago. The Barn Owl *Tyto alba* is a variable taxon, with many subspecies recognised on the basis of geography, size and colour, and the work of Wink *et al.* (2008) provides good molecular evidence that at least some of these should be treated as full species. Two subspecies of Common Barn Owl have been recorded from Britain, namely *Tyto alba alba* and *Tyto alba guttata*. Barn Owls have been introduced into a

TABLE 1. Owl families and the placement of the British species (following Wink *et al.*, 2008).

FAMILY	SUBFAMILY	TRIBE	BRITISH SPECIES
Tytonidae	Tytoninae		Common Barn Owl
	Phodilinae		
Strigidae	Striginae	Bubonini	Eurasian Eagle Owl Snowy Owl
		Strigini	Tawny Owl
		Pulsatrigini	
		Megascopini	
		Asionini	Long-eared Owl Short-eared Owl
		Otini	Common Scops Owl
	Surniinae	Surnini	Northern Hawk Owl Little Owl
		Aegolini	Tengmalm's Owl
	Ninoxinae		

number of regions across the world, complicating our understanding of the genetic structure of local populations.

Relationships within the Strigidae are much more complex than those seen in the Tytonidae – with its two subfamilies and two genera – and there is a great deal of variation across the individual genera. Think how different a 3,000 g Eagle Owl is to a 170 g Little Owl, not just in terms of size, but also diet, ecology and behaviour. The Strigidae has been subdivided into three subfamilies, with the work of Wink *et al.* (2008) recognising the Striginae, Surniinae and Ninoxinae, a slightly different arrangement from that proposed by previous authors (see Table 1). Wink's reassessment suggests that the subfamily Asioninae, containing our *Asio* owls (Long-eared Owl *Asio otus* and Short-eared Owl *Asio flammeus*), would be better placed in the subfamily Striginae, where it would join most of our other owl species as a tribe, the Asionini. The other tribes within the subfamily Striginae proposed by Wink *et al.* (2008) are the Bubonini (Eagle Owl *Bubo bubo* and Snowy Owl *Bubo scandiacus*), Strigini (Tawny Owl *Strix aluco*), Pulsatrigini, Megascopini and Otini.

FIG 4. Little Owl taxonomy has been subject to recent scrutiny, highlighting several distinct lineages and a substantial degree of geographic isolation. (Jill Pakenham)

Long-eared Owl and Short-eared Owl have traditionally been regarded as being closely related. However, the genetic differentiation between the two species is substantial, suggesting a long period of separate evolution, with the Long-eared Owl potentially more closely aligned with the South American Striped Owl *Asio clamator* and the Short-eared Owl showing taxonomic affinity with the Marsh Owl *Asio capensis*. The Eagle Owl and the Snowy Owl cluster within the *Bubo* complex, the latter species showing particular association through common ancestry with the Great Horned Owl *Bubo virginianus* of North America. Discovery of this clustering prompted the recommendation, adopted by the British Ornithologists Union (BOU) in 2004, to correct the scientific name of the Snowy Owl from *Nyctea* to *Bubo* (Sangster *et al.*, 2004). Wink and his colleagues found little differentiation within European Tawny Owl populations but did find evidence which suggested that the form found in Israel should be regarded as a distinct species *Strix butleri*. The Little Owl is placed in the tribe Surnini within the subfamily Surniinae and there is good evidence for several distinct *Athene noctua* lineages, indicative of a substantial degree of geographic isolation. It has, for example, been proposed that Little Owls from Cyprus, Turkey and Israel be recognised as a distinct species, the Lilith Owlet *Athene lilith*, separate from the Little Owls of Western Europe, including Britain.

It is the treatment proposed by Wink *et al.* (2008) that is followed in this book. Thus the American Barn Owl *Tyto furcata* and the Australian Barn Owl *Tyto delicatula* are both treated as a full species, rather than as subspecies of the Common Barn Owl, something that makes interpretation of certain differences in ecology, behaviour and morphology that much clearer. A full revision of the whole *Tyto* genus is badly needed.

THE EVOLUTION OF OWLS

Geologically speaking, birds are relative newcomers to the Earth's fauna. *Archaeopteryx lithographica*, a species for which there are now several well-documented specimens, is regarded by most researchers as being the first known bird. Fossils of the species have been dated to roughly 150 Ma (million years ago) during the Upper Jurassic period. *Archaeopteryx* shares many characters with small bipedal dinosaurs, such as the dromaesaurids and troodontids, and it is widely regarded that it is from these dinosaurs that birds, including modern owls, originated. The question of how far down this evolutionary line *Archaeopteryx* should be placed has stimulated some debate, however, with a number of researchers questioning whether *Archaeopteryx* is actually a bird at all, rather than a dinosaur with feathers. Fossils from the early Cretaceous, notably the turkey-sized *Jeholohis prima*, are unquestionably birds, capable of active flight (Zhou & Zhang, 2002). Other bird fossils from this period have been collected in North America, Spain and China. It is not until the Eocene, however (c. 54 to 47 Ma) that we see quantities of fossil birds from the British Isles.

Although bird bones are highly distinctive and thus separable from other vertebrate remains, they are fragile and this creates a patchy fossil record. Soft silts, such as those associated with wetlands and coastal areas, offer the best chances of fossilisation of delicate bones so the record of our ancient avifauna is dominated by the species linked with these habitats. It tends to be the more robust bones that survive, notably the tarsometatarsus, tibiotarsus, metacarpus and humerus, with the tarsometatarsus being the most commonly used element for species identification and placement within taxonomic groupings. Even so, owls are surprisingly well represented in the avian fossil record and the oldest known fossil that is unquestionably an owl comes from Palaeocene deposits dated to c. 65 to 56.5 Ma. This extinct owl, given the scientific name *Ogygoptynx wetmorei*, was discovered in Colorado, USA, and placed in the family Ogygoptynidae (Rich & Bohaska, 1976). Earlier remains from the Upper Cretaceous, collected in Romania and thought to be from an owl, have since been shown to be from one or more dinosaurs.

An interesting discrepancy arises when you compare the dating of the fossil record for owls (and other species) with that derived from molecular studies. In many cases, molecular evidence produces a date for a given evolutionary event that is substantially earlier than that evident from the fossil record. This discrepancy may be linked to the patchy nature of the fossil record or it could result from a failure in the assumption that a molecular clock should run at a constant rate. Michael Benton tackled this tricky question by using knowledge of gaps within a known lineage to predict the gap that was likely to exist prior to the earliest known occurrence of that lineage. This was then compared with the date generated by molecular evidence to see if the two were now in better agreement. Using this approach, Benton took the earliest known example of an owl (at the time of his work) back from c. 58 Ma to 63 Ma (Benton, 1999). He also came to the conclusion that, even allowing for the presence of missing fossils, the molecular clock was likely to run faster during a period of species radiation, thus breaking the assumption that the rate was constant. Other discrepancies may arise from the incorrect placement of individual specimens within particular families, perhaps because key skeletal elements are missing or from poor work on the part of some early palaeontologists. It has been demonstrated, for example, that some specimens once identified as being from early owls were actually from other avian orders.

FIG 5. The geological timescale against which the evolution and remains of British owls are dated. (Adapted from Yalden & Albarella, 2009)

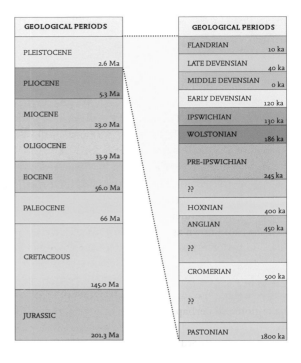

GEOLOGICAL PERIODS	
PLEISTOCENE	
	2.6 Ma
PLIOCENE	
	5.3 Ma
MIOCENE	
	23.0 Ma
OLIGOCENE	
	33.9 Ma
EOCENE	
	56.0 Ma
PALEOCENE	
	66 Ma
CRETACEOUS	
	145.0 Ma
JURASSIC	
	201.3 Ma

GEOLOGICAL PERIODS	
FLANDRIAN	10 ka
LATE DEVENSIAN	40 ka
MIDDLE DEVENSIAN	0 ka
EARLY DEVENSIAN	120 ka
IPSWICHIAN	130 ka
WOLSTONIAN	186 ka
PRE-IPSWICHIAN	245 ka
??	
HOXNIAN	400 ka
ANGLIAN	450 ka
??	
CROMERIAN	500 ka
??	
PASTONIAN	1800 ka

Much of our understanding of the evolution of owls comes from work carried out since the late 1980s. As new specimens are unearthed so our understanding will continue to develop and, quite possibly, change. Our current knowledge underlines that a major radiation occurred within the owls during or just prior to the Eocene (see Figure 5). Cécile Mourer-Chauviré, for example, reviewed material from Eocene, Oligocene and Lower Miocene deposits located at Quercy in southwest France. Mourer-Chauviré's work led to the recognition of three owl families: Tytonidae, Selenornithinae and Palaeoglaucidae, the latter only properly recognised in 1982 when a new, more complete, owl specimen came to light in Germany (Peters, 1992). While the Quercy fossils reveal that the Tytonidae was highly diversified within Europe during the Eocene, it also suggests the absence of the Strigidae, this family not being represented within the fossil record until the Miocene (23.5 to 5.2 Ma), when it occurs in both European and North American deposits. It is during the Oligocene that the family Tytonidae is thought to have split into its two extant subfamilies (Tytoninae and Phodilinae). Further diversification of the owls occurred during the Miocene and Pliocene. It is also at this time that we see a species radiation within presumed small mammal prey and it is likely to be this event that helped to drive the radiation seen within the owls themselves. Evidence from the fossil record additionally suggests that the strigid owls began to supersede the tytonid owls during this period.

Some early specimens thought to belong to the Strigidae have since been placed within the Tytonidae but *Strix brevis* (Lower Miocene, North America) and *Bubo poirrieri* (Lower Miocene, France) are considered to be correctly placed within the Strigidae. The earliest known member of the Tytonidae is probably *Nocturnavis incerta*, collected from Eocene deposits at Eschamps in France. The genus *Tyto* is represented within the fossil record by at least a dozen species, mostly associated with Pleistocene or Holocene deposits but dating back in one instance to the middle Miocene. Many of the fossil *Tyto* species are significantly larger than today's barn owls and some of the island forms are particularly large. There is a wider tendency for island forms to become larger than mainland forms, a trait known as 'gigantism'. An example of this in owls comes from the Gargano Peninsula in Italy, once an island, where Mlíkovský (1998) identified a single lineage of barn owls evolving to larger size, culminating in *Tyto gigantea*. Mlíkovský's work also suggests the disappearance of barn owls from much of Europe during the early Miocene, matching the appearance of the Strigidae in the region and perhaps reflecting changing environmental conditions. We do, however, see their return from the middle part of the Miocene, although this time the fossil record suggests they are restricted to a single genus, *Tyto*.

Early owls in the British Isles

Most of the British Isles was submerged under shallow seas throughout the Miocene, our fossil record for birds not recommencing until the late Pliocene. The few fossils from this period come from seabirds rather than terrestrial species like owls. The Pleistocene (which followed and which covered the last 1.8 million years) in Britain was dominated by a succession of cold periods (the Anglian, Wolstonian and Devensian or 'Late' Glaciations) separated by warmer interludes (the Pastonian, Cromerian, Hoxnian, pre-Ipswichian and Ipswichian Interglacials) from which we see glimpses of a changing avifauna. One of the difficulties associated with studying the avifauna of this period is that the glacial events effectively wiped much of the record away as ice sheets pushed south.

From the Pastonian Interglacial we have our first British record of an eagle owl, the specimen suggesting a form smaller in size than the modern Eurasian Eagle Owl and more similar to the present North African Pharaoh Eagle Owl *Bubo ascalaphus* (treated by earlier authors as a race of the Eurasian Eagle Owl). The other bird species identified from these deposits include Bewick's Swan *Cygnus columbianus*, Mallard *Anas platyrhynchos*, a buzzard *Buteo* sp., Guillemot

FIG 6. Excavations at Boxgrove in West Sussex have revealed some of our earliest records of British owls. (Boxgrove Projects, UCL)

Uria aalge and Razorbill *Alca torda*, suggesting a coastal avifauna of some familiarity. Other eagle owl remains come from the Hoxnian (Swanscombe, Kent), Wolstonian (Tornewton, Devon) and the Devensian (Langwith, Derbyshire). The specimens from both Swanscombe and Tornewton are of similar size to the modern-day form of Eurasian Eagle Owl. Our only definitive record of Snowy Owl comes from Kent's Cavern (Devon) – a Late Glacial site from a period where both Arctic Lemming *Dicrostonyx torquatus* and Norway Lemming *Lemmus lemmus* are present (Harrison, 1987). It is interesting that there are so few examples of either Eagle Owl or Snowy Owl remains from British sites given the extent to which these species have been found at sites from the same period elsewhere in Europe (see Chapter 6).

The first record of Tawny Owl comes from post-Cromerian Boxgrove, a site just inland from the present Sussex coastline and from which there is also evidence of early human habitation. A sizeable list of other species has been drawn up for the site but some of these identifications are best described as tentative because of the limited remains available from which to determine an identification. The avian community suggests an area with some woodland but with extensive wetlands nearby. Many of our other owls also make their first appearance in Late Glacial deposits. At Pinhole Cave (Late Devensian, Derbyshire) Barn Owl appears alongside reported specimens of Short-eared Owl, Tawny Owl, Northern Hawk Owl *Surnia ulula* and Tengmalm's Owl *Aegolius funereus*, the latter two species suggesting the occurrence of a more northern avifauna than present today (Yalden & Albarella, 2009).

The last 15,000 years

As the Devensian Glaciation ended there followed a period of transition towards the warm temperate climate that we recognise today. This transition took roughly 5,000 years (lasting from 15,000 BP – before present – to 10,000 BP) and was associated with both warm and cool interludes. The evidence points to an initial period of tundra-like conditions, the British Isles hosting species such as lemmings, Reindeer *Rangifer tarandus*, Woolly Mammoth *Mammuthus primigenius* and, presumably, some bird species characteristic of the open tundra habitat; Snowy Owl would be a likely candidate. With continued warming we see the development of birch scrub in the southern part of the British Isles and the return of human hunters from what is termed the Upper Palaeolithic cultures. It is in the cave deposits associated with these hunters that we find the remains of birds, including owls. Some of these remains have been radiocarbon-dated,

FIG 7. The retreat of the glaciers and a warming climate saw the succession from open tundra habitats to woodland ones. (Mike Toms)

placing them at 12,600 BP to 12,110 BP (well within the warmer period known as the Windermere Interstadial). From the caves at Cresswell Crags (on the Derbyshire/Nottinghamshire border) we have gamebirds like Ptarmigan *Lagopus muta* and grouse *Lagopus* spp., which dominate the remains, together with Short-eared Owl (two individuals), Tengmalm's Owl and Northern Hawk Owl. Further south, from Soldier's Hole in Cheddar Gorge (Somerset) we find another community dominated by grouse and Ptarmigan, this time with Long-eared Owl and Short-eared Owl represented.

The Windermere Interstadial was followed by a short period of colder conditions, known as the Younger Dryas, most likely forcing the Palaeolithic hunters to retreat south and presumably greatly altering the avian community present. Two cave sites provide a glimpse of the avian communities during this period. Eagle Owl is recorded from Ossom's Cave (Staffordshire) at a date of c. 10,780 to 10,600 BP and a likely Snowy Owl comes from Chelm's Combe Shelter at Cheddar (with a date c. 10,910 to 10,190 BP). The likely Snowy Owl bone – a metacarpal, intermediate in size between the two species – was originally reported as belonging to an Eurasian Eagle Owl, but Stewart (2007), in his review of the fossil remains of the species, suggests that Snowy Owl might be a more likely candidate.

From about 10,000 BP we see the final period of warming, representing the beginning of the Postglacial or Holocene Period. Returning human hunters of the now Mesolithic culture provide us with some of the best sources of subfossil birds. Archaeological excavations at cave sites suggest that the landscape was in transition from the open habitats of the Devensian Glaciation to the wooded habitats of the later Mesolithic. The bird communities identified from the archaeological remains largely reflect this change but it is worth remembering that the species represented will also be influenced through their use by Mesolithic peoples. Quarry species, hunted for food, tend to dominate and smaller – largely passerine – species are likely to be under-represented. One of the most famous sites from this period is Demen's Dale in Derbyshire, from which a diverse bird community has been identified. In addition to the gamebird and waterfowl quarry species we also find the remains of Tawny Owl and the unmistakable tarsometatarsus of a Eurasian Eagle Owl. This individual is the latest certain record of the species in the British Isles as a native. A later record, from the Iron Age Meare Lake Village is of uncertain identity and could not be traced when Stewart came to review published material in 2007.

So what do these records tell us about the owl community at this time and, additionally, going forward further into the Neolithic? As the landscape became more wooded we are likely to have seen Snowy Owl increasingly restricted to more northerly locations, following the retreating tundra habitats. Short-eared Owl may also have retreated further north, though it is likely that populations would have remained established along the coastal margins, where wetlands provided nesting cover and hunting opportunities. Tawny Owl is well represented in the subfossil record and is likely to have been the most common owl within the extensive woodland habitats that were emerging. Yalden & Albarella (2009), using breeding densities derived from Białowieża's 'wild wood' habitats, suggested that the Mesolithic Tawny Owl population was roughly 160,000 breeding pairs, considerably larger than the current population estimate for the British Isles of c. 20,000 pairs. Yalden & Albarella also produced estimates for Eurasian Eagle Owl (c. 450 breeding pairs) and Barn Owl (c. 1,000 breeding pairs). Barn Owl would have been restricted to open habitats, most likely those associated with the coastal fringe of southern Britain, while Eurasian Eagle Owl is likely to have occupied wooded and upland fringe habitats, occurring at a fairly low density. The sparsity of the British records of Eurasian Eagle Owl may, in part, be explained by the low breeding density but it is in sharp contrast to that for Sweden, where the species is well-represented in later Viking burial sites. Since there is good evidence that the species was used as a decoy in falconry, the greater abundance of records from Sweden may reflect cultural differences or, as has been suggested by several authors, the early loss of the species from the British Isles either through persecution or habitat modification.

As the influence of human communities begins to play its part in shaping our owl populations it is time to turn our attentions to other aspects of the British owls and to identify what sets them apart from other bird species. We shall return to the interactions between humans and owls later in Chapter 6, bringing the association up to the present day.

ANATOMY

The owls show a high degree of uniformity in their structure compared to that seen in many other avian families. The skeleton is typically avian in character, additionally displaying a number of the features that reflect a predatory lifestyle, such as the hooked beak and long claws. Another feature associated with the owl as a predator is the shape of the skull. The owl skull is proportionally much broader than that seen in other birds of comparable body weight. This greater width, together with the flattened front face to the skull that is a feature of many small owl species, is linked to the large eyes which provide binocular vision. The width of the skull may also aid sound localisation because the ear openings can

TABLE 2. Dimensions of the skulls of British owls.

Species	Length (mm)	Cranium length (mm)	Cranium width (mm)	Cranium height (mm)	Bill length (mm)	Ratio of length to bill length
Barn Owl	69	40	40	29	29	2.38
Snowy Owl	94	55	63	40	39	2.41
Eagle Owl	100	58	71	41	42	2.38
Tawny Owl	69	44	51	36	25	2.76
Little Owl	50	35	38	25	15	3.33
Long-eared Owl	59	35	43	29	24	2.46
Short-eared Owl	61	37	46	30	24	2.54

be placed farther apart, increasing the lag time between a sound hitting one ear and then the other. The skulls of those owls belonging to the Strigidae have a more rounded appearance, with larger eye sockets, than those of the Tytonidae, the latter being more elongate and with smaller sockets. The bill also tends to be more elongated in the Tytonidae (Table 2).

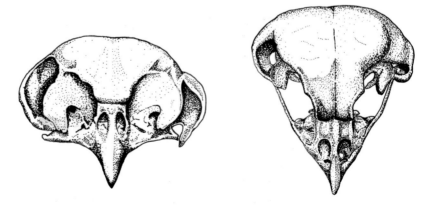

FIG 8. A small number of owls, including this Tengmalm's Owl, show a striking asymmetry to their skulls, linked to their sharp hearing. (Mike Toms, redrawn from Collett, 1871)

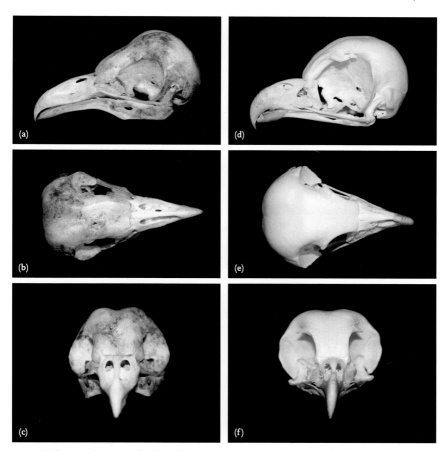

FIG 9. Differences between the Tytonidae and Strigidae can be seen in the shape and structure of their skulls, as these Barn Owl (a–c) and Tawny Owl (d–f) skulls show. (Katrina van Grouw)

Each eye is positioned within a sclerotic tube, something that virtually prevents an owl from moving the eyeball in any way; owls cannot roll their eyes, for example. Owls, therefore, have to rotate their head in order to see what is happening around them, something they can do to a very great extent thanks to a long and flexible neck, rotating through an arc of roughly 270°. Owls may also be seen 'bobbing' their head or moving it from side to side, a behaviour associated with extending the effectiveness of the owl's binocular vision and something to which we will return later in this chapter. A small number of species show a degree of skull asymmetry that is linked to the asymmetrical positioning of the internal ears (see Figure 8). These include: Ural Owl *Strix uralensis*, Tengmalm's Owl and Northern Saw-whet Owl *Aegolius acadicus* and, again, this is something to which we will return later in the chapter.

THE NOCTURNAL HABIT

A number of the features exhibited by owls are associated with their nocturnal habits. Before we explore these features in greater detail we first need to examine nocturnal activity itself, quantifying the extent to which it is exhibited by owls and addressing the reasons why owls might choose to be active at night.

FIG 10. It is with the darkness of night that we associate our owls. (John Harding)

Nocturnal activity, or nocturnality as it is often called, is rare in birds, with perhaps less than 3 per cent of the world's avian species carrying out all aspects of their life cycle between dusk and dawn. The sense that owls are unusual in being nocturnal is further reinforced by our own diurnal nature. Night-time can seem like an alien world to us and this may be one reason why owls feature so prominently in folklore and superstition, belonging as they do to that 'other world' (see Chapter 6).

An examination of the 250 or so owl species – based on König & Weick (2008) – for which information is available, suggests that just over two-thirds of the world's owl species are nocturnal or strictly nocturnal in their habits. A further 12 per cent are crepuscular/nocturnal, leaving 15 per cent as crepuscular/diurnal and just 3 per cent as diurnal. A number of species appear to be active during either day or night. We know very little about the activity patterns of many owl species so it is likely that our knowledge of the extent of nocturnality will develop over time.

Nocturnality in other avian families appears to be restricted to species that utilise open, spatially simple habitats. This is certainly true of the nightjars *Caprimulgus* spp. and the stone-curlews *Burhinus* spp. In contrast, the more strictly nocturnal owls are species associated with well-wooded and structurally complex habitats, while those associated with open habitats (e.g. Snowy Owl and Short-eared Owl) tend not to be so strictly nocturnal and can often be seen on the wing during the hours of daylight. Martin (1990), looking at nocturnal behaviour in birds, defined three groups of owls based on the degree of nocturnal activity and habitat use. Martin also recognised that many owls did not fit neatly into these groups because the degree of nocturnal behaviour was modified by location, season, local habitat and prey availability. Even an essentially nocturnal species like Tawny Owl may, on occasion, be observed during daylight. One of our local Breckland birds was often seen hunting well before dusk during one particularly wet summer (I. Evans, pers. comm.). Diurnal observations may involve birds disturbed from a roost or they may be a genuine response to poor feeding conditions during the previous night. Both Barn Owl and Little Owl certainly show a flexible approach to their activity patterns, with certain individuals of the former species characterised by a tendency to hunt during daylight hours (often late afternoon during the summer, pers. obs.).

A relationship between nocturnal activity and the nature of exhibited territorial behaviour has also been suggested by Graham Martin, who noted that highly territorial and sedentary species tended to be strictly nocturnal in their habits. Martin put forward the Tawny Owl as an example of this, with Snowy Owl and Short-eared Owl offered as examples of species with a more nomadic nature that tended to be less nocturnal in their activity patterns. As we shall see elsewhere in this book, knowledge of a territory (and the likely location of prey within that territory) can be of particular importance to a bird like a Tawny Owl, which is a perch and wait predator. Hunting within the complex structure of a woodland, this is likely to be a more effective strategy for a Tawny Owl than hunting on the wing in the 'dark of night'.

Why might owls be nocturnal?

A number of different reasons have been put forward to explain nocturnality in the owls. These include: i) dietary spectrum, ii) competition for food, iii) reduction of predation risk, iv) thermoregulation and v) the avoidance of biting insects transferring blood parasites. Many owls feed on prey that are themselves nocturnal, such as certain small mammals, together with many insects and other invertebrates. Being active during the night provides access to these prey species at a time when few other avian predators are on the wing. It is interesting to note that some of the more strictly nocturnal owl species (e.g. Tawny Owl) tend to have a wide dietary spectrum, while many of the species that tend to take a reduced range of prey species (e.g. Short-eared Owl) are typically crepuscular or diurnal in habits. Competition with diurnal birds of prey may, therefore, be a more important driver for nocturnality than prey spectrum. The Galápagos Short-eared Owl *Asio galapagoensis* (treated by some authors as an aberrant race of Short-eared Owl) is found on most of the islands within the Galápagos Archipelago. It shares many of the islands with the Galápagos Hawk *Buteo galapagoensis* and where the two occur together the owl is largely nocturnal in its habits and the hawk always diurnal. On those islands where it occurs in isolation, the Galápagos Short-eared Owl is active during both night and day, suggesting that the more dominant hawk limits diurnal foraging opportunities, either through competition or direct interaction.

The potential for competition with diurnal birds of prey can also be seen in the literature surrounding our British owls. During a study of the activity patterns of Short-eared Owls on Orkney, Reynolds & Gorman (1999) recorded 146 prey capture events that occurred during daylight hours. On 11 occasions (7.5 per cent) the researchers witnessed successful food piracy by Hooded Crow *Corvus cornix* or Hen Harrier *Circus cyaneus*. Harassment of the owls by other species (e.g. seabirds and waders) was also noted frequently. There are many other examples of British owls hunting during daylight or twilight and being harassed or robbed by other bird species, including Kestrel *Falco tinnunculus* (e.g. Everett, 1968).

A bigger threat, potentially, is that of predation, with owls known to feature in the diets of certain larger birds of prey, including Golden Eagle *Aquila chrysaetos*, Red Kite *Milvus milvus*, Buzzard *Buteo buteo*, Peregrine *Falco peregrinus* and Goshawk *Accipiter gentilis* (Mikkola, 1976; Ratcliffe, 1993). Owls exhibit relatively slow flight

FIG 11. During winter, Short-eared Owls can often be found hunting during daylight hours over suitable areas of rough grassland. (Steve Round)

compared to their main avian predators and daylight activity is likely to elevate predation risk. A radio-tracking study of Tawny Owls in Denmark, examining roosting behaviour in relation to age and breeding status, found that 73 per cent of the owls which died from natural causes were killed by diurnal birds of prey, notably Goshawk (Sunde *et al.*, 2003a). Examination of roosting behaviour, both within this study and, experimentally, in a later study (Hendrichsen *et al.*, 2006), revealed that the owls generally favoured less exposed roosting sites, often using these repeatedly for months at a time. Adult birds with dependent young were found to roost in more exposed sites, close to where the young were, suggesting that they sacrificed some of the protection afforded by roosting in cover with the greater vigilance needed for defence of the young. Newly independent young roosted in the most exposed locations and at a lower height on average. This could suggest they were less experienced or it could be that they were trading off roosting cover against the need to catch at least some prey during the day. The latter hypothesis gains some support by the fact that newly independent owls roosted in more exposed locations during years of low small mammal abundance than they did when favoured small mammal prey were more abundant. The researchers also discovered that young birds that had been exposed to the presence of a Goshawk subsequently roosted in less exposed locations than youngsters that had not been known to have been in contact with an avian predator.

Diurnal predation may be linked to the mobbing of roosting owls by smaller birds, which is in itself linked to roosting location. Using stuffed Tawny Owls, Ditte Hendrichsen and colleagues found that the probability of being mobbed was six times greater for exposed roost locations than for those with the best cover. Interestingly, the probability of being mobbed was twice as great before noon than after it, suggesting that small birds were more active in the morning. Mobbing of this nature may reduce an owl's fitness through the stress imposed by the need for increased alertness or because it increases the risk of predation by an avian predator attracted to the commotion. Nocturnal activity, coupled with cryptic daylight roosting, may act to counter this risk.

Nocturnal hunting in British owls

British owls feed predominantly on small mammals, favouring Field Vole *Microtus agrestis*, Wood Mouse *Apodemus sylvaticus* and Common Shrew *Sorex araneus*, among others. Shrews, with their high energetic demands, are active throughout the 24-hour cycle and show bouts of activity lasting from 30–120 minutes alternated with periods of rest. Both Common Shrew and Water Shrew *Neomys fodiens* are most active just after sunset and just before sunrise, with the bulk of activity taking place during the hours of darkness. Pygmy Shrews *Sorex minutus* appear to be equally active by day or night (Churchfield, 1982). Field Voles also show regular periods of activity, interspersed by periods of rest, that run throughout the 24-hour cycle. These periods of activity show a periodicity of c. two hours, which is somewhat shorter than the three-hour periodicity noted in the larger Orkney Vole *Microtus arvalis* (see below). Vole activity tends to be greater in the first part of the night (up until midnight) than after. Wood Mouse is a mainly nocturnal species, usually showing a single period of activity, the timing of which is correlated with the time of sunset, and individual mice may spend up to two-thirds of the night active, but this varies with season, habitat quality, moon-phase and the degree of cover available. In North America, moon-phase has been demonstrated to influence predation on the Deermouse *Peromyscus maniculatus* by Short-eared Owls (Clarke, 1983). Deermouse activity is suppressed under the light conditions associated with a full moon and the owls' hunting effectiveness increases with the degree of night-time illumination.

The activity patterns of these small mammals may well drive the patterns of activity seen in the owl species that prey upon them. Reynolds & Gorman

FIG 12. Barn Owls can regularly be seen hunting at dusk, particularly during the breeding season when they have young to feed. (Jill Pakenham)

(1999) found an interesting degree of synchrony between the activity of the Short-eared Owls in their study population and the Orkney Voles upon which they fed. Radio-tracking evidence from this study suggested that the owls were timing their hunting excursions to match the period when the voles were active, with both species showing a short-term periodicity of *c.* three hours. The owls were chiefly nocturnal during the autumn and early winter but showed an increased degree of diurnal activity from March through into July. While nocturnal hunting behaviour appeared to be favoured by these Short-eared Owls, possibly to reduce the level of harassment and kleptoparasitism, the owls may have increased the amount of diurnal activity to target the abundance of voles, counter the shortened hours of darkness and meet the energetic demands of their growing young. Similarly, the amount of diurnal activity seen in Short-eared Owls within a study population on the Scottish mainland also underlines a preference for nocturnal activity. Here, despite territorial birds being present close to all of the observation points used in the study, the owls were found to be active for just 4.8 per cent of the diurnal observation time (Calladine *et al.*, 2010). The related Long-eared Owl is almost entirely nocturnal in habits, with diurnal activity an irregular occurrence outside of the breeding season (Scott, 1997).

A degree of synchrony between other vole predators and their prey has also been noted for Buzzard, Hen Harrier and Kestrel. Within Britain, and indeed within other parts of northern Europe, the Barn Owl is chiefly nocturnal in habits. Most Barn Owls tend to hunt from soon after dusk through until about 2 am, with a secondary bout of activity around dawn. It has been suggested that these peaks in activity are also linked to the activity patterns of voles. Trapping studies have revealed that peaks in Field Vole activity occur at dawn and dusk during the summer months, the species becoming more nocturnal in habits on hot summer days and more diurnal in habits on cold winter days, the latter perhaps a deliberate response to reduce heat loss. These peaks in activity are superimposed upon the series of regular feeding bouts already outlined above for other small mammal species. More generally, the activity of Field Voles and other small mammal prey species may vary with sex or age; for example, adult males tend to be more active than adult females, while juvenile Field Voles tend to be more nocturnal in habits than adults. Differences in small mammal activity patterns may also influence which prey species are taken by owls. For example, Hosking and Newberry, watching prey deliveries to a Barn Owl nest in the 1940s, noted that later into the night the birds were more likely to bring in Common Rats *Rattus norvegicus* than Field Voles, possibly reflecting a change in prey availability or a change in the owl's own hunting behaviour, perhaps with the birds spending more time hunting around the farmyard in which the nest was located during that part of the night when the activity of the voles dropped elsewhere.

Many Barn Owls will, however, indulge in daylight hunting, a behaviour that is typical of some of the birds I have studied in north Norfolk. Certain individuals were regularly watched hunting from early afternoon onwards, often sweeping low over my head as I recorded the sward structure of the rough grassland over which they were foraging. The tendency towards daylight hunting that is seen in some individuals appears to be modified by the level of human disturbance, the food demands of growing chicks and by the weather during the previous night. I could, for example, virtually guarantee early daylight hunting in my local birds following one or more nights of poor weather. Daylight hunting is reported to be quite normal in parts of Scotland and northern England (Bunn, 1972; Taylor, 1994). Bunn *et al.* (1982) observed that while some of their study birds were entirely nocturnal in habits, others invariably indulged in some hunting during daylight. Interestingly, one particular female was a regular daylight hunter over a two-year period before suddenly changing to being strictly nocturnal in habits. This change happened soon after a pheasant feeder was positioned close to the roost site, attracting corvids and, potentially, increasing the amount of harassment faced by the owl and her mate; he, incidentally, had always been a nocturnal hunter.

Little Owl activity peaks at about one to two hours after sunset and again just before sunrise. Exo (1989) found that the activity of individual Little Owls varied between six and nine hours per night, though it also changed with season. During the breeding season, for example, the Little Owls increased the amount of diurnal activity, perhaps in response to the increased demands of rearing a brood of hungry chicks. Activity patterns were also influenced by moon-phase (the owls were more active during a full moon), rainfall (they were less active when it was raining) and wind speed (they were found to be less active when the wind was stronger than a Beaufort Scale score of 3).

Tawny Owls are predominantly nocturnal in habits and, along with the Long-eared Owl, are our most nocturnal species. They will, however, hunt and call from early evening, particularly during the autumn or when they have large young in the nest. Hansen (1952) found that Tawny Owls initiated calling earlier after sunset in autumn than they did in winter, with a slight peak in the intensity of calling noted in the middle of the night. While the results of my own work (Ockendon *et al.*, in prep) support the former point, they contrast with the latter; we found that Tawny Owls became quieter later on at night when we looked at calling behaviour through a UK-wide project that extended over a single winter.

Hunting at night clearly provides some challenges, the most obvious of which appears to be the low levels of light by which a predator can locate and capture its prey. It would be wrong to assume that owls can operate in complete darkness or that night-time is without some degree of background illumination. In addition to light from the moon and stars, there is airglow and zodiacal light, the latter a consequence of the many thousands of meteors that burn up in the Earth's atmosphere each night. Escape from the sprawl of urban light pollution and give your eyes the chance to adapt to the darkness (a process called dark-adaptation and which in humans takes at least 40 minutes) and you will discover how much light is actually available on a typical summer's night. With such large and obvious eyes, you might expect owls to locate prey purely by using their visual apparatus. This is not necessarily the case, however, as we shall see in the follow sections.

OWL VISION

The large, forward-facing eyes which dominate the owl's facial disc suggest a degree of visual sensitivity well in excess of our own. After all, it is easy to assume that an owl must have excellent eyesight if it is to hunt and catch small mammals and other prey at night. Eye size and position are not the only things to determine visual sensitivity, however; the captured image has, for example, to be processed and interpreted. As we shall see, visual sensitivity is something that has been well studied in very few owl species but there is sufficient information available to report on how it compares with our own visual sensitivity and, additionally, that of diurnal birds.

The structure of the owl eye

An owl eye, with its bony sclerotic ring, has a characteristic tubular appearance (see Figure 13). Eye shape, which can be described by the ratio of corneal diameter to axial length, is known to vary with the light conditions under which a species is typically active. A large cornea, which is a feature of species active under low light intensities, allows for a larger pupil, which in turn allows more photons to enter the eye. Measurements of the corneal diameter to axial length ratio for owls show a similar pattern to those seen in other birds; the more nocturnally active species have the highest ratio and crepuscular species show intermediate ratio scores. Interestingly, the two 'diurnally active' owls to have been studied – Short-eared Owl and Northern Hawk Owl – have ratios that are more closely aligned to nocturnal and crepuscular species than expected, suggesting that we are either over-playing the degree of diurnal activity in these species or that it is a behaviour that has only been adopted relatively recently (Lisney *et al.*, 2012).

The tubular shape of the owl eye appears to be related to the owl's nocturnal habits, serving to maximise the size and brightness of the image falling on the retina (Martin, 1982). Which of these two features (image size and image brightness) is the more important has been under debate but, as Graham Martin notes, maximising image brightness is more likely to be 'a secondary consequence of nocturnality, the evolutionary outcome of squeezing an

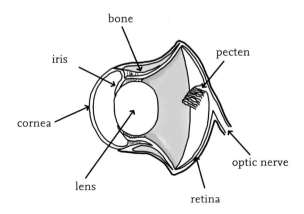

FIG 13. Cross section of owl eye. Redrawn from Harmening & Wagner, 2011.

absolutely large-sized eye into a relatively small skull'. If the owl eye was a more 'normal' rounded shape it would require a much larger skull – it is already too large to fit within the skull properly – adding significantly more weight and, presumably, hindering flight performance. In humans, the eyes occupy less than 5 per cent of the skull's volume but in birds the eyes typically contribute 50 per cent or more. In owls this figure increases to at least 70 per cent (Graham Martin, pers comm.). Because eyes are water-filled structures, examination of their contribution by weight may be more revealing, not least because they are the densest part of the head. A consequence of the eye being so large and tightly fitted within the orbit is a substantial loss of eye movement. Although all six of the extraocular eye muscles are present in owls, only very small movements are possible (a maximum amplitude of about 2° has been reported for Barn Owl, Steinbach & Money, 1973). The restricted degree of eye movement is compensated for by the owl's ability to move its head and to make the most of a long and flexible neck. To some extent the tubular eye can be considered as a cut-down version of a much larger rounded eye, the owl securing some key benefits but at the cost of some disadvantages, notably a reduced visual field width. At roughly 124°, the width of the visual field in Tawny Owl is, for example, some 40° narrower than that of a Starling *Sturnus vulgaris*, reducing the owl's awareness of the world around it. Again, this is something that is countered by the degree of head movement that owls can exhibit.

When we refer to an owl having a large-sized eye, what we are really talking about is an eye with a long focal length – the distance from the lens to the retina. As focal length increases so the size of the image on the retina increases. A larger eye, therefore, increases the distance from the lens to the retina and allows the formation of a larger image. It has been calculated that the Barn Owl eye is almost twice as long as that predicted by the wider relationship that exists between body weight and eye size in birds (Howland *et al.*, 2004). The owl eye achieves the increased distance needed to create a large image but, by using the tubular eye shape, avoids the additional weight and space costs that would come with a conventional rounded eye.

A term familiar to photographers is worth mentioning here and this is the f-number. The f-number gives a measure of the relative brightness of the image produced. It is expressed as a ratio of the focal length of the eye divided by the diameter of the entrance pupil, thus the smaller the f-number the brighter the image. The focal length of a Tawny Owl eye is, at 17.24 mm, only very slightly longer than our own (17.06 mm). With a pupil diameter of *c.* 13.3 mm, the Tawny Owl's f-number of 1.30 works out to be somewhat lower than that of a dark-adapted human eye (2.1) with its rather smaller pupil (*c.* 8 mm). The net effect of these two differences is that, when viewing the same scene, the image produced within the Tawny Owl eye is roughly 2.7 times brighter than that produced in a human eye under similar conditions. For comparison, the f-number of the Barn Owl eye is 1.3 and its focal length is 17.49 mm. The formation of a bright retinal image is a feature generally considered to be an adaptation to a nocturnal lifestyle.

The role of the lens

Light entering the eye is focussed on the retina by the cornea and lens, both familiar enough features of the vertebrate eye. The cornea plays a key role in refraction, while the lens is the primary means for altering the refractive state of the eye during accommodation (changing the thickness of the lens to focus on nearby or distant objects). The avian lens, in contrast to the mammalian one, has an annular pad at its core. It is thought that this pad helps the lens change shape under direction of the ciliary muscle and there is evidence of an interesting relationship between the size of this pad and the extent of accommodative ability in owls. Separate to this is a general relationship between the size of an owl and the degree of accommodation that can be achieved. Small owls tend to show a greater range of accommodation than larger owls, something that is, perhaps, related to the shorter distances over which smaller owls usually deal with food items, together with the generally smaller size of the prey items upon which they feed. Owls appear to be unable to accommodate independently in each eye, leaving them with what is termed 'coupled accommodation', the presence of which suggests that binocular vision is of particular importance to owls.

The optical quality of the owl eye is, in part, influenced by spatial irregularities in the curvature of the cornea and lens. Known as ocular wavefront aberrations, these can affect the quality of the image that is formed on the retina. Measurements of these aberrations in barn owls reveals that the degree of aberration is lower than has been reported in other vertebrates, suggesting that the quality of image projected onto the retina is excellent (Harmening & Wagner, 2011). Similar aberrations measured in human eyes are, on average, some three times greater.

The retina

The retina acts as a two-dimensional array, detecting the visual information that is projected onto its surface via the cornea and lens. Light particles – or more correctly photons – hitting the retinal surface are absorbed by photoreceptor cells, the resulting stimuli passing via the optic nerve to the region of the brain responsible for visual processing. These photoreceptor cells take several forms, the primary division being into rods and cones. The rods provide good sensitivity at low illumination levels – they are 25–100 times more sensitive than cones – but deliver poor acuity; the cones offer good visual acuity at higher light levels and provide colour vision, but perform poorly at low light levels. Needless to say, being nocturnal, the owl retina is dominated by rods – with a rod:cone ratio of roughly 30:3 – while the retina of a typical diurnal bird is dominated by special double-cone cells. Within the owls, there is also a tendency for the more nocturnal species to have fewer cones than those owls exhibiting more diurnal habits (Lisney *et al.*, 2012).

The type and density of the different photoreceptor cells not only differs between species but also varies across the retina of an individual eye. Concentrations of particular photoreceptors may be found at specific points on the retinal surface, typically in small pits known as foveae, and these provide areas of greater visual acuity. Such pits are a feature of primates and some birds, including the diurnal birds of prey, which are usually bifoveate. The presence of a discernible fovea has been confirmed for a number of Strigid owl species but there has been some debate as to whether or not a fovea occurs in any of the Tytonid owls. In all the owl species so far studied the fovea has tended to be small and, uniquely, dominated by rods rather than cones. Another feature of the retina worth mentioning here is the visual streak. This is an elongated area with an increased density of retinal ganglion cells. Diurnally active species living in open habitats tend to show a well-developed visual streak and it is thought that this allows them to view the horizon, over which new visual targets are most likely to appear, with increased resolution and with minimal head movements. Species living in enclosed habitats or which are nocturnal are predicted to have only a poorly developed visual streak. This general pattern is supported within those owls so far studied (Lisney *et al.*, 2012). To date, Snowy Owl has been found to have the best-defined visual streak, while Short-eared Owl and Burrowing Owl *Athene cunicularia* have well-developed streaks and American Barn Owl, Great Grey Owl *Strix nebulosa* and Barred Owl *Strix varia* have poorly resolved visual streaks.

As in other birds (and in contrast to mammals), the vascularisation of the owl retina is reduced and nourishment is received via a feature known as the pecten oculi, which typically has a pleated structure. It is composed almost entirely of blood vessels and projects into the eye chamber. It not only provides an oxygen gradient to the retina but also helps to maintain a constant temperature within the eye. The pecten oculi of owls, like that seen in other nocturnal birds, is quite small, being larger in diurnal birds and particularly large in diurnal birds of prey.

Microspectrophotometry has revealed the presence of several spectrally distinct visual pigments within the photoreceptors of the avian retina, most of which are associated with the cones. These play a key role in colour vision, something which requires the discrimination of objects on the basis of wavelength, rather than intensity. Information on the pigments, coupled with measurements of the spectral absorptance of the oil droplets with which each pigment is associated, has allowed researchers to model how a bird extracts spectral information through its retina. Each oil droplet acts as a filter, enhancing the discrimination of colours and improving colour constancy under different conditions. Some visual pigments are ultraviolet sensitive and there is evidence to suggest that some diurnal birds of prey, sensitive to ultraviolet, can detect and use vole scent marks which are visible in the ultraviolet spectrum (Viitala *et al.*, 1995). There is some evidence to suggest the presence of a similar ability in some owls but more research is needed in this area before more general conclusions can be drawn.

The visual pigment found in the rods of diurnal birds appears well suited to its use during the twilight of dusk and dawn. This pigment is less well suited to the lower illumination levels associated with night-time, however, and you might expect the visual pigment found in owl rods to be shifted towards the longer wavelengths associated with moonlight and starlight. Curiously, the rod visual pigment of owls is not shifted towards these wavelengths but remains similar to that of diurnal birds. One reason put forward to explain this is that extending the wavelength sensitivity of the pigment would increase the receptor's sensitivity to background 'dark' noise and reduce the ability of the bird to discriminate visually contrasting objects at night.

Owls probably use their cones mostly during twilight, something that is supported by the finding that although owls possess spectrally distinct types of oil droplet in their cones most of these appear colourless (just 10 per cent of the cones contain a yellow or orange droplet). Reducing the density of carotenoid pigment in the oil droplets is thought to increase the sensitivity of the cones under twilight conditions, allowing colour vision of a form to be used under these challenging conditions.

The importance of the nictitating membrane

One other important feature of the owl eye is the nictitating membrane, or third eyelid as it is sometimes called. The membrane is a feature shared with other birds but in owls it is particularly robust in structure, being used to protect the eye whenever the owl is engaged in any behaviour that might be considered hazardous. It is, for example, drawn across the eye as the bird comes to strike a potential prey item or when feeding young. Its movement across the eye also appears to be slower and more deliberate than that seen in most other birds.

FIG 14. Owls, such as this Short-eared Owl, typically close their nictitating membrane when dropping onto potential prey. (Steve Round)

How sensitive is the eyesight of owls?

Visual sensitivity is best measured by determining the minimum amount of light that can be detected by an individual, something that involves a process of long and careful experimentation. The resulting figure is known as the 'absolute visual threshold' and this figure has been obtained for the Tawny Owl by Professor Graham Martin. Some researchers have attempted to measure visual sensitivity in other ways by, for example, seeking to assess the minimum illumination levels under which an owl can locate a prey item by sight alone. These alternative methods, although seemingly attractive because of their 'natural behavioural' approach, are difficult to interpret, not least because controlled conditions are very hard to maintain and the owl may be using other cues to locate the prey. Measurement of the absolute visual threshold in the Tawny Owl shows that it overlaps with that calculated for humans. On average, Tawny Owls show slightly higher visual sensitivity than us, but, with the variation in sensitivity noted within species populations, there will be individual people who have greater visual sensitivity than certain Tawny Owls (Martin, 1977). The slightly greater average sensitivity of the Tawny Owl eye can be accounted for by the owl eye's ability to produce a brighter image of the same scene, when compared to a human observer. Importantly, however, the absolute visual sensitivity of the Tawny Owl is roughly 100 times greater than that of a pigeon.

The ability to produce a large and bright image is only part of the visual process. The image has to be decoded as it falls on the retina and the information contained then processed to interpret what it means. One measure of these processes is termed 'visual acuity', which can be defined as the ability to resolve fine-scale details in a visual scene. It has been found that owls, together with many other nocturnal or crepuscular animals, have poor visual acuity. It seems that there is a trade-off between sensitivity and acuity, suggesting that the owls have sacrificed sharp vision for higher sensitivity, something that is clearly advantageous under the challenging light conditions of the night-time world. Some idea of how the visual acuity of owls compares with that of the diurnal raptors can be seen from the following acuity scores: Wedge-tailed Eagle *Aquila audax* (140 cyc/deg), Brown Falcon *Falco berigora* (73 cyc/deg), Barn Owl (6.9 cyc/deg), Tawny Owl (8 cyc/deg) and Little Owl (6 cyc/deg). In case you are interested, 'cycles per degree', or cyc/deg, is a measure of spatial frequency, which is equal to the number of cycles of a grating (one dark and one light band) that subtends an angle of 1° at the eye! It is worth noting that the amount of spatial detail that can be resolved declines as light levels fall. This means that a diurnal bird, such as a pigeon, will have demonstrably inferior spatial resolution under night-time conditions than an owl.

The question of binocular vision

Binocular vision or 'stereopsis' is a direct and highly accurate means of judging visual depth and is likely to play a key role for predators, like owls, looking to target prey accurately. It is not, however, the only means by which visual depth may be calculated. A number of monocular depth cues are known to exist, including pictorial cues (e.g. size and colour), oculomotor cues (e.g. accommodation) and parallax movements (Rogers & Graham, 1979). It is possible, for example, to use the degree of accommodation to calculate the distance to an object, something that has been demonstrated in barn owls under monocular testing conditions (Wagner & Schaeffel, 1991). Stereopsis is likely to be the more important mechanism for owls, however, something that is supported by the associated neural specialisation that is seen in these birds.

Two key requirements for binocular vision are binocular overlap, which is to be found in some bird species that do not have functioning binocular vision, and a degree of visual acuity sufficient for small differences between the images produced by each eye to be identified (known as 'disparity detection'). Robert van der Willigen outlined the problem concisely when he wrote that the brain has to 'pair parts visible from the left eye, with non-corresponding parts as seen from the right eye's vantage point that originate from the same points in three-dimensional space.' Owls appear to have evolved binocular vision independently of mammals and rely on an elaborate neural substrate centred on the visual Wulst, a part of the avian forebrain into which the visual thalamus projects. In those birds with functioning binocular vision the visual Wulst forms a prominent bulge on the dorsal brain surface. An enlarged visual Wulst occurs in the Barn Owl and it has been shown to exhibit a high degree of binocular interaction and selectivity for binocular disparity. Binocular vision might also increase visual sensitivity through the process of binocular summation of the light reaching the eyes. That Barn Owls use binocular vision has been demonstrated by a series of experiments. In these, the owls were presented with random dot stereograms in which the illusion of three-dimensional depth was created. The owls tested were able to discriminate the presence of the illusion, a feat shared with human and primate study subjects (van der Willigen, 2011). Neural pathways clearly have an important role to play in such abilities, something that is better understood in the Little Owl (Bagnoli et al., 1990).

The rather narrow visual field width of owl eyes requires them to be placed in a more forward-facing position in order to generate good binocular coverage. Forward placement comes at a cost to the bird, however, leaving less comprehensive coverage of what is going on elsewhere around it. Interestingly, in contrast to a human observer the eyes of an owl do not face directly forward; instead they diverge at c. 55–60°, leaving a binocular field of c. 48° (see Figure 15).

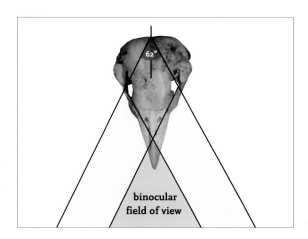

binocular
field of view

FIG 15. Diagrammatic representation of binocular vision in an owl. (Mike Toms)

Our own eyes diverge by 10° and we have a maximum binocular field of 140°. This appears to be a trade-off, the owl moderating the benefits of binocular vision with the need to have some peripheral vision. The outer margin of the binocular field coincides with the feathering of the facial disk and it is interesting to note that the tip of the bill typically falls outside of the owl's visual field. This is in contrast to a bird like a pigeon, where the tip of the bill is placed well within the binocular field. Presumably the pigeon needs to be able to focus on food items taken directly in the bill, while the owl strikes with its feet before passing captured prey to the bill. Payne (1971) demonstrated that as an owl is about to strike its prey the feet are brought up in front of the eyes, forming a straight line from the eyes, through the talons to the prey. It has been noted by some observers that an owl will usually close its eyes when captured prey is passed from the talons to the bill, perhaps to lessen the chance of damage to the eyes.

FIG 16. Barn Owl chicks show a high degree of short-sightedness, their eyes developing with age, growing in length and changing shape. (Mike Toms)

Optical development of the owl eye

In those owl species studied so far, the eye has been found to develop from the starting point of a more rounded shape, the characteristic tubular appearance only developing over time as the chick approaches its adult size and form. In fact, owl eyes undergo an unusually large range of growth during their development, the axial length increasing by a factor of 2.5 or more. Other changes include an increase in pupil diameter and a change in both lens thickness and shape. Such changes will have an impact on the young owl's visual capabilities. For example, when American Barn Owl chicks open their eyes for the first time at c. 12 days of age they show a high degree of myopia (short-sightedness). By 28 days of age the optical qualities of their developing eyes have become substantially better but have still not reached that of an adult (Schaeffel & Wagner, 1996). Since the chick is being provided with food in the relative shelter of its nesting cavity, the temporary short-sightedness is of little consequence. It is also known that the development of owl eyes, and more widely those of other vertebrates, is under visual control. Any perturbation to the quality of the retinal image during this period of growth may bring about longer-term complications. Visual capabilities during this period may also influence the quality of the motor and auditory maps formed within the brain and it is known that owls that have been temporarily and experimentally 'blinded' over their first few weeks of life develop degraded brain maps, altering future perception and interpretation of the visual and auditory world around them (Knudsen, 1988; du Lac & Knudsen, 1991).

The owl eye in the real world

Measurements of the levels of illumination present at night have been derived for several different habitats. It is possible to use these alongside information derived from laboratory work on visual sensitivity to determine how well an owl might be able to see under different field conditions. The levels of background illumination present within open habitats are sufficient to provide a hunting owl with enough light to see its way around and to find food. Underneath the closed canopy of a woodland, however, there may be instances where the levels of illumination fall below the threshold needed by a foraging owl. In particular, the ability to pick out fine detail may fall to a point where the owl is unable to discriminate a prey item from the substrate on which it is sitting (Martin, 1990). Under such conditions, the owl may attempt to counter this problem through both the use of other senses (e.g. hearing) and changes in its behaviour. For example, the Tawny Owl – a species which lives within closed canopy woodland – is well known for its sedentary and highly territorial nature. This lifestyle may enable the owl to use its knowledge of its territory to support the visual information being received. Interestingly, there is evidence that Tawny Owls may, on occasion, collide with obstacles. Graham Hirons once commented that his study owls occasionally flew into branches or even tree trunks if disturbed or surprised at night (Martin, 1986) and Goodman & Glynn (1988) reported that bone fractures were more common in owls than in birds active during the daytime. This might suggest that their vision is fallible under the dark conditions of a closed canopy woodland at night.

It is sometimes stated that owls cannot see very well during the day but this is not true. While certainly inferior to the diurnal birds of prey (and humans), the visual acuity of the owl eye functions at a similar level to that of a pigeon. The owl eye is, however, unable to make fine-scale colour discriminations as well as a diurnal bird, something supported by both behavioural studies and analyses of the visual pigments themselves.

An interesting feature of owls is the pronounced degree of head movement that is often seen, typically where an owl is attempting to make sense of an object in front of it. Such movements are used by the owl to estimate the location,

FIG 17. The use of miniature cameras has revealed how owls direct their gaze in a manner that brings the object of interest to a specific point on the retina. (Shay Ohayon)

distance to and motion of an object through a mechanism known as motion parallax (van der Willigen *et al.*, 2002; Ohayon *et al.*, 2006). The head movements artificially change the location of the object on the owl's retina, increasing the visual information available to the bird. Studies have demonstrated that horizontal movements (termed 'peering') are the most important for the owl, generating a larger motion parallax for objects that are close by as opposed to distant. The owl can then use this information when it leaves its perch to strike at a potential prey item. Such movements are particularly evident in Long-eared Owls (Scott, 1997). Owls have been shown to use such movements for both static and moving prey, underlining that they are not simply tracking the movements of an object. Interestingly, there is evidence to suggest that owls seek to intercept moving prey, rather than simply track it, effectively calculating a point of interception (Fux & Eilam, 2009). A study involving the use of a miniature camera, fixed to the owl's head, has revealed that owls consistently direct their gaze in a way that brings the object of interest to a specific location on the retina where, presumably, there is a particular concentration of photoreceptors (Ohayon *et al.*, 2008).

It seems, therefore, as if the structure of the owl eye is the result of attempting to deliver a large and bright image in order to couple high absolute sensitivity with relatively high spatial resolution at low levels of illumination. However, while the visual abilities of owls are highly sensitive, and indeed close to what is theoretically achievable, there are still conditions under which they are unable to provide a visual representation of the environment within which the owl may find itself. Under such circumstances, can an owl turn to any of its other senses?

OWL HEARING

While the eyes of owls are a large and obvious feature the ears are easily overlooked, hidden as they are behind the ruff of feathers that gives the owls their characteristic facial disc (see Figure 18). Once you understand the importance of hearing to owls, and how sounds are directed towards the ear openings, you come to realise that the facial disc is akin to a parabolic reflector, playing a key functional role in hearing. Although characteristic of owls, it is worth noting that a facial disc of sorts is also found in the harriers *Circus* spp.

The importance of the facial disc was revealed by Roger Payne, who examined its structure in detail ahead of his wider work into the acoustic location of prey by the American Barn Owl. Payne found that the entire facial disc was covered with filamentous auricular feathers; in other birds these normally cover just the ear hole. The auricular feathers have slender shafts, long barbs and, importantly,

FIG 18. The owl's facial disc acts like a parabolic reflector, directing sounds towards the ears. Beneath the feathers are asymmetrically positioned ears and ear flaps. (Mike Toms)

lack barbules, giving the plumage of the facial disc a loose and filamentous structure that allows sound to pass through freely. As Payne himself noted, it is as if 'acoustically-speaking, the auricular feathers are really "not there".' The feathers that form the heart-shaped ruff are, however, important. These are densely packed and highly modified reflector feathers, each displaying a reduced web and rachis (the part of the feather shaft bearing the vane). The skin from which they emerge is also thickened and the whole ruff acts to deflect sound. Not only does the facial disc, including the ruff, direct sound onto the ears, it also appears to act as an amplifier. Masakazu Konishi (1973) calculated that, for sounds of roughly 7 kHz, the Barn Owl's ruff delivers a ten-fold increase in the sound pressure reaching the ear. It is thought that the musculature associated with the ear openings may enable the shape of the ruff to be altered, helping to focus sounds towards the ears.

If you were to remove the feathers of the facial disc from a Barn Owl you would reveal the asymmetrically positioned ears and their associated ear flaps, the latter being square in shape and surprisingly large. Go one stage further and draw a horizontal line through the eyes and you would discover that the centre of the left ear flap sits above this line, while the centre of the right ear flap sits below it. The angle formed between the edge of each ear flap and the line of closure of the bill also differs (by about 15°) between the two sides of the head (Payne, 1971). This is known as bilateral asymmetry of the outer ear and it is found in many other, but not all, owl species. *Asio* owls, like the Barn Owl, show a difference in the vertical placement of their ear openings but consistency in their size and shape. In Tengmalm's Owl, however, the asymmetry arises in the skull rather than in the external ear (see Figure 8), but even here there is never any asymmetry to the structure of the inner or middle ears. As we shall see later in this chapter, this makes a lot of sense, the owl generating variation in when a sound reaches each of the two ears but requiring consistency in the bits of the ear that detect and interpret the sound reaching them in order to allow a proper comparison.

Structure of the owl ear

In common with the ears of mammals, those of birds are made up of three recognisable regions: the outer ear, the middle ear and the inner ear. Pressure waves (sound) reach the outer ear from the environment and are channelled to

FIG 19. The ear opening of a Great Grey Owl; note the nature of the surrounding feathers. (Tim Birkhead)

the middle ear via the auditory canal. Here they reach the ear drum, which is proportionally larger in owls than it is in other birds. The pressure waves are then transformed from airborne vibrations of large amplitude and small force to fluid-borne vibrations of large force and small amplitude within the fluid-filled cochlea that forms the inner ear. This is accomplished through the combination of the ear drum and a single bone (the columella auris); mammals, by way of comparison, have three bones (the malleus, incus and stapes).

While the cochlea assumes a spiral shape in mammals, in birds it is either straight or slightly curved, the latter being the case in the Barn Owl. The spiral nature of the mammalian cochlea secures greater length in a given space than is possible within the straight avian cochlea, something that explains why mammalian cochleas are usually notably longer than those seen in comparable-sized birds. Avian cochlea length also shows a relationship with body size, being, for example, just 1.6 mm in the Zebra Finch *Taeniopygia guttata* but 5.5 mm in the Emu *Dromaius novaehollandiae*. The cochlea of owls break with the body size rule, being substantially longer than those seen in other birds; that of the barn owls, for example, is 9–11 mm (depending on species).

The fluid-filled cochlea contains the basilar membrane to which are attached many thousands of minute hair cells. Vibrations in the fluid are detected by these hair cells, which then send a signal to the brain via the auditory nerve. Sounds of different frequencies reach different parts of the cochlea, stimulating different hair cells to build up a complex picture of the sound being received. It has been found that the Barn Owl has somewhere in the region of 16,300 hair cells, together with a number of modifications not seen in other avian orders, including thickening of the membrane and the presence of an additional sub-type of hair cell (Dyson *et al.*, 1998). More than 50 per cent of the hair cells are devoted to frequencies above 5 kHz, a frequency range where many other birds have poor sensitivity. Barn Owls still retain a similar amount of coverage for the lower frequencies as seen in other birds. One final feature of the hair cells, shared with other birds but not mammals, is the ability to replace them on a regular basis. The loss of hair cells is one of the reasons for the decline in human hearing sensitivity with age, a problem seemingly not encountered by birds.

Sound sensitivity and the importance of asymmetry

The sensitivity of owl ears is not that dissimilar to our own. As with vision, there is a certain amount of overlap between the hearing abilities of human and owl study subjects, such that there are individual humans whose hearing is superior to that of individual owls, and vice versa. Information on the absolute sensitivity to different frequency sounds is available for a dozen or so owl species underlining that their hearing is more sensitive than that of other birds, particularly at frequencies of 5 kHz and above. Payne's experiments, using owls trained to strike at a concealed loudspeaker, found that American Barn Owls were dependent upon frequencies above 8.5 kHz to make an accurate strike and would not attempt a strike at all if all frequencies above 5 kHz had been removed from the sound source.

The absolute sensitivity of the owl ear is probably fairly close to what is theoretically possible, given the evolutionary, physiological and environmental constraints imposed. For example, increased sensitivity beyond the levels currently achieved might introduce a significant degree of background noise, reducing the ability to resolve biologically relevant sounds from other environmental noises. Payne found that the American Barn Owl's sensitivity in its left ear was at a maximum near the line of sight but then fell away gradually as the sound source was moved off in a horizontal plane towards the opposite ear. The upper and lower boundaries of this region of maximum sensitivity dropped away rapidly into two horizontal regions of poor sensitivity. These patterns were repeated in the right ear, this time shifted some 15° vertically, reflecting the asymmetrical placement of the two ears.

Asymmetrical positioning of the outer ears means that each ear receives a slightly different set of information from the same sound source. For example, a sound may reach one ear fractionally ahead of reaching the other (known as interaural onset time), differ in sound spectrum (interaural spectrum) or differ in intensity (interaural intensity). It appears that owls use interaural onset time to identify the horizontal angle of the sound source, relative to the bird, and interaural intensity as a major cue for the vertical (elevational) plane (Poganiatz & Wagner, 2001). Masakazu Konishi's experiments, which involved plugging one ear and then the other, highlighted the importance of interaural intensity (plus, possibly, interaural spectrum) in Barn Owl. Owls with their right ear plugged struck to the left and short of the target; those with the left ear plugged struck to the right and beyond the target. The frequency of the sound being heard may also influence the accuracy by which it can be located. Singheiser et al. (2010), for example, found that Barn Owls were more successful in striking at high frequency targets than low frequency ones, something that is also predicted from examination of the positioning of hair cells within the Barn Owl cochlea.

A number of studies, involving both Barn Owl and Long-eared Owl, demonstrate that asymmetrical positioning of the ears serves to modify the sounds received, the degree of modification varying according to both the location of the sound (relative to the owl) and its frequency (Norberg, 1968; Payne, 1971). Although modification of the sound signal may be key to determining the source of the sound, it is possible that different owls may employ different approaches to resolving this tricky problem.

Hearing and prey location

In order to accurately locate the source of a sound, such as a small mammal moving through the leaf litter of a woodland floor, the owl needs to establish both the angle of the sound relative to its own position and the distance to the source. The angle of the sound (its angular direction) has two components, one in the horizontal plane (termed azimuth) and the other in the vertical plane (termed elevation). How the owl is able to establish these three key components is something that has emerged from a growing body of research that extends back over a number of decades to a key piece of work carried out by Roger Payne and published in 1971. The suggestion that owls might be able to locate prey in total darkness via auditory cues had emerged experimentally a few years earlier when Payne & Drury showed this ability for American Barn Owl, Barred Owl and Long-eared Owl.

The work published by Payne in 1971 centred on a series of laboratory experiments in which he examined how American Barn Owls targeted prey under dark conditions. During the experiment, each owl was housed in a large, light-proof room, the floor of which was covered to a depth of 5 cm with leaf litter. Live mice were released into the room and the behaviour of the owl was viewed. In order to accustom the owls to the experimental set-up, the room was initially kept illuminated. Gradually, over a period of several weeks, light levels were reduced, all the time the owls being fed on live mice introduced into the room. Eventually, the mice were being introduced into a room that was now in complete darkness for 12 hours each day. Payne used an infra-red imaging device to watch the owls (there is no evidence that owls are sensitive to infra-red) and discovered that, although the owl did not feed at all for the first three nights of darkness, it struck directly and accurately on the fourth night that a mouse was introduced. During subsequent days another 16 trials were carried out, the owl striking 16 times, missing on just four of these occasions and then only by a matter of a few inches. In each case the owl left its perch only when the mouse paused and the rustling noise of the leaves ceased.

In order to be certain that the owl was responding to the sound of the mouse moving through the leaf litter, rather than something else, Payne carried out another series of experiments. During the first of these, Payne introduced a dummy mouse (a wad of paper on a piece of thread) and pulled this across the room, through the litter. The owl responded by pouncing on the wad of paper just as if it had been a live mouse. Since the paper was as inert as the background leaf litter, Payne could rule out any possibility that the owl might have been using infra-red vision. Payne then experimentally impaired the owl's hearing with a small wad of cotton, carefully positioning it in one of the ears. Even with the cotton in place, the owl attempted to strike at the live mice but on each occasion missed its target, typically landing about 40 cm short. Payne was unable to determine the extent by which his owls could judge distance. Because they had been kept in the same room over many months prior to experimentation, it is likely that they would have been familiar with the distance to the floor from their perch and thus would already have some measure of the distance once a sound source was heard under blackout conditions. One of the particularly interesting findings of Payne's work was that the owls studied could not capture prey by auditory cues alone if they did not have previous experience of catching prey by using visual cues in the same situation. Once they had experienced a novel situation and caught prey with the aid of visual cues they could then catch prey solely using auditory cues.

Payne also studied the behaviour of the owl and how it targeted and approached the mouse under different lighting conditions. When a mouse was introduced into an illuminated room the owl quickly turned to face the mouse then, leaning forward slightly, it would briefly freeze before leaving the perch in a glide that took it towards the mouse. When it was about a metre from the mouse, the owl would suddenly thrust its feet forward until they almost touched the bill and then pull its head sharply back. The moment of impact, where one foot hit the mouse and the other the ground, was accompanied by the owl shutting its eyes,

FIG 20. Small mammals, such as this Yellow-necked Mouse, may use fallen branches and cover to reduce their chances of being detected by a hunting Tawny Owl. (John Harding)

perhaps to protect them from any risk of damage. When a mouse was introduced into a dark room the owl typically turned its head to face the mouse as soon as it was first heard in the leaf litter. Moving the head to face the sound makes sense, since sounds are located most accurately when they are directly in front of the head and the facial disc, and Payne noted that the owl needed to hear at least one more sound once facing the source before it would strike. This is reflected in the brief pause that was again evident as the owl checked its orientation, before it left the perch. In darkness the approach to the target was made using flapping flight rather than a glide, the bird covering the distance in roughly double the time taken when the room was illuminated. Another characteristic of this slower approach was that the owl swung its feet beneath it, back and forth like a pendulum, until they were brought forward for the strike as before.

Owl hearing in the real world

Various observations in the wild provide evidence of owls hunting prey solely through the use of auditory cues. Perhaps the most often cited example of this behaviour refers to the Great Grey Owl and its ability to accurately target small mammal prey in their runs under continuous snow cover (Mikkola, 1983). There is a report of the same species using a similar approach to take a Pocket Gopher *Thomomys talpoides* from its burrow (Tryon, 1943), plus reports of Short-eared Owl taking small mammals from within continuous dead grass cover (Clark, 1975) and Tawny Owl taking earthworms (Macdonald, 1976). Several parallel pieces of evidence suggest that a quartering owl, hunting on the wing, flies at the optimum height above the ground (c. 3–4 m) to scan and listen for potential prey before pouncing. When you watch a hunting Barn Owl or Short-eared Owl, for example, you will often see it quartering towards the bottom end of this range, sometimes checking its flight to hover briefly at a slightly lower height before pouncing. The sensitivity of an owl's hearing, therefore, suggests that it plays an important role in prey location, being used alongside visual cues to locate and capture prey.

FLIGHT IN OWLS

A general pattern is evident within the owls, whereby those species that hunt on the wing and over open ground tend to have longer and broader wings, while those that hunt from a perch or live within forest or jungle tend to have shorter and more rounded wings. Such differences represent adaptation to the different habitats and modes of hunting. Even though owls belonging to the Tytonidae tend to be longer winged, relative to their body size, than owls belonging to the

Strigidae, a similar habitat-related pattern is evident within both families. These are not the only adaptations related to flight since owls possess other features that aid their predatory lifestyle.

The use of slow flight

As we have just noted, those owls that hunt prey by quartering open ground have relatively long and broad wings. The resulting ratio of wing area to body mass produces a low wing loading that supports flight at the slow speeds suited to hunting from the wing. It has been estimated, for example, that a Barn Owl, which has a wing loading of 0.21 g/cm^2, quarters with a ground speed of up to 16 km/hour (Barn Owl Trust, 2012). Wing loadings have been calculated for Tawny Owl (0.40), Short-eared Owl (0.36) and Long-eared Owl (0.29). A particularly interesting comparison between Barn Owl and the pigeon *Columba livia*, made by Bachmann and his co-workers (Bachmann *et al.*, 2007), highlights this and other adaptations favouring slow flight. The two species are roughly similar in terms of their body weight, with the same number of flight feathers. However, the flight feathers of the Barn Owl are larger and, coupled with a longer wing, this produces a larger wing area and results in a lower wing loading for the Barn

FIG 21. The low wing loading seen in the Barn Owl supports flight at low speeds enabling the bird to quarter the ground for small mammal prey. (Steve Round)

Owl, compared with the pigeon. Not only does this allow the owl to fly at slower speeds, but it also prevents the bird from stalling when it makes a sharp turn and supports the efficient transportation of heavy prey items. A similar conclusion was reached by Neuhaus and colleagues in 1973, when they compared Tawny Owl and Mallard. Bachmann's work also revealed a degree of asymmetry between the two vanes of each Barn Owl wing feather, something not seen in the pigeon. The inner and outer vanes each serve a different function during flapping flight and it appears that the asymmetry seen in Barn Owl flight feathers, coupled with their more porous nature, makes the wing less stiff and more pliant. This might also support slower flight, which in turn reduces energy expenditure – important when hunting from the wing – and reduces flight noise (see below).

Silent flight

It is only when you experience a hunting Barn Owl at close quarters that you truly appreciate the quietness of its flight, the bird drifting low over your head on soundless wings. Silent flight is a feature of many other owl species and its occurrence appears to be related to hunting habits and the spectrum of prey species taken. If owl flight was a noisy affair then it might alert potential prey to the owl's approach, making prey capture all the more difficult. This is likely to be a particular problem where the prey being targeted are small mammals, which are known to have excellent hearing in the ultrasonic range. Many birds other than owls generate ultrasonic sounds during flight, something first noticed by Thorpe & Griffin (1962) during experiments looking at the ultrasonic components of bird vocalisations. Noise generated from the owl's plumage might additionally mask the sounds made by prey and make it more difficult for the owl to pinpoint a meal by ear.

It was more than a century ago that the morphology of owl feathers, and how they might differ from other birds, was first considered. Mascha (1904) revealed the presence of a comb-like structure on the leading edge of the outer primary of the owl wing. This can be seen with the naked eye particularly well on a species like Barn Owl, where the serrations that make up the comb-like structure also extend onto the corresponding primary covert (see Figure 22). In certain other species, e.g. Tawny Owl, Long-eared Owl and Eagle Owl, the serrations can also be found on the neighbouring primary which, in these species, also forms part of the leading edge of the wing. The nature of these serrations has been well studied, often by those working in the field of aeronautics and looking for characters within the natural world that might be transferrable to the domain of aeronautical engineering. Thomas Bachmann and colleagues, working in Germany, have studied these serrations in depth, even using laser scanning

FIG 22. The comb-like serrations on the leading edge of certain Barn Owl wing feathers, coupled with the soft fringe on the trailing edge, help reduce flight noise. (Mike Toms)

microscopy to resolve their precise three-dimensional structure (Bachmann & Wagner, 2011). Each serration is formed from the tip of a single feather barb, its structure curved so that the tip of the serration faces at right angles away from the feather shaft. In the Common Barn Owl the serrations average just 1.8 mm but are slightly longer in the American Barn Owl (Bachmann *et al.*, 2007). Published data on other owl species are lacking.

The serrations of the leading edge are not the only feature to be found on an owl's wing. Graham, working in the 1930s, noted two other features. The first of these was that the trailing edge of the flight feathers was characterised by the presence of a soft fringe, again something that can be seen with the naked eye in Barn Owl (Figure 22). The second feature was the characteristic downy upper surface to the flight feathers. More recent work has, additionally, revealed the presence of a fringe on the leading edge of many flight feathers (though not those carrying serrations). Thomas Bachmann's most recent work (Bachmann *et al.*, 2012) demonstrates that the fringes on the trailing edge of the flight feathers act to remove rough and, therefore, noisy edges, reducing overall flight noise. They achieve this by effectively merging onto the neighbouring feather vanes, slipping into grooves in the underside of the wing. The downy upper surface to the flight feathers is also likely to work in a similar fashion, reducing rough edges and the effect of feathers moving over each other during flapping flight. The downy appearance of the feather surface occurs because of the elongation of the feather barbules.

Over the years, there has been a fair bit of discussion about these different features and how they relate to the aerodynamic functions of the wing and to flight noise reduction. A key question has been which is more important: the owl's ability to fly very slowly or the direct influence of plumage morphology on the physical mechanisms of sound generation (Sarradj et al., 2010)? Both have a role to play, since slow and silent flight is a key adaptation for many owl species. Features associated with silent flight have been found most commonly in owls that prey upon small mammals, but are absent or reduced in those owls that, for example, feed on fish. Owls that typically hunt small mammals from a perch, e.g. Tawny Owl, and then glide towards their prey, also show the serrations and fringing, again suggesting that they are an adaption for silent flight rather than a secondary consequence emerging from features that support slow flight.

SOME OTHER FEATURES OF OWLS

Characteristics of the owl legs, feet and bill

Although the legs of owls are considered short relative to those of bird-eating raptors like Sparrowhawk *Accipiter nisus*, they are comparable in length to diurnal raptor species that feed on mammals. In general, and relative to body size, those of the Tytonidae are longer than those of the Strigidae, although there are exceptions, such as the Burrowing Owl, which is strongly terrestrial in habits. The legs of most owls are feathered, the feathers becoming smaller down the legs, with the feathering often continuing onto the tops of the toes. It is thought that the feathering offers the legs some protection from prey that might bite or scratch. The legs of certain species, notably Buffy Fish Owl *Bubo ketupu* and Blakiston's Fish Owl *Bubo blakistoni*, lack the extensive feathering seen in other owl species.

When a Tawny Owl strikes at a mouse or vole it is the feet, thrust out in front of the bird, that do the killing. The talons are opened fully just prior to impact, providing the maximum possible area for the strike. The momentum of the strike itself is often sufficient to kill the victim but, if not, the subsequent clenching of the talons almost certainly will. As any bird ringer will tell you, the strong grip of a Tawny Owl or Barn Owl can deliver the talons with some degree of force into unsuspecting flesh. The undersides of the toes are rough to

FIG 23. The talon flange of a Barn Owl develops with age and is thought to be used when preening the facial ruff. (Mike Toms)

the touch, highly developed into numerous papillae which aid grip. In many species, for example Barn Owl, the talons and highly moveable toes are somewhat elongated, a feature that increases the size of the area that can be hit by the striking owl. While three toes are usually directed forward, and the fourth backward, owls will sometimes perch with a second toe directed backwards. The inner and central toes of the Tytonidae are of about equal length, while in the Strigidae the inner toe is noticeably shorter than the central one.

Another interesting feature, found in the Barn Owl, is the talon flange that is located on the inner edge of the central toe. This develops with age, starting out as a narrow ridge, before widening to *c.* 1.5 mm and then becoming notched, seemingly with wear (see Figure 23). The flange is thought to be used by the owl to comb the facial ruff but it is certainly less well developed than similar adaptations seen in other birds (e.g. nightjars). The development of the flange has been put forward by some authors (e.g. Johnson, 1991) as a means for ageing Barn Owls but others (e.g. Ramsden, pers. comm.) have questioned the resolution achievable with this approach. Johnson's work, using young from wild broods, road casualties and captive birds of known age, found that the flange was first distinguishable when the owl reached 65–78 days of age. It then developed to reach 1.5 mm in males and 2.0 mm in females some seven months after fledging. There is a suggestion that the talon flange may have a role in reducing the load of feather parasites, though experimental studies are required to test this (Bush *et al.*, 2012).

The hooked bill, with the soft cere at its base and sharp cutting edge, is a feature shared with the diurnal raptors. It is, however, more downward-pointing in the owls than it is in the diurnal raptors and is rather short in profile, perhaps to reduce the extent to which it obstructs the visual field. The cere is usually overlaid with thick bristles, the extent and structure of these varying with species. Bill colour is fairly uniform within the owls and is typically some shade of grey or brown, the former being the more commonly encountered colour. As is the case with most other birds, the owls have a small overhang at the tip of their bill, which could be used to shear through the tough cuticle of feather parasites; again this is something that requires experimental study before firm conclusions can be drawn.

Plumage colour and pattern

Unsurprisingly, given their nocturnal habitats and tendency to hide-up during the day, the plumage of owls is typically cryptic, both in terms of the colour palette and the form of patterning. Plumage colours tend to be a mixture of browns, ochres and greys, with both darker and lighter elements that may serve to break up the outline of the bird when it is roosting. As with other groups of birds, there is a tendency for species and races occupying humid climates to have

FIG 24. The pale colouration of the Lilith Owl is typical of desert-living species. (Mohamed Bin Azzan Almazrouei)

FIG 25. A number of owls, including this Short-eared Owl, show brightly coloured eyes and/or ear tufts. (Steve Round)

darker plumage than those occupying arid environments, a pattern referred to as Gloger's Rule. This trait can be seen, for example, in both the *Bubo* eagle owls and the *Athene* little owls, where the desert and arid-land forms are distinctively paler.

Colour polymorphism is common in owls, occurring in roughly one in three species and to a degree greater than that seen in other bird families (Galeotti & Sacchi, 2003). Tawny Owls, for example, exhibit variation in plumage colour that extends from pale grey to a warm reddy-brown but this is more usually viewed as two colour morphs – one grey and one brown – based on a bimodal distribution. European Tawny Owl populations typically feature both colour morphs and plumage colour has been shown to be a hereditable trait, with offspring resembling the colour of their parents. It is thought that the existence of the two morphs is maintained by fluctuating selection pressures (Brommer *et al.*, 2005) and it has been shown that the two morphs differ in both parasite loads (Chapter 5) and lifetime reproductive success (Chapter 3). Colour polymorphism has also been demonstrated to covary with diet; in Barn Owls, light-coloured morphs differ in the prey species taken from dark-coloured forms (Roulin, 2004a).

In light of the generally cryptic nature of the plumage, one curious feature is the degree of ornamentation on the face and head of many owls. In addition to the presence of ear tufts and/or the brightly coloured irises seen in some species (see Figure 25), many owls exhibit conspicuous 'eye brows' or other features whose shape may, on occasion, be modified in an expressive manner. It has been suggested that these 'ornaments' may be used in communication, either directed towards an owl of the same species or used to startle a potential predator. A review of head ornamentation has been carried out by Paolo Galeotti and Diego Rubolini, who derived an index of head ornamentation for all known owls based on nine different colour cues. These were centred on the ear tufts, iris, front of head, eyebrows, bristles, facial disc, rims, chin and throat. The two researchers, who used pairwise comparisons to control for phylogeny, found that the conspicuousness of the head ornamentation was generally greater in species that lived in open habitats and in those regarded as being more diurnally active. Many of the cues were found to be intercorrelated, such that the presence of ear tufts was often strongly associated with conspicuous eye brows, rims and chin (Galeotti & Rubolini, 2007). Although the authors suggest that the link between head ornamentation and association with more strongly illuminated environments is indicative of a communicative rather than anti-predator role, it could be argued that the impact of predators is also greater in these environments and that head ornamentation could have evolved to startle predators. That ornamentation can have a clear intraspecific communication role can be seen in the throat badge of the Eurasian Eagle Owl. This patch, which is present in both male and female Eagle Owls, is only visible when the bird calls, something that is further emphasised by the posture the bird adopts when calling. We will return to the Eagle Owl throat patch in Chapter 3.

One further result to emerge from the study, namely that there was no evidence that smaller species were more likely to have ornamentation, also lends support to an intraspecific communicative role rather than an interspecific, anti-predation role. One aspect of plumage ornamentation that might have an anti-predator role, however, is that of 'false eyes'. A number of smaller owl species have patches of feathers on the nape that resemble eyes and which might just act to deter predators approaching from behind. The use of 'false eyes' to startle predators has been well studied in certain invertebrates, notably butterflies, but little work has been done on a possibly similar function in owls.

Ear tufts and iris colour

At least a third of the world's owl species sport 'ear tufts' or 'horns', formed on the side of the crown from one or more feathers. Despite the name, these are completely unrelated to hearing but, as we have seen, may serve a role in communication, display or camouflage. It is in the Long-eared Owl that perhaps these 'ear tufts' are most familiar. Each tuft, which is formed from six to eight feathers, is lightly barred and has distinct patterning. When the owl is relaxed, the tufts are flattened backwards over the head but they are often held erect when the owl is alarmed. Scott (1997) noted that the tufts may be held partly raised when the Long-eared Owl is participating in its display flight.

Most of the strigid owls, including Eagle Owl, Little Owl, Long-eared Owl and Short-eared Owl, have brightly coloured irises. These vary from pale lemon yellow, through brighter yellows and oranges, up to a rich warm red-brown colouration. Iris colour in owls may have a communicative or social function or it may, perhaps, provide a signal of mate quality. This is a feature not seen within the barn owls and more work is needed to resolve any underlying function.

Sexual size dimorphism

In common with many other birds of prey, owls often show pronounced size dimorphism, with the female the larger of the two sexes. Heimo Mikkola (2012) examined size differences across 156 owl species for which male and female body size was known, finding that in 92 per cent of cases the female was the larger sex. The extent of size dimorphism varies with species, being just 5 per cent in Barn Owl and roughly 25 per cent in Tawny Owl. There are, of course, seasonal differences in body weight linked to energetic constraints and the breeding cycle. Female Tawny Owls are heavier in winter than in summer, a similar pattern to that seen in males but with the addition of a pronounced spring peak ahead of the first egg being laid.

Sexual size dimorphism in owls and diurnal birds of prey has been linked to diet, with the degree of dimorphism increasing in line with the increasing speed and agility of the main prey (Newton, 1979). Sexual size dimorphism reaches its extreme in small bird-hunting accipiters, like Sparrowhawk *Accipiter nisus*. In a study of North American owls, Earhart & Johnson (1970) found that the degree of dimorphism was correlated with the proportion of vertebrates in the diet. That it has arisen in several different taxonomic groups suggests adaptive significance. Various hypotheses have been put forward to explain sexual size dimorphism in birds of prey and owls, and to explain why it is the female who is the larger of the two sexes. These include the suggestion that it allows greater partitioning of the prey resource between the two sexes, the male taking smaller prey and the female larger, and that while males are able to maximise their hunting success by being closer to their prey in size, females are constrained by the demands of having to produce eggs and brood young and so remain the larger sex. A consequence of the dimorphism is that the female can dominate the prey resources being delivered to the nest by her mate, and has body reserves to support her if conditions are difficult when she is incubating or brooding at the nest. There is certainly the potential for more work in this area, something that can be seen from recently published research, such as that by Geir Sonerud and colleagues (Sonerud *et al.*, 2012).

Vocalisations

Given their largely nocturnal habits, it is unsurprising to find that vocalisations play an important role in the lives of owls. The calls of species like Tawny Owl and Long-eared Owl, most commonly heard at a time of year when few other creatures are vocalising, makes owls a familiar part of the winter soundscape. The main calls are used to advertise ownership of breeding territory or to attract a mate and we will return to these in Chapter 3. Others are used as contact calls, between pair members or between adults and their young. Some may be used to solicit food and others to express alarm or agitation. The sounds made by our owls take many different forms and even within a single species many different sounds can be identified. Not all of the sounds may be vocalisations as some are produced mechanically through bill-snapping or wing-clapping. Again, this is something to which we will return in later chapters.

The vocalisations made by owls are thought to be innate, rather than learned, allowing them to be used in the clarification of species limits and taxonomic relationships, something that is particularly valuable when working with species that are often similar in visual appearance and which sometimes occupy dense forest habitats. In the absence of genetic material for testing, vocalisations have proved very useful in resolving species limits in the genera *Otus* and *Glaucidium*. While the sounds produced by many birds are made at a frequency that matches the peak sensitivities of their hearing range, those of the owls are pitched lower, suggesting that the peak sensitivities are directed at prey location rather than recognition of other individuals of their kind. As we will see later in this book, researchers working on owls have been able to take advantage of owl vocalisations when seeking to monitor the presence, distribution and density of particular owl species.

The various characteristics that we associate with owls, those that 'make an owl an owl', play a wider role in the lives of owls than simply enabling us to recognise them. As we will see in the following chapters, it is these features that enable owls to locate and secure their prey, to establish and maintain a breeding territory, attract a mate and to produce a new generation of owls. These features have also shaped our relationship with owls, influencing our beliefs and contributing to our own culture heritage. It is easy to see why so many of us display such affection for these enigmatic birds.

CHAPTER 2

Foods and Feeding

T HE NOTION THAT OWLS are purely nocturnal predators, taking just
mice and rats, is a misleading one. Owls take an incredible range
of prey items, from small rodents and bats through to amphibians,
reptiles, invertebrates and, perhaps surprisingly, fish. Even the familiar British
species show a diversity of prey selection that highlights an ability to utilise
locally abundant prey and favourable feeding opportunities. For example, a
Tawny Owl might feed on earthworms, taken from a suburban lawn on a wet
night, or a Little Owl maintain a larder stocked with the remains of dozens of

FIG 26. Small mammals, especially voles, are the most important prey for many of our owl
species throughout the year. (Mark Hancox)

Storm Petrels *Hydrobates pelagicus*. The use of such prey is likely to surprise many people, not least because it goes against the traditional image of the owl as a simple hunter of small mammal 'vermin'.

The diets and feeding behaviours of the British owls have been well studied, at least in broad terms, and can be used to examine how the different species exploit available resources and minimise the degree of competition that might otherwise exist between them. An understanding of owl diet can also be used to examine the link between food availability and important components of the owl's life cycle, such as breeding success and overwinter survival. A number of researchers have, additionally, utilised owl diets to reveal the occurrence patterns of prey species within the wider environment or to construct a picture of ancient mammal communities, as revealed from owl pellets preserved at archaeological sites. Before we can properly interpret the diets of our British owls, it is first necessary to examine how information on diet is collected.

STUDYING OWL DIET

Owl diets have been variously determined through the analysis of stomach contents, examination of prey remains collected at nest sites, observations of prey delivered to young chicks and the study of pellets. The analysis of stomach contents, typically from birds shot for the purpose, is a technique that has little relevance today. In addition to justifiably being viewed as inhumane, the method invariably suffers from biases associated with small sample size and prevents the collection of material from the same individual over longer periods of time (Errington, 1932). However, an examination of the stomach contents of birds found dead (such as those picked up as road casualties) can sometimes produce useful material, occasionally expanding our knowledge in unexpected ways. Macdonald & McDougall (1972), examining the stomach contents of a road casualty Tawny Owl from near Jedburgh, found (and measured) 22 larvae of the Large Yellow Underwing moth *Noctua pronuba*, together with the remains of *Lumbricus* and *Allobophora* earthworms and the Marsh Slug *Deroceras laeve*, although given the habitat preferences of the latter species, this may have been a misidentified field slug *D. reticulatum* (Chris du Feu, pers. comm.). Recovering evidence of these species within Tawny Owl diet would not necessarily have been possible through other means of analysis.

Prey remains are often found at owl nest sites and, to a lesser extent, where owls roost. Additionally, a number of owl species may cache surplus prey at or near the nest (Baudvin, 1980; Taylor, 1994). For example, Little Owls regularly

FIG 27. Surplus prey may build up at the nest, as shown by these remains taken from a Barn Owl nest in the Lincolnshire fens. (Mike Toms)

make use of a 'larder', the male taking food from here to the female as she needs it (Meade-Waldo, 1912; Lockley, 1938) and several owl species may even establish prey caches outside of the breeding season (Blanc, 1958). Collections of prey remains allow the researcher to determine the range of species taken within the diet and, if used in conjunction with observations of the prey being delivered to the nest, can give an indication of the quantitative importance of different prey groups. It is widely acknowledged that the use of prey remains usually leads to an overestimation of the amount of large or conspicuous prey taken (Rosenberg & Cooper, 1990). However, the flip side of this is that it is these larger prey species which are often absent from pellet remains. Luigi Marchesi and colleagues, working on Eagle Owls nesting in the Italian Alps, found that the prey remains approach failed to detect the family Muridae, which accounted for a third of the items present within pellets collected from the same sites (Marchesi et al., 2002). The Eagle Owl prey remains were dominated by the conspicuous skins of Hedgehogs Erinaceus europaeus and uneaten parts of various birds, many of which were not represented in the pellet sample. The use of prey remains certainly gives a more complete picture of bird prey taken by Eagle Owls but smaller items tend to be missed. The same pattern is almost certainly true of our other owl species, especially in relation to bird remains.

FIG 28. Hedgehog is one of the more unusual prey species to be taken by owls, in this case by Eagle Owl. (Mike Toms)

The value of owl pellets

It is apparent from the published literature that most of our knowledge of owl diet is derived from the examination of pellets, with many hundreds of papers covering a wide range of owl species from across all continents. These studies may involve the examination of very small collections of pellets or the collation of samples from many dozens of different sites and totalling many thousands of individual prey items. While the examination of pellet samples often involves the laborious process of breaking open individual pellets and extracting all the skeletal and invertebrate material they contain, it is possible to examine whole batches in a more industrial manner. As well as revealing information on the diet of the owls, pellet analysis can also provide valuable information on the prey species themselves, including that on the age or sex classes present within the population – possible because of age- or sex-related differences in patterns of tooth wear or pelvis morphology in small mammals (Clevedon Brown & Twigg, 1969; Saint Giron, 1973). More recently, advances in the isolation and amplification of DNA have allowed researchers to recover genetic information from the prey remains found in owl pellets, allowing detailed studies of population structure for shrews and other small mammal species (e.g. Poulakakis *et al.*, 2005).

The most complete picture of owl diet comes from an approach which combines the examination of owl pellets with the collection of prey remains from nests and, ideally, video capture of the prey being delivered. Of course, recording what is being delivered to owl nests is invariably very time-consuming and, additionally, only really tells you about what owls feed to their chicks, something which may differ significantly from what the owls are feeding on at other times of the year. This is where pellet remains can be particularly useful.

Pellet formation and function

The production of pellets is something that is not unique to owls; it has been observed in more than 60 bird families, involving in excess of 350 species worldwide. All of the British owls produce pellets and differences in pellet size, colouration and deposition sites may be used to identify the species which produced them (see Table 3). There is, however, a fair degree of variation in the

TABLE 3. The pellets produced by British owls.

Species	Length (mm)	Width (mm)	Description
Barn Owl	30–70	18–25	Compact pellets, glossy black in colour when fresh but fading with age. Usually with rounded ends. Freshest pellets are sticky to the touch.
Snowy Owl	52–113	22–35	
Eagle Owl	43–129	21–42	
Tawny Owl	30–70	18–25	Looser textured than Barn Owl and paler in colour when fresh. Old Barn Owl pellets may appear similar in colour to those of Tawny Owl.
Little Owl	30–40	10–15	Small, grey in colour and rounded at both ends. Superficially similar to those of Kestrel, but latter often shows a more tapered end. Birds feeding on earthworms may produce pellets that are sandy in appearance.
Long-eared Owl	35–65	15–25	Similar to Tawny Owl in colour, but often narrower. Observation of the bird itself is most reliable means of identification.
Short-eared Owl	45–80	20–25	When fresh, black in appearance and not dissimilar to Barn Owl. However, they lack the glossy 'varnished' appearance of Barn Owl pellets and, additionally, they often fragment into segments.

FIG 29. Pellets are often deposited at regular roost sites, as is the case with Barn Owl, allowing the researcher to collect a large sample of study material. (Mike Toms)

size of pellets produced by an individual, a reflection of meal size and the meal to pellet interval (see below). A pellet is typically composed of the undigested components of a bird's food; in the case of the owls these components are dominated by fragments of bone, tooth and insect exoskeleton, all bound within a matrix of fur and, sometimes, feather remains. The pellet is formed in the ventriculus (or 'gizzard'), which effectively takes over the role of mammalian teeth in the mechanical digestion of food. The thick, muscular walls of the ventriculus compact material too large to pass through the pyloric opening into the small intestine. It is not just the small size of the pyloric opening that is behind the incorporation of bone and other fragments into pellets that are then regurgitated; the feeding behaviour of owls and the relatively poor digestive efficiency of their gastric juices also have a role to play.

Owls typically feed on small prey items, such as mice and voles, and these are invariably swallowed whole, the owl ingesting the entire skeletal framework of the prey item. Diurnal raptors, on the other hand, usually take larger prey items and remove sections of flesh from the carcass, ingesting only small fragments of bone. Even where diurnal raptors do feed on small prey items and ingest most of the carcass, the greater digestive efficiency of their gastric juices leaves few bone remains intact (Duke, 1997). As already noted, some owl species, for example Tawny

Owl, Snowy Owl and Eagle Owl, will tackle large prey items and these may be torn apart prior to ingestion in a similar manner to that seen in other predatory birds.

Newly formed pellets are passed from the gizzard into the proventriculus where they remain until egestion. This movement of the pellet from the gizzard into the proventriculus may explain the apparent confusion in the older literature over the exact site of pellet formation. Although the process of pellet egestion has not been widely studied in owl species, the pattern revealed in Great Horned Owl is probably similar to that which occurs in the British owl species. Gary Duke and his co-workers found that a pellet was formed by a series of vigorous gastric contractions about 12 minutes prior to egestion and then moved into the lower oesophagus. It was then delivered by reverse peristalsis to the mouth, a process which took some 8–10 seconds in the Great Horned Owl. Although some authors have described owls 'vomiting up' pellets, the process of pellet egestion differs from vomition in that it does not involve contractions of the abdominal muscles.

The behaviour associated with pellet production has been documented for several owl species. Chitty (1938) described the process in one of his captive Short-eared Owl study subjects, noting that the owl appeared:

> to be shaking all over. After a few seconds the neck was stretched out once; then again further and the beak opened wide. [The] owl tried unsuccessfully to produce pellet (which could be seen in the oesophagus); then relaxed neck, closed beak slightly, and after a pause brought up pellet with apparently considerable effort.

FIG 30. Barn Owl pellets a glossy black when fresh and slightly sticky to the touch but they fade with age as they dry out. (Mike Toms)

Bunn *et al.* (1982), writing of a Barn Owl, described how a bird that is about to eject a pellet 'looks decidedly miserable and listless' and 'lowers its head a little and shakes it from side to side; after a moment the pellet appears between the parted mandibles and is dropped.' Heaver (1987) observed pellet egestion in wild Little Owls on two occasions, describing how a bird was seen to

> bend forward so that its body was horizontal and the crown of its head could be clearly seen. The bill was then opened and two pellets were produced one after the other. The bird then straightened up and flew off.

Various authors have noted that a captive owl can be prompted to regurgitate a pellet when presented with another food item. However, there appears a minimum period that must elapse between the time of last feeding and pellet production; this is known as the 'meal to pellet interval' (MPI). Smith & Richmond (1972) were able to test this interval experimentally with their captive American Barn Owl and determined that roughly 6.5 hours would have to elapse before the bird would regurgitate a pellet in response to the presentation of a fresh meal. The ingestion of further prey items within this period served to delay pellet production, with remains from the various meals combined into a single pellet. Meal to pellet intervals have been shown to vary between the different owl species, the interval being noticeably shorter for smaller owls, and with meal size, where the interval is shorter for relatively smaller meals across all species so far studied. Additionally, Dennis Chitty noted that meal to pellet intervals were longer at night than during the day for a captive Short-eared Owl being fed on a controlled diet. It has also been shown experimentally that both the presence of a conspecific and the degree of fasting may also have a bearing.

In the wild, pellets produced by owls typically contain the remains of more than one individual, indicating that multiple prey captures take place within the window over which a pellet is normally produced. One would expect an owl that has had a successful night's hunting to digest the prey remains and produce a pellet following a period of diurnal rest. Interestingly, for comparison, falconiformes tend to egest their pellets at dawn, a pattern that may reflect their diurnal habits and the benefits of beginning a new day's hunting with an empty stomach. The number of pellets produced during a 24-hour period by wild owls is difficult to determine, even where individual owls make use of regular roosting sites. Studies of pellet production in captive birds, fed on a diverse range of prey items (from laboratory mice to small passerines) would suggest that Barn Owls and Long-eared Owls produce, on average, fewer than two pellets per day, while a captive Little Owl (fed twice a day) typically produced two pellets per day, each roughly 11.5 hours after it had been fed (Hanson, 1973; Marti, 1973). This Little Owl would occasionally, on presentation of its next meal, either wait to eject a pellet before tackling its meal or eat straight away and hold the pellet over. In the latter case, a 'double' pellet was formed which readily broke into two after egestion. Such 'double pellets' are often found at Little Owl roost sites.

Digestive efficiency

The degree to which the prey remains present within owl pellets reflect the prey actually taken is dependent upon a number of different factors. We have already seen that owls tend to swallow prey whole, though the degree to which this happens is determined by the size of the prey item relative to the size of the owl. For example, one captive Little Owl was found to tackle small mammals by first decapitating them, the head being eaten and then the body split into three or four pieces prior to ingestion (Hanson, 1973). The hindquarters and tail of the small mammal were invariably swallowed last. Small birds were treated in a similar manner, the head being swallowed first, followed by the body, legs and wings. This particular individual was also observed in its treatment of a Blackbird *Turdus merula*, a large prey item for a Little Owl. The head was first removed and the brains eaten; then the wings and legs were severed and cleaned before the breastbone was stripped of its flesh. Even where a small mammal may have been swallowed whole, there is invariably some degree of mechanical damage to the bones; there is likely to be more bone breakage in a small mammal eaten by a

FIG 31. Kestrels and other diurnal birds of prey have more acidic gastric juices than owls. (John Harding)

small owl than is the case when the same small mammal is eaten by a larger owl (Andrews, 1990). Mechanical damage may not only make individual bones more difficult to locate or identify during pellet analysis but it may also increase their susceptibility to chemical damage from the gastric juices.

The digestive efficiency of owls, in terms of the digestion of bone remains in the stomach, is lower than that seen in other predatory birds, such as diurnal raptors and herons (Glue, 1970a). Duke *et al.* (1975) determined that the basal pH value for owls ranged from 2.2 to 2.5, compared with 1.3 to 1.8 for a number of diurnal raptors. In physiological terms this leaves owls with roughly six times fewer hydrogen ions per millilitre in their basal gastric secretions, which led Gary Duke and colleagues to conclude that the greater acidity of the gastric juices in diurnal raptors was sufficient to explain the paucity of bone remains in the pellets they produced. Owl pellets contain a larger proportion of the meal from which they originate than is the case with raptors, a pattern that is primarily the consequence of the occurrence of more bone material in owl pellets.

Although some authors (e.g. Shawyer, 1998) have suggested that there is little or no chemical modification to bones recovered from owl pellets, the work of Peter Andrews (1990), using a scanning electron microscope, has revealed that chemical modification is frequent and the cause of complete bone digestion in many cases. Andrews also revealed that the effects of digestion on small mammal remains are most readily seen on the teeth, since the tooth enamel is the most highly mineralised component of the small mammal skeleton and, hence, the one most readily affected by the acidity of the gastric juices. Across owl species there is variation in the degree of bone digestion, with, for example, less damage seen in Barn Owl prey remains than in Tawny Owl (Raczyński & Ruprecht, 1974; Mayhew, 1977; Lowe, 1980; Bocheński *et al.*, 1993). The generalisation sometimes seen in the literature, that owls do relatively little damage to bones during digestion, may actually stem from the fact that the initial work on this topic was carried out on owl species in which the degree of digestive efficiency was low.

Digestive efficiency and age

Racyński & Ruprecht (1974), feeding wild caught mice and voles to captive birds, determined that the greatest losses of bone were found in young Tawny Owls (up to 50.8 per cent), followed by young Long-eared Owls (45.9 per cent) and then young Barn Owls (34.2 per cent). It is plausible, as Mikkola (1983) suggests, that the greater degree of bone digestion seen in young Tawny Owls and Long-eared Owls is related to the relatively short period of time that they spend in the nest compared to Barn Owls. Racyński & Ruprecht also calculated losses in terms of the number of prey items presented in the diet and then returned in the pellets;

this gave a slightly different picture, with losses of 20.9 per cent (Long-eared Owl), 16.2 per cent (Tawny Owl) and 8.2 per cent (Barn Owl). Hardy (1977) and Lowe (1980), both feeding wild-caught mice and voles to captive Tawny Owls, calculated loss rates for individual prey items of 20.4 per cent and 19.1 per cent respectively. Lowe demonstrated that the degree of loss varied both with the age of the owl and the age of the prey. Young Tawny Owls showed a greater digestive efficiency than adult birds, something that is likely to reflect more acidic gastric juices in young birds and, perhaps, a greater need for calcium during a period of growth. This difference has also been noted for Barn Owl (Bruderer & Denys, 1999). It is also worth noting that young mice and voles have softer bones, with a lower degree of ossification than adults, and these are likely to be digested more thoroughly in the owl's stomach as a consequence.

Other factors influence digestive efficiency

The degree of digestion may also vary with the type of bone involved. Small or fragile bones, such as small mammal ribs and the delicate bones of passerine birds, may be digested more readily than robust ones. Within small mammals, it is the jawbones that are the most robust and so they are also the ones that give the best picture of what has been ingested. The poor representation of bird bones within many pellet samples may be a consequence of their fragile nature, combined with the greater incidence of dismemberment prior to ingestion. Some indication of this can be seen from a study by Flegg & Cox (1968), who examined a sample of nearly 100 Long-eared Owl pellets from a winter roost located within an area of mixed deciduous woodland where they were also carrying out a ringing study. Although they found some bird remains in their pellet sample, the presence of several other individuals was only revealed through the occurrence of metal leg rings, fitted to the birds as part of the wider ringing study.

Even within an individual owl there may be variation in the degree of bone loss and it is not unusual to find heavily damaged bones in the same pellet as ones that appear undamaged or which still retain some undigested cartilage or sinew. While this may be linked to the nature of the bone material (young or old, robust or fragile), it may also stem from the degree of exposure to the gastric juices. To some extent the question of exposure has already been touched on through discussion of the meal to pellet interval. However, it is worth noting that various researchers have found that some prey remains may be held in the stomach for up to 48 hours. The retention of prey components and presentation in a later pellet (a process known as 'multirejection') could explain the large differences in the degree of digestion sometimes observed within a single pellet, the more heavily digested components having been held for longer in the stomach during carry-over from one pellet to the next. Exposure may also be influenced by the weight of food eaten and it has been shown that food is less well digested when the quantity ingested is greater. Hence, variation in the degree of damage to individual bones, or indeed to different parts of the same bone, may indicate that damage is determined by the extent to which the bone is in contact with the gastric juices and the degree of dilution of those juices by other material (Mayhew, 1977).

Smith & Richmond (1972), using a captive Barn Owl, were able to demonstrate that the acidity of the gastric juices varied over time; acidity declined with time elapsed since the ingestion of a meal, presumably as the juices became diluted by digested food. Digestion may therefore be more complete when an owl is struggling to find food, i.e. when there is less food in the stomach, than when food is plentiful. There may also be a lower degree of 'stimulation' to promote pellet ejection. You will note that these discussions have centred on the effect of stomach pH on bone, rather than the effect of digestive enzymes. This is because it is the acidity in the stomach that is responsible for bone digestion; the digestive enzymes themselves appear to have little role in bone modification.

The findings from these studies into the digestive efficiencies of owls have important consequences for any examination of owl diet, especially where the research emphasis is centred on a comparison between diets (i.e. pellet samples), either across species, seasons, habitats or prey spectrums. Given that most of the published papers on owl diet are based on pellet samples, and that most seek to make such comparisons, it is important to understand the biases that might be associated with each study. For example, an attempt to compare the winter and summer diets of a Barn Owl, using pellets from a nest site (summer) and roost site (winter), could be biased by (i) the different ages of birds likely to have produced the pellets, (ii) the greater degree of mechanical damage at the nest site (trampling, effects of parental provisioning), (iii) seasonal differences in the age groups of the prey taken and (iv) differences in the quantity of material ingested. There is also the question of whether the pellet sample collected is complete or not, with the possibility that birds may regurgitate some pellets at other sites. How, then, might we begin to build up a suitable comparative picture of owl diets?

ADDING IT ALL UP

Interpretation of owl diet requires consideration of what the prey items present in the sample actually represent. In most instances the researcher is seeking to determine the number of individuals represented within the material presented in the pellets. Should the researcher simply count the number of skulls or is a

FIG 32. Large prey items are often under-represented in owl pellets, because little or no bone material is ingested. (Vicenzo Penteriani)

count derived from a combination of bone fragments more reliable; and should the researcher treat each pellet as a distinct sampling unit or lump groups of pellets together and count the number of individual prey components across the sample as a whole? This next section looks at the techniques that have been employed and evaluates the approaches used in the study of pellet contents.

Dealing with numbers

A count of the number of individual prey items within a pellet or a sample of pellets is the simplest way to represent the diet of an owl. However, one consequence of bone loss is that certain skeletal components may be over- or underestimated because of differential digestion. Of the larger more readily identifiable small mammal bones, the pelvis is the one most likely to be damaged or missing in pellet remains, with up to 80 per cent missing, followed by the skull (up to 35 per cent missing) and then mandibles (up to 25 per cent missing). For bird bones, Bocheński & Tomek (1994) determined that the humerus and ulna provided the most robust measure of the number of individual prey items present in the pellets of Tawny Owl, Eagle Owl and Long-eared Owl.

Establishing which bones to use then allows you to derive the 'Minimum Number of Animals per taxon' by determining the greatest number of identical bones per taxon. This measure, the MNAt, is synonymous with the MNIt often quoted by taphonomists and zooarchaeologists and defined as the 'Minimum Number of Individuals per taxon'. Lyman *et al.* (2003), examining 107 published collections of Barn Owl pellets, together with their own pellet sample, explored how the sampling protocol might influence the calculation of MNIt. Treating pellets as individual sampling units and deriving values for MNIt on a per-pellet basis, which are then summed across the entire pellet sample, was found to produce a different MNIt value to one obtained by lumping all the pellets together into a single sample first and then deriving a MNIt value for this sample. This difference primarily stems from the way in which individual prey items are grouped within pellets or samples of pellets, i.e. multirejection, where the bones from one animal may be spread over more than one pellet. However, the biggest difficulty in interpreting published values for MNIt remains the lack of consistency in the methods adopted, a problem which can reduce the value of attempts to produce a synthesis of diet for a given owl species.

Prey Units and other conversion factors

One problem with using MNIt to assess the contribution that a particular prey species makes to the diet of an owl is that it is misleading to treat a small prey item exactly the same as a larger one. This problem was first identified by Southern (1954), who was working on a Tawny Owl population in Wytham Wood, Oxford. Southern recognised that the energetic contribution of a 16 g Bank Vole *Myodes glareolus* was going to be greater than that of an 8 g Common Shrew and so he derived a system of Prey Units. He took the mean weight of a typical small rodent (calculated to be 20 g) to represent a 'Prey Unit' and then adjusted the values for other (smaller or larger) species accordingly (Table 4). Southern's system has been almost universally adopted in subsequent work, although there has been some re-evaluation of the approach and of the values assigned for particular species (e.g. Morris, 1979; Fairley & Smal, 1988). The most obvious problems with Southern's original proposal were the allocation of a Prey Unit score of 5 to the Common Rat, suggestive of a mean prey weight of 100 g and the allocation of a score of 1 to any birds taken. Wild rats may weigh 20 g when they first leave the nest, reaching 790 g or more as a mature adult (Leslie *et al.*, 1952), representing scores that range from 1 to 40. Quite clearly, a 300 g Barn Owl is unlikely to tackle a large rat but it was unclear exactly what size rat a Barn Owl would actually take. Pat Morris looked at this question by first examining the

TABLE 4. Prey Units and other conversion factors used in pellet analysis.

Species	Mean weight (g)	'Prey Unit'	Source
Bank Vole	18	1.00	Southern, 1954
Field Vole	21	1.00	Southern, 1954
Water Vole	200	5.00	Southern, 1954
Wood Mouse	19	1.00	Southern, 1954
House Mouse	12	0.60	Yalden, 1977
Common Rat	60	3.50	Morris, 1979
Mole	110	5.00	Southern, 1954
Common Shrew	8	0.50	Southern, 1954
Pygmy Shrew	3.5	0.18	Grainger & Fairley, 1978
Water Shrew	15	0.75	Southern, 1954
Weasel	95	5.00	Southern, 1954

FIG 33. Common Rats weighing up to 160 g may be taken by Barn Owls. (John Harding)

relationship between body weight and structural size in the Common Rat. He derived an equation to describe this relationship, using a standard measure of lower jaw length:

Log weight = (4.7170 × log jaw length) – 4.2923

and then determined the size range for rat jaws (lower mandibles) recovered from Barn Owl pellets. This revealed that the smallest rats to be eaten by the owls had a predicted body weight of 25.9 g and the largest 163.6 g. The mean derived from calculating a predicted size was 66.5 g, significantly lower than the arbitrary value ascribed by Southern. Of course, it is important to note that Southern's Tawny Owls may have been able to tackle larger rats than the Barn Owls studied by Morris, additionally highlighting the dangers of using Prey Unit values across different predator diets. While useful, the equation derived by Morris still does not tell the whole story because he found that young rats, with one or more teeth yet to erupt, did not fit the pattern so well. Because of the range in estimated body weights for rats taken by the owl, Morris proposed that researchers should estimate rat body weights separately for each individual taken, rather than adopting a mean Prey Unit value of 3.5 (Morris, 1979). This method has been used to similar effect for mice and voles, even though when dealing with smaller prey species the margin of error resulting from an inaccurate Prey Unit value is much reduced (Tome, 2000).

A similar approach has been adopted to derive a more robust means of determining the size of bird prey taken by owls (Morris & Burgis, 1988). Small passerines are the birds most frequently represented in the diets of British owls (Glue, 1974; Yalden, 1985; Birrer, 2009) and, as a group, show a generally similar build and body structure. Using fresh carcasses of known weight, Morris & Burgis established that there was a very strong relationship between body weight and humerus length across 28 different bird species. The resulting equation:

Log weight = (2.4221 × log humerus length) – 3.8027

can be used to determine prey weight for passerine species recovered from the pellets of British owls. Morris & Burgis also examined other bird bones (deriving tarso–metatarsus length, sacral width, cranial width and sternum height) but their relationships with body weight were less strong. This approach has the added advantage that it does not require the identification of the bird species concerned, something which is often difficult when dealing with owl pellets because feathers are often poorly represented within pellets and characteristic

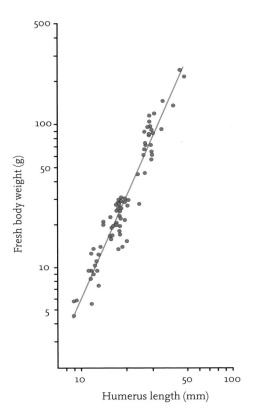

FIG 34. The relationship between log. humerus length and log. body weight for a sample of 82 passerine birds of 28 species. Redrawn from *Bird Study* 35: 147–52 (Morris & Burgis, 1988) with permission from the British Trust for Ornithology.

skulls often missing or badly damaged (Andrews, 1990). Paul Johnson developed this approach further, using material from the Natural History Museum to produce a table of mean bone dimensions for a range of passerine species encountered in the diets of British owls. More recently, Derek Yalden and Umberto Albarella produced a very useful review for those wishing to get to grips with the identification of bird remains.

Small mammals and birds are not the only prey species to appear in owl pellets and attempts have been made to derive conversion factors (which is essentially what Prey Units are) for frogs (Fairley & Smal, 1988, using pelvic girdle length), beetles (Yalden & Warburton, 1979; Smal, 1987) and earthworms (Yalden & Warburton, 1979). Earthworms can be an important prey item in the diet of certain owl species, notably Tawny Owl, but leave little obvious evidence of their presence in pellet remains, unless you have access to a microscope and can search for their chaetae (Wroot, 1985). Derek Yalden also examined to what extent it was possible to determine the dietary contribution of earthworms to particular owl diets. However, his technique, which uses the knowledge that 10 g of earthworms yields roughly 1 g of sand once digested, could only be applied where the pellet being tested just contained earthworms and no other prey.

A number of authors have derived other conversion factors, either simple ones based on the mean weights of prey species trapped in the area over which owls were thought to be hunting or from bone measurements of such animals. The various conversion factors represent an improvement on the use of the number of individuals present in a pellet sample and, indeed, on the use of an arbitrary and untested Prey Unit value. They have the potential to improve our understanding of how owl diet varies with season, location or between species but their limitations and underlying assumptions need to be kept in mind when making such comparisons. There are, for example, instances where the body weight of an individual may differ substantially from the population mean or from that predicted by some measure of its structural size (such as jaw length); a heavily pregnant Field Vole will weigh more than one that is not pregnant, while a small passerine about to set off on migration will carry significantly greater fat reserves than one that has recently arrived. Nevertheless, an examination of the diets of our owl species, based on Prey Units or other conversion factors, remains worthwhile, enabling us to determine how they differ from one another in broad terms, and from populations elsewhere within their wider range. It is these that we will examine next.

THE DIETS OF BRITISH OWLS

Collectively, the British owls have been recorded taking prey species that vary in size from small beetles and earwigs to Brown Hare *Lepus europaeus* and Pheasant *Phasianus colchicus*. The diversity of prey species taken by individual owls also suggests a certain flexibility and opportunism when it comes to feeding opportunities. However, certain prey groups dominate the diets of each of our owls, with small mammals seemingly the most important prey group numerically for all of our owls, except Little Owl (although even here they have an important seasonal role and make a major contribution energetically). The relative contribution of the different prey groups to the diet of British owls can be seen in Table 5, which pulls together information from various published studies. Diets for Ireland and offshore islands are displayed separately because of the different prey spectrums available (Table 6).

TABLE 5. The diets of British owls, as revealed by studies of pellet material. Figures shown are percentage contribution to diet, derived from number of prey items recovered. There has yet to be a significant analysis of Little Owl diet within Britain, though the work of Sutcliffe, 1990 (see Table 6) and Hounsome et al., 2004, provide an indication of the likely importance of different prey groups.

Prey	Barn Owl	Tawny Owl	Short-eared Owl	Long-eared Owl
Source	Love et al., 2000	Southern, 1954	Glue, 1977	Glue & Hammond, 1974
Type	National	Local, woodland	National	National
Bank Vole	4.7	30.7	0.4	11.0
Field Vole	38.7	13.3	64.5	47.4
Water Vole	0.3	0.1	<0.1	0.3
Wood mice*	22.7	29.3	9.5	18.0
Common Rat	0.5	0.8	8.9	3.0
Common Shrew	18.5	12.0	2.5	2.6
Pygmy Shrew	9.3	1.8	1.9	1.3
Water Shrew	0.6	0.4	<0.1	0.1
Bat	<0.1	<0.1	<0.1	0.1
Other mammal	3.6	6.4	2.1	1.2
Bird	1.0	5.1	9.9	15
Amphibian/ reptile	0.1	0.0	0.0	0.1

* both Apodemus sylvaticus and A. Flavicollis

Most of the vertebrate prey taken falls within a narrow range of weights and body sizes. Most prey is taken from the ground and, since owls are not adapted for pursuit, it is normally taken unawares. The main prey groups taken by British owls are small mammals, small birds and large invertebrates, although other groups may be exploited where opportunities arise. This next section reviews the relative importance of these different prey groups and examines how their relative importance varies between owl species, with habitat and across the seasons.

TABLE 6. The diets of British owls, as revealed by studies of pellet material from islands. Figures shown are percentage contribution to diet, derived from number of prey items recovered (items). Where known, the season is given.

Barn Owl	**Ireland (Fairley & Clark, 1972):** Wood Mouse (49.0%), Pygmy Shrew (29.5%), House Mouse (10.1%), Common Rat (4.6%), Common Frog (3.8%), bird (3.0%)
	Ireland – all year (Walsh, 1984): House Mouse (35.0%), Wood Mouse (28.0%), Common Rat (18.0%), birds (11.1%), Pygmy Shrew (7.2%)
	Skomer (Clevedon-Brown & Twigg, 1971): Bank Vole (69.05%), Wood Mouse (24.5%), Common Shrew (6.6%)
	Skomer (Plant, 1976): Bank Vole (51.4%), Common Frog (21.5%), Common Shrew (10.3%), Pygmy Shrew (9.3%), Wood Mouse (4.7%), Starling (2.8%)
Little Owl	**Skomer – Summer (Sutcliffe, 1990):** Bank Vole (10.4%), Wood Mouse (1.8%), *Sorex* spp. (1.0%), other mammals (3.7%), Storm Petrel (3.7%), Meadow Pipit (<0.1%), beetles and other invertebrates (79.4%)
Short-eared Owl	**Ireland – Winter (Walsh & Sleeman, 1988):** Redwing (35%), Snipe (20%), Wood Mouse (12.5%), Skylark (12.5%), Dunlin (12.5%), Water Rail (2.5%), Song Thrush (2.5%), unidentified thrush (2.5%)
Long-eared Owl	**Ireland (Fairley, 1967):** Wood Mouse (82.5%), House Mouse (6.8%), birds (4.9%), Common Rat (4.8%), Pygmy Shrew (0.9%)
	Ireland (Hillis *et al.*, 1988): Wood Mouse (81.6%), House Mouse (7.3%), birds (7.2%), Common Rat (2.7%), Bank Vole (0.2%), bats (0.2%)
	Ornkey (Okill & Ewins, 1978): Wood Mouse (81%), House Mouse (8%), birds (8%), Common Rat (2%), Rabbit (1%)

MAMMAL PREY

Mice, voles and shrews (known collectively as 'small mammals') are the main mammal prey to be taken by the British owls. Larger species, such as Rabbit *Oryctolagus cuniculus*, Grey Squirrel *Sciurus carolinensis* and Hedgehog, may feature on occasion in the diets of Tawny Owl (Rabbit), Snowy Owl (Rabbit) and Eagle Owl (Rabbit, Grey Squirrel and Hedgehog). The importance of small mammals to the diet of British owls reflects both their availability (they are common across the habitats hunted over by owls) and their patterns of activity (most are active throughout the 24-hour cycle). An additional consideration is the size of small mammals relative to their predators; at 28 g, an adult Field Vole should pose little

FIG 35. Bank Vole (pictured) populations appear not to cycle in the way that Field Vole populations do. (John Harding)

problem to a 300 g Barn Owl, but a 500 g Grey Squirrel almost certainly would. Changes in the availability of small mammals can have a pronounced impact on owls and, in particular, their breeding success, highlighting their importance within the diet. For example, Taylor (1994) found that both average clutch size and fledging success in Scottish Barn Owls were correlated with Field Vole abundance. Similarly, the nomadic nature of Short-eared Owl populations in some northern habitats has been linked to the cyclic fluctuations of microtine (vole) populations, a trigger also seen in continental Barn Owl populations, where long-distance dispersal of young birds occurs in years following an abundance and then crash in the vole population (termed 'Wanderjahren' by von Sauter, 1956).

Small mammals dominate the diet of British Barn Owls, with five species making up more than 90 per cent of the prey taken (Love *et al.*, 2000). These five are: Field Vole, Bank Vole, Common Shrew, Pygmy Shrew and wood mice *Apodemus* spp. (primarily Wood Mouse but with some Yellow-necked Mouse *Apodemus flavicollis* featuring in southern Britain; the two can be difficult to distinguish and until recently were usually grouped together in pellet analysis). The most frequently encountered prey of Barn Owl is the Field Vole,

FIG 36. Rough grassland habitat, such as this damp, riverside meadow, can hold high densities of Field Voles, providing good hunting opportunities for Barn Owls and Short-eared Owls. (Mike Toms)

contributing a median percentage frequency in excess of 40 per cent in both of the national Barn Owl pellet analyses (Glue, 1974; Love et al., 2000). Where it occurs, the Field Vole is also the dominant prey item in the diets of Short-eared Owl (representing 64.5 per cent of prey items nationally, Glue, 1977a) and Long-eared Owl (where it is the main item by weight in 40 of the 47 mainland Long-eared Owl diets examined by Glue & Hammond, 1974). Field Voles are associated with rough grassland habitats, such as lowland wet meadows, unmanaged ditch banks and newly established plantation woodland. The key habitat feature appears to be a well-developed and dense sward structure, dominated by grasses and within which the vole can feed and establish its network of runs.

Where Field Voles are less abundant, such as in areas of arable farmland, on certain islands and in Ireland, the three owl species mentioned will exploit secondary prey species, notably Wood Mouse and Common Rat (arable areas in Eastern England), Pygmy Shrew (Rhum), Common Vole (Orkney) or Wood Mouse and Pygmy Shrew (Ireland). The same pattern is also true in relation to changes in the seasonal or multi-annual pattern of Field Vole abundance, with other species becoming more important when Field Vole numbers are low (see seasonal variation in diet, below). It was once thought that Barn Owls found shrews unpleasant and so avoided them when hunting (e.g. Mitford, 1876) but they are clearly an important secondary prey item in some areas.

The Wood Mouse is something of a habitat generalist, utilising a wide range of different habitats (including both coniferous and deciduous woodland, arable margins and even urbanised land – although its populations in the latter are heavily influenced by the level of cat predation) and this may be one reason why it is such an important secondary item for several of our owl species. Along with Bank Vole, a species which favours thick ground cover, the Wood Mouse is the primary prey item taken by woodland Tawny Owls. Southern (1954) found that Wood Mouse and Bank Vole were the most important prey taken by his woodland Tawny Owls, representing 29.3 per cent and 30.8 per cent of the diet numerically. Tawny Owls appear to catch proportionally more Wood Mice than Bank Voles in relation to their availability, as defined by live trapping, something that may well reflect the greater use of open areas by Wood Mice and the preference for cover that is seen in Bank Vole. Southern's Tawny Owls also preyed upon Field Vole, taking them from more open areas, and all three of the mainland shrews. The presence of Water Shrew within woodland is something that may surprise some readers but the species can occur sporadically in grassland and woodland,

FIG 37. Moles may be exposed to owl predation when active above ground, something that is a not unusual occurrence in early summer. (Amy Lewis)

often up to 3 km from water. I have taken them fairly regularly in woodland, including from an area of extensive Sweet Chestnut *Castanea sativa* coppice several kilometres from the nearest water source. An equally surprising component of woodland Tawny Owl diet is the Mole *Talpa europaea*, a species which contributed 4.9 per cent by numbers in Southern's study. Moles were originally inhabitants of woodland but have taken advantage of agricultural landscapes; sizeable populations still occur within deciduous woodland where their earthworks are hidden from our gaze by the leaf litter. Although Moles remain within their extensive tunnel systems for most of the year, there is a period of surface dispersal during early summer and this greatly increases the availability of predominantly juvenile Moles to the owls at this time of the year.

Common Rats become a feature of owl diets in certain habitats; for example, in the arable landscapes of Eastern England they can be important for Barn Owls and in suburban habitats they are often taken by Tawny Owls. As noted previously, it is the smaller, younger, rats that are tackled by Barn Owls, with fully grown animals seemingly too large for the bird to handle. Southern's work on Tawny Owls also suggests a preference for younger individuals, though presumably a Tawny Owl would be capable of tackling a larger rat. A similar pattern exists with Water Vole *Arvicola terrestris* (Barn Owl) and Rabbit (Tawny Owl), with fully grown individuals unlikely to be taken by the owls.

While small mammals may not be numerically important in many British Little Owl diets, they are important when viewed in relation to their contribution to prey biomass. Field Voles form a significant part of the diet in areas where Little Owls have access to rough grassland but appear to make a much reduced contribution in intensively managed agricultural landscapes, a pattern studied in greater detail on the Continent. It has been found that Little Owls become more specialised in their diet in these intensively managed landscapes, taking – for example – large numbers of earthworms. As well being energetically less rewarding than mammalian prey, the high water content of earthworms can result in nests becoming very wet, something which might have implications for Little Owl fledging success (Luder & Stange, 2001). Access to small mammal prey, notably microtine voles, has been linked to breeding success in the Little Owl. Illner (1991a), for example, found a strong relationship between Little Owl productivity and the percentage contribution of Common Vole to prey biomass. Voles can make a significant contribution to Little Owl diet in other parts of Europe (e.g. France 70 per cent of biomass, Germany 76 per cent and Switzerland 51 per cent). The relative contribution of small mammals to Little Owl diet has, additionally, been found to vary with geographical location, with invertebrates increasing in importance as you move further south within the range.

FIG 38. Brown Long-eared Bats *Plecotus auritus* are occasionally taken by hunting owls, presumably at their roost. (Mike Toms)

Bat remains are only rarely encountered within owl pellets. John Speakman reviewed published diets for British owls and found that bats accounted for just 0.035 per cent of the prey taken, with Barn Owl, Tawny Owl and Long-eared Owl the species feeding most frequently on bats. Speakman used these figures, alongside those for population size and energetic requirements, to estimate how many bats might be lost to predation each year. The three owl species mentioned were estimated to account for nearly 188,000 bats annually, representing roughly 10 per cent of the estimated annual mortality of British bats, a not insignificant contribution (Speakman, 1991).

One of the interesting aspects revealed by an examination of bat remains in pellet samples is that the level of predation is not evenly spread across the samples but is instead linked to particular birds or sites. Some 53 of the 57 bats found in David Glue's 1974 study of Barn Owl diet were from a single Cumbrian site, where they made up 25 per cent of the diet. A similar pattern was found in the 1997 Mammal Society study of Barn Owl pellet remains, where 6 of the 12 bats found (out of nearly 49,000 vertebrate prey items) were from a single site in Wales. Patty Briggs (pers. comm.) noted a Greater Horseshoe Bat *Rhinolophus ferrumequinum* site in the southwest, where a local Tawny Owl had discovered the relative ease by which it could pick off the bats as they emerged from their roost. Elsewhere in Europe, the contribution of bats to owl diet reached almost 39 per cent at a site in Germany – largely due to very heavy predation on a roost of Natterer's Bat *Myotis nattereri* in one particular year of a four-year study (Sommer *et al.*, 2009), although this is a value that is far in excess of what has been recorded at other Central European sites (Ruprecht, 1979).

Mammal prey also feature strongly in the few Eagle Owl diets that have been examined in Britain. Pellets collected from an Eagle Owl nest site in the Peak District during the 1990s, and examined by Derek Yalden, revealed a diet that included Mountain Hare *Lepus timidus*, Rabbit and Hedgehog. Rabbit also featured in the breeding season diet of a pair of Eagle Owls inhabiting the Forest of Bowland and the species is an important component of Eagle Owl diet elsewhere within Europe. In fact, Eagle Owl populations in southern Europe specialise on Rabbits, only switching to other (usually smaller) mammals when Rabbit populations are low. In such instances, the loss of Rabbits as the primary prey item may also lead to later and less productive breeding attempts (Penteriani *et al.*, 2002). Eagle Owl populations from further north in Europe, e.g. Germany, also take other medium-sized mammals, with Hedgehog and Brown Hare important. Although the very few Eagle Owl diets studied in Britain have come from northern areas, often associated with upland habitats, we might expect Hedgehog and Brown Hare to feature if these birds become established in southern Britain. Here, they might additionally take Grey Squirrel – a species which would seem to fit the size and habitat profile exploited by the predator (Toms, 2009).

Grey Squirrels are sometimes taken by one of our smaller owls. David Glue (Glue, 1973a) recorded Grey Squirrel remains from Tawny Owl pellets collected in the Chilterns. He also discovered that his local Tawny Owls were exploiting the introduced population of Edible Dormouse *Glis glis* established in the area. Perhaps shaped by his audience, David's paper appearing in the *Quarterly Journal of Forestry*, he wrote that 'Regrettably, larger avian predators like the Eagle Owl … do not occur and one suspects that there is a niche available for a carnivore of this type'; it seems he might, just, get his way.

Rabbits appear to have made an important contribution to the diet of Snowy Owl on the few occasions when individuals or pairs have appeared in Scotland. Seven intact pellets and five pellet fragments, collected in July 1972 from the Isle of Lewis and originating from one or more of at least three different individuals, were found to contain the remains of at least 13 juvenile Rabbits. Measurements of the long bones revealed that the Rabbits varied in weight from 139 g to 700 g, the pellet sample suggesting that the birds fed exclusively on this prey species (Marquiss & Cunningham, 1980). Robinson & Becker (1986) highlighted the importance of Rabbit for the Snowy Owls breeding on Fetlar between 1967 and 1975. Young Rabbits

FIG 39. Rabbit may be an important prey species for both Eagle Owl and Snowy Owl. (John Harding)

were the main prey item during the breeding season up until 1970, when the arrival of Myxomatosis brought about a crash in the population. Over the next few years the Snowy Owls were forced to switch to alternative prey, predominantly wader and skua chicks, and the owls, breeding success dropped dramatically. The Fetlar Snowy Owls were noted to include Wood Mouse in their diet during the winter months, a period when they would sometimes hunt close to the crofts. Another small mammal, Field Vole, featured in the diet of a female Snowy Owl which summered on the Cairngorm Plateau in 1987, although the contribution to diet was small (just 3 per cent by weight) as Mountain Hare and Ptarmigan dominated.

BIRD PREY

Small passerines appear to constitute a greater proportion of the diet in both Tawny Owl and Long-eared Owl than is the case for our other widespread owl species. However, bird prey certainly feature in the diet of all our owls. Little Owl, for example, has been recorded taking adult birds in daylight and out in the open, including Starling, Dunlin *Calidris alpina* and, perhaps surprisingly, Jackdaw *Corvus monedula*. Bird remains were found in 90 per cent of the Long-eared Owl pellet samples analysed by Glue & Hammond (1974), accounting for 15 per cent of the 7,761 prey items recovered; in four of the pellet samples examined, birds were the main food item by weight. House Sparrow *Passer domesticus* and Starling were the most frequent of the bird remains identified. Southern's work on Tawny Owls in Wytham showed avian prey accounted for 5 per cent of the 9,494 prey items recovered, with Chaffinch *Fringilla coelebs* by far the most commonly taken species and accounting for over half of the avian remains identified to species. Other species to feature included Great Tit *Parus major*, Robin *Erithacus rubecula*, Greenfinch *Carduelis chloris*, Bullfinch *Pyrrhula pyrrhula*, Blackbird and Song Thrush *Turdus philomelos*, collectively contributing a third of the remains identified to species. The largest species taken were Jay *Garrulus glandarius*, Jackdaw and (probably) Woodpigeon *Columba palumbus*. Interestingly, the dominance of Chaffinch might reflect the fact that it often roosts communally in winter, affording the Tawny Owls with an opportunity to take them at roost when they are easier to catch.

Both Short-eared Owls and Barn Owls may also take more bird prey during the winter months, something which may explain the dominance of birds in the diet of those Short-eared Owls roosting on the Berkshire downs during the early 1970s, where they accounted for roughly 45 per cent of the prey items taken.

FIG 40. Species which roost communally, such as House Sparrow, may be more vulnerable to owl predation. (John Harding)

During a very cold spell during January 1973, with associated snow cover, the pellets of a Short-eared Owl hunting over some Hampshire saltmarsh included a number of bird remains (including Dunlin, Ringed Plover *Charadrius hiaticula*, Snipe *Gallinago gallinago* and Skylark *Alauda arvensis*). A similar picture was noted in a pellet sample from elsewhere in Hampshire in February 1939 (Glue 1970b). Short-eared Owls have also been recorded feeding on migrating birds attracted at night to coastal lighthouses. Baxter & Rintoul (1953) record them taking birds up to the size of a Common Tern *Sterna hirundo* in this manner.

Glue (1972) reported that while bird remains accounted for a tiny percentage of the vertebrate prey taken by Barn Owls, they were found in 65 per cent of the 165 samples he examined. In none of the samples were birds found to account for more than 8 per cent of the vertebrate prey remains. For those bird remains that could be identified to species it was apparent that House Sparrow and Starling were the two species most frequently taken. Documented declines in British populations of these two species may explain the fall in the median percentage frequency of birds within the diet of mainland Barn Owls between 1974 and 1997 observed by Love *et al.* (2000). Many of the bird species taken by Barn Owls roost communally outside of the breeding season, a habit that might make them vulnerable to owl predation.

There is a strong suggestion from the BTO's Little Owl Food Inquiry (Hibbert-Ware, 1938) and the observations of Mitchell (1994) that Little Owls increase the proportion of bird prey in their diets during the nestling period. Mitchell observed her local pair work hedgerows and trees in order to locate nestling passerines, which were then taken back to their own developing young. This was confirmed by David Glue, who noted that the majority of birds taken by Little Owls are predated from mid-April through into July. Tawny Owls have also been reported taking birds from their nests (Harrison, 1960). Individual Little Owls may take advantage of opportunities where small birds are readily available. The severe winter of 1939/40 saw a resident Little Owl exploit visitors to a garden feeding station, where Blackbirds and other thrushes had been attracted by windfall apples, the owl seemingly making kills on an almost daily basis. R. M. Lockley (quoted by Alice Hibbert-Ware in 1938) reported that a pair of Little Owls, which established themselves on Skokholm Island in 1934, predated a large number of Storm Petrels over several seasons. These tiny seabirds nest in holes in walls on the island, arriving at the end of April. Since the birds are active around their nest holes shortly after dusk, they would seem an obvious target for the Little Owls and this may explain why so many of their remains were found in and around the owls' nest. Outside of the Storm Petrel breeding season, the Skokholm Little Owls were thought to feed on young Rabbit, House Mouse *Mus domesticus*, Common

FIG 41. Little Owls present on Skokholm and Skomer have taken large numbers of Storm Petrels in the past. (John Harding)

Frog *Rana temporaria* and, possibly, Slow-worm *Anguis fragilis* (Lockley, 1938). The predation of Storm Petrels by the Little Owls established on Skomer Island NNR caused concern over the possible impacts that they may have been having on the Storm Petrel colony, something to which we will return in a later chapter.

That larger species of owl can take larger birds as prey is self-evident, with Pheasant and Red Grouse *Lagopus lagopus* documented from British Eagle Owl diet and Red-legged Partridge *Alectoris rufa*, various pigeons *Columba* spp. and other birds of prey featuring elsewhere in Europe (Mikkola, 1983; Martinez & Zuberogoitia, 2001; Dalbeck & Heg, 2006). The extent and impact of owl on owl predation is discussed is Chapter 5. Bird prey appear to be of importance to British Snowy Owls in some circumstances, with Ptarmigan the dominant prey item in the diet of Snowy Owls summering on the Cairngorm Plateau (Marquiss *et al.*, 1989) during the 1980s. However, birds appear to have been a secondary prey item for the Snowy Owls breeding on the Isle of Lewis and on Fetlar. In the latter case, birds (in the form of Oystercatcher *Haematopus ostralegus*, Whimbrel *Numenius phaeopus* and Arctic Skua *Stercorarius parasiticus* chicks) only really featured in the breeding season diet in those years when Rabbit populations were at a low. The Fetlar owls did not take wader chicks in relation to their availability but selectively preyed upon those species mentioned, with Lapwing *Vanellus vanellus* and other waders under-represented in the diet. Interestingly, the owls completely ignored those small passerines nesting within their territory, but they did sometimes take young Common Gull *Larus canus* and Great Black-backed Gull *Larus marinus* chicks (Robinson & Becker, 1986).

It is interesting, however, to note that the 'smaller' owls (in terms of body weight) will sometimes tackle large birds. Derick Scott found the remains of a Moorhen *Gallinula chloropus* in an unusually large Long-eared Owl pellet, something which prompted him to write that he had once come across the partly eaten remains of an adult Moorhen in a Long-eared Owl's nest located 6 m off the ground (Scott, 1997). An adult Moorhen (weighing between 326–400 g) would have proved quite a challenge for a Long-eared Owl (weighing 285–345 g). Short-eared Owl has been recorded taking Water Rail *Rallus aquaticus* on Orkney (Gilbert, 1947) and, as we have already noted, Little Owl has been recorded tackling Blackbird and Snipe.

As we have seen with the Little Owls and Storm Petrels already mentioned, there are occasions where individual owls may exploit particular opportunities and target bird prey. Glue & Langley (1993) reported on a Tawny Owl that systematically targeted a Cornish dovecote and its Fantail Pigeons during the months of April and May, each year from 1990 to 1992. The identity of the predator remained unknown until the owl was trapped in 1992 and it appeared that this bird would target the doves only when it had growing young of its own in a nearby nest.

INVERTEBRATE PREY

For some of our owl species invertebrates are uncommon within the diet and appear to be taken opportunistically. However, it should be noted that many insect prey items are likely to go unrecorded, either because they suffer complete or near-complete digestion or because researchers disregard them during pellet analyses. Some authors have made the effort to identify and quantify invertebrate prey remains. For example, Beven (1965) recovered the skins of five Lime Hawkmoths *Mimas tiliae* from Tawny Owl pellets in London and Alice Hibbert-Ware went to great lengths to identify invertebrate prey remains in Little Owl pellets for the BTO's Little Owl Food Inquiry. Greater attention to the pellet matrix, together with the more widespread use of binocular microscopes, might reveal mandibles and other hard parts from various invertebrate species that would otherwise go undetected.

Both Tawny Owl and Little Owl show a greater degree of utilisation of invertebrates within their prey spectrums than our other owls; in the case of Little Owl, the numerical contribution of invertebrate prey is maintained at around 30 per cent throughout the year. Some 121 different beetle species, together with other insects, earthworms, spiders and millipedes, were recovered from pellet samples examined by Alice Hibbert-Ware. Five insects stood out on account of their abundance within the pellets: *Melolontha melolontha* (Cockchafer), *Geotrupes stercorarius* (a dor beetle), *Pterostichus madidus* (a ground beetle), *Forficula auricularia* (Common Earwig) and various crane-flies (*Tipula* spp.). Although as many as 30 or 40 earwigs were found in individual Little Owl pellets fairly frequently by Hibbert-Ware, there was one abnormally large pellet from which the remains of 343 different individuals were recovered. The dominant invertebrate prey taken was found to vary throughout the year, tracking the seasonal abundance of particular species – e.g. Cockchafer was dominant in summer and Common Earwig in autumn. The dominance of invertebrates is soon lost, however, once you switch from the numerical contribution of individual prey species to their biomass value. For example, the contribution of invertebrates to the summer diet of Austrian Little Owls is 67 per cent numerically but only 2 per cent when viewed in terms of biomass.

Southern's (1954) study of woodland Tawny Owls revealed the numerical importance of invertebrates for this species, with earthworms an important component of the diet within some Tawny Owl territories. He also found that several beetle species, namely Cockchafer, various dor beetles and several of the larger ground beetles (mainly *Carabus nemoralis*), were taken by the owls. As with Little Owl there is a degree of seasonality in terms of the invertebrate species taken, with Cockchafer dominant in late summer and dor beetles important somewhat earlier in the year. As previously noted, the presence of earthworms in Tawny Owl diet can be readily determined if brown fibrous pellets are found. These differ from the more usual grey pellets that contain the bones of small mammals within a matrix of fur. Since earthworm chaetae stain yellow when a few drops of picric acid (2,4,6-trinitrophenol) are added to a macerated suspension of the pellet, it is usually relatively easy to recover them and to quantify their contribution to diet. Southern (1954) examined the ratio of brown to grey pellets and found that the proportion of brown pellets in his samples was often in excess of 50 per cent for those Tawny Owl territories bordering open fields. He also noted that peaks in this proportion coincided with wet nights, presumably on which the worms were more surface active. Invertebrates are only occasional constituents in the diets of our other owls, but it is worth mentioning that earthworm chaetae have been identified in two Long-eared Owl pellet

FIG 42. All of our owls, including this Short-eared Owl, may take invertebrate prey from the ground. (Steve Round)

samples examined by Glue & Hammond (1974) and, additionally, Scott (1997) notes seeing a Long-eared Owl feeding on earthworms at a farm compost heap. Bavoux *et al.* (2001) note Barn Owl, and Fernandez & Pinedo (1996) note Eagle Owl, both preying on the Red Signal Crayfish *Procamburus clarkii*, presumably caught on land at night.

SOME UNUSUAL PREY ITEMS

Fish

There have been occasional reports of fish appearing in the diets of British owls. For example, David Glue recovered the remains of several Perch *Perca fluviatilis* and Roach *Leuciscus rutilus* from a Tawny Owl nest located 10 feet up in a decaying Elm *Ulmus procera* close to the Grand Union Canal, near Tring in Hertfordshire. Beven (1965) also notes Tawny Owl taking fish; he recovered the bones of two Goldfish *Carassius auratus* from pellets dropped by a Tawny Owl which regularly roosted close to a pond known to contain these ornamental fish. In May 1963, Keri Williams went one better and photographed a Tawny Owl delivering fish to its nest at Penderyn, Breconshire. Keri spent several nights watching the nest and first saw the male Tawny Owl arrive with a small fish on the night of 25 May, followed by a second later the same night. Again on 29 May, the male was seen twice bringing fish to the nest, one of which was a small Brown Trout *Salmo trutta*. On the night of the 1 June both adults brought fish to the nest, the female one and the male two, the latter involving at least one Miller's Thumb *Cottus gobio*. These birds had clearly discovered a feeding opportunity nearby (Williams, 1964). Although it is not clear if the Barn Owl described hunting low over Sheerness harbour by Henry Saxby, who was stationed on HMS *Devonshire* at the time, actually caught a fish, he does note that he once found fish remains in the stomach of a Tawny Owl (Saxby, 1862).

Amphibians and reptiles

Several amphibian and reptile species feature in the diets of British owls and there are even cases where individual birds appear to specialise on them for short periods (Colin Shawyer pers. comm.). These include Barn Owl, specialising on Common Frog. Little Owls have also been recorded feeding on Common Frog, together with Grass Snake *Natrix natrix* (an immature some 20 centimetres in length – Buxton, 1947) and Smooth Newt *Triturus vulgaris* (Trimnell, 1945). Interestingly, the presence of a number of untouched newt carcasses in the nest

FIG 43. Common Frogs may be taken opportunistically by hunting owls. (John Harding)

to which this record relates, together with a single undigested carcass in the pellet remains, led Bernard Tucker to suggest that Little Owls might find newts unpalatable.

Grass

John Ash, writing in 1955, was one of a number of authors to note the presence of partially digested vegetable matter in the stomachs of both Little Owl and Tawny Owl. He argued that, while this may have been ingested accidentally with invertebrate prey, the quantity present in some of the birds was such that it suggested deliberate ingestion. David Poulter measured the largest of the grass stems recovered from a Little Owl, dug out and killed by his dog in 1952, at just over nine inches, which again would suggest deliberate ingestion; the other stomach contents on this occasion were predominantly remains of the beetles *Carabus violaceus* and *Necrophorus vestigator*. It is known that captive owls will deliberately ingest binding material, including grass, to aid the formation of the pellet matrix, especially in the absence of other binding material (e.g. small mammal fur). Perhaps the greater use of invertebrate prey by Tawny Owl and Little Owl necessitates the occasional ingestion of a binding material because of the low amount of small mammal fur in the diet. The need for binding material might also explain an odd note by E. L. Roberts who, writing in 1945, attributed the sheep's wool recovered from two Tawny Owl pellets from Lincolnshire to the bird feeding on carrion.

SIMILARITIES AND DIFFERENCES BETWEEN DIETS

Derek Yalden is one of the few authors to examine the diets of multiple owl species using the same geographical area within Britain, in this instance the Peak District (Yalden, 1985). His findings show a strong degree of similarity in the diets of Barn Owl, Long-eared Owl and Short-eared Owl, something that is largely due to the predominance of Field Voles in the diet (see Figure 44). The diets of Little Owl, Snowy Owl and Eagle Owl are sufficiently distinct to suggest little competition between these species and our other owls. However, the apparent similarities between the diets of Barn Owl, Long-eared Owl and Short-eared Owl require a more detailed examination. Yalden's study revealed that Barn Owl and Short-eared Owl showed the greatest similarity in their prey spectrum, sharing 76.4 per cent of their diet. He concluded that the differential use of the habitats available in the Peak District effectively restricted competition between the two species. While the Short-eared Owl favoured moorland and young forestry

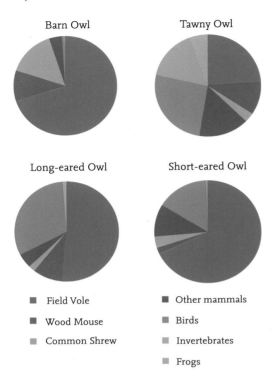

Barn Owl

Tawny Owl

Long-eared Owl

Short-eared Owl

- Field Vole
- Wood Mouse
- Common Shrew
- Other mammals
- Birds
- Invertebrates
- Frogs

FIG 44. Dietary separation in four species of British owl within the Peak District. Adapted from data published in *Bird Study* 32: 122–31 (Yalden, 1985) with permission from the British Trust for Ornithology.

plantations at altitudes in excess of 300 m above sea level, the Barn Owl worked rough grazing at lower altitude. Yalden also noted the similarity in diet between the two *Asio* owls, highlighting evidence within the diet (such as the importance of Pygmy Shrew, Skylark and Twite *Carduelis flavirostris* to both owls) which suggested that Peak District Long-eared Owls also hunted over open moorland. This finding conflicts with Southern's (1954) assertion that the Long-eared Owl is essentially a woodland species. Dietary overlap between Long-eared Owl and Tawny Owl, placed at 65.2 per cent by Yalden, is almost certainly not as extensive as it first appears.

Yalden also reworked published national datasets in order to examine how the degree of dietary overlap might differ at the national level. Although he had to make one or two assumptions (particularly with regard to Tawny Owl for which national data were limited), his findings are similar to those obtained from the analysis of the Peak District diets (and also to those presented by Mikkola, 1983).

FIG 45. During the winter months, Short-eared Owls may hunt alongside Barn Owls on lowland grazing marsh. (Steve Round)

Barn Owl and the two *Asio* owls shared diets with between 73 and 77 per cent similarity, this time with the two *Asio* owls showing the greatest degree of overlap. It appears therefore, that while Short-eared Owl and Barn Owl have similar diets, they reduce the degree of competition between them by utilising different habitats for much of the year (though competition may be greater during the winter, when both species may be seen hunting over the same lowland habitats). Long-eared Owl appears to occupy a position that is intermediate between Barn Owl/Short-eared Owl and Tawny Owl, both in terms of diet and habitat use.

While there may seem to be some obvious division of prey species through the utilisation of different hunting habitats between the owl species, with Tawny Owl a woodland species, Long-eared Owl woodland or open country depending on season, Short-eared Owl an upland open-country species and Barn Owl a lowland open-country species, it must be remembered that these are only general patterns and that individual owls may deviate from these patterns. For example, Tawny Owl populations using isolated woodlots and farmland in Aberdeenshire were found to hunt extensively over open farmland and field margins, with Field Vole the primary prey species. Examination of the range of prey species taken by British owls may also explain why Tawny Owl is the one species to have colonised suburban habitats. It shows a more diverse prey spectrum than the other owls and utilises a number of prey species that may allow it to make a living within urbanised landscapes. Interestingly, elsewhere in Europe, the Eagle Owl has also shown itself able to occupy secondary habitats modified by humans, including working quarries and residential areas (Toms, 2009).

SEASONAL VARIATION IN DIET

Throughout the previous sections we have touched upon the seasonal variation in prey selection that is evident with the diets of the British owls. In particular, we have noted how birds vary in their seasonal importance for our larger owls. Much of this information comes from the comparison of pellet samples collected during different seasons and from different sites. However, there have also been studies which look at the seasonal changes in diet at individual sites and, in many ways, these are potentially more interesting since they effectively control for differences in the local habitat around sample sites.

Monthly pellet samples from a roost site in Westfield, East Sussex, and collected over a three-year period, enabled Love et al. (2000) to look at seasonal variation in Barn Owl diet. Seasonal changes in the primary prey species (Field Vole) were found to be the same in all three years, with the percentage of Field Vole remains decreasing through spring to an early summer trough before increasing again in the autumn. This pattern follows the known seasonal changes in Field Vole populations, which increase markedly from a late spring trough to an autumn peak following a successful breeding season. When Field Vole declined within the Barn Owl pellet sample it was replaced by either Common Shrew (most seasons) or Wood Mouse (summer/autumn). Both of these species have been previously described as being important alternative prey for Barn Owl. These results underlined those found by Webster (1973), who also examined seasonal variation in Barn Owl diet, this time in the north of England.

Glue & Hammond (1974) were able to compare breeding season and non-breeding season diets of Long-eared Owls by using pellet samples from 20 sites at which methodical pellet collections took place. Examination of these samples revealed that the contribution of birds to the diet increased three-fold from the breeding to non-breeding season. The authors ascribed this to a greater reliance on communally roosting passerines, such as House Sparrow, during the autumn and winter months. Interestingly, the bird species taken during the breeding season tended to be those more closely associated to the woodland habitats where the Long-eared Owls nested.

ANNUAL VARIATION IN DIET

There have only been two attempts to compare changes in the diets of British owls over longer periods of time, both of which relate to the Barn Owl (Glue & Jordan, 1988; Love *et al.*, 2000). Glue & Jordan had access to a large quantity of Barn Owl pellet material recovered from a chimney stack that had been capped in 1913 and only opened again in 1986. The presence of bones from both adult and young Barn Owls, plus fragments of Barn Owl eggs, revealed that this had once been a Barn Owl nest site. An examination of the material yielded the remains of 813 prey items, from which Glue & Jordan were able to construct the diet of the birds using the site at the turn of the previous century. The diet was found to contain a wider spectrum of prey than seen in 'modern' counterparts, with the presence of Weasel *Mustela nivalis*, Natterer's Bat, Water Shrew and Common Dormouse *Muscardinus avellanarius*, all uncommon or rare in modern diets. The second important finding was that, although the Field Vole was both numerically and nutritionally the most important prey species, House Mouse, wood mice, Bank Vole and Pygmy Shrew all made a substantial contribution. Glue & Jordan attributed the difference between the two periods to a progressive loss of suitable hunting habitat, noting that those owls hunting in the early 1900s would have:

> been able to hunt along field hedges and woodland for Field and Bank Voles and wood mice, over damp ground and ponds for shrews, Water Voles and frogs, and around stables and rickyards for House Mice, Brown Rats and seed-eating birds.

More recently, the sample of 34,051 prey items collated by David Glue for the British Trust for Ornithology (Glue, 1974) was re-analysed alongside a new Mammal Society sample of 48,996 items collated by Alasdair Love. Love and his co-workers restricted their new analyses to sites on the British mainland and from which at least 40 pellets had been submitted. This enabled them to compare the median percentage frequency of individual components of the two diets and also relate these to region and landscape type. They found that Barn Owl diet differed significantly between the two periods and that this was the result of changes in the occurrence of particular prey species. Significant increases in median percentage frequency were noted for the wood mice *Apodemus* spp. (+5.5 per cent), Bank Vole (+1.5 per cent) and Pygmy Shrew (+3.2 per cent), while a significant decrease was noted for Common Shrew (-9.1 per cent). Differences were also observed for some of the minor prey items, notably birds. The most pronounced change related to the wood mice and this was predominantly linked to a large increase seen in Eastern England. The authors suggested that the increased occurrence of Wood Mouse in this region might have been linked to the introduction of set-aside in 1988 which, although heralded as providing habitat for small mammals in general, is really only used by Wood Mouse (Rogers & Gorman, 1995; Tattersall *et al.*, 2001).

That Love and his colleagues failed to find any change in the frequency of Field Vole in the diet is particularly interesting given the general view that Field Vole populations in Britain have undergone a substantial decline as a consequence of agricultural change (Toms, 1994; Harris *et al.*, 1995). The loss of their preferred rough grassland habitat has been substantial and the likely decline in their abundance has been implicated in the decline of Kestrel populations within southern Britain. This decline is likely to have been the most pronounced in the arable areas of eastern Britain and it is in these areas where we see a significant increase in the frequency of Wood Mouse in the diet.

FIG 46. Harvest Mouse may now be more vulnerable to predation by owls because its preferred habitats have become fragmented. (Mike Toms)

These changes in the diet of Barn Owls over time are thought by many authors to reflect changes in the relative abundance of prey, with owls switching between prey items depending upon their availability within the environment. While this is likely to be true in most cases, it is worth noting that relative abundance is not a straight surrogate for population size. By definition, relative abundance must include some measure of the susceptibility of the prey species to owl predation, perhaps linked to habitat use or activity patterns. Changes in either of these may also influence the degree to which the species turns up in an owl's diet. Love *et al.* (2000) reported an increase in the proportion of Harvest Mice *Micromys minutus* in the diet of Barn Owl between the two sampling periods; this was unexpected because of the widely accepted view that there has been a decline in Harvest Mouse populations over the same period. The Harvest Mouse is regarded as being something of a habitat specialist and it may now show increased vulnerability to Barn Owl predation because it is increasingly restricted to small fragments of suitable habitat.

ISLAND DIETS

As can be seen by the treatment of owl diets presented in Table 6 (p. 74), the spectrum of prey species available to owls in Ireland differs from that available within Britain. This pattern is paralleled in a wider sense, with islands generally supporting a reduced, and often different, small mammal fauna to that present on nearby larger landmasses (Table 5, p. 73). Faced with such differences, the owls generally continue to exploit prey species in relation to their relative availability, either taking the small mammal species that are present or making use of other prey groups (e.g. seabirds). It is worth briefly exploring how island diets may differ from those of mainland populations.

Ireland
Ireland has a reduced terrestrial mammal fauna when compared with Britain, something that is particularly apparent when looking at the small mammal species present. Only Wood Mouse, House Mouse, Common Rat and Pygmy Shrew are widespread, with Bank Vole and Greater White-toothed Shrew *Crocidura russula* recent introductions showing a restricted range. Bank Vole, the more widespread of the two introductions, is restricted to the southwest of Ireland and appears to be spreading at a rate of c. 3 km per year from the site of introduction. Ireland also has a reduced number of owl species; Little Owl and Tawny Owl are absent as breeding species, with just a handful of confirmed records. Short-eared Owl is only an occasional breeder, but occurs more widely during the winter months. This leaves Barn Owl and Long-eared Owl as the two widespread breeding owl species. The diet of both of these owls has been studied extensively in Ireland, revealing the importance of Wood Mouse and Common Rat as the primary prey species (Fairley, 1967; Glue & Hammond, 1974). Barn Owl diets from within the range of Bank Vole show that it makes an important contribution, the species representing between 15 per cent and 22 per cent of the diet by weight. Similarly, pellet analyses of Short-eared Owls breeding within the Bank Vole's restricted range in the 1970s showed that this species contributed roughly 75 per cent of the diet by weight. It has been suggested that Irish Bank Voles utilise more open habitats than their counterparts on the UK mainland,

possibly because they are freed from competition with the larger Field Vole, and this might make them a more accessible prey species to those owls hunting over areas of rough grassland within the area of colonisation.

Other islands

The Field Vole is present on many of our smaller islands, including most of the Inner Hebrides, but is absent from many others. Where it does occur, it invariably becomes a major contributor to owl diet (e.g. Jeal, 1976). It is replaced on Orkney by the Common Vole, known locally as the Orkney Vole (Harris & Yalden, 2008), and this species dominates the diet of Short-eared Owls breeding on the island and Long-eared Owls wintering there (Glue & Hammond, 1974; Reynolds & Gorman, 1999). Wood Mouse is the most widely distributed of our small mammals across the various islands and it is likely that it has been accidentally introduced to many of these islands from visiting ships and their cargo. Again, it features widely in the diet of those owl species using the islands.

Offshore islands also support other potential prey species, including various seabirds, and these may feature in the diet of local owls. We have already highlighted the exploitation of Storm Petrel breeding colonies by Little Owl

FIG 47. Island-living Little Owls have been recorded taking limpets and other shellfish from the intertidal zone. (Steve Round)

on Skokholm, a pattern repeated on Skomer (Sutcliffe, 1990) and mirrored on Bardsey, this time with Manx Shearwaters *Puffinus puffinus* targeted – there are fewer than 50 apparently occupied Storm Petrel nest sites on the island (Heaver, 1987). Saunders (1962) noted two occurrences on Skomer of other owls feeding on young seabirds. In July 1962 he flushed a Short-eared Owl from an area of clifftop bracken; the owl was carrying a young Puffin *Fratercula arctica* and had been seen to hunt regularly over the Puffin colonies on the island during previous weeks. In August of the same year Saunders flushed a Tawny Owl from a cave in which he found the remains of three young Kittiwakes *Rissa tridactyla* and a series of Tawny Owl pellets, the latter containing the skulls of seven young Kittiwakes. This was only the second record of a Tawny Owl on the island and this bird had clearly been roosting in the cave that happened to support the island's largest Kittiwake colony.

One final group of prey species taken on certain offshore islands are intertidal invertebrates. Unsurprisingly, it is just Little Owl that has been found to utilise this resource, with a number of molluscs recovered from pellet samples taken on Bardsey and Skomer (Heaver, 1987; Sutcliffe, 1990). Included in these were Common Limpet *Patella vulgata*, the periwinkles *Littorina saxatilis* and *L. littorea* and the freshwater snail *Planorbis planorbis*.

HOW DOES DIET RELATE TO PREY AVAILABILITY

Throughout this discussion of owl diet we have touched upon the idea of the 'relative availability' of particular prey species. This idea implies something more than just which prey species happen to be present in a particular area. Instead, it suggests some sense of accessibility that might mean particular prey (either species or individuals) are more accessible to a hunting owl, either because they are more active, more likely to use microhabitats hunted over by the owl or are selectively targeted by the owl. A number of authors have suggested that owls sample prey in relation to their availability and, to an extent, this assumption underpins much of the work looking to reconstruct historical or ancient small mammal faunas from pellet samples collected at archaeological or fossil sites (see Andrews, 1990; Yom-Tov & Wool, 1997). However, as Iain Taylor (1994) notes when discussing prey selection in the Barn Owl, it would be quite wrong to take the considerable degree of flexibility seen in some owl diets as evidence of non-selective (random) foraging. Taylor quite rightly expected Barn Owls to forage and select prey in a way that improved the efficiency of their predation. Of course, testing this in the field presents its own problems, not least because attempts to determine prey 'availability' have their own inherent sampling biases. For example, the live trapping of small mammals has been shown to be biased by season, weather conditions, trap-response (some species are shy of novel objects), trap position, trap spacing, trap density and even the odours left by previous inhabitants. Even if we could sample prey availability in an unbiased way, there remains the question of whether the pellet or prey samples examined are themselves a random sample of the owl's catch. As we saw at the start of this chapter, in our discussions of the mechanisms for studying owl diet, how you study owl diet will determine what you can say about it.

Those attempts that have been made to examine the question of whether or not owls select certain prey species preferentially, have used live trapping as the means to establish 'availability' of the prey within the wider environment. Despite the potential pitfalls already mentioned, it does appear that owls do preferentially take certain prey. Carl Marti (1974), working on American Barn Owl, showed that voles were preferentially taken over mice. While some of this selection for voles may have occurred as a consequence of the owls preferentially hunting over areas of rough grassland, it seems almost certain that an additional level of selection was in operation. This might have been linked to capture rates, since Derting & Cranford (1989) discovered that capture success was greater in strikes made on voles (84 per cent) than in those made on mice (50 per cent). Mice tend to be more agile than voles and have larger eyes and ears, suggesting they are better equipped to evade capture. This then raises the question of whether owls can identify particular prey species prior to launching an attack? Recent work, looking at the mechanics of attack behaviour in Barn Owls (see Chapter 1) suggests that owls can target the launch of an attack to very specific cues (Fux & Eilam, 2009), so they may well be able to distinguish between particular prey types.

Other apparent selection can be linked to small mammal behaviour. For example, the selection of adult male voles by Barn Owls during the breeding season is likely to be linked to the fact that male voles are more active than females at this time of the year and also more vocal. The 'selection' of Harvest Mice in the autumn and early winter may simply result from the fact that these mice are arboreal for much of the year, living within standing vegetation and difficult to capture, but are forced down onto the ground once the vegetation is cut or dies back. Selection of prey can therefore happen at several levels, with the choice of hunting habitat one of the main elements in determining which prey species are targeted. This selection of hunting habitat has a behavioural basis, with birds preferentially targeting those habitats supporting the greatest abundance of accessible and profitable prey species. Rough grassland habitats in Britain support the highest densities of Field Vole prey and are preferentially targeted by Barn Owls and Short-eared Owls. Although we will return to the question of habitat selection in later chapters, we will consider certain other aspects of hunting behaviour here.

HUNTING BEHAVIOUR

As we have already seen in Chapter 1, during our examination of the nocturnal habit, our owls show clear peaks in their hunting activity, many of which are associated with peaks in the activity of their prey. The type of prey taken and the habitat within which a hunting owl operates, will both influence hunting behaviour. Although there are clear differences in the hunting behaviour of our various owls, there is also a significant degree of flexibility within those behaviours exhibited by individual species or even individual birds. Barn Owls, for example, may hunt from a perch or quarter open ground; sometimes they will even attempt to flush prey from the cover of bushes or shrubs. Some of these differences may relate to the time of year (the use of perches by Barn Owl appears to be more prevalent during the winter months), to the prey being targeted or to the success or otherwise of the hunting owl. Bunn *et al.* (1982) noted one particular Barn Owl which would switch to 'post hopping' after 30 minutes or so of unsuccessful hunting on the wing. This might suggest a trade-off between the energetics costs of quartering on the wing versus hunting from a perch, against the likely returns. Hunting on the wing remains, however, a favoured strategy for several of our owl species.

Hunting in flight
Three of our owl species regularly hunt by quartering open ground, these being Barn Owl, Long-eared Owl and Short-eared Owl. All three species have a low wing-loading score (see Chapter 1) and are able to cover substantial amounts of ground with the maximum degree of energetic efficiency. The Short-eared Owl hunts by using a combination of flapping and gliding flight and typically operates between 0.5 and 2 m above the ground (Glue, 1977a). Short-eared Owls will sometimes make a more direct and higher flight (10 m or more above the ground), reminiscent of that adopted by a hunting harrier and during which the wing beats are usually regular and steady, with the wing tips following a wide arc. Like the Short-eared Owl, the Long-eared Owl will quarter areas of suitable hunting habitat, often straying closer to the ground, and mixing rather deep wing beats (which don't tend to lift above the body) with longer periods of gliding flight (Davis & Prytherch, 1976). Long-eared Owls tend to glide on flat wings, while

FIG 48. Hunting Barn Owls often 'quarter' an area, flying just a few metres above the ground. (Steve Round)

Short-eareds show a shallow 'v' to the wing position. Although the Long-eared Owl will quite happily hunt over open ground (such as areas of upland rough grazing, lowland rough grassland, chalk escarpments and forest rides) it appears equally at home hunting within woodland, remaining well below the canopy and occasionally pausing on suitable vantage points (Glue & Hammond, 1974). A hunting Barn Owl adopts a similar approach to the Short-eared Owl, although to my mind the flight appears more buoyant and better controlled. Certainly, Barn Owl appears the more dextrous when it comes to hovering, a behaviour that often punctuates the quartering flight. Hovering is presumably triggered when the owl detects movement on the ground below it, the bird halting its progress in order to better pinpoint a potential meal. Hovering may be followed by a dive directed towards the prey item, the bird's wings held back in a deeply shaped 'V'. Long-eared Owls have also been noted to hover, though they do so less frequently (and less gracefully) than either Barn Owl or Short-eared Owl.

Little Owls will sometimes catch prey in flight, acting in a flycatcher-like manner from a suitable perch and taking aerially active insects with some degree of dexterity. In this manner they have been seen to take insects up to the size of a Cockchafer, typically returning to the perch to either swallow them whole or to pull them apart with their beak (Beven, 1979). In contrast to those owls which regularly hunt over open ground, the Little Owl rarely hovers. Several authors have implied that the species is decidedly clumsy when it does hover but T. C. Gregory, writing in 1945, observed a Little Owl working an area of wet ground in a Kestrel-like fashion, alternating between quartering flight and hovering, before successfully dropping down to the ground to take a Lapwing chick.

A hunting owl will sometimes attempt to flush roosting birds from the relative security of a scrubby bush or hedgerow. This behaviour has been recorded in Long-eared Owl (Ticehurst, 1939; Scott, 1997), Barn Owl and Tawny Owl (Witherby *et al.*, 1938; Beven, 1965) and may involve the owl deliberately banging its wings against the bush. The technique seems to be targeted against species that roost communally, for example Starlings, sparrows and finches, and is most commonly reported in winter.

Hunting from a perch

The use of a perch, from which to scan for suitable prey, is an energetically efficient hunting technique but also one that depends on suitable prey coming within range of the owl. Such an approach is likely to require a high level of prey abundance in order to produce an encounter rate that will meet the energetic demands of the owl. At low prey densities the owl will need to cover a greater area of suitable habitat and this may, instead, favour the use of a quartering flight. Hunting from a perch is most commonly seen in Tawny Owl, Snowy Owl, Eagle Owl and Little Owl but it can be a feature of our other owl species at certain times of the year.

Most British researchers would tell you that Tawny Owls favour hunting from a perch over all other techniques. This observation, while certainly true for the majority of British birds, may be influenced by the habitat preferences of the species within Britain. Here, woodland is the favoured habitat and it naturally provides plenty of perches from which the bird can wait quietly before dropping onto unsuspecting prey. Interestingly, radio-tracking studies of Tawny Owls, living within more open habitats in southern Sweden, have revealed a much greater incidence of hunting in flight (Nilsson, 1978). Ingvar Nilsson, who carried out the work, found that his radio-tagged Tawny Owls devoted about a third of their active time to hunting on the wing. On those moonlit nights when he was able to watch the birds as well as track them, Ingvar found that they would fly some two to three metres above the ground, using a slow flight, interspersed with glides and only used in open habitats. The birds would work an area of open ground carefully, the bouts of hunting on the wing broken by periods when

FIG 49. 'Post-hopping' can be an energetically efficient hunting technique for Short-eared Owls during the winter. (Emma Perry)

the birds were either resting or hunting from a suitable perch (it was not always possible to tell which of these two activities the owl was indulging in). At between 89 and 146 hectares, the territories of these Swedish birds are significantly larger than those of British Tawny Owls living within woodland habitats (see Chapter 3) and are suggestive of lower prey densities.

Barn Owls will often hunt from a perch and this behaviour tends to be observed more commonly outside of the breeding season, especially during periods of poor weather. Fence posts are used fairly regularly, though birds will often seek a more sheltered perch (tucked into the leeward side of a tree or hedgerow) if it is raining or windy. In addition to the energetic savings this approach offers, of particular importance during the winter months, it is also worth noting that small mammals may make greater use of linear features, such as fence rows, at this time of the year. With mid-field vegetation often much-reduced during winter, fence rows offer a greater degree of cover and increased feeding opportunities for small mammals. Movement into fence lines, hedgerow bases and ditch margins by Field Voles was evident on my small mammal trapping grids in rural Norfolk during the late autumn and winter months.

It can, as Iain Taylor found in his studies of Scottish Barn Owls, be difficult to make a clear separation between perch hunting and flight hunting. His birds were found to exhibit perching phases that lasted anywhere from 15 seconds to just over eight minutes. While birds would sometimes drop directly from the perch onto a prey item, they more commonly took to the wing first, hovering as if to pinpoint the prey before dropping onto their target. At other times, when the birds appeared to be moving between perches, they would suddenly latch onto a mouse or vole and pounce. Taylor argued that the birds were using the perch for initial scanning and rough prey location but needed to take to the wing to pinpoint the exact location of the prey before a strike could be made. Such an approach would offer some energetic savings and, as outlined above, the use of perches would seem a more rewarding strategy in winter, when energetic costs are of increased significance. Taylor's birds were found to increase their use of perches significantly from 54 per cent in summer to 87 per cent in winter (Taylor, 1994). One other aspect examined by Taylor was the question of the optimum height for hunting. In the context of perch use, it is worth noting that Barn Owls do not use telegraph posts for perch hunting (Kestrels do so regularly and Long-eared Owls have been recorded doing so), suggesting that they are unable to pinpoint prey from this height. Barn Owls inhabiting Malaysian Oil Palm *Elaeis guineensis* plantations not only utilise perches to a far greater degree than our birds, they also hunt from perches located up to five metres above the ground (Lenton, 1984). The race found on the Malay Peninsula, *Tyto alba javanica*, is a structurally bigger bird, with a wider talon spread, and is able to catch much larger prey (mainly Malayan Wood Rat *Rattus tiomanicus*) which can presumably be detected at greater range. Long-eared Owls typically make use of perches located at a height of between 1.6 and 6 m off the ground. Some individuals may make greater use of perches than others, with Derick Scott commenting on a male Long-eared Owl in Lincolnshire which used 1.5 m high fence posts as his main means of securing a meal. The posts were located between a wood and a small rural road and the bird was observed to use them over a four-week period, arriving in the half-light of dusk and demonstrating a strike rate of one in every three to five attempts.

Taking food on the ground

Little Owls seem at ease when hunting on the ground and will often run or hop in pursuit of prey. Quite often they will combine hunting methods, using a perch to locate prey before flying down to the ground and making the final approach on foot (Mitchell, 1994). In this way, Little Owls will take earthworms, beetles and earwigs. In some parts of their range, notably Kazakhstan and Russia, Little Owls

FIG 50. The Little Owl seems comfortable on the ground, whether hunting or, as in this case, drinking. (Mark Hancox)

regularly enter the burrow systems of small mammals to take gerbils, a behaviour that has ecological parallels with the Burrowing Owl. Records of Little Owls within Rabbit burrows in Britain are more likely to represent breeding sites than feeding ones. The presence of rocky-shore molluscs in Little Owl diet on islands also suggests that the species is happy to forage on the ground within some inter-tidal areas. Tawny Owls also seem at home on the ground and will readily spend some time here when feeding on earthworms. Macdonald (1976) described how a Tawny Owl hunting earthworms would sit motionless on the ground until it seemingly heard a sound, whereupon it would rotate its head and crane its neck to pinpoint the source of the noise. The bird would then hop forward several paces at a time, pausing to check the location of the sound, before finally bounding forward with wings partially outspread, to snatch up the worm. As anyone who has been out with a torch on a damp night will know, many worms only partially emerge from their hole (and can retreat with surprising speed) and a Tawny Owl may find itself in a tug of war with the worm, often breaking it in two as it attempts to extract the worm from its burrow. After eating a worm, the owl may sit motionless for many minutes before picking up the sound of another meal and beginning the process again. While Tawny Owl predation on earthworms is predominantly a nocturnal pursuit, a letter published in *The Times* in 1964 revealed the curious diurnal behaviour of one particular Tawny Owl. This bird was found to be following the plough:

> It waits in a thick hedge at the side of the field and every time I pass flies out to search the new furrows, mingling oddly with the gulls. After examining a few yards of earth it returns to its perch to wait for the tractor to pass again.

Presumably this bird was after earthworms or soil-dwelling larvae. Records of our other owls actively hunting on the ground are rare. Godin & Loison noted a Long-eared Owl actively pursuing a Harvest Mouse on foot one afternoon, while Derick Scott reports one feeding on earthworms at a farm compost heap.

Dealing with prey

Although the mechanics of prey location and capture have already been covered in Chapter 1, we still need to examine how owls actually deal with prey once they have caught it. The majority of the prey items taken by owls appear to be caught unawares and quickly subdued by the impact of the strike. This is certainly what happens in the case of small mammals and small birds. Field observations of owl behaviour, coupled with evidence derived from an examination of the damage to skulls recovered in owl pellets, suggests that owls kill small mammals by nipping through the back of the cranium. Captured prey is often devoured immediately but it may be carried a short distance to a favoured perch or more sheltered location before being tackled. An owl may mantle a prey item, in a similar manner to that more commonly seen in diurnal raptors, spreading its wings slightly over the kill and sometimes adopting an aggressive posture. This behaviour is common in the Long-eared Owl (Scott, 1997) but appears less frequently in the literature in regard of our other owl species. Heimo Mikkola notes a Barn Owl that mantled a prey item in response to a pair of Carrion Crows *Corvus corone*, which had taken an interest in the activities of this particular daylight-hunting bird.

Owls may occasionally be killed when they tackle larger prey items. J. H. Gurney, writing in the *Zoologist* in 1876, reported an incident that took place on a farm at Leigh, near Tonbridge in Kent. A farmer's wife had picked up a dead Barn Owl from the floor of a barn, next to which was a very large rat, also dead. Both animals showed injuries which suggested that they had died as a result of a failed attempt by the owl to tackle such a large prey item. Other mammal species may also prove problematic and it is interesting to note the presence of both Stoat *Mustela erminea* and Weasel in several of our owl diets.

BEYOND FOOD AND FEEDING

This exploration of the diet and feeding habits of our owls, and of how we study them, is only part of the story. The spectrum of prey that our owls exploit has important consequences for the key components of an owl's life cycle. Prey availability may determine breeding success or, indeed, whether individual birds will attempt to breed in the first place. It will shape the survival chances of newly fledged young, perhaps even influencing how far they disperse from their natal sites, and it will also have a bearing on their future success. Because of this, mention of food and its availability will enter into our discussions on these other aspects of owl ecology throughout the next three chapters. First though, we shall turn our attentions to breeding ecology.

CHAPTER 3

Breeding Ecology

REPRODUCTION IS CENTRAL TO the owl's year, its timing shaped by natural selection to deliver the maximum number of young into the breeding populations of subsequent years. In some birds the timing of breeding aligns the period of greatest food demands for growing chicks with the seasonal peak in prey abundance. In owls, however, there is evidence to suggest that the peak in prey abundance comes later in the year and is more closely matched with the period when newly independent young are learning to find food for themselves.

As we shall see in this chapter, the timing of breeding may vary with species, location or even between individual birds. Its success or failure may be linked to the availability of resources and it is competition for these resources (including nest sites and potential mates) that may underpin the establishment of breeding territories. Selecting the right mate also has an influence on breeding success and, as we will discover, individual owls may advertise their suitability in a number of different ways. Reproduction is energetically costly, so birds may need to get into 'breeding condition', sometimes falling short and failing to make an attempt in a given year. The allocation of resources to breeding by an individual represents a trade-off between the returns it receives from reproducing, the amount of resources required and how these balance against the likelihood of a future breeding attempt and the individual's own survival chances. It is a complex business, which is one of the reasons that it has proved so interesting to researchers.

NESTING HABITAT

Any birdwatcher will be able to list the habitats that you would need to visit if you wished to see our native owls. The association of individual species with particular habitats reflects underlying differences in ecology, foraging behaviour, competition and the prey spectrum taken. Habitat associations within a species may vary with season; for example, while a visit to the uplands of Scotland in summer might reveal breeding Short-eared Owls, these birds will be absent come winter, foraging instead over coastal grazing marshes or on lower-altitude grassland. Habitat associations are of particular interest to our examination of the breeding ecology of British owls, for it is during the breeding season that habitat requirements include both an abundance of prey and a suitable place in which to nest. While there are certain similarities in the nesting requirements of our owls, there are also some key differences and it is these that allow apparently similar species to co-exist alongside one another. For example, three species that exploit microtine rodents – Barn Owl and the two *Asio* owls – show differences in the habitats they utilise, how they use them and where they choose to nest, something we have just touched upon in the previous chapter.

Prey availability and the nesting habitat

The British owls have to find substantial quantities of prey for their growing chicks and prey availability may ultimately determine reproductive condition and shape breeding success. Individuals, then, are likely to select breeding habitats on the basis of prey abundance but they may also be constrained by nest site availability or some other aspect of their ecology. Short-eared Owls and Snowy Owls, which nest on the ground and which are not tied to the presence of suitable tree cavities or disused stick nests, can make a nesting attempt wherever prey are most readily available. Both species show nomadic movements and may cover vast distances between subsequent nesting events in order to locate the best feeding opportunities. These are often found in open landscapes, like moorland or large expanses of rough grassland, where vole populations can reach very high densities. Other species, such as Barn Owl and Tawny Owl, are more sedentary in nature, perhaps tied to habitats where suitable cavity sites are available and conditions over-winter are more favourable.

Most microtine voles are associated with grassland habitats, in particular mature grassland and its tussocky, well-developed sward structure with a deep litter layer. The well-developed structure is important because it is within this that the voles construct a network of runways and nesting chambers. Vole densities have been found to display a negative relationship with grazing intensity, such that increased stocking levels are likely to have reduced the quality of much pasture grassland within the UK for hunting owls (Schmidt *et al.*, 2005). Large expanses of rough, tussocky grassland are now uncommon across much of Britain and in many areas vole populations are restricted to smaller blocks, often those present alongside ditch edges, woodland margins, hedgerows or within stands of newly planted woodland. With Field Voles prominent in so many of the Barn Owl

FIG 51. Increased stocking densities of sheep and other livestock restrict the development of the dense sward structure favoured by voles. (Mike Toms)

diets studied within the UK, it is perhaps unsurprising that so much emphasis has been placed on the availability of rough grassland within the foraging ranges used by this species. Colin and Val Shawyer, for example, stressed that Barn Owls required 40 ha of unimproved grassland within their foraging range in order to breed successfully (Shawyer & Shawyer, 1995). During the period when the release of captive-bred Barn Owls was being licensed by the UK government, the Department of the Environment (DoE) guidelines were that 50 ha of rough, permanent pasture were 'usually necessary for permission to release Barn Owls into the wild to be granted'. Despite this, there are many successful nest sites from which chicks are fledged year after year but with little rough grassland present locally. In many arable areas, where foraging opportunities appear limited because of the lack of rough grassland, it is the Wood Mouse that becomes an important secondary prey species. This adaptable species is found across many different habitats, including farmland, but peak densities are associated with woodland.

Woodland mice, together with Bank Voles, are important for nesting Tawny Owls. Shrews, another secondary prey species for some of our owls, reach their highest densities in habitats similar to those favoured by voles. Although small mammals are important for breeding Little Owls, the use of invertebrates and other food types allows a wider range of nesting habitats to be exploited, though woodland and large expanses of intensive agriculture are avoided. Grassland is very much a favoured habitat for Little Owls, particularly when part of a mosaic of habitat types, and sward height appears to be important in allowing access to favoured invertebrate prey. During the breeding season, when the growth of vegetation may limit foraging opportunities, access to areas of short sward or bare ground may be particularly important. One radio-tracking study, for example, found that Little Owls spent 85–95 per cent of their time at locations where the ground vegetation did not exceed 20 cm (Grzywaczewski, 2009), a pattern repeated in other studies (Šálek & Lövy, 2012). Our Eagle Owl population is too small to allow examination of nesting habitats in relation to prey availability, but experience from elsewhere within Europe suggests that prey availability is important in shaping the breeding distribution, although disturbance and persecution may also play a role in some populations (Donázar, 1988).

The influence of habitat on the breeding success of British owls is something that has only really been studied in relation to the Barn Owl. The results to emerge from this work have been somewhat mixed, at least in terms of what they tell us about the importance of unimproved grassland. Several analyses, using information collected from local studies, have failed to find evidence that the amount of rough grassland within the hunting range of a breeding pair might influence breeding success (Bond *et al.*, 2004; Meek *et al.*, 2009). In contrast, a nationwide study found that nest boxes located within grassland areas had a higher degree of occupancy, a greater proportion of pairs that attempted breeding and had females that were heavier than those associated with farmland or improved pasture habitats (Leech *et al.*, 2009; Dadam *et al.*, 2011). In addition, this national study found that birds breeding in arable areas laid smaller clutches and, as a consequence, produced smaller broods. This suggests that rough grassland, and the Field Vole populations that it supports, does have an influence on Barn Owl breeding success, with attempts to examine this at a local level possibly hindered by the habitat differences between successful and unsuccessful sites being too small to be tested fully. We can get some indication of habitat quality and its influence on our breeding owls by looking at territory size and ranging behaviour, something to which we will turn shortly. A high quality habitat, perhaps one with an abundance of small mammal prey, is likely to support more breeding pairs and these are likely to have smaller territories than is the case in a habitat where prey are less abundant. At 18 ha, the Tawny Owl territories in deciduous woodland are much smaller than those in coniferous woodland (46 ha), for example, suggesting that prey are present in higher densities within deciduous than they are within coniferous woodland (Hirons, 1985).

The nesting habitats of British owls

We tend to split our five common owl species on the basis of breeding habitat into those associated with lowland farmland (Barn Owl and Little Owl), those associated with woodland (Long-eared Owl and Tawny Owl) and those associated with moorland (Short-eared Owl). These, of course, are generalisations and the actual habitats used by our owls show a far greater degree of diversity. All of the British species are part of wider populations found elsewhere across Europe or beyond and individuals in some of these populations occupy very different habitats to those used within Britain, underlining a degree of adaptability providing that sufficient food is available and nest sites present. The semi-desert habitats used by breeding Little Owls in North Africa, for example, are very different from the mixed-farmland habitats of south-east England.

The range of habitats available within the British Isles is more limited and we see a degree of overlap in the habitat use of our different owl species. The Barn Owl, which has long been associated with the agricultural habitats of lowland Britain, is a case in point since the species may also be found breeding in young conifer plantations alongside Short-eared Owl. The association of the Barn Owl

FIG 52. Set in a modern arable landscape, this barn might seem unsuitable for nesting Barn Owls but there is sufficient small mammal prey in the patches of rough grassland and ditch banks that remain to allow successful breeding. (Mike Toms)

with farmland derives from a period when farming was less intensive in nature and areas of rough grassland, coupled with an abundance of small mammals around stack yards during winter, afforded the species a more comfortable living than is perhaps available today. Rough grassland is an important foraging habitat because it supports good populations of Field Voles and this is why the Barn Owl may exploit both young conifer plantations and damp valley bottoms. Favourable grassland swards and their Field Vole populations are often absent or highly fragmented within the more intensive modern agricultural systems of lowland Britain. Agricultural practices, such as mowing and grazing, further damage sward structure and lower vole populations, leaving the owls breeding here more dependent upon secondary prey species (Tattershall *et al.*, 2001; Askew *et al.*, 2007). Additionally, the sedentary nature of the Barn Owl, coupled with high levels of mortality during poor winter weather, appears to limit this owl altitudinally and it rarely breeds above 300 m above sea-level. Scottish populations around the Black Isle are some of the most northerly in the World.

Like the Barn Owl, the Little Owl is also chiefly to be found breeding in lowland habitats, particularly those associated with farmland. It does not, however, occupy the young plantation habitats used by Barn Owl and is, additionally, absent or less abundant in the pastural landscapes of south-west Britain, where the Barn Owl appears to be doing well. Within its wider breeding range across Britain, now largely restricted to England and the Welsh borders, modelled abundance from *Bird Atlas 2007–11* suggests a patchy distribution for this introduced species (Balmer *et al.*, 2013). There is a suggestion that damp pasture could be important to breeding Little Owls, as might parkland with mature trees and mixed farmland with well-developed hedgerows. The avoidance of upland areas can be seen from both distribution maps produced through *Bird Atlas 2007–11* (see Figure 153) and an examination of BTO Nest Record cards, the latter revealing that 85 per cent of the nests studied are below 122 m above sea level (Glue & Scott, 1980). The species may sometimes be found breeding in areas lacking trees, such as coastal sea cliffs, dune systems and on islands, where seabird burrows and clefts between rocks may be used.

Short-eared Owls may occasionally be found breeding on lowland farmland in the more southerly parts of their European range, although this only tends to happen in years of very high vole numbers. In Britain, lowland farmland, in the form of large expanses of coastal grazing marsh, still holds some breeding pairs but more typical habitats are the rough grassland of young conifer plantations, heather moorland, upland bogs and areas of rough grazing. The afforestation of large parts of northern and western Britain appears to have benefited breeding Short-eared Owls during the initial few years following planting. Many upland grasslands were formerly grazed by sheep and it is their removal which has promoted the development of a dense tussocky sward of the type favoured by Field Vole populations. These, in turn, have attracted Short-eared Owls to settle and establish territories in response to local prey densities. Peak vole densities are reached after the plantations have been established for three to seven years, the numbers then declining as the canopy closes. The owls appear to require large expanses of habitat for breeding and have not, for example, been able to exploit small blocks of rotational clear-fell. In a study of Short-eared Owls breeding in south-west Scotland, Geoff Shaw found that the smallest such block to be used was 62 ha in size (Shaw, 1995). Shaw also found that the density of breeding owls declined with patch age, though with a clear peak at about five years post-planting, matching the period of peak small mammal availability.

The Long-eared Owl uses a range of wider habitat types. These include heath and moorland, woodland, farmland and coastal margins, the owls utilising small plantations, shelterbelts and hedgerows for placement of the nest site itself. Both deciduous and coniferous woodland are used, sometimes where these exist as extensive blocks – in which case the birds favour the edges – and often where they are present as small clumps or even isolated trees, sometimes even including those to be found in larger gardens. Although Long-eared Owls have been recorded nesting in excess of 500 m above sea level, they are more commonly encountered in the lowlands, where some form of woodland or dense hedgerow is bordered by areas of rough grassland, fen or other open habitat and supporting good populations of their favoured small mammal prey. The small and sometimes short-lived breeding populations on the Western Isles, Orkney and Shetland have, at times, nested in the more open habitats associated with Short-eared Owls, such as the heather-dominated open hill country of Shetland. The establishment of conifer plantations on some of Scottish islands, for example Lewis and the Uists, may have increased nesting opportunities over recent years but it may also increase the degree of competition from Tawny Owl in the longer term.

Competition with the Tawny Owl is thought by some researchers to limit the distribution of breeding Long-eared Owls more widely but there are instances where the two species have been found breeding within the same small area of woodland. A study in West Norfolk concluded that there were definite signs that the two species could not co-exist. This conclusion was based on the fact that the closest together that calling young from 34 Long-eared Owl and 46 Tawny Owl nests were found was 500 m and that a traditional Long-eared Owl site was abandoned following the arrival of breeding Tawny Owls (Kemp, 1981). The association of breeding Long-eared Owls with smaller woodlands and shelterbelts might also be suggestive of competition with the Tawny Owl. Tawny Owls favour mature woodland with suitable nesting cavities, which are less commonly found in small blocks of younger-aged woodland, leaving the Long-eared Owls to breed undisturbed. In Ireland and on the Isle of Man, where Tawny Owls are absent, Long-eared Owls are reported to breed in a wider range of woodland types – including more extensive woodland blocks – than seen here in Britain. Competition between Tawny Owl and Barn Owl is sometimes mentioned in the literature but again there are examples of the two species nesting in close proximity. Andy Dowell and Geoff Shaw described two cases where Tawny Owls and Barn Owls bred successfully within 40 m of each other and I have had birds breed just 16 m apart in neighbouring oak trees in Norfolk parkland in the early 1990s.

The Tawny Owl is dependent upon trees for nesting, roosting and, to a significant extent, hunting. It is, after all, a perch and wait predator and is generally considered to be a 'forest' owl. Despite this reliance on trees, which sees a strong association with large blocks of deciduous, mixed and coniferous woodland, Tawny Owls may also be found breeding in more open landscapes, including some parts of the East Anglian fenlands. Steve Redpath, for example, found the species to be present in all woodlands blocks of 4 ha or larger in size, with a third of the woods smaller than a hectare also supporting the species. The smallest occupied block in which Tawny Owls roosted and made a nesting attempt was just 0.3 ha (Redpath, 1995). These fenland owls have large home ranges, typically taking in several blocks of woodland, but they will also use the surrounding matrix, sometimes feeding from isolated hedgerow perches or from the ground in patches of rough grassland. Hardy (1992) found a similar pattern in his study populations occupying Aberdeenshire farmland, with its small woodlots. Tawny Owls may also be found nesting in the well-wooded parts of some of our cities, a behaviour that is also seen in other European countries (Galeotti, 1990; Luniak 1996; Ranazzi et al., 2000)

Of the owl species breeding within Britain it is the Eurasian Eagle Owl that perhaps shows the greatest breadth of habitats across its wider range. The species may be found breeding in rocky and mountainous habitats, in deserts, farmland, deciduous forest and scrubby steppe. It may even be found breeding alongside people in some European cities. Within Britain, the small number of nesting attempts documented have tended to be in rough upland or upland margin habitats, the birds nesting on a ledge or in the cover of an overhang. The nesting attempts made by Snowy Owls within Britain have been made in areas characterised by rough terrain and little human disturbance. The pair found nesting on Fetlar in 1967, the first substantiated breeding record for Britain, settled on the Hill of Stakkaberg, an area of boulder-strewn slopes and rocky outcrops, dominated by rough grass and heath and reminiscent of the tundra habitats favoured further north (Tulloch, 1968).

NEST SITES

As with our examination of nesting habitats, the nest sites used by our British owls can also be divided into core types, namely: cavities (Barn Owl, Tawny Owl, Little Owl), old stick nests (Long-eared Owl) and ground/ledge nests (Short-eared Owl, Eagle Owl, Snowy Owl). Each species shows its own preferences, even within a particular type of nest site, but there may also be variation linked to the opportunities available. In my own work on Barn Owls, for example, I have encountered nests in tree cavities, on the floor of attic roof spaces, in bale stacks, in the ducting of an underground hospital, in an old-fashioned milk churn and in various types of nest box. Interestingly, there is an underlying pattern of regional variation in the nest site types used by breeding Barn Owls within Britain. Through Project Barn Owl we discovered that the majority of recorded

FIG 53. Little Owls favour smaller cavities for nesting and are able to make use of opportunities not available to other nesting owls. (John Harding).

nest sites in the western half of Britain were in buildings, while in the East of England up to 80 per cent of reported sites were in tree cavities. This does not necessarily imply any form of selection for a particular type of nest site but rather highlights the regional variation that, most likely, exists in site availability. Radio-tracking studies and the recapture of ringed birds at the nest refutes the misconception sometimes heard that birds reared in a particular type of site will select for that site type as breeding adults.

Cavity-nesting owls

Natural cavities in oak, Ash *Fraxinus excelsior* and willow are important for a number of cavity-nesting species, including both Barn Owl and Little Owl. Barn Owls favour larger cavities, matching both their larger size and the size of brood produced. Many are deep within the trunk of hollow trees, the nesting chamber often several feet below the entrance hole. The cavities which form in mature fruit trees provide additional opportunities for nesting Little Owls and the association between Little Owls and old orchards has been well documented. David Glue and Derick Scott found that nearly one in five of the 482 sites used in their study were in fruit trees (Glue & Scott, 1980). Fruit trees appear to play an even more important role in some parts of continental Europe where, for example, they may make up more than a quarter of the sites used. Further south in its European range the Little Owl can often be found nesting among the piles of stones that are cleared from agricultural fields.

The small size of the Little Owl allows it to exploit small cavities, unavailable to other owl species. These may include those in mature timber, accessed by spherical holes or vertical cracks, or in man-made structures such as stone walls and outbuildings. The small size of some sites prevents human access and may reduce the number of such sites that are monitored by researchers and nest recorders, such that published figures on site types may be biased towards those more readily inspected. Little Owls also seem to prefer cavities that provide a nesting chamber some distance from the external entrance hole. An examination of Little Owl nesting chambers by Glue & Scott (1980) revealed that most were reached by a narrow, winding passage some 50 to 130 cm in length. Modern designs of Little Owl nest box have tried to emulate this and to produce a nesting chamber that is dark and out of direct sight of the entrance hole.

Another habit of some Little Owls is to nest underground, the birds using clefts in rocks, chambers under stone walls or at the base of trees and, on occasion, Rabbit burrows; the latter sites are a feature on some coastal cliffs and islands. There is a suggestion that Little Owls might prefer an elevated nest site over a subterranean one. Roy Leigh, a Little Owl fieldworker in Cheshire, noted how one of his study pairs moved into a Rabbit burrow following damage to the nest box, placed five metres up in an oak tree. The following year the nest box was replaced and the owls returned to use it, seemingly in preference to the burrow that appeared unchanged from the previous year. The small size of the Little Owl also affords a degree of adaptability and the species has also been recorded nesting among stacked bales, under an active railway track and inside pipework. Nests made in corn-stacks, using disused rat runs, were fairly common in the 1940s. In some countries the nest sites used by Little Owls shape the bird's local name. In parts of central Europe the species is known as 'Stockeule' (willow owl) and in southern France it is 'Chouette des tuiles' (roof owl) (Schönn et al., 1991; Barthelemy & Bertrand, 1997).

Tawny Owls often occupy tree cavities that are intermediate in size between those favoured by Barn Owl and Little Owl. Of the three species they are the one most likely to be encountered in a more open setting, the cavity not always complete and sometimes exposed to the elements – for example where the trunk has broken off to the leave a hollow 'chimney'. The cavities favoured are usually below 12 m in height above the ground, although Tawny Owls will nest higher than this, particularly where they have chosen to occupy the old stick nest of another species (e.g. Magpie *Pica pica* or Carrion Crow). This is not an uncommon habit and is one that is shared with the Long-eared Owl. Tawny Owls will sometimes nest in a suitable cavity in a building, most often a chimney, and may sometimes be found nesting on the ground (e.g. in coniferous woodland, among tree roots or a snag) or among rocks. Like both Barn Owls and Little Owls, Tawny Owls will take to suitable nest boxes (see later in this chapter). While work carried out in Kielder Forest demonstrates that Tawny Owls prefer nest boxes over natural sites in the coniferous forests of northern England, work in other habitats, and indeed in other countries, shows that this is not always the case. Kielder's Tawny Owls took readily to boxes for nesting but did not seem to use them at other times of the year, presumably because there were other roosting opportunities available. In contrast, Tawny Owls breeding in urban Milan (northern Italy) were found to prefer natural sites for breeding, with the boxes instead used extensively for roosting during the winter months (Sacchi et al., 2004).

Open-nesting owls

Unlike our other tree-nesting owls the Long-eared Owl favours the open nests of other bird species, utilising those of corvids, Woodpigeon and various raptors. In some instances a nest will be used by a succession of species over several years, perhaps being constructed by a Carrion Crow, added to by a Sparrowhawk and then used by a Long-eared Owl. Individual pairs may use the same site over a

FIG 54. Used by nesting Sparrowhawks in one year, this nest may be used by breeding Long-eared Owls in a future season. (John Harding)

number of years, also using it for replacement clutches. Long-eared Owls will also use old squirrel dreys and natural platforms formed from 'witches brooms'. Ground-nesting and cavity-nesting have both been recorded on occasion and the species has also been coaxed into woven baskets erected as nest sites by researchers (see later in this chapter). In some parts of the Netherlands the species has also taken to using Kestrel boxes. There is a suggestion of local preferences with, for example, Magpie nests favoured in certain Yorkshire plantations and Carrion Crow on some Lancashire mosslands (Glue, 1977b). However, such 'preferences' might simply reflect local availability and it seems likely that the Long-eared Owl makes use of what is available. It is worth noting that Little Owls may also occupy the empty nests of Magpie, as appears to be a fairly common practice in parts of Moldavia.

The platforms used by Long-eared Owls are normally those located high in the upper branches of conifers (notably Scots Pine *Pinus sylvestris*) but they will nest lower down in dense deciduous growth, such as a hawthorn thicket. Research carried out in Slovenia demonstrates that coniferous trees are preferred over deciduous ones because of the cover they provide early in the year, at the time when Long-eared Owls are nesting (Tome, 2003). Davorin Tome tested predation rates in the different types of tree by using hen eggs and found rates in deciduous trees to be significantly greater than those seen in conifers. Predation risk has been shown to influence nest site choice in this species, with Spanish Long-eared Owls found to select for dense canopy cover around the nest and high shrub cover below it (Rodríguez et al., 2006). The degree of shrubby cover below the nest was found to be positively related to nest productivity, suggesting that it provided newly fledged young with a greater degree of protection against predators.

Derick Scott found the average height of the 200 Long-eared Owl tree-nests he monitored in Britain to be about 6 m, a little lower than the figure of 6.7 m calculated from BTO Nest Record cards by David Glue. Favoured tree nests are usually those with good all-round visibility and with easy access through the surrounding trees. Ground nests tend to be found where suitable nest platforms are absent, the bird making a simple nesting scrape at the base of a tree or alongside a suitable snag. Such scrapes are often given some protection by bramble, heather or dead bracken cover. Eric Hosking once photographed an unusual nest placed among reeds. Female Long-eared Owls may adapt their chosen nest platform, perhaps removing the grass or wool lining added by its previous corvid occupant, and adding new material in the form of small twigs (a behaviour also seen in the male prior to egg-laying and, rarely, during incubation). James Cairns, for example, reports the presence of green pine needles and dead fronds of 'hard' fern in some of the Scottish Long-eared Owl nests that he visited (Cairns, 1915). Cavity-nesting owls appear to do even less work on their nest, the female simply forming a shallow scrape within the nesting chamber, perhaps within a bed of old pellets from previous years. Where the nest site is being used for the first time the eggs may be laid directly onto the floor of the cavity resulting, in some cases with Barn Owls, in eggs laid onto plasterboard and even loft insulation.

While both Tawny Owl and Long-eared Owl have been recorded nesting on the ground (Gurney & Turner, 1915; Scott, 1997), this is the exception rather than the rule, with ground nesting the domain of Short-eared Owl, Snowy Owl and Eagle Owl. The ground-nesting owls also appear to show some clear preferences in the placement of their nests. Those of the Short-eared Owl are usually placed within some taller cover, typically that provided by heather, grasses, bracken or rushes. Although Short-eared Owl nest sites are associated with open habitats, suggesting the birds seek visibility from the nest site, Geoff Shaw found that pairs nesting in blocks of conifer restock tended to place their nests within 75 m

FIG 55. Eagle Owl nest scrape in the Forest of Bowland, northern England, placed on the ground. (Michael Demain)

of the nearest forest edge, despite the fact that the blocks were large enough to allow the birds to place the nests more centrally and at a greater distance from the margin. Britain's breeding Snowy Owls have tended to site their nests so that the incubating female has a commanding view of the surrounding landscape. The site used on Fetlar in 1968 was typical, although it did have some blind spots, which the male covered through his choice of look-out (Tulloch, 1968). Elsewhere within their breeding range Snowy Owls have been shown to favour mounds for nest placement, which Denver Holt and colleagues suggest provide drier conditions at the nest and greater vigilance against predators; they may also reduce the unwanted attentions of biting insects because they tend to be more exposed to the wind (Holt *et al.*, 2009). The Snowy Owl nest site is a shallow scrape to which dead grasses may be added as incubation proceeds. Eagle Owl nest sites also take the form of a scrape; these are often placed on a cliff ledge, which appears to be the preferred location. In the absence of a suitable cliff or quarry site, the species will nest on the ground – often strongly sloping – perhaps, under an overhang or close to a tree trunk or boulder. Eagle Owls may make use of the abandoned stick nests of larger birds.

Site selection and use

Being long-lived birds, it is perhaps unsurprising that 'traditional' sites may be used by our owls over many years, sometimes with a short break in occupancy. This suggests that a particular site might be attractive in wider terms, presumably because of its location, structure and local food availability. Dianne Mitchell reported on a site in a Hampshire Ash tree that was used by breeding Little Owls from 1977 to 1992, with nesting attempts made every year except for 1982. In every year that the tree was used, except for the last, the birds used the same nest hole (Mitchell, 1994).

Site selection may also be modified by the presence of particular predators, with owls nesting in areas with more predators likely to seek out better-concealed nest sites. Experimental manipulation of predation risk, through the presentation of models of the Spanish Montpellier Snake *Malpolon monspessulanus* to cavity-nesting Little Owls ahead of the breeding season, was found to alter nest site selection between years. Little Owls were more likely to re-occupy a territory if it was 'safe' rather than 'risky' (the latter being those where model snakes had been presented) and selected 'safe' nest boxes over 'risky' ones. This study also demonstrated how early in the breeding season the assessment of territory quality is made (Parejo & Avilés, 2010).

Some unusual nests

The ornithological literature contains a good few examples of owls nesting in unusual locations. I have, for example, already mentioned the Little Owl nesting under a railway track being used by trains, one of two such examples published in the journal *British Birds* (Masefield, 1928; Vickers, 1935). There are several examples of Tawny Owls breeding in open corvid nests and H. B. Cott described how one had taken possession of a Rook *Corvus frugilegus* nest in a Scot's Pine. Some of the other Rook nests in the tree were occupied by Rooks (Cott, 1921).

Owls may sometimes share their nest sites with other species. Major Tony Crease once encountered a Barn Owl nesting in the rotten stump of an elm *Ulmus*, which had to climb over an active Jackdaw nest in order to reach its own nest further into the main cavity (Crease, 1992). Bernard Starley and H. G. Wagstaff were surprised to discover a female Long-eared Owl in a tenanted Magpie nest; the owl was incubating a clutch of five Magpie eggs and one of her own (Starley, 1912). Perhaps the strangest account of this kind concerns a Tawny Owl that was found nesting on a Scottish corn-stack, alongside which a newly hatched chicken was discovered. With the aid of a ladder Leslie Smith made a more detailed examination and, pushing the owl aside, discovered she was brooding another newly hatched chicken and a mixed clutch of chicken and owl eggs (Smith, 1925).

NEST BOXES

Nest boxes deserve special mention in our discussion of the nest sites used by breeding owls, in part because of the sheer number in use by owls nesting across Britain. The use of nest boxes has enabled researchers to collect large amounts of information on the breeding ecology and population dynamics of owls, information that has proved far more difficult to collect from most natural cavity sites. The study of owl populations through the use of nest boxes is, however, not without its own problems (Lambrechts *et al.*, 2012).

The impact that the introduction of nest boxes can have at the local level can be seen from work on the breeding Tawny Owls and Barn Owls of Kielder Forest, north-west England. Information collected prior to the introduction of boxes revealed that Tawny Owls breeding within the study area were using tree cavities (38.6 per cent), man-made structures (22.8 per cent), crag and ground sites (26.3 per cent) and stick nests (12.3 per cent). During the first year that nest boxes became available, 1980, some 83 per cent of all nesting attempts were made in

FIG 56. A nest box, such as this one for Little Owl, may provide a new nesting opportunity in an otherwise unsuitable location. (Mike Toms)

them and by 1983 all natural sites had been abandoned. Just one clutch, out of 317 found, was subsequently made in a natural site. Steve Petty and his fellow researchers found that the number of Tawny Owl territories in the study area also increased following the introduction of boxes, from 40 territories annually to 66 in 1991, but they concluded that this was a consequence of improving feeding opportunities as clear-cuts became available for Field Voles, rather than of the boxes themselves. The story was different for Barn Owls, where an increase in breeding numbers was felt to result from the erection of nest boxes. The number of Barn Owl pairs in boxes increased from zero to 37 pairs over the period 1985–93, while the number of pairs using 'natural sites' – these were man-made structures like buildings – remained stable (Petty et al., 1994).

Various researchers have examined key breeding parameters to find out whether differences might exist between natural cavity sites and nest boxes. Paul Johnson, whom I worked alongside in north Norfolk, found that Barn Owls using his nest boxes produced significantly larger clutches than those breeding in natural cavities or in buildings. Interestingly, Barn Owl pairs using boxes did not produce more fledglings than other site types (Johnson, 1994), although this has been documented for Little Owl (van Nieuwenhuyse et al., 2008). Looking beyond those parameters linked to the breeding attempt itself, Ákos Klein found the short-term survival of young Barn Owls fledged from nest boxes to be lower than that of young fledged from church tower sites. Ákos suggested that this difference was a result of chicks raised in boxes having insufficient space to exercise and develop their flying skills, something that a space within a church tower offered with some degree of security (Klein et al., 2007). David Ramsden of the Barn Owl Trust has also raised the issue of nest box design, highlighting how a poorly designed box might lead to higher levels of chick mortality. Young Barn Owls may make excursions around the nest area before they are three weeks of age and, as they get older, they jump, pounce and increase their area of exploration. Since young Barn Owls usually start to fly from around 56 days, there is a period of several weeks during which they could fall from the nest and be unable to return. Adult Barn Owls appear to ignore chicks that have fallen from the site. This suggests that nest boxes that have an entrance hole at the same level as the nest may put chicks at risk, increasing the chances of a fall. For this reason, the Barn Owl Trust recommends that the minimum depth from the nest hole to the nest should be 460 mm. Since pellet debris builds up in a well-used box, the box should also be emptied annually.

A review of the use of nest boxes and their design in the study of owls and other birds of prey has also highlighted the difficulties that can exist in drawing more general conclusions from different studies. The main problem appears to be the great variation in nest box designs used in the different studies and in the failure of many authors to publish details of the designs used when producing peer-reviewed papers. There is evidence that box design can influence some of the parameters under study, making it impossible to make fair comparisons between different pieces of work, even if carried out on the same species and within the same habitat and geographic location. There is, for example, evidence that the prevalence of blood parasites may be influenced by the size of entrance hole used on the box, presumably because a larger entrance hole may afford increased access for the insect vectors that transmit such blood parasites (Peter Sunde, unpublished data). We need to understand how nest boxes influence breeding parameters and, in particular, productivity if we are to use them for conservation purposes. There is the potential to use boxes to provide nesting opportunities in areas where prey species are abundant but nest sites lacking, something put to good effect in Israel where the provision of nest boxes has allowed farmers to employ Barn Owls as biological control agents (Meyrom et al., 2009).

We should also include nesting platforms when we consider artificial sites, with the wicker nesting baskets provided for Long-eared Owl at Woodwalton Fen National Nature Reserve in the Huntingdonshire fens perhaps the best British example (Garner & Milne, 1997). The baskets, purpose-built to an internal diameter of 300 mm and a depth of 150 mm, were made from 'brown' willow and untreated Osier *Salix viminalis* rods with the bark left on. Durability was increased through the application of two coats of yacht varnish and the baskets were then sited in Hawthorn *Crataegus monogyna* bushes at a height of 3.5 to 5 m. The owls first bred in baskets at the site in 1981 and some 77 nesting attempts were made over a six year period, including a number of attempts which were replacements and one which appeared to be a genuine second brood. Nine attempts were made in natural sites over the same period and similar baskets have now been deployed at many other sites.

TERRITORY

The requirements for breeding – namely a mate, a nest site and sufficient food – form a key resource that may be defended against other individuals, either by the male on his own or by the pair together. In its most extreme form a breeding territory *is* this defended area, with its clearly defined boundaries and intention of exclusive use. Ownership of the territory may be advertised through display and vocalisations often reserved solely for this purpose, although some of these may also be used to attract a mate or to reinforce the pair bond. Under other circumstances a territory may be less strongly defined, such that there is overlap between neighbouring pairs and any defended area is restricted to something more closely focussed on the nest site itself. In some circumstances the degree of overlap between neighbouring pairs may be virtually complete and territorial behaviour almost absent. To some extent, the form that territorial behaviour takes will be influenced by the nature and availability of the resources required for breeding. In the British owls we see some clear differences in the extent to which a territory is defined and defended, from the virtual lack of territorial behaviour in the Barn Owl to the clearly marked boundaries defined by breeding Short-eared Owls and Tawny Owls.

The term 'territory' is usually applied to those circumstances where there is a defined boundary to an area used by the breeding pair, one that is advertised and defended. In situations where an obvious boundary is lacking, perhaps because of a lack of any overtly territorial behaviour, the term 'home range' may

FIG 57. Territorial skirmishes may sometimes end in the two birds coming together. (Steve Round)

TABLE 7. Home range/territory size of British owls, where known, during the breeding season.

Species	Location	Habitat	Range size (ha)	Method*	Source
Barn Owl	Scotland	Mixed farmland	313.4	rt	Taylor, 1994
	England	Mixed farmland	550	rt	Barn Owl Trust, 2012
Tawny Owl	England	Deciduous woodland	18.2	w	Hirons, 1985
	England	Coniferous woodland	46.1	w	Hirons, 1985
	England	Farmland	37.4	w	Hirons, 1985
	Scotland	Farmland	53	rt	Hardy, 1992
	England	Woodland (fragmented)	107	rt	Redpath, 1994
	England	Woodland (unfragmented)	24	rt	Redpath, 1995
Little Owl	England	Water meadows	35		Mikkola, 1983
	England	Mixed farmland	38		Mikkola, 1983
Short-eared Owl	Scotland	Moorland	16.2	w	Lockie, 1955
	Scotland	Moorland	71.6	w	Village, 1987

* Method: rt = radio-tracking; w = watching

be used and you may also see mention of a 'core range' highlighting that bit of the home range where most of the pair's activity takes place. The use of these different terms, sometimes interchangeably, can make comparison of territory/home range sizes across species that much more difficult (see Table 7). Defended areas (territories) are more readily defined and thus measured, while the limits of undefended home ranges may be harder to resolve.

The calls of Tawny Owls on cold November evenings are a real feature of the British winter and indicate the presence of birds holding claim to a breeding territory. The first calls may be heard in late September, once the birds have completed their moult, and these calls increase in frequency over the following weeks. The main call, the territorial hoot, is used to proclaim ownership but it may be backed up by threatening behaviour or direct attack if an intruding bird attempts to press home an incursion. Short-eared Owls also have a reputation for being strongly territorial during the breeding season. A number of displays are used by the species to denote territory ownership and to advertise boundaries. These include the use of exaggerated wing beats, the bird raising the wings high above its back and then dropping them deep below, sometimes bringing the two wings together to generate a wing-clap (Lockie, 1955). These two behaviours overlap with those used during courtship, something underlined by the observation of birds sometimes displaying with exaggerated wing beats and wing-clapping above the nest site, even in the absence of any intruder. If the display is insufficient and fails to drive an intruder away, the male engages in a 'butterfly-like' fluttering skirmish. Such skirmishes appear to be short-lived and the birds rarely come to blows.

The Little Owl is another species that, like the Tawny Owl, maintains a sedentary lifestyle on a year-round territory. It too, is advertised through territorial hooting, with a peak in nest defence evident during the spring courtship period. Neighbouring breeding territories are exclusive and do not overlap, the neighbouring males able to discriminate between the calls of known neighbours and intruding or newly established birds (Hardouin et al., 2006). Territory size and ranging behaviour in the Little Owl does, however, vary with season and with breeding status. A radio-tracking study in northern Spain revealed that, although the owls occupied exclusive territories while breeding, home range overlap was frequent outside of the breeding season. Additionally, pairs whose nesting attempts had failed were found to increase the size of their foraging range and were often recorded hunting over areas used by neighbouring pairs (Zuberogoitia et al., 2007).

Although Long-eared Owls appear to be territorial in their habits, there is a degree of fluidity that results from food availability and the location of good hunting habitat. Under the right conditions birds can nest at very high densities and Derick Scott has found pairs nesting as little as 15 m from one another (Scott, 1997). Andrew Village recorded a peak of 18 pairs within 10 km² in his Scottish study (Village, 1981), while Derick Scott additionally logged six breeding pairs in a 2 km² study site in Nottinghamshire. Male Long-eared Owls, therefore, maintain a territory that often just covers the area immediate to the nest. Individuals may forage over 2.5 km away from their nest, or further if food is scarce (Scott, 1997), and often share this with other individuals or other owl species (e.g. Barn Owl or Short-eared Owl).

Barn Owls are the least territorial of the British owls, with aggression towards other individuals largely restricted to occasional incidents where a male bird enters the nest site of another male. Radio-tracking studies undertaken by John Cayford (1992) and Iain Taylor (1994) demonstrate that the home ranges of breeding males may overlap extensively. Such evidence supports observations made by myself and other fieldworkers of males from neighbouring sites seen foraging within a few dozen metres of one another without any signs of aggression. The spatial nature of the small mammal prey resource may enable the Barn Owls to share foraging habitat, while still retaining a degree of territorial exclusivity around the nest site, with the male effectively mate guarding his female to secure parentage of the resulting offspring. Intruding females may be tolerated at the nest site, as suggested by some authors, but it is worth noting that cases of infanticide have been documented, where an intruding bird raids a neighbouring nest and takes the young.

Home range and territory size

The quality of a breeding territory or home range, in terms of the resources that it holds, is usually reflected in its size. Where prey resources occur at a low density, then the territory is likely to be significantly larger than where the prey are more abundant and occur at a higher density. Of course, territory size will also be influenced by the availability of other resources, including nest sites, and it may also be modified by predation risk and/or levels of human disturbance or persecution. Territory size in the Short-eared Owl, again determined by food availability, may vary from one year to the next, even within the same areas. Such changes reflect changing prey abundance (think of Field Voles and their roughly four-year cycle of abundance). Andrew Village, for example, saw mean territory size in his Short-eared Owl study population increase from 80 ha (range 49–138 ha) in 1976 to 122 ha (range 45–242 ha) in 1977, when vole populations crashed. Territory size came down again the following year to 62 ha (25–102 ha), as vole populations recovered (Village, 1987).

Tawny Owls living in areas of open woodland or farmland with small patches of woodland have larger home ranges and breeding territories than those living within continuous woodland. Steve Redpath's work in Cambridgeshire revealed that the size of the 'core patch' – that where breeding took place – and the distance to the neighbouring patch, accounted for 80 per cent of the variation in the home range size of the male Tawny Owls in his study area. The smaller and more isolated the woodland patch that was occupied the larger the home range of the bird involved. Interestingly, Redpath's farmland Tawny Owls called less often than those living in a nearby block of continuous woodland cover, suggesting that the territories were either more fluid or less heavily defended by the owls. Small woodlands within farmland are known to support higher densities of small mammal prey than larger blocks of continuous woodland, suggesting that these farmland Tawny Owls may be trading off the increased costs of covering a larger home range against the benefits of reduced territorial defence and higher prey densities.

If territory size is linked to prey abundance, it then follows that it is also linked to habitat, since prey densities vary between different types of habitat. While Southern's (1970) study of the Tawny Owls in the closed woodland structure of Wytham Wood, Oxford, had an average territory size of just 12 ha, those studied by Petty & Pearce (1992) in the coniferous Kielder Forest were some 70 ha. One study of Norwegian Tawny Owls suggested a mean territory size in excess of 100 ha, most likely a result of the much lower prey densities available to these birds so far north in the breeding range.

The importance of hormones

The hormone testosterone is known to influence the territorial and mating behaviour of male birds. Testosterone levels increase as breeding territories are established and increase again when mating takes places, taking them well above the baseline levels seen outside of the breeding season. Increased levels have been linked with increased levels of calling behaviour, the adoption of more elaborate courtship displays and with increased aggression. Male Tawny Owls with the highest levels of testosterone are those with several years' breeding experience, occupying better quality territories of smaller size within areas of high Tawny Owl density. Females paired to these 'high quality' males are more tenacious in their defence of the territory and prey provision to the nestlings is also higher, presumably because the territories occupied by these birds have a greater abundance of prey (Sasvári et al., 2009).

THE BREEDING SEASON

As indicated at the beginning of this chapter, the timing of the breeding season is aimed at delivering as many young as possible into the future breeding generations. This aim may, however, be tempered by the parent's own future reproductive opportunities. The timing of our owls' breeding seasons differ between species, something that may be linked to things other than just the prey species taken and their pattern of seasonal abundance. Our owls differ in where they nest and species nesting in cavities, which are more sheltered, may be able to initiate their breeding attempts earlier than those using more exposed sites. Additionally, species maintaining a year-round territory (e.g.

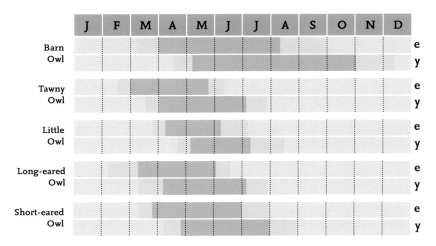

FIG 58. The breeding seasons of British owls. The seasonality of nests with eggs (e) and young (y) are shown as horizontal bars. The darker component indicates the period over which 90% of eggs or young respectively are produced, based on laying dates recorded between 2000 and 2009. The paler component represents the typical duration of the season nationally. Adapted from Ferguson-Lees *et al.* (2012), with permission from the British Trust for Ornithology.

Tawny Owl) may be better placed to predict future prey abundance because of their familiarity with the site, while those arriving to breed at a new location (e.g. Short-eared Owl) may require some time to 'test' prey availability before then attempting to attract a mate.

Advertising ownership of a territory

The vocalisations made by owls may serve a number of different functions, some of which may advertise the presence of an occupied breeding territory and its boundaries. Other calls may, however, serve to attract a mate and/or strengthen the pair bond. The use of clear, far-carrying calls may be of particular importance for species that are nocturnal in habits and which tend to occur at relatively low densities. Density can influence the degree of territorial calling, as can the nature of settlement patterns and their timing. While it is generally the male owl who is the more vocal of the two sexes, advertising his territory, females often produce calls of their own and will sometimes 'duet' with their mate. The familiar '*hooo hu huhuhuhooo*' call of the male Tawny Owl, for example, is often answered by the female with a '*keewik*' contact call, this sometimes overlapping with the end note of the male's call. Female Tawny Owls sometimes produce a similar call to the male's hoot, though it is higher in pitch, more coarse in nature and with less precise phrasing. That female owls will duet with their mates in response to an experimentally simulated intrusion (through the use of audio-playback) implies that they also take an active role in defence of the breeding territory. In experiments using call-playback, some 43 per cent of Tawny Owl responses were found to involve both members of the pair (Appleby et al., 1999a). Duetting is likely to present a more 'unified' response to an intruder, underlining that not only is the territory occupied but that it is also occupied by a pair of birds. Female Tawny Owls are more likely to initiate a response to the call of a bird of their own sex than to a male call, but males are equally likely to respond to either sex (Appleby et al., 1999a). There is one interesting addition to this general finding, however. Male Tawny Owls that have previously bred successfully with their mate are significantly more likely to respond to a strange female call than males that have been unsuccessful. Since breeding success in this species is influenced by the experience of the female partner, a male who has been successful with a particular female is likely to value her more highly and show a greater degree of territorial response against any intruding female.

The structure of specific calls has been found to differ between individual owls, something that enabled Bridget Appleby and Steve Redpath to correctly attribute 98.6 per cent of the English Tawny Owl calls that they recorded during a study looking at three different populations. Although they found no evidence of a specific component within the call acting to identify the individual, the overall characteristics of the call did allow identification (Appleby & Redpath, 1997). There is good evidence that owls can also identify individuals from their calls. Both Tawny Owls and Little Owls have been found to react more strongly to the calls of strangers than those of known neighbours. In fact, Little Owls not only discriminate against strangers but they also react in the same way to the calls of neighbours, if those calls come from an unexpected location – i.e. not from the usual boundary between the two territories (Hardouin et al., 2006). It has been suggested that because territorial defence is a costly activity, individuals should direct their efforts towards new or unknown challengers rather than the well-known individuals with which they share a stable boundary. Interestingly, even though female Tawny Owls discriminate in a similar manner to their mates when presented with an intruder, they show a quite different response, reacting more slowly but more aggressively.

If an individual owl can be identified from its call, could the call then be used to broadcast other information about an individual to prospective mates and territorial rivals? Numerous studies looking at other bird families have

FIG 59. Tawny Owls advertise territorial ownership through their characteristic hooting call. (John Harding)

demonstrated that calls and calling behaviour can provide an honest signal of some measure of the bird's quality – perhaps its suitability as a mate or its size and social status. A bird is thought to incur a cost when it participates in vocal display, perhaps because the display occupies time that could be spent feeding or because it increases the chances of the individual being targeted by a predator. An individual that can call for long periods may, therefore, be of better 'quality' than one that can only afford to sing for short periods.

The pitch of a call has been found to be inversely related to body mass in male Tawny Owls and, additionally, it is known that the ending 'vibrato' section of the advertising call is longer in larger males than it is in smaller ones. A relationship between call characteristics and blood parasite loads has also been found in Tawny Owls with, for example, those owls carrying high parasite loads showing a smaller range of frequencies within the main territorial call (Redpath *et al.*, 2000). A study carried out on Tawny Owls breeding elsewhere in Europe revealed that successful males produced hoots comprised of significantly longer notes than those produced by males that were unsuccessful (Galeotti, 1998).

An implied consequence of vocal display carrying a cost is that birds should only invest in territorial display where it is needed, reducing calling activity under circumstances where they are not being challenged by the presence of other pairs. A suggestion that this is the case can be seen in the work of Victor Penteriani, working on Eagle Owls in southern France. Penteriani found that the shorter the distance between neighbouring pairs the higher the call duration for the male calls. Since he could find no evidence for differences in the quality of either the territories or the males between his high density and low density populations, he concluded that the variation in call duration was a consequence of density, with birds in a low density population reducing the cost associated with calling activity by calling less often (Penteriani, 2003).

Calling behaviour and weather conditions

Studies on the calling behaviour of individual birds or study populations have revealed that calling behaviour may be modified by external factors, such as temperature and weather conditions. Work in Denmark, for example, found that Tawny Owls were more likely to call on warmer nights, reducing calling activity on nights that were cold or windy. Some years ago we investigated the calling behaviour of this species at a much larger scale, using a network of 3,409 'citizen scientists' spread across Britain. We found that Tawny Owls were more likely to be heard calling on warmer nights and on those nights when a greater fraction of the moon's disc was visible. Related to this latter finding, was a negative relationship with the degree of cloud cover – birds were less vocal on cloudy nights (Ockendon et al., unpublished). Calling behaviour in Eagle Owls has also been found to be strongly related to moon-phase, with less activity noted on dark nights (Penteriani et al., 2010).

The visual display of territory

The display flights mentioned earlier in this chapter may provide a visual signal of territory ownership as well as a vocal one. Such visual displays have long been regarded as being less significant than vocalisations, not least because of the perception that owls are nocturnal. However, many owls show peaks in activity around dawn and dusk and recent work on Eagle Owls has demonstrated that visual cues may be important in territorial behaviour. Eurasian Eagle Owls have a white throat badge that is only visible during vocal displays, when it is repeatedly exposed with each call. Experimental studies, in which the size of the badge was manipulated, have revealed that the badge plays an important role in visual communication during territorial display, with individuals using the size of an opponent's badge to gauge whether or not they should respond with a call of their own (Penteriani et al.,

2007a). The importance of such visual communication may explain why this species is most vocal at dawn and dusk – or later if there is strong moonlight. It may also explain why territory-holding males select more visible and dominant perches from which to call than non-territorial 'floaters' (Campioni *et al.*, 2010).

The early part of the breeding season

Long-eared Owls begin their territorial activities in early winter, with the males marking their territories from late October or early November. Although resident pairs maintain the territory year-round, this upturn in activity is probably driven by the settlement period of young birds which occurs about this time, following the end of their natal dispersal (see Chapter 4). Activity then falls away again, picking up markedly from late January (Garner & Milne, 1997). A similar pattern can be seen in our breeding Tawny Owls, with a peak in calling activity in late autumn followed by a second that occurs from December through into January prior to egg-laying. While it is the sedentary male Long-eared Owls that tend to be vocal from late January, those returning from communal winter roosts are most vocal from March to April. Continental birds may still be present at this time, roosting communally before spring departure in April or early May, so the presence of owls at a site may not necessarily indicate that breeding will take place. The period of peak display, in which birds may be seen making display flights, usually begins a month before the first egg is laid. British Long-eared Owls breed early in the year, with most pairs on eggs from the end of the first week of March through until the start of June. The mean first egg date falls in late March. In some years, the first eggs may be laid as early as mid-February, although such early nests may struggle because of poor weather conditions, and there is a British record of a nest with young found on 3 March, which would indicate a first egg date falling in January.

Early in the year, in the weeks leading up to egg-laying, Tawny Owl pairs appear to visit the nest sites available within their territory before, as egg-laying approaches, selecting one and hollowing out a deep scrape. All of the pairs in an area appear to go through this process even if they do not eventually go on to breed. This upturn in activity directed at the nest site follows on from the territorial advertisement that was a feature of early winter, a pattern also seen in Britain's Little Owls but beginning somewhat later. Little Owls begin to display increasing amounts of territorial activity from the start of February, the male calling with the '*gooock*' call from favoured perches to advertise his presence. The level of activity seen, and its timing, is influenced by the weather.

As is the case with Little Owl, some Barn Owl pairs may roost together at the nest site throughout the year but most probably only share the roost for part of the

FIG 60. Little Owl pairs spend increasing amounts of time around the future nest site as the breeding season approaches, with activity continuing until the chicks fledge. (Steve Round)

year, during the period of courtship and egg-laying. Iain Taylor examined roost fidelity in Scotland by marking a series of Barn Owl pairs with dye, revealing that individual birds typically used one to three daytime roosts and that most pairs (22 out of 24 pairs) roosted apart for most of the year. Some individuals were found to roost more than two kilometres from the nest site with which they were associated and, on average, males were found to roost farther away from the site than females. Individual Barn Owls increasingly begin to roost at the nest site in the two months leading up to egg-laying, with females taking up residence earlier than their mates.

Courtship and display

Like the Tawny and Long-eared Owls already mentioned, Eagle Owls also show a strong seasonality to their calling behaviour, with a change in emphasis and call structure clearly evident as the breeding season proper approaches. During late autumn/early winter, male Eagle Owls generally initiate calling behaviour from a prominent perch located near to the nest site before moving to other perches located further away and often positioned closer to territorial boundaries, where neighbouring males are calling. During late winter, termed the 'sexual period', the male spends more time in close-proximity courtship dialogues with his mate. Although there is still some territorial calling, the focus switches to the nest and the female and is accompanied by increasing levels of female calling, display and pair duets. Male vocalisations during the sexual period are significantly longer than those of the territorial period and the call rates are higher, suggesting that the calling may either be a form of mate guarding or that it may consolidate the pair bond and stimulate copulation (Penteriani, 2002).

Little Owl courtship involves much calling, the male uttering a loud '*hooo-oo hooo-oo*' call which is usually answered by the female through a series of shrieks and yelps. This is a species with a wide repertoire of calls, many of which are put to use during the pre-laying period. The pair bond may then be reinforced by the pair flying together and perching together within the same tree, sometimes accompanied by the presentation of prey. Vocal activity increases as the breeding attempt approaches, the pair often duetting, and this is then followed by visits to the chosen nest site and increasing amounts of copulation. Although the male presents different nesting options to his mate, it is she who appears to make the decision as to the site that will be used.

Vocalisations are also a key feature of Tawny Owl courtship, the female uttering a wide range of different calls and the male, additionally, sometimes wing-clapping. The male also appears to display at the female while perching near her. This display may involve swaying movements and the male may also fluff up his plumage, adopting a larger and more rounded appearance. Such displays may occur throughout the pre-breeding period, but their incidence increases as the pair select their nest site (it is thought that the female is responsible for this) and spend increasing amounts of time together, including at roost. Courtship feeding is also a feature of this period, the presentation of prey increasingly directed at the future nest site.

The presentation of prey is also a feature of Short-eared Owl courtship. In this species, the provision of food often precedes copulation, which takes place on the ground. A male that has returned to the breeding territory with food will call at his mate, who calls back before she approaches him to take the food. After copulation the female may fly to the nest scrape and, even if egg-laying has yet to begin, she may settle onto the scrape as if incubating. Alongside this courtship feeding and calling there are wider displays, which may also serve to indicate territorial ownership to neighbouring pairs. These displays involve wing-clapping and the use of exaggerated wing beats, not dissimilar to those seen in Long-eared Owl.

Long-eared Owl display flights normally begin after dusk but they can, on occasion, begin earlier. The male will fly circuits above the breeding site, advertising his presence through a combination of wing-claps (a feature of the *Asio* owls more widely) and occasional calling, using the '*oooo*-ing' call. Wing-claps, which are produced by the bird bringing its wings together beneath the body, may be produced every few wing beats. The flight tends to be rather varied, the male dipping and rising on stiff wings and occasionally swooping low over the canopy. He may be joined by his mate, the two birds flying together and using exaggerated wing beats and again with the accompaniment of wing-clapping. Display flights may be broken off, the male leaving to hunt and then returning with prey which he will offer to his mate. One individual of the pair may sometimes alight on a suitable perch, typically the top of a prominent tree, while the other bird continues to fly around them. If it is the male who has perched then he may lower his wings and sway slightly from side to side while making a sighing sound. If it is the female who has adopted this pose then the male may sometimes hover in front of her before alighting on her back and attempting copulation. Display flights in this species may also take place below the canopy, the birds calling and following one another through the trees, often at speed and always with dexterity. Such chases often culminate in the birds perching, face to face, before more swaying movements, often followed by copulation.

In line with the absence of any overt territoriality, courtship in the Barn Owl appears strongly focussed on the pair and the nest site, rather than any wider area. The pair will roost together in the period leading up to egg-laying and will indulge in allopreening, often accompanied by a subtle series of soft calls. At times, the two birds may fly excitedly around the nest site, entering and leaving with much calling and excitement. Unpaired individuals, in contrast, direct their efforts towards the attraction of a mate. In the Barn Owl this results in a song-flight, often of some duration, in which the bird repeatedly calls with a plaintive and drawn out screech, described by Bunn (1974) as '*shrrreeeeee*' and lasting for two to three seconds. Such flights appear to be undertaken by birds of both sexes, although I have only witnessed this on one occasion where the sex of the bird was known. Paired birds may also utter the screech, with some males delivering a series of subdued screeches prior to emergence from roost at dusk. The female, if present, may join her mate in calling. Some observers have witnessed other interactions between the breeding pair. Derick Scott and Tony Warbuton, among others, have seen male Barn Owls hovering in front of their mates and delivering soft wing-claps. Hosking & Smith (1943) describe a remarkable display in which a male was seen to stretch his neck forwards, puffing out the throat feathers and to then sway and roll his head in a serpentine manner. This prompted the female to sway and to utter the hissing call note.

Copulation

As we have just seen, copulation often follows on from display, perhaps also involving the presentation of food by the male. Although it may take place during the early stages of courtship it becomes a more regular occurrence in the days leading up to the first egg being laid. Observation of Little Owl pairs, resident on their territory throughout the year, indicate that mating may occur in the months leading up to the breeding season proper. Diane Mitchell (1994), for example, noted her local birds mating on several occasions during both December and January. Copulation in the Long-eared Owl is frequent during the laying period, continues through the incubation and early nestling stages, even occurring occasionally much later in the breeding cycle, including after the chicks have left the nest. Nest box cameras have revealed that copulation in the Barn Owl is frequent during both the laying and incubation periods, often following the delivery of prey to the site by the male (Barn Owl Trust, 2012) and sometimes following a series of short, mellow screeches, described by some authors as

FIG 61. After copulation, the female Short-eared Owl may fly to the nest scrape while her mate remains nearby. (Jill Pakenham)

'purring'. Female Little Owls also make a series of 'begging' calls – similar to those produce by the chicks – when courting. These prompt the male to respond by feeding his mate with any prey that he has caught. The hissing calls used for begging appear to have a wider function and are perhaps better considered as a form of self-advertisement; they may be used as a contact call; for example, by a male Barn Owl returning to the nest site. Alloopreening, where one bird preens another and which may serve to reinforce the pair bond, may also be seen during the act of copulation. Copulating Long-eared Owls may sometimes nibble each other's plumage, typically the feathers of the crown and facial disk, both before and after copulation.

Although poorly studied, the copulation behaviour of Little Owls appears to be preceded on occasion by a display involving swaying of the body and bobbing of the head, with the two birds facing one another and in a manner not dissimilar to that already described for some of our other owl species. More usually, however, Little Owl copulation appears to follow a bout of mutual preening. The female may then lower her body slightly, adopting a more horizontal position, before the male mounts. Copulation is often accompanied by soft, almost 'conversational' calls, including a delicate 'ker-rep' but it can also be more frantic. Havershmidt (1946) reported how a male Little Owl alighted on a favoured perch, calling repeatedly with increasing intensity and volume. He was then joined by the female who remained silent. Without any further uttering the male mounted the female, who then lent forward so that her body was horizontal and her tail raised slightly. The male pressed down onto her before copulation occurred, accompanied by much wing-flapping. While, as in this case, it is usually the male who takes the initiative, perhaps at some small signal from the female, Derick Scott described how the female Long-eared Owl may occasionally encourage her mate, sometimes aggressively, into copulation. She may, on occasion, even mount him briefly before the roles are reversed.

Courtship feeding and prey caches

The provision of prey by the male during courtship, egg-laying and incubation may serve two purposes. First, it may provide a measure of prey availability and the male's ability to provide for his mate. Second, it may provide the female with resources that can be used to produce any clutch of eggs that may follow. Male Long-eared Owls do not appear to stockpile prey in nearby caches of the kind occasionally seen in Little Owl and Tawny Owl. They do, however, in common with Barn Owl, sometimes deliver more food to the incubating female than she can cope with. In the case of Long-eared Owl the female will discard unwanted prey by dropping it over the side of the nest.

Increasingly, the nest site becomes the focus of the female's attention and, as she spends more time here, so the male will provide her with more and more food. If conditions are favourable and the male can find sufficient prey, then the female will put on the weight necessary to produce a clutch of eggs. At this stage, just prior to the first egg being laid, a female Barn Owl, for example, might attain a weight in excess of 420 g, an increase of 15–20 per cent on the weight of a non-breeding female at this time. This weight gain is driven by the accumulation of body fat and, to a lesser extent, protein. On average, female Barn Owls begin to increase their body weight some 19 days before the first egg is laid, reaching a maximum weight on the day that this initial egg is deposited, and the female may gain 5 g per day in weight over this period (Durrant *et al.*, 2010). The development of the female reproductive organs has also been found to be correlated with body weight and Hirons *et al.* (1984) discovered that Tawny Owl females in poor condition (i.e. with low body weight) did not attain the degree of ovarian development required for breeding to occur, a pattern also seen in the males. Graham Hirons, therefore, considered that extra food was required for a female Tawny Owl to acquire the reserves necessary for breeding, with courtship feeding by her mate essential to this process. The findings of Hardy *et al.* (1981) also suggest that any failure to attain sufficient spring weight may constrain egg production and delay or halt breeding in this species.

The work of H. N. Southern, which involved a long-term study of a Tawny Owl population breeding in Wytham Woods near Oxford (1947–59), established that breeding success in this species was dependent on the numbers of Wood Mouse and Bank Vole available to the owls. In years when mice and voles were particularly scarce the owls made no attempt to breed even though the number of pairs holding territory remained roughly stable. Even in those years where conditions were far more favourable there were a number of non-breeding pairs, this proportion rarely falling below 30 per cent. Southern also found that a significant proportion of the eggs that were laid failed to hatch because they became chilled during incubation or were abandoned. Female Tawny Owls incubate the eggs alone and rely on the male to deliver food to the nest. Females which receive sufficient food from their mate are attentive to the job of incubating the eggs, only leaving the nest briefly each night to defecate. Those females receiving insufficient or irregular deliveries of food spend longer away from the nest and are more likely to desert. Nest failures at the egg stage in this species increase with the more wet nights there are during the incubation period.

Examination of the weights of female Barn Owls caught at nest box sites being monitored for the UK Barn Owl Monitoring Programme (BOMP) revealed

FIG 62. Off-nest bouts provide a chance for the bird to preen and defecate. (Steve Round)

that the mean weight of non-breeding females was lower than breeding females, and that those incubating were heavier than birds that had one or more young in the nest (Dadam *et al.*, 2011). Daria Dadam's work also highlighted that weather conditions during the preceding winter (November to March) were correlated with differences in female body weight; females were heavier after mild, dry winters and lighter after colder and wetter ones. This suggests that provision of prey during the period leading up to (and during) egg-laying in this species may be particularly important. The quantity of food delivered to the female during the laying period may be considerable. Male Barn Owls, for example, have been found to deliver an average of 16.4 prey items per 24-hour period when the female is laying. This is similar to the peak levels seen during provisioning of the chicks (Langford & Taylor, 1992).

Daria Dadam and other authors have also found a relationship between prey abundance and the proportion of a population initiating a nest attempt and laying eggs, a pattern also found in other studies. Iain Taylor, for example, found that 7 per cent of his breeding Barn Owl pairs did not make a breeding attempt in years when vole abundance was low (Taylor, 1991; 2002). Steve Petty found that

96 per cent of his Tawny owl population laid eggs in a year of high Field Vole numbers but only 9 per cent laid eggs when the vole population was at its low point just two years later. He also found average clutch sizes to be smaller in poor vole years and laying/incubation to start later.

Monogamy and other relationships

Most owls are monogamous, forming short-term pair bonds that last for at least one season. In species like the Short-eared Owl, which tends to be nomadic and which breeds at widely different sites in subsequent years, individuals pair with a new mate each spring. The formation of longer-term pair bonds, lasting over several seasons, is typically seen in sedentary species living within well-defined territories, for example Eagle Owl, Tawny Owl and Little Owl. A long-term study of the lifetime reproductive success of Finnish Tawny Owls, for example, revealed that most females (67 per cent) made breeding attempts with just one male over their reproductive lifetime; 24.9 per cent had two male partners, 6.4 per cent had three and just 1.7 per cent had four partners, underlining both the low rate of mate replacement and the need to select a suitable mate at the first attempt (Brommer *et al.*, 2005). Trapping studies suggest that, as a general rule, Little Owl pairs are maintained from one year to the next and traditional sites may be occupied over many years.

Features of monogamous mating systems more widely are extra-pair copulations (EPCs) and extra-pair fertilisations (EPFs), where an individual mates with multiple partners but is otherwise faithful to the socially monogamous pair bond. These behaviours are thought to arise because both individuals in the pair have the potential to increase their lifetime reproductive success by seeking other matings with high quality partners. The extent of EPFs among bird species has only recently come to light, thanks to the arrival of new molecular techniques; it appears that, on average, roughly one in ten offspring will have been sired outside of the pair bond. In contrast to this wider pattern, the extent of EPFs in owls is thought to be very low. Wendt Müller, for example, found no evidence of EPFs among 53 Little Owl nestlings produced by 16 breeding pairs and Jeffery Marks detected no EPFs in 59 Long-eared Owl nestlings from 12 nests in a semi-colonial breeding situation (Marks *et al.*, 1999; Müller *et al.*, 2001). Later work by Marks *et al.* (2002) did, however, reveal a case where a female Long-eared Owl produced two broods in a single season with two different males. This behaviour is known as serial polyandry, the female leaving her first mate to finish rearing the chicks of the first attempt while setting up for a second attempt with a different male. In this case, the female had started her first attempt particularly early in the year and prey availability was high. Derick Scott also notes two cases of polygamy in this species from Britain (Nottingham and Lincolnshire), this time with more strongly overlapping nesting attempts.

Polygamous relationships have been found in a few other owl species, including Snowy Owls breeding on Shetland and Tawny Owl, but they remain rare events, most likely to occur under the favourable conditions provided by a peak in small mammal prey populations. Polygamy is probably most common in Tengmalm's Owl, where between 9 and 14 per cent of the males in some study populations form bigamous relationships. Cases of polygamy in Barn Owls have been noted from some long-term studies carried out in Britain. Iain Taylor, for example, recorded seven instances of bigamy out of 419 nesting attempts made in his Scottish study area. The two nests were generally some distance apart (up to a maximum of 1 km), with one female receiving far more attention from the male than the other, but Taylor recorded one instance where two females shared the same site, nesting just centimetres apart. Taylor also recorded two cases of serial polyandry.

The low occurrence of polygamous pairings in owls could well be a consequence of the male owl's central role as provider. Food provision by the male owl begins well before egg-laying and continues through to the end of the breeding attempt, the female only taking on some of the responsibility once the chicks are a week or more old. The demands of caring for two broods simultaneously appears to be too much and so polygamy is only seen under very favourable conditions. The success of a breeding attempt is influenced by the male's provision of food, including during the period pre-laying, and this may also have a bearing on EPFs, the female reluctant to risk the nesting attempt by visiting other males. Another factor that might be linked to the low levels of EPFs is the low density at which most owls breed, making it less likely that a female will encounter another male.

Jeffery Marks' record of serial polygamy in Long-eared Owl mentioned earlier also involved an apparent case of an additional individual helping to feed the young of one of the two nesting attempts. This individual, a male, was not the father of the chicks in either nest. However, he was related to the nesting female – being either her brother or one of her offspring. The presence of 'helpers' has been documented in at least ten different species of owl and is also known from many other families of bird. The behaviour has been documented in Eagle Owl on more than one occasion, with the suggestion that helpers are unpaired individuals with little or no breeding experience. Such individuals are known to interact with territorial adults occupying lower quality territories. José Martinez watched one female Eagle Owl 'helper' feed the remains of a hare to a brood of chicks while the parents sat nearby seemingly unconcerned (Martinez *et al.*, 2005).

Incest

As we will see in Chapter 4, the dispersal of young birds away from their natal site reduces the chances of inbreeding. There are, however, documented cases of inbreeding for British owls. Steve Petty and colleagues, for example, recorded an incestuous pairing between a female Barn Owl and one of her offspring. Unusually for a breeding adult, this female had moved some distance away from her earlier nest site and it may have been this movement that brought her into contact with one of her offspring (Petty *et al.*, 1986).

The age of first breeding

As can be seen from Table 8, the majority of our breeding owls first breed in the year after hatching. In larger, longer-lived species the age of first breeding is later, a pattern also seen more widely across birds and mammals. In some instances there may be a tendency for one sex to become sexually mature before the other. Bunn & Warburton (1977) report a female Barn Owl, born in 1971, who laid a total of 16 eggs the following year, in three ultimately unsuccessful nesting attempts. Work on Scandinavian Tawny Owls has revealed that most of the offspring

TABLE 8. Breeding parameters of British owls. Clutch size shows the typical clutch size, followed in brackets by the observed range.

Species	Clutch size	Incubation (days)	Fledging period (days)	Number of broods	Age of first breeding	Source
Barn Owl	3–8 (3–10)	30–34	49–56	1 (2)	1	BTO Nest Record Scheme
Snowy Owl	5–6 (4–10)	32–34	50–60	1	2	Robinson & Becker, 1986; Mikkola, 1983
Eagle Owl	2–3 (1–5)	32–35	55–70	1	2	Mikkola, 1986
Tawny Owl	2–3 (1–5)	28–30	32–37	1	1	BTO Nest Record Scheme
Little Owl	3–4 (2–5)	27–29	30–35	1	1	BTO Nest Record Scheme
Long-eared Owl	3–4 (1–6)	27–29	30–40	1	1	BTO Nest Record Scheme
Short-eared Owl	4–8 (3–14)	26–28	24–27	1 (2)	1	BTO Nest Record Scheme

hatched during the increase phase of a vole cycle go on to breed the following year, while most of those hatched during the decrease or low phase do not start breeding until they are two years of age. Adults breeding for the first time show a much lower productivity than older birds, regardless of the stage of the vole cycle.

Nest defence and similar behaviours at the nest

Defence of a nest containing eggs or chicks, or of fledged but still dependent young, is seen in many species of bird. The behaviour has the potential to reduce the level of nest predation and to increase the chances of a successful breeding outcome but it brings with it the risk of injury or death to the adult bird. The degree of nest defence should, therefore, involve some balancing of benefits against risks, with individuals more likely to defend the nest when they have invested more in the nesting attempt. Parental defence in Long-eared Owls has, for example, been shown to be greater for older chicks than it is for young chicks or eggs (Galeotti et al., 2000). The same researchers also found that female Long-eared Owls defended nestlings more often and with more vigour than their mates, perhaps reflecting that females spent more time at the nest and/or were the larger of the two sexes.

In my experience, individual owls may also vary greatly in their behaviour at the nest, particularly when a monitoring visit is being carried out and regardless of the stage that the nesting attempt has reached. Some individuals may sit tightly, some are docile, others slip away quietly upon your approach and a few are aggressive. Individual birds may 'hiss' or 'bill-snap' the latter sound possibly produced by the tongue rather than by the bill coming together. The reactions to human observers show similarities to the responses directed towards other species. For example, although some Long-eared Owls tolerate other birds of prey and corvids within their territory, perhaps accepting them nesting just metres away, other individuals are aggressive and will attempt to drive them away whenever they appear. Intruding Jays, for example, may be killed but larger birds usually manage to escape. On occasion this intolerance may be directed at mammals, with recorded attacks on foxes, hares, dogs and even humans. Little Owls have been seen to chase away Grey Squirrels and even cats (Mitchell, 1994), underlining that the size of the attacker may have little bearing.

Lockie (1955) reports a similar pattern of responses to human observers for Short-eared Owl, additionally noting a particularly aggressive bird that would strike at the head of visiting fieldworkers. The male may sometimes make a distraction display, rising from a favoured perch often located within 30 m of the nest. Female Tawny Owls probably have the worst reputation for attacks on human observers and are decidedly more aggressive than Eagle Owls, which

FIG 63. Both Long-eared Owls and Short-eared Owls will raise their ear tufts if agitated by the approach of a human observer. (Steve Round)

have something of an undeserved reputation within the UK because of a well-publicised incident involving a birdwatcher with a dog who got too close to a nest containing young. Female Tawny Owls, on the other hand, will not uncommonly strike at an intruder, often causing injury and, in the case of the photographer Eric Hosking, the loss of an eye. Aggression towards human observers may be more pronounced where the species has been exposed previously to persecution or to high levels of disturbance.

Nest defence is not the only behaviour used to protect the nest. Birds may become more secretive around the nest when they have eggs or young chicks. Little Owls, for example, usually go quiet when the female begins incubation, with only occasional calling, and when the eggs hatch visits to and from the nest hole appear more cautious. When incubating or brooding, female Short-eared Owls will half-close their eyes, presumably in an attempt to conceal their glaring yellow iris. They may also, if feeling threatened, change their facial expression to make their pupils appear large, the face narrowing and the ear tufts becoming erect.

FIG 64. While some female Little Owls may sit tight, others may leave the box upon the approach of a visiting fieldworker. (Richard Castell)

EGGS AND INCUBATION

The egg is a complicated structure and the key feature of avian reproductive biology. A female owl hatches with all of the egg cells (ova) that she could lay in her lifetime already present within her ovary. Once she becomes sexually mature, hormonal changes initiate the development of some of the ova, which then develop in sequence; as each ovum develops and enlarges so recognisable yolk is deposited. The yolk is formed over a number of days, typically just two to three days in many birds but, at an average of 11.2 days, this takes significantly longer in the Barn Owl (Durant *et al.*, 2004b). The mature ovum then passes into the mouth of the oviduct and it is here that it will be fertilised if suitable sperm are present. Regardless of whether or not fertilisation occurs, the egg then begins to move down the oviduct ahead of the formation of the albumen (egg white) proteins, the addition of the shell membranes and the hydration of the albumen, 'plumping' the shell-less egg to assume its natural shape. The shell is then formed over the outer membrane before the egg is passed and 'laid' by the female. In the Barn Owl the whole process, from yolk development to laying, takes roughly two weeks.

Egg quality and size
That the Barn Owl has a much slower rate of yolk deposition than expected for the size of its egg is not the only thing that is odd about it. The yolk's energy content is also lower than predicted, meaning that Barn Owl chicks hatch in a rather under-developed state. The slow rate of deposition, coupled with a reduced energy content in the yolk, allow a female Barn Owl to deposit yolk in several developing eggs at the same time and, additionally, may provide a buffer when food resources are limited. It also gives the female some flexibility in the number of eggs that she can produce – there is little or no decline in yolk quality as the number of eggs produced by a Barn Owl increases – and this flexibility can also be seen in the fact that she will develop more ova than are actually ovulated. In experiments where eggs are removed from a clutch, a female Barn Owl will keep on producing new eggs until she has what she considers to be a complete clutch. Birds able to do this are referred to as 'indeterminate' layers.

Egg weight in birds usually shows a very tight relationship with female body weight. This relationship is allometric, meaning that egg weight is related logarithmically to female body weight and as female body size increases, so individual eggs represent an ever smaller percentage of body weight. In Barn Owl, each egg equates to just under 5 per cent of body weight and in Little Owl it is roughly 7 per cent. In an examination of the relationship between egg mass and female body weight, Iain Taylor found that cavity-nesting owls showed a different relationship to open-nesting species, possibly because cavities provide greater protection and allow cavity-nesting species to produce less-developed young that then spend longer in the nest. Interestingly, when Taylor (1994) restricted his analysis to just cavity-nesting species, he found that the eggs produced by Barn Owls were smaller than predicted – just 17.5 g rather than the 25.5 g expected. Could the small size of Barn Owl eggs, coupled with their lower quality yolk, allow Barn Owls to produce larger clutches and exploit years of good prey availability?

There may be a downside to reducing the degree of investment made to individual eggs. Eggs sometimes fail to hatch, perhaps a consequence of incubation behaviour or the degree of parental investment in the contents of the egg. It is known, for example, that egg failure rates, aside from those related to predation, may vary between species in a consistent manner. A comparison of failure rates for Barn Owl, reported to be in the range of 15–30 per cent in some studies, exceed those seen in Sparrowhawk, something that it is believed may be linked to differences in the allocation of nutrients to the eggs (van den Burg, 2002). With less investment in egg quality, Barn Owls may be prone to lower rates of hatching success than other birds and indeed to many other owls.

FIG 65. The eggs of our owls are white and unmarked. Perhaps there is no need of camouflage because the females begin incubation so early during the laying period. Short-eared Owl nest. (James Bray)

TABLE 9. Egg dimensions of British owls.

Species	Length (mm)	Width (mm)	Weight (g)
Barn Owl	39	32	21.2
Snowy Owl	57	45	59.0
Eagle Owl	60	50	69.3
Tawny Owl	48	39	39.0
Little Owl	34	29	15.6
Long-eared Owl	40	32	23.0
Short-eared Owl	40	31	21.3

Although they vary greatly in size, the eggs produced by British owls are fairly similar in appearance, being white, unmarked and rather rounded (see Table 9). The eggs of many cavity-nesting species, though not all, are white and unmarked and it has been suggested that markings are unnecessary given the security that cavity-nesting offers. But what of those owl species that do not use cavities but which, instead, nest on open ground? Unlike many birds, owls initiate incubation with the first egg and, with the female sitting on top of the eggs, perhaps there is no requirement for camouflage.

Clutch size

Given that at least some of our owls are indeterminate layers, able to keep on producing eggs, how does a female gauge when to stop laying? How many eggs should she produce in a particular season if she is to maximise her reproductive success? The number of eggs that an owl produces, known as clutch size, has implications for the outcome of the breeding attempt. Produce too many eggs and the parents may discover that there is insufficient food to rear the resulting young, potentially prejudicing the prospects of the wider brood and impacting on the survival of the adults themselves. Produce fewer eggs than the available resources can support and the parent is not maximising its productivity. Additionally, there is some evidence that increased egg production might have longer term effects on female condition and future reproductive potential. Clutch size may vary in relation to female age, although this has been little studied in our British owls. In other species (e.g. Tengmalm's Owl, Laaksonen et al.,

2002) or other populations (e.g. Little Owl and Barn Owl on the Continent, van Nieuwenhuyse *et al.*, 2008; Altwegg *et al.*, 2007), there is a tendency for clutch size to increase with age to a peak, after which it begins to decline again (see also, 'Breeding performance', p. 169).

The weight of the female, or to be more precise the reserves she is carrying, appears to be important in determining that breeding will occur, but does it also determine the number of eggs produced? Clutch size in Barn Owls has been found to be positively related to the pre-laying body mass of the female (Taylor, 1994; Durrant *et al.*, 2004a). However, given the relatively small investment made in each egg and the prey surpluses typically delivered to the nest by the male, does female body weight in the pre-laying period really determine how many eggs she will produce? Could it be some other cue that is involved? Durrant *et al.* (2010) suggest an alternative, at least for Barn Owl, in which the female is predicted to use the amount of food being provided by the male as a measure of wider prey availability and/or his ability as a provider. She can then use this information to gauge the optimum number of eggs to produce. It is an interesting idea and one that certainly warrants further study.

A number of different studies have revealed relationships between clutch size in our owls and various external factors. Iain Taylor, for example, found a relationship between clutch size and food availability in his Scottish Barn Owls. Given what we have just discussed, it should be unsurprising that food availability should play some key role in determining the number of eggs produced. In turn, food availability may be influenced by other factors, so we might expect to see relationship between clutch size and these. Gassmann & Bäumer (1993), for example, found Little Owl clutch size to be correlated with the amount of rainfall in March, preceding egg-laying, and other researchers have found links with laying date, population density and geographic location. UK Barn Owl clutch sizes are also smaller in those years following poor weather, in this case colder and wetter winters (Dadam *et al.*, 2011). Interestingly, the clutch size of British Barn Owls is larger, on average, in the north of Britain than it is in the south (Dadam *et al.*, 2011), a pattern seen in many other species and thought to be linked to spring food availability and the level of overwinter mortality. The tendency for clutch sizes to increase along a gradient from south to north has also been demonstrated in the Tawny Owl (Overskaug & Bølstad, 1998). The clutch sizes of Barn Owls nesting in arable areas within Britain have been shown to be smaller than those of birds nesting in grassland-dominated areas, again underlining a potential link with prey availability.

Laying dates

In addition to influencing clutch sizes, we also see some of these external factors shaping the laying dates of British owls. Egg-laying usually begins in February for some pairs of Tawny Owls and Long-eared Owls, although both species begin more widely from March when the first pairs of Short-eared Owl and Barn Owl also start laying (see Figure 58). Little Owls breeding in Britain appear to have a fairly restricted and somewhat synchronised laying period, with egg-laying almost entirely limited to April and May. In an analysis of BTO Nest Record cards, Glue & Scott found that 83 per cent of Little Owl clutches were initiated between 11 April and 10 May, the mean first egg date being 28 April. The earliest recorded through the scheme was 16 March.

Studies of Little Owl have demonstrated earlier laying in years of peak vole abundance and later laying in years when snow cover remains for longer than is usual. Poor weather conditions may restrict hunting opportunities and increase energetic costs and, as a consequence, reduce the ability of the female to put on the reserves necessary for production of her clutch. Poor conditions ahead of clutch initiation may also limit the number of eggs that can be produced, resulting in reduced clutch sizes in some years. Work elsewhere in Europe

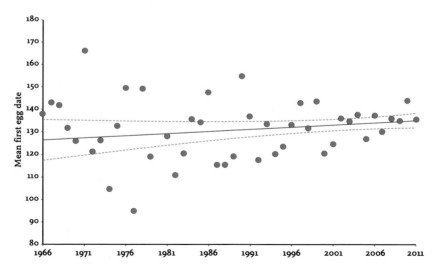

FIG 66. Mean laying date in Julian days (1 April is day 90) for British Barn Owls. Smoothed line shows date predicted from model and the confidence intervals associated with this. Redrawn from Baillie *et al.* (2012), with permission from the British Trust for Ornithology.

suggests that female Little Owls will lay an additional 1–1.2 eggs during peak vole years (Exo, 1992) and that these larger clutches tend to be initiated earlier in the year (Bultot et al., 2001).

Iain Taylor found that the laying dates of Barn Owls in his Scottish study area were earlier in those years when spring temperatures were high and prey more abundant. Prey abundance was the more significant factor, although collectively the two variables explained 86 per cent of the annual variation seen in laying dates. Examination of data collected through BOMP underlines that weather conditions ahead of the breeding season can have a significant influence on productivity and the timing of egg-laying. The mean first egg date – a standard measure for analyses of breeding ecology in birds – for British Barn Owls was later following colder and wetter years, perhaps suggesting that female Barn Owls either found it more difficult to reach breeding condition in such years or that possible external cues used to initiate breeding (e.g. food availability) were delayed by the poor weather. Data from BOMP also indicate that average laying dates may have got earlier over time, a pattern seen in many other bird species and linked to the rise in average early spring temperatures associated with global climate change (Crick et al., 1997). Advancement in the average laying dates may also be a feature of our other breeding owls but the small numbers of nests monitored annually – for which laying date can be calculated – prevents this from being formally tested.

Laying intervals
Little Owls usually produce one egg each day, although some eggs may be laid on alternate days, the female initiating incubation before the clutch is complete. Although Glue & Scott (1980) state that incubation usually begins with the first egg, studies elsewhere in Europe have suggested that it may begin after the second or third has been laid (Exo, 1983). Some authors have even found incubation to begin with the penultimate egg or once the clutch is complete. Such variability might be linked to clutch size or to the development of the brood patch. If this is the case, then incubation might begin earlier with smaller clutches than with larger ones.

Long-eared Owl eggs are laid on alternate days as a rule, though the interval may be longer, and the female normally starts incubating from the first egg. A similar pattern is seen in Barn Owl, Short-eared Owl and Tawny Owl, with the laying interval tending to be greater in the latter two species; Tawny Owls often lay their eggs at two-day intervals, sometimes with a gap of four days ahead of the last egg being laid. Gaps in a sequence of laying dates may result from a period of poor weather, as is shown by the Snowy Owls nesting on Fetlar in 1968 (Tulloch,

1969). The pair, in their second year at the site, appear to have laid their six eggs on 12, 13 or 14, 15, 20, 22 and 23 or 24 May, the pause part way through coinciding with a short period of bitterly cold northerlies and rain.

Asynchronous hatching

While many birds begin incubation with the final egg, our larger owls initiate incubation as soon as the first egg has been laid. This has an important consequence in the form of asynchronous hatching. Each chick that hatches will be a day or two older than its next oldest sibling. If a species produces a clutch of seven eggs, laying one egg every two days but incubating from the first egg, then the last chick to emerge will be nearly two weeks younger than its oldest sibling. In reality, since incubation periods show a small degree of flexibility, the eggs usually hatch somewhat closer together than the laying dates would suggest. Even so, this still puts the youngest chicks at a competitive disadvantage, as they are only likely to secure a meal once all the other chicks in the brood have had their fill. This strategy is thought to increase the chances of at least some chicks surviving if feeding conditions deteriorate. If all the young hatched on the same day then, under conditions where food was scarce, the weakest chicks would take longer to die but maybe still receive some food and reduce what was available for other, stronger individuals, thus weakening the whole brood.

Rigging the competitive abilities of the chicks in this skewed manner can, therefore, be regarded as an adaptation to the presence of an unpredictable food supply, favouring whole brood survival during boom times and quickly reducing brood size to a more appropriate level during lean times. The parents are only likely to rear the entire brood in those years when food is readily available. That this is what happens in the wild can be seen from the work of Iain Taylor and his Scottish Barn Owls. Taylor (1994) found that mortality fell disproportionately on the youngest chicks within a brood. In years of prey abundance, when just 5–10 per cent of the chicks died, it was invariably the youngest chick or chicks that were lost. In years of low vole abundance, when up to 45 per cent of chicks died, the mortality of the last hatched chicks was 94 per cent while that of the first hatched was just 20 per cent. In the case of the Barn Owl, at least, the relatively small investment made to each egg probably facilitates this strategy, the female risking only a small amount of additional investment in the hope of larger returns if conditions prove favourable.

Asynchronous hatching is also seen in the diurnal birds of prey, where it can be taken to an extreme in what has become known as the Cain–Abel conflict, where the older chick mercilessly attacks and ultimately kills its younger sibling, thereby securing access to all of the food that is delivered by the parents. It is

FIG 67. The range of ages in a brood of Barn Owls underlines the degree of asynchronous hatching. (Mike Toms)

not a feature of small birds of prey nor of the British owls, so cases where the smallest chicks in a brood of owls disappear are almost certainly the result of necrophagy rather than fratricide. Video footage of nesting Tawny Owls has revealed the tentative manner in which the brooding female may determine that a chick is dead before it is then fed to the remainder of the brood. This involves a switch from brooding and preening behaviours, with their associated calls, to the treatment of the dead chicks as if it is just another prey item.

Incubation

The process of incubation provides the heat necessary for the successful development of the embryo forming inside the egg. It also allows the female to guard her investment, protecting the eggs against would-be predators. The eggs receive heat, transferred from the bird via her brood patch, an area of bare skin that is rich in blood vessels and which forms during the egg-laying period. The female will also tend the eggs, turning them from time to time and adjusting her position to make sure that the clutch remains in contact with the brood patch. On average, an incubating Barn Owl will make 4.48 turns per hour (Epple & Bühler, 1981).

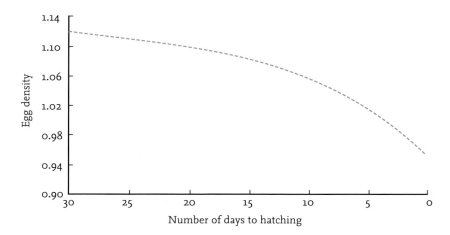

FIG 68. Egg density curve for Barn Owl showing the decline in egg density as hatching approaches. (Redrawn from Toms, 2007)

Incubation is almost entirely the responsibility of the female, the male delivering prey to her during the period that she remains in the nest site. However, Derick Scott has recorded male Long-eared Owls incubating or brooding on a number of occasions, including one occasion where he observed the male deliver prey to the female, who then carried it away from the nest to eat elsewhere; the male began to brood the chicks, leaving seven minutes later when the female returned and took over.

A female Little Owl will leave the nest two or three times during a 24-hour period to cast pellets and defecate. If her mate is struggling to find sufficient food for her then she may leave the nest more often, perhaps ultimately abandoning the nesting attempt, a pattern also seen in Short-eared Owl in one Scottish study and, more widely, in studies of Tawny Owls. The extra body reserves that female owls lay down ahead of a breeding attempt, which are important for initiating the clutch, are also carried through into the incubation period. These reserves might buffer incubating birds against occasions where, perhaps because of poor weather, the male is unable to deliver sufficient prey to the nest. In the Tawny Owl, for example, where small mammals are so important, wet nights can greatly reduce the male's chances of catching a sizeable meal and he may switch to taking earthworms. Even if he can provide large numbers of worms for the female there will still be a substantial shortfall in the weight of prey delivered –

Hirons calculated that the amount of prey delivered to his Tawny Owl nests on wet nights was just 70 per cent of that brought in on dry ones (Hirons, 1976).

A number of changes occur within the egg as it develops, one of which is of particular use to researchers monitoring owls at the nest. This is the loss of water vapour from a developing egg, which occurs at a relatively steady rate through diffusion and evaporation. The loss of the water vapour leads to a predictable reduction in egg weight through the incubation period, making it possible to predict when an egg is due to hatch from its weight (once calibrated against egg size and shape) and reference to what is known as an egg density curve (see Figure 68). Since some owls are thought to be sensitive to disturbance around the time of hatching, knowing when this is going to happen can be very useful to the researcher. Egg density curves have been produced by the BTO in support of those studying UK populations of Tawny Owl and Barn Owl (Percival, 1990; Toms, 1997).

Egg losses and predation across the breeding season

As we have just seen, an incubating female may abandon her eggs if the male fails to provide sufficient food, resulting in the loss of the entire clutch. Iain Taylor found that complete hatching failure (excluding seven infertile clutches) occurred in less than 4 per cent of the nesting attempts made by his Scottish Barn Owls

FIG 69. Corvids, such as this Carrion Crow, may take the eggs or small chicks of owls. (John Harding)

(Taylor, 1994). The loss of individual eggs within a wider clutch is more common, again something noted by Iain Taylor, who found a failure rate of 22 per cent in a study of marked eggs in 38 clutches. The majority of these failed eggs were either the last egg to be laid or the penultimate one, suggesting that perhaps they did not have sufficient resources committed to them or were infertile. The failure rates for British Little Owl eggs (including the loss of full clutches) were calculated by Glue & Scott (1980) at 43.6 per cent and by Leigh (2001) at 13.1 per cent.

In addition to failures in the eggs themselves, nesting attempts may also fail because of predation of the eggs or any resulting chicks. It is known, for example, that ground-nesting Short-eared Owls can suffer high levels of nest predation. Lockie (1955) reported that just one in five nests in his study area survived to hatching, with a good proportion of the failures taking place before the nest was even visited by fieldworkers. Eggshell remains implicated avian predators (most likely Carrion Crow and/or Hooded Crow) together with Red Fox *Vulpes vulpes*, the latter also taking adult birds off the nest.

Predation events at the nests of hole-nesting species, such as Tawny Owl, tend to be more common during the chick phase, presumably because of greater levels of activity at this stage (which may increase nest conspicuousness) and because the presence of the female during incubation may deter some nest predators. In some owl populations, nest predation has been found to increase where pairs nest at higher densities, where the pair are less experienced breeders and where adverse weather conditions occur. The latter finding can be linked to adverse weather increasing the level of chick calling behaviour (because individuals are hungry) and to predators seeking alternative prey because other prey become unavailable (e.g. mustelids switching because favoured small mammal prey are hidden by snow cover). As we will discover later, a number of mammalian predators have been implicated in the predation of incubating or brooding females nesting in vulnerable locations. Elsewhere in Europe this may be more of a problem than it is within Britain, with, for example, the Beech Marten *Martes foina* thought to be an important predator of nesting Barn Owls.

CHICKS AND FLEDGING

Hatching

Young owls call from inside the egg during the hours prior to hatching, a behaviour which – in the case of Barn Owl – prompts the female to utter a soft chattering call that is also used with newly hatched chicks. There is some suggestion that the female owl may help the young out of the egg by nibbling at

FIG 70. Female Tawny Owls are attentive parents, sitting tight and keen in their defence of the nest and its contents. (Richard Castell)

the shell to remove small fragments around the hole that the chick has created with its egg tooth. Once the chick has hatched the discarded shell may be eaten, left in situ or carried away, the latter seemingly an uncommon behaviour in owls. Unhatched eggs tend to remain in the nest, where they may be buried by the accumulating debris or else cracked by the activities of the growing young.

Development of the young

From an average weight at hatching of just 13–14 g, a Barn Owl chick is likely to reach a peak weight of just under 400 g (at around day 40) before it subsequently leaves the nest at a body weight of between 340–350 g (at around day 60), a significant transformation. Long-eared Owl chicks are heavier at hatching, with a mean weight of 18.4 g, but they leave the nest at a lower body weight (around 250 g). Such differences are thought to be linked to the nesting habits, with cavity-nesting species often developing more slowly than open-nesting ones. The general pattern of growth seen in our owls, and indeed in other owls and many raptors, is for a period of morphological development and slow weight gain over the initial days

FIG 71. Young Tawny Owl chicks huddle together for warmth in the absence of their mother. (Richard Castell)

following hatching, followed by a period of rapid growth and weight gain. This period may see the young owl grow from just 10 per cent of the peak weight that it will achieve to 90 per cent of this peak weight over a short period; the process takes roughly three weeks in the Barn Owl. There is then a second period of slower development, followed by a decline in chick weight ahead of leaving the nest. The decrease in body weight prior to fledging comes about because the young owl reduces its rate of food intake, even though plenty of food is still being delivered to the nest. The timing of the weight reduction in the oldest chicks overlaps the period of peak food demand in some of its younger siblings, suggesting that it might be an adaptive strategy improving the productivity of the brood as a whole (Durant & Handrich, 1998).

With a brood of perhaps four or five young to look after, the parents face a busy few weeks providing food, warmth (initially) and protection. An owl chicks hatches from its egg in a relatively undeveloped state. Helpless, blind and unable to regulate its own body temperature, the chick is entirely dependent upon the support that it receives from its parents. Young owls tend to rest on their belly or chest, the head supported by the bill resting against the substrate. The patchy down that covers the fragile-looking pink body is initially white, fine in structure and appears to offer very little insulation. The eyes open after a few days (four to six days in Long-eared Owl, four to seven days in the Eagle Owl), the pupil having a creamy-bluish tinge initially before darkening with age. The egg tooth, so important in helping the chick to break out from the egg, is usually lost during the first week but may remain for longer; in the Little Owl it is usually visible until 13–15 days of age. Young owls do not gape but take small pieces of food when offered. Since their eyes are closed, very young chicks must sense the food as it touches the bristles present at the base of the bill. With the chicks unable to look after themselves during these early days, the female remains at the nest with them, receiving food delivered by the male and tending to the needs of her young and incubating any unhatched eggs.

Owl chicks appear to sleep for long periods and, when small, remain under the brooding female. If she leaves the nest then the young may be seen huddled together in an attempt to reduce the amount of heat loss. The growing demands of the older chicks may see the female leave the nest to forage while the youngest chicks are still unable to regulate their own body temperature or feed. If the female is away for much of the night hunting, then the youngest chicks might not receive any food until she retires to the nest site with the approaching dawn; during the day such chicks may be fed from any surplus of prey present within the nesting chamber. Within a week of hatching the formerly rather scanty down

FIG 72. The wing feathers of a Barn Owl chick will only have reached 80 per cent of their final length by the time it leaves the nest. (Mike Toms)

has become more plentiful, covering the body and the first down is replaced by the mesoptile down from 10–14 days (Long-eared Owl). It is around this time that the female ceases to brood the young regularly. Young Short-eared Owls are brooded until the young are roughly 12 days of age, although the female might cease brooding somewhat earlier if feeding conditions are poor and she is not receiving sufficient food from her mate.

Wing and tail feathers start to emerge from the second or third week in most of our owls, though beginning earlier in the smaller Little Owl, and the facial disk undergoes a period of rapid development, presumably because of the key role that this plays in how the owl perceives the world around it (see Chapter 1). Development of the facial disk is completed by day 33 in the Long-eared Owl, with a defined facial disk evident from day 16 (Seidensticker *et al.*, 2006). Once the flight feathers emerge from the skin they will continue to grow until after the chick has left the nest. In fact, the main wing feathers of Barn Owls may only have reached 80 per cent of their final length by the time that the young owl is ready to fledge. Skeletal growth, however, is completed much earlier than this; in Barn Owl, for example, the humerus and tibia reach c. 98 per cent of their final length by day 40.

Prey provisioning
Parent owls have clearly defined roles related to their gender, the male responsible for most of the prey provision and the female responsible for care of the young at the nest. As long as the female is at the nest brooding the young owls, the male will be solely responsible for the prey that is delivered. Even after this time, once the female has joined her mate to hunt for prey, the male continues to hold the primary role, responsible – in the case of the Barn Owl – for roughly two-thirds of the prey that is delivered. Interestingly, it is known that males and females may respond differently to the begging calls of their chicks, something that can lead to the chicks themselves begging more intensely at one parent than the other. It has been demonstrated, for example, that Barn Owl chicks direct more begging calls at their mother than their father. Even though female Barn Owls may spend more time in the nest when visiting with prey, they hand over the prey to a chick more quickly than the male does in his shorter visits (Roulin & Bersier, 2007).

High levels of prey delivery are a feature of Barn Owl nests, with rates increasing from 8–11 items per 24-hour period at hatching to reach a peak of 14–16 items per 24-hour period when the first chick is roughly a month old, equating to roughly four items per chick or just over 100 g per chick (Langford & Taylor, 1992). Much of the prey delivery in this species takes place during the first part of the night, the parent's arrival greeted with a chorus of begging calls. Those of young Barn Owls are a drawn out hissing sound, something that can be heard over some distance and providing useful evidence that a nest site contains an active nest with young. The begging calls of young Barn Owls have been studied in some detail by Alexandre Roulin and colleagues, who have been examining the degree of competition that may occur between siblings in the nest.

Competition between nestling birds may take several different forms. As we have already highlighted earlier in this chapter, an older sibling may attack, or even kill, a younger individual in order to secure sole access to the food being provided. More commonly, however, and certainly the typical case in most songbirds, the nestlings indulge in scramble competition, jostling with each other to be in the best position to take food from a returning parent. Such jostling involves much calling and there is good evidence for some bird species that the female will feed the chick that is begging the loudest. Young Barn Owls are surprisingly vocal even when the parents are away from the nest, though not as vocal as when a parent returns with food. Alexandre Roulin has demonstrated that the calling behaviour that occurs prior to a feeding visit also plays a key role in determining which chick will get access to the food (Roulin, 2001, 2004b; Roulin et al., 2009). Through experimental studies, Roulin revealed that the chicks use the degree of calling behaviour to judge how competitive their siblings will be when a parent later arrives with food. If the largest chick is being particularly vocal, then its younger and smaller siblings know that they stand little chance of securing the next prey item to be delivered and so will then beg less intensely when that delivery arrives. Roulin termed this 'sibling negotiation', with senior chicks also using this calling behaviour to deter junior chicks from begging. Individual chicks 'negotiate' by responding to the calls made by siblings. An individual may respond to the long call made by one of its siblings by producing a long call of its own. For calling to provide an honest signal of intent it must carry some inherent cost and, with an average of 1,800 calls per day made by each chick in the absence of its parents, it seems that it probably does. Those individuals that call more loudly and with greater frequency when the parents are absent are more likely to receive food first.

As an aside, it is worth just mentioning here that it is not just vocalisations that might shape successful begging behaviour. Interesting research by Vincenzo Penteriani and colleagues suggests that the pale feathering around the mouth of young Eagle Owls may provide an important visual cue for their parents, stimulating food provision during the period in which the young first leave the nest (Penteriani et al., 2007b). In many ways, if this is supported by more research, it could be considered not that dissimilar to how the chicks of many passerine species stimulate feeding through their brightly coloured gapes.

FIG 73. Large prey items, like this young Water Vole, may be over-represented in prey caches at the nest. This was one of three individuals at a Barn Owl site. (Mike Toms)

Calling by young Barn Owls also continues after a prey item has been delivered and it is thought that the chicks may also signal their willingness to defend a food item that they have just received. This circumstance occurs because most prey items delivered to the young owls are large and cannot be eaten instantly. A chick that has just received a prey item may attempt to hide in the corner of the nest chamber, perhaps turning its back on its siblings; it may sometimes even sit on the prey item. Nestling Barn Owls are unable to tear up a large prey item without help from their mother until they are at least 25 days of age. Once beyond this age they will often prefer to tear at a carcass, swallowing smaller portions that can, presumably, be digested more readily. If a chick fears that the prey it has received is going to be stolen by a sibling then it may swallow the prey whole, rather than risk losing it (Roulin *et al.*, 2008).

A visit to an active Barn Owl or Tawny Owl nest will often reveal the presence of uneaten prey items. Some authors refer to these as 'prey caches', suggesting that their presence is an intentional act, rather than the result of the parents delivering food at a rate above that which it can be eaten by the developing chicks and without any attempt to measure how much food is available within the nest. At least three different hypotheses have been put forward to explain the presence of such 'stores'. The 'large prey' hypothesis, put forward by Korpimäki

(1987), proposes that nestlings have difficulty in tackling larger food items so preferentially feed on the smaller items and take time to dismember large ones. There is good evidence that large prey items are over-represented in Barn Owl nest sites. A second hypothesis – the 'insurance' hypothesis – proposes that parents store food to buffer against temporary shortages that may result from adverse weather conditions (Baudvin, 1980). A third hypothesis, the 'feeding time' hypothesis (Roulin, 2004b), is a special form of the 'insurance' hypothesis, since it proposes that parents may use food stores to allow the chicks to feed when they are hungry and to spread meals over the entire 24-hour period. Hunting activity in the Barn Owl, for example, is confined to part of the 24-hour cycle, with much of the prey delivered in the first three hours of night-time activity. By caching what they catch when they can hunt, owls may be allowing the chicks to continue feeding during the rest of the day, when hunting does not take place.

Parental roles

As we have seen, a common pattern among the British owls is for the male to feed the female while she is incubating and brooding young chicks, after which both members of the pair catch and deliver prey, though with the male typically continuing to be the main provider. Male Little Owls, for example, have been shown to cover more distance and have fewer periods of inactivity than their mates during the period of chick rearing, underlining their contributing to the breeding attempt (Holsegård-Rasmussen et al., 2009). A similar pattern is seen in Tawny Owls, where the male forages at a greater distance to the nest than his mate (Sunde et al., 2003b). Young Snowy Owls, still in the nest scrape, are fed by the female if she is present but larger chicks, which sometimes rush at the arriving male, may be fed directly by him. In Eagle Owl, the female spends most of the day at the nest while the chicks are less than a month of age, again with the male responsible for prey provision and nest defence, but once the chicks are older, the female will increasingly tend to use a different roost – though close enough to be able to see the nest site. This feature is also seen in other owl species, for example Barn Owl. The decision made by the female on when to leave the nest and join her mate in provisioning the young appears, in the Barn Owl at least, to be made on the basis of the balance between the amount of food being provided by the male and the requirements of the young. Durant et al. (2004a) found that brooding female Barn Owls make their first hunting trip about two weeks after the first egg has hatched, just about matching the time at which the amount of prey being delivered by the male falls below what is required by the growing chicks.

Nest hygiene and sanitation

Nest sanitation is an important component of the parental care seen in owls and it begins as soon as the female occupies the nest. Female owls usually leave the nest to defecate or cast pellets elsewhere, although sometimes these are simply deposited over the side of the nest, as is sometimes the case in incubating or brooding Long-eared Owls. This is not necessarily an option for cavity-nesting species. Owl chicks do not produce a faecal sack of the kind seen in passerines; the faeces of young chicks, too small to defecate out of the nest, may be ingested by the female, particularly during the first few days after hatching. As platform-nesting Long-eared Owl chicks get older, so they continue to defecate out of the nest. Inevitably they sometimes miss and the rim of the nest becomes increasingly stained with faeces, a feature seen in other open-nesting birds of prey. Prey remains may collect in the nest during the final days of occupancy, attracting flies and making the nest appear particularly unsanitary. The brooding female will preen young chicks very gently, removing small pieces of uneaten prey that have become attached to the chick's beak or feathers. As the chicks grow older so they begin to exercise and they may also be seen to preen, scratch and to bob their heads. They may occasionally preen their fellow siblings.

FIG 74. Young Tawny Owls leave the nest and 'branch' while still very much dependent on their parents for support. (Mike Toms)

Leaving the nest

The length of time that young owls remain in the nest varies between species, with cavity-nesting species (and the Barn Owl in particular) tending to spend longer in the nest than open-nesting species (see Table 8). Young Tawny Owls, for example, are well-known for their habit of leaving the nest at a stage where they are still dependent upon their parents, a behaviour sometimes referred to as 'branching' and shared with nestling Long-eared Owls. Once they have left the nest the chicks will call for food throughout the night, the characteristic 'squeaky door' call of Long-eared Owl chicks familiar enough to those working its favoured forest habitats. The call of a young Tawny Owl is equally characteristic and best described as '*ke-serp*' or, at slightly higher pitch, '*ke-suip*' (Muir, 1954). As we shall see in the next chapter, parental care does not end when the chicks leave the nest; instead, the adults continue to provision the chicks through into the post-fledging dependency period.

REPLACEMENT CLUTCHES AND SECOND BROODS

Following the failure of a breeding attempt, a pair of owls may have the opportunity to try again, either in the same nest or at a new site elsewhere. The question of whether or not a replacement clutch is to be laid will be influenced by the timing of the failure (can the birds fit another attempt in?), the condition of the female and the current environmental conditions (including food availability). Replacement clutches following failure in nesting Eagle Owls appear to be fairly common, with a figure of 80 per cent derived for one long-running study (Bettega *et al.*, 2011) but in other species they are less typical. In the Little Owl, for example, the average replacement rate derived from a number of European studies comes out at just 1.7 per cent (25 cases out of 1,446 clutches). An examination of replacement clutches more widely, looking across a range of bird species, suggests that the 'quality' of the replacement nesting attempt is often lower than the initial attempt, with a smaller number of eggs laid and chicks produced. However, this is not always the case as Chiara Bettaga demonstrated in Eagle Owl, where clutch size, brood size, body condition and immune condition of replacement attempts were all found to be similar to those of the first attempts. Bettega suggested the result could have been influenced by the early season timing of the replacement attempts and the quality of the pairs involved, which might also explain the high incidence of replacement clutches made in this study. Second broods are, at the very least, rare in Eagle Owl and have yet to be proved beyond doubt for European populations.

Long-eared Owls will replace lost clutches but again only rarely produce a genuine second brood (Glue, 1977b). If the eggs are lost during the early stages of incubation then the female will often produce a replacement clutch within a few days and in the same nest. If the loss happens towards the end of the incubation period, or once the eggs have hatched, then a replacement clutch is far less likely. Where one is produced then this tends to follow a period of display and courtship, the new clutch not appearing for several weeks. A genuine second brood recorded by Derick Scott involved a pair whose first breeding attempt was made unusually early, with small young present in the nest on 3 March 1960. The pair then went on to produce a clutch of two eggs in the same nest. These hatched at the end of May and the resulting young left the nest at a time when two individuals from the previous brood were still with their parents.

Although second broods are not uncommon in British Barn Owls they do appear to be dependent on prey availability, being more common in years and areas when prey are abundant. In such years, the Barn Owls can begin breeding that much earlier in the year and this appears to provide an opportunity for a second nesting attempt later in the year. There has been something of a tendency for Barn Owl second broods to go unreported in the past, but the growing recognition that they do occur has seen more effort directed to late-season visits by those involved in monitoring Barn Owl nest box schemes. Iain Taylor found that the average interval between starting the first and second clutches in his Scottish study area was 98 days, the birds initiating the second attempt a week or more before the young from the first attempt had fledged.

In some double-brooded species, one member of the pair may desert the nesting attempt before the chicks gain independence, leaving their partner to complete the job. In such cases the individual that has abandoned their first brood may begin another nesting attempt with a different partner. It is usually the partner that contributes less in the latter stages of the breeding attempt that deserts and, for our owls, this is likely to be the female. Studies of breeding Barn Owls support this. Roulin (2002a) found that, among individuals producing a second brood, 46 per cent of females and 4 per cent of males deserted to mate with another partner. What is interesting about Alexandre Roulin's work was the finding that although the clutches produced by deserting females were larger and produced two weeks earlier than those second clutches produced by females which stayed with their mate, there was no difference in nesting success. The case of a Barn Owl pair in Devon producing three clutches in just five months, and reported by Pearce (1986), is untypical as the birds in question were part of a breeding and release programme and were receiving supplementary food on a daily basis. It does, however, underline how food availability can influence the number of broods that a pair might produce in a season.

BREEDING PERFORMANCE

One measure of breeding performance is provided by the number of chicks that fledge from the nest. However, the success of a breeding attempt should not just be judged by how many young leave the nest; instead it should be judged by the number of young that are recruited into the breeding population in future years. Brood size at fledging, although ultimately determined by the number of eggs that have been laid and which then go on to hatch, will be determined by food availability. If feeding conditions deteriorate during the course of the nesting attempt then, as we have seen, the strategy of asynchronous hatching adopted by our owls will lead to brood reduction. Threatened with deteriorating feeding conditions, the parent owls could attempt to up their investment in the breeding attempt by increasing the amount of time that they spend hunting; this, however, is something that might compromise their own survival prospects and curtail future reproductive opportunities. Since owls are relatively long-lived species you might expect them to place longer-term opportunities above short-

FIG 75. Breeding performance in British Barn Owls has been found to vary with the nature of the landscape within which the birds are nesting. (Emma Perry)

term risks, favouring the acceptance of brood reduction over the increased risk to themselves of increasing their efforts to provide more food. That this is what happens in the wild is supported by work in which the brood sizes of Barn Owls have been manipulated experimentally (Roulin *et al.*, 1999). The results of this work demonstrate that parents do not increase their investment in the breeding attempt when broods require extra parental effort; Roulin and his co-workers found that adult condition and subsequent reproductive success were not impacted by the change in brood size; nestling quality, however, was reduced. Similar findings have been revealed for the Tawny Owl (Sasvári & Hegyi, 2010a).

Breeding ecology and the importance of prey abundance

As we have seen throughout this chapter, the abundance of preferred prey species is a key driver, shaping many aspects of the breeding ecology of our owls. At the start of the chapter we saw how prey abundance was influenced by the nature of the habitat, the knock-on effects of which can be seen in comparisons made between the breeding success of owl populations occupying different habitats within Britain. Iain Taylor's work in Scotland has, for example, revealed that Barn Owl pairs breeding in areas of young conifer plantation consistently raise larger broods than pairs using farmland within the same general area. He suggested that these differences were a consequence of the different prey populations that the two habitats were able to support. This was further emphasised by his finding that the productivity of individual pairs breeding in farmland was related to the density of suitable grassland hunting habitat within a 1-km radius of the nest (Taylor, 2002). This underlines the importance of particular habitat types and the small mammal populations they support.

Data collected through the BTO's Barn Owl Monitoring Programme (BOMP) also underline the important role that habitat plays in determining the number of chicks produced per breeding attempt, this time at the national level. The number of chicks produced was found to be greater in areas of semi-natural or natural grassland than in areas of more intensive agriculture. Occupancy rates of study sites were also found to follow this pattern, being lower in arable areas (Leech *et al.*, 2009). Similarly, Project Barn Owl revealed that the proportion of Barn Owl pairs rearing at least one young to fledging was higher – at 86 per cent – in the grassland-dominated south-west of Britain than it was in the largely arable east of England, where the proportion was just 61 per cent (Toms *et al.*, 2000).

Prey abundance doesn't just vary with habitat but, as we have seen, it also varies from year to year. Vole populations are known to fluctuate in a cyclical manner over time, the periodicity of the cycles tending to increase as you move further north; cycles peak roughly every three years in the temperate zone but every four

FIG 76. Tawny Owls may find prey abundance more stable within lowland deciduous woodland in southern England than in the conifer plantations of northern England. (Steve Round)

to five years in the northern boreal zone. Additionally, vole population cycles are not necessarily synchronised over large areas, meaning that the conditions faced by owls breeding in one area may be very different from those faced by owls breeding in a similar habitat elsewhere. The cycles tend to be more pronounced in more northerly latitudes and may be barely discernible further south. There is also evidence that the strength of the cycles is fading, particularly in more northerly latitudes. Faced with such cycles, our breeding owls have two options; either to stay where they are as residents and switch to alternative prey or move to an area where feeding conditions are more favourable. It is difficult to pick out the effect of this regional variation in cycle amplitude when looking just within Britain but a hint of its influence might be seen in the fact that Tawny Owl populations breeding in lowland deciduous woodland in southern Britain (Southern, 1970) show a relatively high degree of stability, with a maximum difference in the number of breeding pairs from one year to the next of 15 per cent. In contrast Steve Petty found that his Tawny Owl population, inhabiting coniferous woodland in northern England, changed by up to 24 per cent between years (Petty, 1992).

The impact of changing prey numbers over time can also be seen by looking at a single population over many years. This has been done in a number of British studies, bringing together information on breeding success – typically expressed as the number of chicks fledged – with that on prey populations. Petty & Pearce (1992) did just this for Tawny Owls nesting in Kielder Forest on the border between England and Scotland. In those years when Field Vole numbers were low the Tawny Owls fledged an average of just 0.20 chicks per territory, compared with 2.58 chicks per territory in years when the Field Vole population was at its peak. By studying this population over a number of years the researchers were also able to examine how the quality of individual territories varied and they were also able to identify habitat characteristics that might predict territory quality. The best territories for rearing chicks during years when Field Voles were abundant were also among the best when vole populations were low. However, the most successful territories in low abundance years were not necessarily among the best territories when it came to the better years. Habitat diversity was found to be of particular importance during those years when vole numbers were low, enabling the owls to better exploit other food sources (e.g. birds and amphibians). The poorer quality territories did well in years with low vole numbers because they contained other habitat types and the owls could use the alternative prey species associated with them. However, these territories did not do well when conditions were more favourable because they did not have enough of the habitats favoured by the voles and so the breeding owls were unable to take advantage of the peak in prey abundance.

How our owls respond to changing prey abundance

The two main responses to changes in prey abundance are to switch to alternative prey or to move elsewhere, and you can see how our British owls may be categorised according to which of these two strategies they adopt. For example, while Barn Owls and Tawny Owls remain where they are, but switch to alternative prey, our Short-eared Owls move elsewhere to seek out areas where favoured prey are more abundant. There are, additionally, a number of other responses to changing prey abundance that may be seen in our owls. Birds may begin breeding earlier in those years where prey are more abundant, something that may, as we have seen, allow some species to make more than one nesting attempt within the season. Females may show higher body weights, lay more eggs or even lay larger eggs, potentially increasing the productivity of the nesting attempt. Barn Owl pairs breeding early in the season have been shown to produce larger brood sizes and are more likely to recruit at least one of their offspring into the breeding population (Roulin, 2002b). We may also see a greater proportion of the population breed in those years when prey are more abundant,

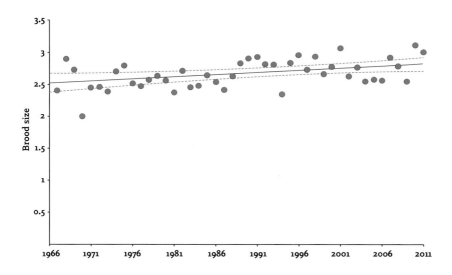

FIG 77. Mean brood size for British Little Owls, 1966–2011, from BTO Nest Record Scheme submissions. Smoothed line shows brood size predicted from model and the confidence intervals associated with this. Note how mean brood size varies between years. Redrawn from Baillie *et al.* (2012), with permission from the British Trust for Ornithology.

with more young birds represented within the breeding population and better adult survival coming into the breeding season. In those years when prey are less abundant it appears to be the higher quality, experienced pairs that manage to breed successfully, although with reduced productivity.

There is another, rather interesting, response to changing food conditions that has been documented in several Tawny Owl studies. Appleby *et al.* (1997) working on a British Tawny Owl population, found that offspring production was biased towards female young under favourable feeding conditions but biased towards the production of male young when pairs were facing poor feeding conditions. Although this finding has been replicated in work carried out elsewhere in Europe (Sasvári & Hegyi, 2010b), there have been other studies where no such effect has been found (Kekkonen *et al.*, 2008). Female Tawny Owls are larger than the males and, therefore, likely to prove more costly to produce. Selection may, therefore, favour the production of males in some owl species when conditions are difficult because they are less costly to produce.

Breeding performance and the weather

Within this chapter we have seen how weather conditions can influence breeding success and productivity, most notably in relation to birds coming into breeding condition. Weather conditions may also modify or counter the influence of prey availability during the breeding season itself, perhaps by restricting access to prey populations (e.g. when heavy rain prevents Barn Owls from hunting or windy conditions make it more difficult to hear the movements made by small mammals on a woodland floor) or by directly altering the trajectory of their populations. For example, a sudden drought, appearing part way through the summer may limit grass production and curtail the growth of vole populations, which would usually increase from an early spring trough to a late summer peak. The effects of weather conditions is something to which we will return in Chapter 5 when we look at mortality.

Breeding success and the individual

Breeding is an energetically demanding part of the owl's annual cycle and we would expect to find that it is isolated from other components, such as moult or migration. In the Tawny Owl, for example, breeding, moult and territory establishment are all separated from one another. Most adult Tawny Owls begin the moult of their wing feathers in early June, when the breeding season has ended, with a strong suggestion that failed breeders initiate their moult earlier than breeding birds (Hardy *et al.*, 1981). Lasting an average of 77 days, the moult

FIG 78. The reproductive lifespan of a Barn Owl is influenced by its sex, with females starting later and showing a shorter reproductive lifespan than males. (Emma Perry)

is then completed before the establishment of territories from early winter. Breeding, therefore, has consequences for the individual and the amount of resources that it puts into a breeding attempt will be influenced by various things, including age and experience. A long-term study of Hungarian Tawny Owls has, for example, revealed that older, more experienced males are better at pin-pointing alternative prey sources than young males during those years when favoured prey species are less abundant (Sasvári et al., 2000). This makes them more likely to fledge young during a year of low prey abundance and they may be more likely to undertake a nesting attempt and to prove successful in it. The success of Tawny Owl pairs increases with age and it seems to be individuals breeding for the first or second time that do less well than older individuals.

The breeding success of an individual is best measured over its whole lifetime, rather than on the basis of a single breeding season. This measure of breeding success is often referred to as 'lifetime reproductive success' and is determined not just by the number of breeding attempts made and their outcome but also by the survival of the bird itself (something to which we will return in Chapter 5). Lifetime reproductive success may vary between individuals, populations and species; it may also vary by sex. Res Altwegg and colleagues have found, for example, that male Barn Owls had a longer reproductive lifespan on average than females (Altwegg et al., 2007). In part this is because females have lower survival rates than males but it is also a result of females tending to start reproduction later. Breeding success has been shown to change with age. The number of young Barn Owls produced per brood and the probability of producing a second clutch during a season is higher for older birds than it is for birds making their first breeding attempt, suggestive that experience might be important (Res Altwegg again). Beyond two years of age, the number of fledglings produced has been found to increase with female age but to decrease with male age. This fall in productivity with increasing male age may, in part, be a consequence of reduced fertility in older males. However, Altwegg also found that older males were associated with reduced clutch sizes. This may seem surprising, given that the female controls clutch size, but it may be that older males are less good at provisioning their mate and that she adjusts her clutch size accordingly, something that has been demonstrated in other bird species. In English Tawny Owls, both male and female reproductive performance has been found to increase with age to a peak, after which it declines. In females, this peak was reached at around nine years of age but in males it was much earlier, at three years (Millon et al., 2011).

The success of an individual appears to be influenced, in part, by the start that it gets in life. Body mass at fledging has, for example, been shown to have a bearing on future prospects. In a Norwegian study of fledging behaviour in Tawny Owls it was found that fledglings that died or disappeared (and were assumed to have died) during the first ten days after leaving the nest had a 16 per cent lower body mass than those that survived this period (Overskaug *et al.*, 1999). Additionally, it has been shown that a Tawny Owl fledgling was more likely to recruit into the breeding population as a high quality individual if it had fledged alone, although at the cost of the siblings that failed to make it. Results from a Scottish study (Taylor, 1994) revealed that young Barn Owls (both male and female) that had fledged before the median fledging date for the population had a higher probability of being recruited into the breeding population than those that fledged after the median date. It seems that there is a pressure to breed early and for the resulting young to get a good start in life.

Breeding performance is just one component contributing to population size. Although it is a particularly important component, we need to turn our attention to what happens to an individual after it has left the nest before we can examine owl populations more fully and unravel the factors that drive changes within them.

CHAPTER 4

Movements

A S A FAMILY, THE OWLS EXHIBIT most of the different types of
movement strategy shown by other birds. Some species are resident
within a year-round territory but others are nomadic or irruptive in
habits and may appear in areas well outside their normal range. Although no owl
species is considered to be completely migratory, a few populations of certain
species are known to undertake migrational movements. Additionally, young
owls move away from their place of birth to settle in other areas and, once settled,
show varying degrees of attachment to a breeding site over future seasons.

FIG 79. Our owls undertake a range of different movements; Little Owls are, for the most part,
a rather sedentary species. (Mark Hancox)

The British owls demonstrate a reduced range of movement strategies. Once the period of natal dispersal has ended they can be loosely grouped into those that are either essentially sedentary (e.g. Tawny Owl, Barn Owl, Eagle Owl and Little Owl) or which show varying degrees of seasonal movement in at least some components of the British population (e.g. Snowy Owl, Short-eared Owl and Long-eared Owl). For some species, notably Long-eared Owl, we know very little about the movements that are made by our breeding birds and what knowledge we do have may be clouded by the movements of birds from elsewhere, arriving here for the winter. Individual species may also adopt different strategies in different parts of Britain, so it is important to interpret the findings of localised studies with care. As we shall see, while there is much that we do know about the movements of the British owls, there is still a great deal to learn.

NATAL DISPERSAL

Having left the nest, there is a strong tendency for a young bird to move away from where it was born. This process, known as 'dispersal', is thought to reduce the chances of inbreeding and allows the youngster to settle elsewhere, where there may be less competition from already established birds and greater access to resources like food and nest sites. Inbreeding, which may be a particularly strong driver for dispersal, has been documented in British owls on occasion (Petty et al., 1986; Shaw & Dowell, 1989), but is probably a rather rare occurrence. The chances of inbreeding may be reduced even more if there is a tendency for one sex to move further than the other during the dispersal phase, something to which we will later return. The flip side of moving away is the risk that the bird may find itself in unsuitable habitat and separated from others of its kind, reducing the chances of locating a suitable mate.

Exactly what triggers this movement away from the natal site has been of particular interest to ecologists. It has, for example, been established that the dispersive movements of insects are influenced by a hormone (known as the 'juvenile hormone'), but there is no evidence of a directly comparable hormone operating in birds or mammals. Other hormones, notably the nongonadal steroid hormone corticosterone, have been implicated in natal dispersal but their exact role has yet to be resolved and they may not be the proximate driver. Corticosterone, which is produced by the adrenal glands, has been shown to affect body composition, stimulate feeding and initiate locomotor activity (Dufty & Belthoff, 2001), so it may prepare the body for dispersal rather than drive it. Physical condition may be important, with older, more socially dominant chicks perhaps able to secure greater access to food resources in the nest and thus be able to leave the nest at an earlier date. It is known that older and more socially dominant Western Screech Owl *Megascops kennicottii* chicks leave the nest before their subordinate siblings (Ellsworth & Belthoff, 1999), something that also appears to happen with other owls. This, in turn, may prompt younger siblings to leave the nest prematurely, possibly with costly consequences for their future survival chances. Age at fledging in young Tawny Owls has been shown to influence predation risk, with younger birds more likely to be taken by mammalian predators during the first few days out of the nest (Sunde & Markussen, 2005). Since mortality events linked to predation by mammals are often clumped within Tawny Owl broods, premature fledging may put other siblings at risk.

It is possible that the trigger to move away might come from the parent birds, perhaps because they have ceased to provide food and support to their offspring or because they actively drive the young away. The parent–offspring conflict over the duration of parental care was something that Peter Sunde examined in his study of a Tawny Owl population (Sunde, 2008). Using radio-tracking, Sunde found that young Tawny Owls stopped begging for food some 8–12 weeks after leaving the nest – or some 13–18 weeks after hatching. It then took another one to two weeks before the young owls first roosted away from their natal range. So it seems that young Tawny Owls gain independence (i.e. cease to beg for and receive food) before they leave the natal area, which suggests that the parents do not chase them away but that they leave on their own initiative.

The first steps towards independence

When a young owl first leaves the nest it is likely to require ongoing support from its parents and many young leave the nest before they are able to fly. Young Eagle Owls, for example, which typically leave the nest at 40–45 days of age, have wing and tail feathers that are only 80 per cent and 40 per cent of their final length respectively, with many of the developing feathers still encased in protective sheathing (Penteriani *et al.*, 2005). This means that they can walk and jump but not take to the wing. Over the coming days and weeks the young owls increase their mobility, exploring a wider area while, at the same time, their parents reduce the level of support that is provided. This phase, which precedes dispersal proper, is known as the post-fledging dependence period. Rather little work has been done on this phase in the lives of young owls, but it is likely to be a critical period for the young as they make the transition towards independence. The two species for which the most work has been done – and which are relevant to our study of British owls – are the Tawny Owl and the Eagle Owl. Young Eagle Owls initially focus their activities within the immediate area around the nest but as they get older they increase the area over which they range and gradually move away from the nest site. In turn this leads to an increasing distance between siblings, although individual Eagle Owl chicks may sometimes be found roosting together. Increasing distance from the nest with age is also a feature of Tawny Owls and is probably typical of other British owls too. Young Barn Owls, for example, may roost in buildings or trees adjacent to a nest site as soon as they are able to fly.

Tawny Owls are well known for leaving the nest at an early age, with shallow cavity or open sites vacated earlier than those of a more sheltered nature. Most young leave the nest at around 25–30 days of age, the first few days out of the nest often spent on or close to the ground, where the owlets have to rely on their parents for both food and protection. Chicks from the same brood rarely roost together. It is during this period that young Tawny Owls appear to be particularly vulnerable to mammalian predators like Red Fox (Petty & Thirgood, 1989) and Pine Marten *Martes martes* (Overskaug et al., 1999), both of which may be attracted by the youngsters' begging calls. For example, Sunde (2008) found that all mammal-induced deaths in his study population of 72 young – from 41 broods – occurred during the first two weeks after leaving the nest, with two-thirds of these incidents occurring on the night that the chicks first left the nest. Although drawn from a much smaller sample, just 12 individuals, Petty & Thirgood (1989) found a similar pattern in their study of Scottish Tawny Owls.

Young Tawny Owls fly poorly when they first fledge and are usually to be found within 50 m of the nest, but after ten days or so they begin to fly more strongly and are increasingly able to roost off the ground. At this stage they favour thicker cover, often roosting close to the trunk during the day but moving to lower and more exposed branches at night, presumably to increase the chances of an adult delivering food to them. Predation by raptors like Goshawk and Common Buzzard *Buteo buteo* occurs throughout the post-fledging period but may be a particular problem for late broods, gaining independence during June, when the raptors have young of their own to feed and show an increase in hunting activity (Sunde, 2008). Interestingly, a study examining the behaviour of 71 newly fledged Tawny Owls in a lowland deciduous woodland (Wytham Wood in Oxfordshire) found little evidence of predation, perhaps because the site supported only a very low density of mammalian predators and neither Buzzard nor Goshawk were then established in the wood (Southern et al., 1954). Predation appears to be less of an issue for young Eagle Owls, their larger size and fearsome parents presumably affording greater protection. Even so, 8 per cent of the 74 chicks radio-tracked by Maria Delgado and colleagues in Spain died during the post-fledging dependency period (Delgado et al., 2010).

FIG 80. Young Little Owls increasingly explore their wider surroundings as they progress towards independence. (Mark Hancox)

There is some evidence that food availability may be an issue for newly independent owls. Starvation has, for example, been found to be a prominent cause of death in some – but not all – Tawny Owl studies. Where it has been reported as being a significant cause of mortality it tends to occur later in the post-fledging dependence period, as the young owls become truly independent and have to find food for themselves (Hirons *et al.*, 1979; Coles & Petty, 1997). This pattern has also been observed in Long-eared Owls (Tome, 2011). Food availability may also influence predation risk because hungry young are more likely to make the begging call. Calling rates are, on average, lower when food is superabundant, which means that both territory quality and between-year variation in prey abundance can influence chick losses post-fledging (Sunde & Markussen, 2005).

Other hazards face young owls during the first few weeks of life, including disease and, curiously, suffocation – several studies have reported finding dead Tawny Owl young with a vole part-swallowed and seemingly stuck in the throat (e.g. Petty & Thirgood, 1989). Characteristics of particular nesting sites may also pose a risk. Bendel & Therres (1993), working on a population of American Barn

Owls nesting in off-shore duck blinds in Chesapeake Bay, saw many of their radio-tagged youngsters drown in the sea. All of the known survivors came from duck blinds situated less than 400 m from the shore, suggesting that the fledglings were unable to cover a distance much greater than this during their first flight. While the duck blinds offered excellent protection from nest predators, they posed a real risk to the young. The presence of electricity pylons within 200 m of the Eagle Owl nests studied by Fabrizio Sergio (Sergio *et al.*, 2004) was found to increase the likelihood of partial or complete brood loss during the post-fledging period, with an estimated 17 per cent of young falling victim to electrocution.

Parental care appears to be largely restricted to the provision of food and defence against predation and there is no evidence that the parents train the young in how to hunt or to catch prey. This observation is supported by the successful establishment of young Barn Owls that have been raised in captivity and released as part of reintroduction programmes within Britain (Meek *et al.*, 2003). Food provision may be directed towards the chick or it may, as is often the case with Barn Owls, be directed towards the nest site, the parents often bypassing chicks loitering outside the nest entrance. Young Barn Owls that are too weak to return to the nest site for feeding are usually ignored by the parents and face a bleak future. Parental duties may be split if the pair initiates a new nesting attempt, the female incubating the new clutch while the male continues to feed the young from the previous attempt. In other cases the female may cease her involvement with the brood for different reasons. It has been noted, for example, that female Long-eared Owls may abandon fledged young when they are six to ten weeks of age, leaving the male to continue feeding for an additional few weeks on his own, even though the female has not initiated a new nesting attempt.

An interesting aspect of the post-fledging dependency period is the occasional instances where the young from one brood move into the home range of a neighbouring pair, where they may remain for a period before dispersal proper. This has been termed 'brood-switching' by some authors, although it is not clear if the young actually receive any food from the resident adults. Brood-switching has been documented in Eagle Owls, the authors suggesting that youngsters may be attracted into a neighbouring range by the begging calls of the resident chicks (Penteriani & Delgado, 2008).

Moving away

The process of natal dispersal can be loosely divided into three different components, each of which is associated with particular behaviours and each of which may have different triggers. The first is 'departure', the owl moving away from the natal area; the second is 'transience', during which the owl explores

a wider area through a series of wandering movements. The final phase is
'settlement', the owl establishing itself within a future breeding territory or as a
non-territorial floater (the latter is of particular relevance in species where the
age at first breeding is two or more years). This three-phase partitioning of the
dispersal process is best applied to owls that are essentially sedentary as breeding
adults, finding a territory and then remaining within it in future seasons. It is
less suitable for species with a nomadic or migratory lifestyle, where it becomes
more difficult to separate dispersal from the other forms of movement that are
taking place.

Dispersal behaviour can vary greatly between individuals, with some moving
away over a relatively short period and others settling locally for a time before
moving off elsewhere, often through a series of short-distance movements
interspersed with further periods of temporary settlement (Seel et al., 1983;
Delgado et al., 2010). Young owls may make a series of exploratory movements
during this early stage, perhaps returning to the natal area after several days
away. Eick (2003) saw such behaviour in some of the Little Owls that he was
radio-tracking in Germany, with individuals revisiting the natal site following
excursions typically lasting from three to five days. During these excursions
the young birds would cover up to 41 km per night. In the Little Owl, such
exploratory movements increase with age (Zens, 2005) before departure proper
occurs during early autumn.

On average, Eagle Owl chicks begin to disperse from their natal areas at
170 days of age, but some may leave at 131 days and others as late as 232 days
(Delgado et al., 2010). For comparison, dispersal begins at 48–154 days in Tawny
Owl (Coles et al., 2003) and 70–98 days in Long-eared Owl (Tome, 2011 and
supported by rather limited ring-recovery data from the UK). Young Barn Owls
leave their natal areas soon after fledging and disperse rapidly thereafter (Toms,
2002; Huffeldt et al., 2012). Individual Barn Owls may vary in when they begin to
disperse, as revealed by radio-tracking work in Devon, where one bird did not
move away until it was 116 days of age (Barn Owl Trust, 2012).

There is no evidence of a strong directional component to the movements
made by dispersing chicks in any of the British owl species, something that is
largely supported by work elsewhere in Europe and in North America. Local
habitat features may, however, influence the pattern of dispersal. For example,
dispersing Tawny Owls have been shown to actively select woodland and forest
habitats over open country (Coles & Petty, 1997; Overskaug et al., 1999) and birds
may orientate along the axes of valley systems (e.g. Tawny Owl, Coles et al., 2003)
or avoid high ground (e.g. Barn Owl, Taylor, 1994; Mátics, 2003). However, the
often-repeated suggestion that dispersing Barn Owls follow river corridors or

FIG 81. Barn Owl ringing in Nottinghamshire. Ringing can reveal the pattern of dispersal and other movements made by owls. (Mike Toms)

other linear features has not yet been supported by radio-tracking work. In fact the movements of 12 young Barn Owls followed by the Barn Owl Trust in Devon, suggested that local movements were completely unrelated to linear habitat features (Barn Owl Trust, 2012). Interestingly, while some dispersing Eagle Owl chicks – tracked from nest sites within the Alps – initially orientated their movements along valley features, most eventually crossed ridges or high mountain passes, including some above 3,000 m, during their dispersal phase (Aebischer *et al.*, 2010).

For a number of owl species it is thought that large waterbodies may inhibit dispersal movements (Frylestam, 1972). There have been, for example, no overseas recoveries of British-ringed Little Owls or Tawny Owls and just six overseas recoveries of British-ringed Barn Owls (BTO). Dispersal movements of Barn Owls ringed on islands like Anglesey and the Isle of Wight also suggest a general reluctance to cross large expanses of water (Seel *et al.*, 1983; Gloyn, 1990). Movements across water do happen though; for example, a young Barn Owl ringed on the Isle of Wight was recovered the following spring in Bedfordshire and other individuals ringed on the island have been recorded in later years in

Kent and France (Gloyn, 1990). Large waterbodies do not present a barrier to Long-eared Owls, Short-eared Owls or Snowy Owls.

Information from ring-recoveries, radio-tracking or the use of satellite tags can provide an insight into the process of dispersal, charting the distances moved by individual owls and the period over which these movements take place. For example, an examination of ring-recovery data for British Barn Owls found that the median distance between ringing location (the nest site) and subsequent recovery location was just 3 km for birds recovered in the second month after ringing as a chick. This rose to 7.5 km in the third month after ringing and 12 km in the fourth, by which stage the process of dispersal appeared to be complete as median recovery distance then levelled off (Toms, 2002). The phase of transience or 'wandering' may sometimes see birds return towards their natal area. Ullrich (1980), working on Little Owls in Germany, found three cases where juveniles that had moved away in the autumn later returned to settle near their natal area. One of these birds returned from 36 km away. The speed of movement during the dispersal phase may depend on condition (owls in poor condition have been shown to move shorter distances and to travel more slowly when dispersing) and habitat (unfavourable habitats may be crossed more rapidly, the owls only lingering in more suitable habitats), as well as individual behaviour (Delgado *et al.*, 2010).

FIG 82. The dispersal of young Eagle Owls may be influenced by local habitat features. (Vincenzo Penteriani)

Settlement

The point at which a dispersing youngster decides to settle is dependent on a range of different factors; the presence of suitable habitat and adequate food resources are obviously key, but the presence of other owls – either potential mates or competitors – may also be important. In species like Little Owl, where pairs exhibit year-round territoriality, the young owl will not be tolerated if it attempts to settle in an already established territory. Territory owners show a peak in defence behaviour during this period of dispersal and, as well as advertising ownership through their calls, they will actively chase juveniles and other non-territorial 'floaters' away (van Nieuwenhuyse *et al.*, 2008).

As with the two earlier phases of the dispersal process, settlement behaviour and timing is best understood through the use of radio-telemetry and satellite-tracking, since these provide the most complete picture of the movements made and how they relate to features on the ground. The limitations of these methods are centred on the small sample sizes that can be secured and this is why information gathered through bird ringing can be particularly useful. The large sample sizes that can be attained through the recovery of ringed birds enables the production of a more rounded picture of dispersal behaviour and settlement patterns. However, ring-recoveries fail to provide detail on what has happened between the ring being fitted and the bird being recovered.

When it comes to interpreting the movements revealed through the examination of ring-recoveries it is also worth bearing in mind that the circumstances under which the ringed bird is found may have a bearing on the representativeness of the movement made. Birds that are killed through collision with road traffic are more likely to be reported than those that die of starvation. Additionally, birds that are killed by road traffic may, following impact, be carried on the vehicle for some distance. I once followed a lorry that appeared to have collided with an owl for many miles before, having stopped at a set of traffic lights in the middle of a town, the lorry drove off leaving a dead Barn Owl in the middle of the road. Iain Taylor found that road-killed Barn Owls from his study population had travelled significantly further than those reported through other causes of mortality (Taylor, 1994). Taking transportation to an extreme, the finding of a dead British-ringed Barn Owl at an airbase in Afghanistan was thought to have involved the accidental transportation of a bird that had been roosting in a hanger here in Britain.

The pattern of recovery distances over the months following ringing as chicks provide an indication of how quickly birds reach the settlement phase. In the case of the Barn Owl, this appears to be within four months of leaving the nest. However, individual birds may settle more rapidly than this. Iain Taylor found that some of his Scottish birds settled into their future breeding sites within two months of fledging. One particular female was found at her future nest site within five weeks of fledging, roosting next to an established, though unpaired four-year-old male in a good quality habitat. The young female even occupied the nest chamber for a couple of weeks, but the pair did not breed until the following year. Where sample sizes are large enough similar explorations of the settlement phase and its timing can be made for our other owls. For other species, e.g. Eagle Owl – where there have been few recoveries of ringed nestlings, we have to look elsewhere if we are to build up a picture of settlement patterns. We know, for example, that the mean age of Spanish Eagle Owls at beginning the settlement phase is 395 days, having initiated dispersal at a mean age of 170 days (Delgado et al., 2010), but the extent to which a similar pattern might occur in the small but expanding British population remains to be seen. The use of satellite transmitters could be particularly useful if we are to establish dispersal patterns in British Eagle Owls.

The distance moved

The distance between the nest site where the chick was raised and the point of settlement is referred to as the 'natal dispersal distance'. This figure is widely used in demographic studies and is often derived from ring-recovery information. It can be more strictly defined as the distance between the natal site and that of the place of first breeding (Newton, 2008). Examination of ring-recovery information from British owls provides a rather limited picture of natal dispersal distances, largely because of the small number of birds ringed as

TABLE 10. Dispersal movements made by British owls, where known. Derived from recoveries of ringed birds (Wernham et al., 2002).

Species	Natal dispersal	Breeding dispersal
Barn Owl	12 km (0–103 km)	3 km (0–84 km)
Tawny Owl	4 km (0–29 km)	0 km (0–16 km)
Little Owl	7 km 0–92 km)	0 km (0–182 km)
Long-eared Owl	42 km (0–122 km)	Insufficient data
Short-eared Owl	Insufficient data	Insufficient data

FIG 83. Tawny Owls generally settle close to where they were born and less than 10 per cent of natal dispersal movements for British Tawny Owls exceed 20 km. (Steve Round)

chicks that have been recovered during the following breeding season. Only for Barn Owl and Tawny Owl are the sample sizes sufficient for a more robust examination (see Table 10).

The median natal dispersal distance of 12 km calculated for British Barn Owls is lower than that reported for populations elsewhere in Europe and certainly much lower than that seen in the American Barn Owl, where the median distance has been calculated to be 60 km (Marti, 1999). As we will see later in this chapter, dispersal movements made by young Barn Owls in continental Europe are characterised by years in which long-distance movements become more commonplace.

A median natal dispersal distance of just 4 km highlights that British Tawny Owl chicks generally settle and establish breeding territories close to their natal site; in fact, less than 10 per cent of natal dispersal movements made by British Tawny Owls exceed 20 km (Wernham *et al.*, 2002). Ringing data suggest that Little Owls also settle close to their natal site, something which may help to explain the pattern of Little Owl colonisation seen within Britain following its introduction.

Initial movements were incremental in nature, the species establishing clusters of nesting pairs following introduction and then expanding from these at a slow rate. More widely, a similar pattern can be seen across other European studies. Generally, only a few Little Owls disperse over distances exceeding 50 km, although Exo & Hennes (1980) found that nearly 9 per cent of the juvenile birds in their study settled more than 100 km away from the natal site. The longest movement made by a British Little Owl chick was 152 km. Occasional long-distance movements in excess of 200 km (as noted elsewhere in Europe) may give rise to unexpected records of vagrancy, including perhaps the handful of Little Owl records for Britain that pre-date the importation of individuals for release, together with records from Helgoland, Ireland and the far north of Scotland.

Our breeding Long-eared Owls appear to show less attachment to the natal area, with a median natal dispersal distance of 42 km calculated by Wernham *et al.* (2002), although this was based on just a dozen birds. Studies from elsewhere in the breeding range suggest that some Long-eared Owls (notably males) may settle somewhat closer to where they were born (Marks, 1985). In contrast, the opportunistic nature of Short-eared Owl populations would seem to indicate very low fidelity to the natal area, with young birds breeding for the first time at sites many hundreds of kilometres from where they were born. Although young Short-eared Owls are reported to remain near the breeding site for several weeks before departure, the median distance for recoveries made in the second month after ringing as chicks rises to 9 km and then to 61 km, 228 km, 418 km and 490 km in subsequent months. Despite the number of young Short-eared Owls that have been ringed, the preference for breeding in remote areas and the difficulties of catching breeding adults on territory mean that there are insufficient records to calculate median distance values for either natal dispersal or breeding dispersal. The use of wing-tags and satellite telemetry may prove particularly informative for this species. Satellite-tracking may also aid our understanding of Eagle Owl movements which is currently based on a handful of recoveries of ringed birds. Three of the four Eagle Owl chicks to have been recovered at the time of writing, out of 42 ringed in Britain, covered relatively large distances. Two of these movements fall within the period of natal dispersal – the other spanning a longer period – and both exceed 200 km.

Natal dispersal, food availability and competition

If one of the drivers behind dispersal away from the natal area is the prospect of increased competition for resources, then we might expect to discover correlations between food availability or population density within the natal area and the dispersal distance moved. As we shall see later in this chapter, food availability can also influence other aspects of owl movements, most notably contributing to nomadic or irruptive behaviours. Within the context of natal dispersal, however, it appears that the distance moved tends to be greater in those years when food supply declines sharply either during or soon after the rearing phase (Coles *et al.*, 2003). Additionally, Coles *et al.* (2003) found that vole abundance within their study area explained roughly a quarter of the variation in the time that young Tawny Owls remained within the natal area.

One of the features of Barn Owl movements within continental Europe is occasional years when there are pronounced long-distance movements of young birds away from their natal areas. The term *Wanderjahren* has been applied to these years, a number of which have been documented by researchers working across Europe (e.g. Schifferli, 1949; von Sauter, 1956; Laursen, 1997). Pronounced dispersal of young birds takes place during the summer and appears to be completed by late November; associated with this is an increase in mortality reports and ring-recoveries, suggesting a successful breeding season followed by a crash in Common Vole populations which forces young birds to move away over greater distances. Iain Taylor, pulling together information from different sources, suggested that young Barn Owls, fledged in years of high vole abundance, do not have to disperse far in order to find unoccupied areas containing abundant food. In years when vole populations are at a low, the young owls have to disperse that much farther. The *Wanderjahren* documented in 1990 by Laursen (1997) saw 39 birds recovered in Denmark that had been ringed as young in Germany and the Netherlands during the 1990 breeding season. While most had arrived from northern Germany

FIG 84. This particularly dark female Barn Owl was found breeding in Nottinghamshire; part of the natural variation in plumage colour or an indication that birds of the dark-breasted race *guttata* sometimes reach our shores? (Mike Toms)

a few were from nest sites located farther south. Many unringed individuals were also reported, including some of the white-breasted race *Tyto alba alba*, which had not been previously recorded in Denmark. At least 11 birds were reported from Sweden, where the Barn Owl population had previously gone extinct in 1984 and birds were also found in Finland and Norway. Single ringed birds from Germany and the Netherlands were also reported in Britain over the following winter, one of which – found dead – was mounted and sits in my study (Toms, 2002). Years of increased dispersal within continental Barn Owl populations might also explain the occasional reports of dark-breasted Barn Owls from parts of Britain and Ireland (see Chapter 7).

Population density may influence dispersal, although it can be difficult to disentangle its influence from that of food availability. For instance, Huffeldt *et al.* (2012) found that young Barn Owls from larger broods appeared to leave their natal area sooner than young from small broods. However, since brood size is related to food availability, it could simply be that young from larger broods were better fed and, therefore, in better condition to disperse at an earlier time.

Sex-related differences in dispersal movements

Small sample sizes and the difficulty in sexing the chicks of some owl species, makes it difficult to test for differences in the dispersal movements made by males and females. It is known, however, that (on average) female Eagle Owl chicks make longer natal dispersal movements than males, although the absolute difference between the two sexes is relatively small, even if statistically significant (Delgado *et al.*, 2010). A similar pattern is seen in Scottish Barn Owls, where a small but significant difference was found between males and females, again with female birds moving slightly farther than males (Taylor, 1994).

BREEDING DISPERSAL

While natal dispersal is the process by which a young bird moves from its natal site to where it will make its first breeding attempt, breeding dispersal is the term applied to movements made between successive breeding attempts. Related to this term is another, that of site fidelity, which describes the extent to which an individual remains faithful to a single breeding site or territory. Once an owl has found a suitable site at which to breed there are a number of factors that may, in the case of resident species, cause it to move to a new site in a subsequent year. Breeding failure is one of these, with birds that have failed more likely to move than those that have succeeded in a given season; another is mate loss. Young

FIG 85. Catching female Barn Owls as they emerge from a nest box about to be inspected enables the collection of valuable information and reduces the time that any young or eggs are left unattended. (Mike Toms)

birds may be more likely to move than older birds, perhaps because they are less experienced (and so more likely to fail), because they are unable to hold onto the territory (being of lower social rank) or because they move to take over a better quality territory that has become available to them.

Information on the movements made between breeding attempts comes mainly from detailed studies, where individual birds are radio-tracked or recaptured at the nest as a matter of course. Ring-recoveries provide some additional information but sample sizes are considerably smaller than those available for examination of natal dispersal. Many of the ringers who ring nestling owls do not make an effort to catch the adult birds, sometimes for fear of desertion. Providing that known sensitive periods during the breeding cycle (e.g. prior to clutch completion or when eggs are hatching) are avoided, then catching adults at the nest is generally considered to be safe. In fact, being able to catch a female Barn Owl on the nest often allows you to return the bird to the nest and to allow her to settle, without flying off and leaving the nest unattended. This is likely to reduce the risk of nest predation or eviction by another bird. Increasing numbers of ringers now catch adult Barn Owls at the nest, following efforts to promote the value of doing so (Toms, 1997).

Ring-recovery information supports the notion that Barn Owl, Little Owl and Tawny Owl are essentially sedentary once they have settled on a breeding territory (see Table 10), something that is reinforced by intensive local studies. Iain Taylor, working in Scotland, found that all but one of the 137 male Barn Owls that he caught in two successive years was occupying the same nest site. A similar pattern of site fidelity was seen in the females, with just seven of 150 females moving between the two years. Taylor's work also provides an insight as to why these few movements actually occurred. Six of the birds (the male and five of the females) moved following the loss of their mate, while two females moved having previously bred as the second female in relationships with bigamous males. Mate loss has been found to influence movement patterns in other owl species but, while we might see increased levels of movement following mate loss, birds may choose to remain within the existing territory because it represents a valuable resource. This is something that might be particularly relevant for species where both members of the pair take part in territorial advertisement and/or defence (e.g. Tawny Owl).

Movements between breeding attempts may also be driven by the abundance and/or reliability of small mammal prey populations, something that is particularly evident in nomadic species like Short-eared Owl, to which we will turn next. For sedentary species, like Barn Owl and Tawny Owl, however, the response to low prey populations is not to disperse elsewhere but to forego breeding and remain on the existing territory (see Chapter 3).

IRRUPTIONS, NOMADISM AND OTHER SEASONAL MOVEMENTS

While none of the owl species found breeding in Britain can be said to be truly migratory, there is clear evidence that our breeding populations of Long-eared Owls and Short-eared Owls are joined by winter visitors from further north. Whether individual birds joining us for the winter months undertake migrational movements every year or only move in response to particular conditions (e.g. food availability or climatic events) is unclear. However, counts made at bird observatories highlight that arrivals in some years are well in excess of those witnessed in others, something that would tend to support the hypothesis that these movements are made in response to external events whose influence varies between years (see Figure 86).

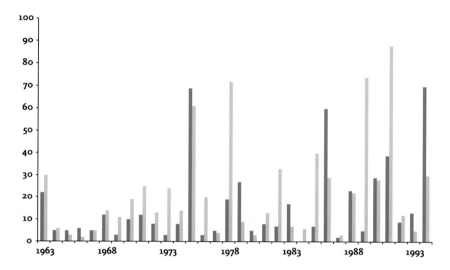

FIG 86. Numbers of Long-eared Owls arriving at Spurn (green) and Fair Isle (yellow) bird observatories.

Irruptive movements

Irruptive movements, triggered by food availability, have been demonstrated in a number of owl and other raptor species. These species tend to specialise on particular small mammal prey – notably voles and lemmings – whose own populations follow a cyclical pattern of abundance. Because the small mammal populations in question cycle over time, typically peaking every three to five years, and because these cycles are not synchronised over very large areas, the owls will vacate former breeding grounds as prey numbers fall, seeking out opportunities elsewhere. Both Short-eared Owl and Snowy Owl are known to respond to peaks in small mammal populations by breeding at very high densities (Goddard, 1935) and the Short-eared Owl is known to vacate large areas of tundra and boreal nesting habit if small mammal numbers here crash (Korpimäki & Norrdahl, 1991). A rather apt description for the movement patterns exhibited by Short-eared Owls comes from Géroudet (1965), who once noted that Short-eared Owls were 'nomads who camp where the table is laid'.

The occurrence of 'vole plagues' in Scotland, famously described by Adair (1892), provide a colourful picture of how Short-eared Owls respond to a sudden surge in prey numbers. These vole plagues appear to be a thing of the past within Britain. Once a feature of the coastal marshes of lowland England, they increasingly became restricted to parts of Scotland at the turn of the last century and, even here, are no longer seen at the scale that they once were. It would be incorrect to think of all Short-eared Owl populations as nomadic and there is good evidence to view some as being rather settled, supported by a regular and largely predictable food supply. Even so, the rapid increase in Short-eared Owl numbers following an increase in prey populations at sites within the UK does suggest that they may arrive from overseas if conditions are favourable here but poor elsewhere within the breeding range. As we have already discussed, movements of Short-eared Owl nestlings ringed in Britain show a greater degree of dispersal than is evident in our other breeding owls and chicks ringed here have been found during the following autumn and winter in Belgium, France, Morocco and the Faeroes, highlighting both the sizeable movements undertaken and the degree of variation in direction travelled (Robinson & Clark, 2012).

Winter arrivals

Northern populations of Short-eared Owls are strongly migratory, moving south with the approach of winter, and it is these birds that can be seen to arrive along the east coast of Britain during the autumn months, beginning in late August and

FIG 87. Many of our wintering Short-eared Owls are thought to arrive from overseas. (Mark Hancox)

peaking from mid-October through into November (Davenport, 1982). Ringing-recoveries reveal the origins of these individuals to include birds from Iceland, Norway, Sweden, Germany and the Low Countries.

Bird ringing studies indicate that most of the Long-eared Owls arriving to winter in Britain originate in Fennoscandia, with smaller numbers arriving from Eastern Europe and beyond into Russia. Variations in ringing effort between countries may influence this pattern, so some caution is needed when interpreting the origins of the birds wintering here. Movements appear to be undertaken at night; autumn arrivals on the British east coast are typically seen from dawn and extend through into late morning when birds may be noted coming in off the sea. Although many of these owls are likely to remain in Britain for the winter, some may push further south into France and Spain. One of the largest Long-eared Owl influxes took place in the autumn of 1975, with passage birds noted almost daily throughout late October and early November at some key coastal sites (Glue, 1976), and other peak years for this species include 1978, 1991 and 1993. There is a suggestion of an underlying cyclical pattern to winter arrivals of Long-eared Owls at mid-latitude locations within Europe. Harvey & Riddiford (1990), for example, noted a three- to four-year cycle to the arrivals on Fair Isle and Schmidt & Vauk (1981) recorded a similar pattern on Helgoland. Rob Williams (Williams, 1996) found that arrivals on the British east coast were correlated across widely separated sites.

Within some parts of the extensive breeding range the movements of Long-eared Owls demonstrate differential migration, the females wintering further south than the males. Evidence of this can be seen from the sex ratios of Long-eared Owls caught by bird ringers at Britain's network of coastal bird observatories. Harvey & Riddiford (1990), for example, found a ratio of 1:3.5 (males:females) in birds trapped at Fair Isle during the 1980s, while Williams (1996) produced a ratio of 1:4.6 from records collected at Landguard Bird Observatory in Suffolk. The pattern is repeated more widely within Britain, with ratios of 1:5.25 seen in birds found dead during the winter and submitted for post-mortem (Wyllie et al., 1996) and 1:7.5 evident from an analysis of museum skins (Williams, 1996). Sex ratios in the Netherlands, western Denmark and northern Germany match those seen in Britain (Erritzøe & Fuller, 1999). In contrast, a sex ratio strongly biased in favour of males is evident in Long-eared Owls wintering within southern Norway and ratios appear to approach parity in Sweden and eastern Denmark (Overskaug & Kristiansen, 1994).

A recent review of Short-eared Owl movements across Europe, drawing upon 330 ring-recoveries held in the EURING database, found a general trend for decreasing distances between ringing and recovery locations since at least the 1970s (Calladine et al., 2012). This trend, as the authors note, has coincided with marked reductions in the Short-eared Owl breeding populations formerly present along the North Sea coast and within the eastern half of continental Europe, and quite possibly within Britain itself, coupled with a possible dampening of the vole cycles that were once a feature across parts of the Short-eared Owl's range. The resulting lower population densities and reduced variability in prey populations could have lowered the level of intra-specific competition and reduced the need to move. Alongside this we have seen a general amelioration in winter weather conditions, which could also favour wintering further north than was previously possible.

Nomadic movements

The most nomadic of the British owls is undoubtedly the Snowy Owl, at least within a global context. The species has been shown through the use of satellite telemetry to cover vast distances along the coastlines of Arctic Russia, Canada and the USA (Fuller *et al.*, 2003), with females sometimes heading out onto the sea ice, crossing large expanses of ocean or even switching from the north coast of Alaska to the south. All of the tagged owls from this study frequented areas that they had visited previously, but evidence of any fidelity to previous breeding or wintering locations was missing. It appears that the movements of these stunning birds allow them to exploit food resources that occur for only a short while and in a patchy and unpredictable manner. Periodic invasions of Snowy Owls to the northeastern USA have been known for more than a century, with years of peak arrival occurring roughly every four years (Newton, 2002).

The Snowy Owl remains a scarce but almost annual visitor to northern Britain, with individuals often staying for prolonged periods at sites on the Western Isles, on Orkney or Shetland. Although the birds may be present at any time of the year, the pattern of new arrivals shows a clear spring peak (April to May) and it is widely assumed that these birds originate from the Arctic regions of Scandinavia or Russia. This assumption is supported by the recovery of an adult female, ringed in Hordaland, Norway, in April 1992 and found injured on North Uist just under two months later (BTO, pers. comm.). There was a period during the 1960s and 1970s when increased numbers of Snowy Owls were reported from Orkney and Shetland, resulting in a successful breeding attempt on Fetlar in 1967 (Tullach, 1968).

Other seasonal movements

As we have seen, the movements of our *Asio* owls and of Snowy Owl appear to be driven by food availability, highlighting the rather specialised nature of their diets and, in particular, their dependence on the availability of microtine rodents.

FIG 88. Some British Barn Owls are known to make altitudinal movements in winter to avoid the impact of poor weather conditions. Periods of prolonged snow cover may be a major problem for the species. (Mark Hancox)

Our other owl species have diets that are more varied overall and, therefore, more stable from one year to the next. Such stability may support a more sedentary lifestyle, with relatively short natal dispersal distances and a high degree of fidelity to breeding sites in future years. This may well be why we do not see large-scale movements in Little Owl, Tawny Owl or Barn Owl.

Interestingly, while Little Owl populations within Britain and most of Europe are considered to be sedentary, elsewhere within their breeding range they may undertake regular seasonal movements. In Kazakhstan, for example, they are considered to be nomadic, deserting parts of the range during the cold winter months to winter further south where conditions are, presumably, more favourable. The suggestion by Geoffrey Holroyd that some northern European Little Owls might be migrating to Spain and the Balearic Islands in autumn is unsubstantiated, and quite possibly incorrect, but does require further study (Holroyd & Frefry, 2011).

British Barn Owls are known to make altitudinal movements, abandoning elevationally marginal sites in the winter months for the more sheltered conditions of lowland marshes and valley bottoms. Even so, the indications from those monitoring Barn Owls within the UK are that poor winter weather sees the loss of birds from known sites rather than movements away and subsequent return. In contrast, there is evidence that some populations of the American Barn Owl migrate south during the autumn. Trapping and ringing studies at Cape May Point, New Jersey, have revealed a seasonal passage of American Barn Owls through the site, which separates Delaware Bay from the Atlantic and is known for its autumn migrants, in October and early November. In fact, the American Barn Owl is the third most commonly encountered owl at the site in autumn, behind Northern Saw-whet Owl and Long-eared Owl (Duffy & Kerlinger, 1992). The bulk of the American Barn Owls passing south are young birds (averaging c. 80 per cent) and these tend to peak slightly later than is the case with the adults. From what we have said of the link between diet and movement pattern, we might predict that more migratory populations of American Barn Owl show greater dependence on microtine rodent populations and a less diverse diet than is the case with populations living elsewhere.

SUMMARISING THE MOVEMENTS OF BRITISH OWLS

As we have seen from this chapter, our owls undertake a range of different movement patterns, from simple dispersal away from the nest to the complex processes that influence the arrival of visiting birds during the autumn. There remains a great deal still to discover, however, and new and emerging technologies are likely to play a key role over the coming years. Interchange between populations, sites and habitats is likely to influence breeding success and survival rates, not just here within Britain but over a wider area. As we will see in the next chapter, our owls face varied threats and we need to develop our understanding of their movements in order to underpin and evaluate conservation action directed towards these.

CHAPTER 5

Mortality

MORTALITY HAS PROVED TO BE one of the most challenging aspects of owl ecology to study. With only a fraction of dead birds ever found, even within intensive field studies, it becomes very difficult to quantify the levels of mortality experienced by different populations and to determine which mortality causes are the most important. Perhaps the biggest difficulty comes from the fact that the chances of a dead bird being found may be linked to how it has died. An adult owl that has died from starvation in a tree cavity roosting site is far less likely to be found than a young bird that has died from collision with a motor vehicle and lies in the open by the side of a road. Such biases can be seen in the recoveries of ringed owls from Britain, where those associated with road mortality dominate the returns for which the finding circumstances are known (see Figure 89). As we saw in the previous chapter, the cause of mortality may also bias our interpretation of other aspects of owl ecology, most notably dispersal movements, either because it biases the chances of the bird being recovered or because it actually transports the dead bird to a different location.

There have been few attempts to quantify the degree of bias that might be associated with particular causes of mortality. Iain Taylor, working on a population of Barn Owls in Scotland, made extensive efforts to recover all of the dead owls found within his study area. By carrying out systematic searches of known roosting sites, driving local roads and asking those out and about in the countryside to look for birds, Taylor was able to recover nearly one in five of the young birds raised within the study area. Of these, just over half were found dead by the side of a road and a further third were found dead at known roost sites. The pattern was different for the adult birds collected, with two-thirds found in an emaciated condition at known roost sites and just one in five found dead by a road (Taylor, 1994). This work demonstrates that, were you to only look at a single mortality cause, there is a real risk of misinterpreting its ecological importance for particular age or sex classes. Taylor recognised that even his

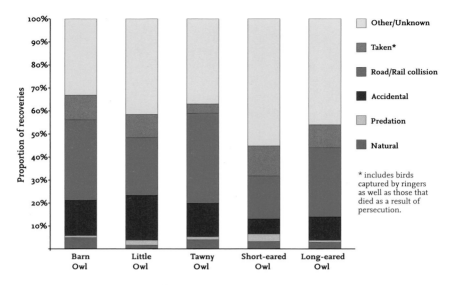

FIG 89. Finding circumstances of ringed owls in Britain, grouped into broad categories.

intensive study suffered from a degree of bias, in that young owls tended to roost in less predictable places than established adults, leading to the under-reporting of young birds that may have died from starvation.

Given that recoveries of ringed birds are the main means by which we currently estimate mortality rates, it is important to keep in mind the biases that might be associated with them. Even the assumption that such biases will remain constant over time is unlikely to be true, hindering the interpretation of temporal trends in mortality rates over longer periods of time. For example, an expanding road network, with increasing volumes of fast-moving traffic, is likely to both increase the number of owls killed on roads and the associated reporting rate, the latter also being biased by road type – observers are more likely to stop on a minor road to collect a dead owl than on a motorway, where stopping is illegal. With fewer people now working on the land, the reporting rate for owls found dead in barns or along field margins is likely to have fallen and one-off events, such as the 2001 Foot and Mouth outbreak, may limit the number of corpses reported during a particular period. Reporting rates may also vary spatially, from region to region or from country to country. Our understanding of the movements of migratory Short-eared Owls, for example, is almost certainly biased by spatial variation in both ringing effort and hunting pressure/persecution. More of our wintering Short-eared Owls may come from Russia than is apparent from ringing studies because ringing effort in Russia is considerably lower than it is in Scandinavia.

Studies using radio-telemetry may give a more representative understanding of the different mortality agents affecting owls but they suffer from the small sample sizes achievable and from the quantity of fieldwork required to deliver them. As we saw in the previous chapter, radio-tracking studies have tended to be used on young owls, dispersing away from their natal site, but they still provide useful information on mortality during what is an important but rather short window during their longer lives. Eick (2003), for example, was able to identify Goshawk, Red Fox and Sparrowhawk as three of the five predators that took radio-tracked Little Owls. Even with such technology it can sometimes prove difficult to establish the ultimate cause of death and some mortality agents may go undetected.

Chick mortality

The asynchronous hatching that we discussed in Chapter 3 has a major role in shaping the nature of chick mortality within the nest. Levels of mortality may be linked to food availability, being greater in years of prey shortage. Iain Taylor's work on Barn Owls in Scotland, which showed levels of chick mortality ranging from 5 per cent in years of peak vole abundance to 45 per cent in years of low vole abundance, highlighted that most of the mortality fell on the youngest chicks. Baudvin, working in France, found a similar pattern, with 80 per cent of chick mortality falling on the last or second last chicks to have hatched (Baudvin, 1978).

The age at which Barn Owl chicks die also shows an interesting pattern. In those years when vole numbers are low, the mortality can be seen across the entire period that the chicks are in the nest, with some birds on the point of fledging even succumbing. Most of the mortality, however, occurs during the first three weeks after hatching. In years when voles are abundant, the majority of mortality happens within the first ten days and very few chicks older than three weeks of age go on to die in the nest.

Mortality of Little Owl chicks also appears to fall disproportionately on the youngest chicks and during the initial days after hatching. A study in northwest England, involving the monitoring of 15 Little Owl nest boxes over an eight-year period (Leigh, 2001), calculated chick mortality to be 4.5 per cent, with 90 per cent of this mortality happening within five days of hatching. Chicks either died from starvation, chilling or, possibly, predation by siblings (cainism). Leigh observed that chick mortality was highest in those years when prey availability was low but research carried out elsewhere suggests that poor weather conditions might also exert an influence. Adult Little Owls, hunting surface-active earthworms under wet conditions, often return to the nest with wet plumage. If this moisture transfers to the young chicks then they may chill and die. Work elsewhere in Europe has underlined the impact of poor weather on chick mortality in Little Owls; Lederer & Kämpfer-Lavenstein (1996) found that high rainfall amounts in May and June were correlated with high levels of chick mortality and reduced fledging success. It is worth just emphasising that Roy Leigh's results, notably the very low mortality rate for chicks at the nest, may not present a typical picture of the pattern of chick mortality more widely.

David Glue and Derick Scott's examination of BTO Nest Record Scheme data revealed that, of 156 Little Owl clutches initiated, 28 per cent failed during laying and a further 26 per cent failed after clutch completion but before chicks fledged from the nest. The authors also found that losses of entire broods were not infrequent, although 46 per cent of pairs raised one or more young to fledging (Glue & Scott, 1980). A German study (Zens, 2005), involving a much bigger sample of 412 Little Owl broods, produced a mortality rate (across both eggs and chicks) of 49.9 per cent (Roy Leigh's combined figure was 17 per cent), which was composed 27 per cent eggs and 73 per cent chicks. Predation at the nest was clearly a major contributory factor for egg and chick losses in this German study. On the Continent the Beech Marten is an important predator. Being a generalist predator and an agile climber, the Beech Marten is able to access many Little Owl nest sites, including nest boxes. This problem has been addressed by some researchers through the use of anti-predator devices, fitted to the nest box. In one study the predation rate fell from 9.45 per cent to zero following the addition of these devices (van Nieuwenhuyse et al., 2008). Work on Tawny Owls in Scandinavia over a 14-year period revealed that 91 per cent of 300 breeding attempts that reached the chick stage resulted in one or more young fledging successfully (Karell et al., 2009).

A number of mammalian predators of Little Owl chicks and eggs have been identified within Britain, including: Hedgehog, Common Rat, Stoat, Red Fox, feral cat and domestic dog (Glue, 1971; Glue & Scott, 1980), with other failures linked to starvation, weather events or disturbance. Owl chicks may also die from starvation or be taken by predators, having fallen from the nest site. This may be a particular problem for some types of nest site – for example, certain designs of Barn Owl nest box. Concerns over the risk of young Barn Owls falling from the nest box has prompted the Barn Owl Trust to develop deeper boxes from which the chicks can emerge only when able to fly (Barn Owl Trust, 2012).

We have seen that mortality may fall disproportionately on particular chicks, either because of their age or because of their position within the brood. There is a suggestion that, under certain circumstances, it might also fall disproportionately on one sex over the other. In owls, the female is the larger of the two sexes and this implies that a female chick will require more resources than a male one. In seasons where food is less abundant it might pay to invest more in male chicks because by doing so would increase the chances of successfully fledging at least one offspring. There is some evidence to support this for Tawny Owls, where low quality parents with small broods have been found with a male-biased sex ratio. In broods where all of the nestlings raised by high quality parents, a female-biased sex ratio was found among the young hatched (Sasvári et al., 2010).

Adult mortality

The patterns of mortality seen in immature and adult owls vary between species and with season. Some mortality agents act on particular components of the population or only operate at certain times of the year. David Glue, in his review of seasonal mortality in four small birds of prey, found that adult Barn Owl mortality peaked between December and April, while that for adult Little Owls peaked in May and June, when most birds were either incubating eggs or feeding young. Peak mortality for Tawny Owls was March and April (Glue, 1973b). Glue

FIG 90. Collision with motor vehicles is thought to be a major cause of mortality in young Barn Owls. (Mike Toms)

found different patterns when he looked at immature birds, patterns that largely centred on the timing of fledging and the period of subsequent dispersal.

Human-related mortality agents dominate the findings of most of the mortality studies carried out in Britain and Ireland. This is particularly evident for those that draw on the recovery of ringed birds, where roughly three-quarters of the recoveries for which cause of death is known can be linked to agents such as collision with road traffic, deliberate persecution and poisoning (see Figure 89). Although less is known about 'natural' mortality agents, for example predation, starvation and disease, these are likely to play an important role in population limitation and we need to develop methods that enable us to study their impacts more effectively.

A number of studies have examined the mortality patterns of owls that have either been released following rehabilitation or as part of captive-breeding and release programmes (Fajardo *et al.*, 2000). Naïve birds, released into the wild, often suffer higher levels of initial mortality, with starvation an important cause of post-release mortality.

COLLISION WITH MOTOR VEHICLES

Collision with motor vehicles is the most commonly reported cause of mortality for British owls, a pattern repeated in many other European countries and one that highlights our dependence upon ring-recoveries to generate information on mortality. As we have already noted, birds killed on roads are more likely to be found and reported than those dying elsewhere, biasing our understanding of the relative importance of this particular mortality agent. Undoubtedly, however, collision with motor vehicles is an important cause of death for several of our owl species and it may be *the* most important agent for some populations. Ramsden (2003), for example, found that the construction of a new 22 km section of dual carriageway in south-west England resulted in the loss of Barn Owls from all of the previously well-used roost sites within 500 m of the new road. Similarly, Shawyer & Dixon (1999) attributed the 'great scarcity' of breeding Barn Owls within 2.5 km of a 50 km stretch of the A303, an area that was otherwise suitable for the species, to the high levels of road mortality that they witnessed. Both of these studies suggest that Barn Owls may be unable to maintain breeding populations within the vicinity of major roads. Perhaps the most compelling evidence for such an effect comes from recent Canadian work, carried out in the Fraser Valley, British Columbia (Hindmarch *et al.*, 2012). This study, which examined the influence of landscape features on the continued presence of

American Barn Owls at known sites, found that the only landscape variables to consistently predict continued site use were changes in traffic volume and the length of highway present within a 1 km radius of the roosting or nesting site. The probability that a site remained occupied was approximately 90 per cent if there had been little or no change in traffic exposure over the study period but this dropped to 60 per cent for sites with the largest increases in traffic exposure.

Thanks to a wide range of studies, both here, elsewhere in Europe and in North America, we now have a good understanding of road mortality in owls and how it varies with species, season and age-class. We also know how it is influenced by the nature of the road and its surrounding landscape. Owls may be hit by traffic either when they cross a road, when they rise up from its surface or when they are pulled in by the backdraft of a passing lorry. Consequently, different species may be susceptible for different reasons (e.g. Short-eared Owls hunting on the wing and crossing a road or Little Owls feeding on large beetles taken from the road surface). Birds that have been in collision with a motor vehicle tend to show the bruising and broken bones characteristic of trauma, both of which are evident on post-mortem. Post-mortem examinations of road-casualty owls, such as those carried out by Newton et al. (1991), also allow a more detailed examination of road mortality patterns in relation to sex and body condition. Overall levels of road mortality, as suggested by the recovery of ringed birds or the submission of carcasses for post-mortem study (e.g. Newton et al., 1991; Barn Owl Trust, 2012) put road casualties at between 40–50 per cent of all deaths reported through established monitoring schemes.

Because studies of road mortality vary in the length of road examined and the time period covered, you will often find the number of casualties reported as deaths per 100 km stretch per year. Expressed in this manner it is also possible to make comparisons between different owl species. Few such figures are available for British owl populations but with more figures published from elsewhere in Europe it is possible to form a picture of the numbers of owls likely to be killed on British roads. British studies do, however, reveal that the Barn Owl is the most frequent victim of collision with motor vehicles; Shawyer & Dixon (1999) recorded 102 dead Barn Owls in their study of a 50-km stretch of the A303 in southern England, equivalent to 68 deaths/100 km/per year and comprised of 67 per cent immature and 33 per cent adult birds. This pattern is repeated elsewhere in Europe where, additionally, the Little Owl is thought to suffer from high levels of road mortality.

Two peaks in owl–vehicle collisions are evident from ring-recovery and other data, one in late autumn and a second in late winter. While the autumn peak corresponds with the time when young owls are moving away from their

FIG 91. European research suggests that Little Owls may suffer from high levels of road mortality. (John Harding)

natal sites, the late winter peak may reflect birds having to extend their foraging ranges to find food. In Barn Owl, road casualties from late autumn (August to November) are dominated by immatures (e.g. Newton *et al.*, 1991; Shawyer & Dixon, 1999). Road deaths in most European Little Owl studies, including Britain, show a peak in July–August, again suggesting a link with post-fledging dispersal and supported by the dominance of young birds (Hernandez, 1988; Bultot *et al.*, 2001). Massemin *et al.* (1998), looking at Barn Owl casualties on French motorways, derived a figure for this period of 84 per cent, based on dissection and examination of the bursa of Fabricius (the nature of which can be used to age birds through into early spring). Massemin and his co-workers found that percentage of immatures then fell to 46 per cent in early winter and 35 per cent in late winter. Interestingly, throughout the year as a whole, immature females were the most frequently encountered casualties, followed by mature females, immature males and then mature males. This may reflect the tendency for immature females to disperse further than immature males, placing them at greater risk of encountering a road. An examination of mortality causes in British Long-eared Owls (Wyllie *et al.*, 1996) revealed a late-winter peak in traffic collisions, matching similar findings from Denmark and Germany (Erritzøe,

1999). It may be that late winter is a particularly difficult time for Long-eared Owls – there is some evidence that they increasingly turn from small mammals to birds at this time of the year – or it may indicate the presence of larger numbers of immigrants moving around and seeking suitable prey-rich habitats.

Factors linked with owl–vehicle collisions

As is the case with other avian families, owl collisions with motor vehicles are not random occurrences. Instead they show a pattern of spatial clustering, something that has enabled researchers to examine the extent to which particular landscape features (verge characteristics and the nature of surrounding habitat) and road-related factors (e.g. traffic volume and traffic speed) play their part in the risk of collision (Gunson *et al.*, 2010).

Traffic speed and volume

Within Britain, the proportion of finding circumstances for ringed owls attributable to road mortality has increased with time (see Figure 92). In Barn Owl, for example, 6 per cent of ring-recoveries collected over the period 1910–54 were of birds found dead on a road, this figure rising then to 15 per cent for the period 1955–69 (Glue, 1971). Newton *et al.* (1991), looking at the period 1963–89, derived a figure of 42 per cent from birds submitted for post-mortem examination through

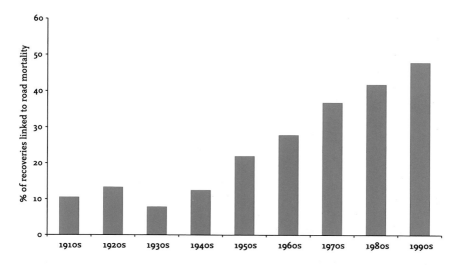

FIG 92. Proportion of ring-recoveries of British owls attributable to collision with road traffic, summarised by decade (1911–99). (BTO)

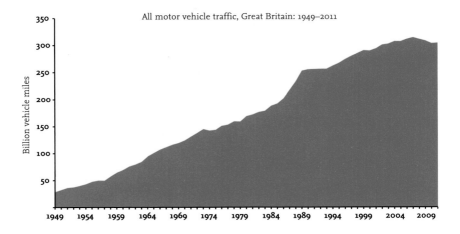

FIG 93. As the volume of road traffic has increased, so the number of miles driven annually in Britain has also increased. (National Road Traffic Survey, Department for Transport)

the Predatory Bird Monitoring Scheme operated by the Institute for Terrestrial Ecology (now the Centre for Ecology and Hydrology). We have seen a significant increase in traffic volume and the size of the road network over the last hundred years, something that is likely to have brought more of our owls into contact with road traffic. Data from the Department for Transport's National Road Traffic Survey show that the total vehicle miles driven within Great Britain has increased from 28.9 billion in 1949 to 303.8 billion in 2011 (Figure 93). Private cars account for the bulk of this change, with periods of particular growth in car ownership falling within 1953–71 and 1984–89. Traffic speeds have also changed over time, often in tandem with expansion of the road network and the opening of new dual carriageways and motorways. Since the first motorway opened in 1959 we have seen our motorway network expand to cover some 2,705 miles and it now carries nearly 62 billion miles of vehicle journeys annually.

Illner (1991b) found highly significant differences between the mortality rates recorded for Barn Owl and Little Owl on roads where traffic speeds were regularly in excess of 50 miles per hour and those where speeds were lower. While traffic speed is likely to have an important role in collision risk – it is more difficult for a bird to take avoiding action when faced with a vehicle moving at high rather than low speed – it is important to understand that high-speed roads, like motorways and dual carriageways, are likely to have different verge and boundary characteristics from other road types, something which may confound any attempt to isolate the effects of traffic speed from other factors. What little comparative information is available does, however, demonstrate different levels of mortality on different types of road. Figures produced by David Ramsden (2003) indicate that Barn Owl mortality rates on country lanes of <0.01 deaths/100 km/year are substantially lower than those for A/B roads (0.2 deaths/100 km/year) and dual carriageways and motorways (3.6 deaths/100 km/year). The same study also collected information on live sightings, revealing that Barn Owls encountered on major roads were three times more likely to be reported dead than alive, while those encountered on minor roads were 57 times more likely to be encountered alive than dead.

Interestingly, the seasonal pattern of Barn Owl mortality noted by Massemin *et al.* (1998) – see above – was found to correlate best with the seasonal difference between sunset time and peak traffic, rather than with total traffic volume. This suggests that it is the timings of when peak volumes of traffic are on the road that are more important than traffic volume per se. As the autumn nights begin to draw in there will be a greater degree of overlap between the initiation of owl foraging activity and the volume of traffic on the road, making collisions more likely. Couple this with a period of dispersal of young birds and you begin to see the potential for a problem.

Verge and boundary characteristics

The nature of the verge or boundary running alongside a road can exert a significant influence on the risk that it poses to owls. A rural lane in a county like Devon, often sunken and with high hedgerows and no verge, is unlikely to pose much of a risk to a hunting Barn Owl, which is forced up and over the road when crossing from one side to the other. In contrast, a fast fenland road in Cambridgeshire, typically raised above the surrounding landscape and bordered by sloping grassy verges and ditches, not only places a passing owl at car level but may actually attract a hunting bird by virtue of the small mammal populations that the verge supports. Massemin & Zorn (1998), working in north-western France, found the highest levels of Barn Owl mortality along raised (embanked) sections of road, lacking hedgerows and passing through open arable landscapes. Hugues Baudvin, also working in France, found a similar pattern for both Barn Owl and Long-eared Owl (Baudvin, 1997). In addition, he also found that sunken stretches of road produced significantly fewer casualties, something underlined by the work of Peter Pons, who revealed that the relative probability of collision (across all birds, not just owls) increased as bank height decreased (Pons, 2000). The open, flat landscapes of parts of East Anglia, well-used by Barn Owls and

wintering Short-eared Owls, are known for owl road casualties. For example, an
8 km stretch of the A47, passing through Halvergate Marshes, yielded at least 15
Short-eared Owl victims during the winter of 1982/83 (Harding, 1986).

There has been some discussion of the influence of verge width on collision
risk, in part stemming from the findings of Shawyer & Dixon (1999) and their
subsequent interpretation by other authors. Verge width might influence how
close a hunting owl is to passing cars but it is also likely to be related to other
factors, such as management and habitat type. Verge width has been found to be
an important predictor of verge use by diurnal raptors and the same may be the
case for owls (Meunier *et al.*, 2000). Management of the verge may be of particular
importance. For example, a grass-dominated verge, allowed to develop a thick
sward structure, will suit *Microtus* voles and, as a consequence, attract vole-eating
owls and other birds of prey. Baudvin (1997) noted that owls were sometimes
attracted to roadside verges in his study area by the presence of small mammal
prey and Bourquin (1983), working on a 37-km section of the Geneva–Lausanne
highway, blamed high vole densities and the presence of suitable perches for
the high levels of owl and raptor mortality he encountered. Common Vole
densities at his site were estimated at 250–400/ha during the winter months and

FIG 94. The nature of any roadside verges, the height of the road in relation to surrounding
habitat and other boundary features may all influence the risk posed to local owls. (Mike Toms)

were, most likely, even higher during late summer. It is not just Bourquin who has implicated the presence of roadside fenceposts as a contributory factor in mortality events. During the winter months a number of owl and raptor species will use fenceposts as perches from which to hunt small mammal prey. This is thought to be an energetically efficient strategy for the birds, particularly during the demanding winter months, so an area of rough grassland with fenceposts may prove especially attractive to a hunting owl.

Habitat mapping of the roadside verges in Shawyer & Dixon's study of the A303 suggested that nearly two-thirds of the linear verge length provided rough-grassland suitable for Field Voles and for use by hunting Barn Owls. Road mortality incidents for 70 per cent of the owls were found to have occurred at the interface between this rough grassland and tree or shrub belts, the latter features perhaps diverting the owls from their line of flight and out into the road itself.

Finally, it is possible that the degree of illumination along a road may influence collision risk. Mauro Hernandez found that the presence of illumination, in the form of street lighting, decreased the level of road mortality in a Little Owl population (Hernandez, 1988). However, this effect may have been confounded by the presence of other variables, perhaps correlated with the degree of illumination (e.g. habitat type). Hernandez suggested that bright headlights in an otherwise dark environment might produce temporary blindness in a hunting owl, much as in the same manner that powerful flashlights are used by bird ringers to dazzle and capture waders and other birds at night.

The influence of the wider landscape

The spatial clustering of owl–traffic collisions along particular sections of road is a feature of most studies, a pattern repeated for many other vertebrate families (Gunson et al., 2010). This suggests that wider landscape features may also have a role to play, contributing to collisions by bringing individuals into contact with the road or its immediate surroundings. Shawyer & Dixon (1999) found this to be the case for Barn Owls on the A303, and other British studies have found similar clustering in their results (e.g. Dunthorn & Errington, 1964). The lack of such clustering in some British studies (e.g. Ramsden, 2003) might be because these studies used casual reporting rather than systematic searches of a section of the road network. Shawyer & Dixon (1999) suggested that collision hotspots were linked to areas where grassy corridors associated with stream, river and ditch banks bisected the road. Tawny Owl traffic collisions in Iberia have been linked to hotspots where roads bisect high quality woodland habitats, with young Tawny Owls being killed during the period of dispersal as the young move through

FIG 95. The presence of suitable perches may increase the attractiveness of roadside verges to a hunting owl, increasing the risk of subsequent collision with a motor vehicle. (John Harding)

increasingly fragmented blocks of favoured habitat (Pereira *et al.*, 2011). In north-eastern France, Long-eared Owls and Barn Owls were found dead more often on sections of road bordered by arable fields than the availability of this habitat would suggest had collisions occurred randomly with respect to surrounding habitat (Baudvin, 1997). Work in Portugal also highlights the association of Barn Owl collisions with grassland habitats of the sort likely to hold sizeable populations of *Microtus* voles (Gomes *et al.*, 2009). The same study associated Little Owl collision hotspots with areas holding low densities of trees, such as olive orchards.

Is road mortality the ultimate cause of death?

It has been suggested by some authors (e.g. Taylor, 1994) that while some road traffic victims are within the normal weight range for a healthy individual of the species, many (or most) are in poor condition, suggesting that low condition birds might be more susceptible to collisions. It has been argued that such individuals may be less able to take avoiding action when faced with a motor vehicle or that they are forced to hunt along roadside verges or to spend more time hunting. Iain Taylor compared the weights of Barn Owl collision victims with those of adult birds caught during the winter months in his study area, finding the weights of road killed birds to be intermediate between those of healthy adults and birds that were known to have died from starvation. In contrast, other studies have found that road casualties are not necessarily different from other individuals. Massemin *et al.* (1998) found that the body masses of dead immatures (after stomach contents had been removed) were not significantly different from captive Barn Owls during the autumn dispersal period. There was one exception to this pattern and that was the finding that immature females killed on roads were lighter (by about 8 per cent) than comparative captive birds. In adult birds it was different; mature females killed by collisions were lighter than their captive counterparts at each period throughout the autumn and winter, while mature males were significantly lighter only in late winter. Low body mass is a reported feature of non-breeding female birds of prey during the early breeding period, perhaps suggesting that at least some road-killed owls were unpaired birds searching for a suitable territory, perhaps following the loss of their partner during the winter.

In addition to the possibility that poor body condition may make birds more susceptible to road mortality, it is worth noting that many road casualty Barn Owls have been found to have detectable levels of Second Generation rodenticides in their bodies upon post-mortem examination, including some birds for which residue levels were sufficient to suggest that, were it not for the collision, they would have died of poisoning (Newton *et al.*, 1991). We know very little about the sub-lethal effects of these compounds in owls and it is possible that their presence may inhibit an owl's ability to hunt effectively or avoid road traffic. More work is clearly needed in this area.

Impacts of road mortality at the population level

Attempts have been made to estimate the impact of road mortality on owl populations, both locally and at the national level. David Ramsden, for example, has used Shawyer & Dixon's (1999) figure of 68 Barn Owl deaths/100 km/year to estimate the total number of birds killed each year on Britain's roads at just under 7,000 individuals. This is not that dissimilar to Shawyer's (1987) estimate of 3,000–5,000 individuals, produced at a time when the Barn Owl population was almost certainly smaller than it is today. Shawyer & Dixon calculated that 17 per cent of adult and 24 per cent of juvenile Barn Owls are likely to be lost to road mortality each year. Illner (1991b) examined how road deaths related to the known breeding populations of owls living within his 125 km² study area in Germany, calculating that 6.5 per cent of adult Barn Owls, 4 per cent of adult Little Owls, 1.5 per cent of adult Long-eared Owls and 1 per cent of adult Tawny Owls were killed annually. The figures for young birds during dispersal would have been considerably greater. Both Long-eared Owls and Short-eared Owls probably face similar risks when hunting to those seen in Barn Owls, although the overall levels of mortality are likely to be lower because these birds occur at lower densities and tend to use more remote habitats. There may, however, be problems at certain sites, for example where roads pass through an area of coastal marsh, wet fen or young conifer plantation.

Work on the American Barn Owl has taken examination of road mortality one stage further through the development of life history models. From these Moore & Mangel (1996) predicted that when road traffic collisions account for 27 per cent of first-year mortality, or 48 per cent of adult mortality, then the population growth rate would fall below one and the population would begin to decline. Shawyer & Dixon's estimated figure for juvenile Barn Owls, of 24 per cent, might indicate that road mortality is having an impact on the British Barn Owl population. Certainly, more efforts should be focussed to derive a robust measure of the contribution of road mortality on this species within Britain and to establish any potential role in population change.

It is also worth keeping in mind that it is not just through direct mortality that roads may impact on owl populations. Roads may cause birds to modify their behaviour or may, perhaps, even act as barriers, isolating populations and increasing local extinction risk. Little Owls have, for example, been shown to reduce roadside hunting activity when the volume of road traffic is high (Fajardo *et al.*, 1998), a pattern also suggested by Shawyer & Dixon's study of English Barn Owls. Importantly, roads have been shown to influence habitat quality in surrounding areas, the road's 'footprint' sometimes extending several kilometres out from the road itself (Forman, 2000). Where a network of roads occurs within a landscape, the net result may be one of saturation, such that there are few potential territories that remain unaffected by the presence of a road. The high road densities evident in some parts of Britain may fragment suitable owl breeding and foraging habitat to the extent that populations are limited by the level of road mortality that results.

COLLISIONS WITH RAIL TRAFFIC

Very few records of owls killed in collision with trains are to be found in the databases associated with national ringing schemes. Such paucity of records is a consequence of a much reduced level of reporting for birds killed in this manner. Unlike our road network, railways are inaccessible and there is little or no opportunity to undertake regular searches of the kind needed to calculate mortality

FIG 96. The scale of owl mortality associated with railways is unknown but may be important for some species in certain areas. (Mike Toms)

rates. K. G. Spencer collated a number of reports from three different sources and concerning 116 birds that were identifiable. Among these were 27 Tawny Owls, 12 Barn Owls and one each of Long-eared Owl and Little Owl. A letter printed in the February 1965 issue of *Rail News* elicited a handful of responses, all of which suggested a regrettably high level of avian mortality on the railways (Spencer, 1965).

During the mid-1990s, while running Project Barn Owl, I was contacted by a train driver who shared a simple list of the collisions he had with owls while serving on railways around Norfolk and Suffolk. Over a period of several years he collided with many dozen owls, including Barn Owl, Long-eared Owl and Short-eared Owl, with the greatest number of incidents coming from those lines that ran across the relatively flat and exposed parts of eastern Norfolk around the Broads and the coastal marshes. The terrain along the railways themselves may provide suitable hunting habitat for owls and other birds of prey and it is likely that we have greatly underestimated the numbers of owls killed by rail traffic annually. Perhaps the earliest record of a collision with a train was of a Barn Owl which collided with the funnel of a locomotive running between Kelso and Roxborough in 1876 (Shawyer, 1998).

STARVATION

The impact that a run of adverse weather can have on some owl populations is perhaps best illustrated by the Barn Owl. This is a species whose breeding distribution within Britain appears to be limited by winter weather conditions; it is, after all, on the northern limit of its breeding range and it is also restricted altitudinally, with less than 7 per cent of the population thought to breed in excess of 150 m above sea level (Shawyer, 1987). Taylor (1994) puts the altitudinal limits of the breeding range in Britain at 250–300 m. Increased levels of mortality have been reported during periods of particularly poor weather within Britain (Ticehurst & Hartley, 1948; Dobinson & Richards, 1964) and the number of days of lying snow may be important, restricting access to favoured small mammal prey and either leading to starvation or a change in behaviour. John Nuttall, for example, observed an altitudinal shift in roosting location of a Lancashire Barn Owl during the 1968–69 winter. As the weather deteriorated over the New Year, the bird moved from its usual roost at 275 m above sea level to an agricultural building at 150 m. Even here, examination of the bird's pellets, suggested that it was struggling to find sufficient food. Barn Owls are able to catch Field Voles through light snow cover, but deep snow appears to prevent hunting. As we saw in Chapter 2, another behavioural change seen in Barn Owls during the winter

FIG 97. Heavy snow cover may have disastrous consequences for Barn Owls. (Mike Toms)

months is an increased use of post-hopping, the birds switching from active quartering to a sit and wait strategy.

Anecdotal evidence suggests that wild Barn Owls can tolerate seven or eight days of complete food deprivation during winter (Piechocki, 1960; Schönfeld *et al.*, 1977), something that is supported by laboratory work carried out in North America. Yves Handrich and colleagues carried out a detail examination of the effects of starvation on a series of captive Barn Owls, monitoring body weight and identifying metabolic changes evident from the composition of the birds' droppings (Handrich *et al.*, 1993). Three phases to starvation were identified, the second and third characterised by increasing mobilisation of lipid and protein reserves in the body. The findings of this work suggest that, for wild birds, rates of body mass loss could vary between 6–11 g per day. Allowing for the influence of sex, initial body conditions, behaviour and weather conditions, this provides an estimate for starvation tolerance of 3–15 days.

One interesting feature of some of the birds, coming in the latter stages of starvation and just prior to refeeding, was the production of black, bile-like droppings. The appearance of these droppings is similar to the bile-like substance found by Shawyer (1987) in some road casualty birds of low body weight. In one case Handrich found that a male, weighing just 212 g and which had produced such droppings, was unable to digest a mouse given during subsequent refeeding eight hours later. Although the bird ingested the mouse it was regurgitated intact ten hours later; the bird did manage, however, to digest a skinned mouse fed subsequently. This suggests that some wild birds at the limits of starvation tolerance may be able to hunt but have lost the ability to digest prey. David Ramsden has noted Barn Owls able to fly less than 24 hours before dying of starvation. Other characteristics of starvation victims presented at post-mortem include severe atrophy of the pectoral muscles, no visible intra-abdominal or subcutaneous fat and atrophy of liver and digestive system (Marti & Wagner, 1985). Esselink *et al.* (1995), looking at body condition in starved Barn Owls, suggested that fat reserves are only found when protein reserves exceed 15 per cent of body mass. Newton *et al.* (1991) define Barn Owl starvation victims as birds weighing less than 240 g (male) or 250 g (female) on post-mortem examination. Of 44 birds taken to the Barn Owl Trust for rehabilitation because they appeared to be underweight, with no other sign of injury/illness, the mean body weight was 257 g (range 180–307 g). Following rehydration and force-feeding, Barn Owls as light as 180 g have been successfully rehabilitated (Barn Owl Trust, 2012).

Cold winters with snow cover can also produce substantial losses in Little Owls, as was seen during the 1962–63 winter in England and in other years elsewhere in Europe (Dobinson & Richards, 1964). Severe winters, when a large number of Little Owls are lost, may result in a substantial decline in the breeding population the following year. Studies in Germany and France showed a decline of roughly one-third following a severe winter (van Nieuwenhuyse *et al.*, 2008). Our *Asio* owls appear better adapted to adverse winter weather than either Barn Owls or Little Owls because of a willingness to switch to other prey species, notably small passerines. Wintering *Asio* owls also appear to have an increased option to move away from the poor weather conditions. The suggestion that Barn Owls might carry smaller fat reserves than similarly sized owl species (notably Tawny Owl and Long-eared Owl) has been disproved by examination of birds killed by trauma (Massemin & Handrich, 1997). Barn Owls do, however, appear to have a higher metabolic rate than the other two species, something that might arise from a lower insulation efficiency (calculated from feather mass scaled to skin area). Barn Owls feet are unfeathered and the tarsi only sparsely feathered, another difference from both Long-eared Owl and Tawny Owl. Since Barn Owls are most strongly associated with tropical and sub-tropical habitats, those present in Britain at the northern limit of their range may be more vulnerable to the poor weather conditions that sometimes characterise the northern winter.

FIG 98. Winter snow can prove challenging for Little Owls and, in some circumstances, lead to a substantial decline in the breeding population the following year. (Mark Hancox)

Steve Percival, using BTO ringing data for Barn Owls, found that weather conditions explained 61 per cent of the variation in adult survival rates and 41 per cent of the variation in first-year survival rates. Adult Barn Owls' survival rates were particularly influenced by winter rain and low spring temperatures (Percival, 1990). A long-term study of the Swiss Barn Owl population, covering the period 1934–2002, revealed that snow cover explained 49 per cent of the variation in adult survival rate and 19 per cent in the juvenile rate (Altwegg *et al.*, 2006). Winters with long-lasting snow cover led to decreases in survival and catastrophic declines were noted following the severe winters of 1952–53 and 1962–63, when snow cover remained for 57 and 61 days respectively (Altwegg *et al.*, 2003, 2006). Interestingly, the same authors found that snow cover had no significant effect on brood size during the following season. Cold weather may have a greater impact on one sex than the other; in those owl species where the female is the larger sex, for example Tawny Owl, the female may be better able to survive a period of bad weather than her smaller mate, who cannot carry as much in the way of reserves.

Starvation is not just a feature of the winter months; it is also a reported cause of death for young owls in the nest (see Chapter 3) and during the period when young owls first gain independence. During a study of the fate of 101 fledgling

Barn Owls, the Barn Owl Trust found that half of the birds reported as starved were found within two months of leaving the nest, suggesting that they failed to become self-sufficient. This mortality represented c. 3 per cent of the total mortality for this cohort of fledglings.

PREDATION

In general, the available evidence supports the notion that owls sit at the top of the food chain and only rarely fall prey to other predators. However, as we have seen in Chapter 4, recently fledged young may be vulnerable to both avian and mammalian predators as they gain independence, something that may be a particular problem during the period before they are able to fly strongly. There is also a suggestion that predation of owls by other owl and raptor species may be more extensive than is evident from the current literature, because predation incidents tend to happen within the wider countryside where contact with the human population is much reduced (Sergio & Hiraldo, 2008). Fewer than one in 50 ring-recovery reports for British owls, for instance, refers to predation as the cause of death. A certain amount of information may be gleaned from published literature concerning the diets of potential predators, both from Britain and elsewhere. This highlights the potential for species like Goshawk and Buzzard to take owls as prey (Tubbs, 1974). There is also the potential for larger owls, notably Eagle Owl, to predate our smaller species.

Colin Shawyer, during his study of Barn Owl mortality, received four records of Goshawk taking Barn Owl, plus additional records involving Buzzard and a female Sparrowhawk. Populations of Goshawk and, to a lesser extent, Eagle Owl have increased in Britain over recent years and it is likely that these two species now exert a greater impact on our other owl species than previously, something which requires further study. For example, although there is relatively little evidence of Eagle Owls and Goshawks taking Long-eared Owls within Britain (Petty et al., 2003), the picture from elsewhere in Europe demonstrates that both are significant predators of this species in some parts of their overlapping breeding range. Heimo Mikkola cited 768 records of Eagle Owl and 317 of Goshawk taking Long-eared Owl, making this the most frequently predated owl in his literature-review of the interactions between different owl species. In a study of Long-eared Owls breeding in west Norfolk, Kemp (1981) failed to find any pairs within 1.5 km of breeding Goshawks, even though the habitat within such areas looked suitable. Mikkola (1983) also adds Tawny Owl and Ural Owl to the list of Long-eared Owl predators, although these last two species seem to be

FIG 99. Goshawks may take an increased number of owls when they have young of their own to feed. (Mike Toms)

very minor players. Nestling Long-eared Owls are taken by a range of predators, including Red Kite, Sparrowhawk, Common Buzzard, Magpie and Carrion Crow.

Tawny Owl joins the Long-eared Owl as a frequent victim of Goshawk and Eagle Owl predation, most likely a reflection of similar preferences for wooded habitats. In some areas the presence of nesting Eagle Owls has been shown to reduce the productivity of nesting Tawny Owls, a pattern that is exacerbated under high Eagle Owl densities (Sergio *et al.*, 2007). There are also records of Tawny Owls being taken by Ural Owls and a British record of a Tawny Owl feeding on another adult Tawny Owl, but whether this was a case of predation or scavenging is unclear (Dawson, 1997).

Five of the British owl species (Barn, Tawny, Little, Short-eared and Long-eared) have been reported as being taken by Peregrine Falcon here in Britain but they are very rare victims. Of the five, the Short-eared Owl is probably the most vulnerable, often hunting during the day and sharing the same open-country, upland habitats as used by breeding Peregrines. Ratcliffe (1993) notes how a Barn Owl pair that had the temerity to use a Peregrine crag quickly paid the price, the pale remains of one individual scattered below the eyrie. Although the remains of a Short-eared Owl have been found in the nest of a Hen Harrier, the two species usually co-exist and may be seen to tussle occasionally on their shared breeding areas (Watson, 1977). Short-eared Owl has also featured in the diet of Golden Eagle within Britain (Watson, 1997) and, more widely, in the diets of Eagle Owl, Snowy Owl, Rough-legged Buzzard *Buteo lagopus* and Gyrfalcon *Falco rusticolus* (Mikkola, 1976).

Barn Owls tend to feature in the diet of other avian predators less often than either Long-eared Owl or Short-eared Owl. This is likely to reflect their absence from the upland and well-wooded areas used by key predatory species, coupled with their largely nocturnal behaviour and cavity-nesting habits. In 2009, however, the Barn Owl Trust received a series of several reports involving Buzzards catching daytime active Barn Owls in flight, suggesting that these were inexperienced juveniles. You might expect nesting Barn Owls to be susceptible to mammalian predators but there are few recorded instances of adults taken at the nest. Shawyer (1998) implicates Mink *Mustela vison*, Stoat, Weasel and Common Rat in the predation of incubating or brooding Barn Owls nesting in vulnerable locations. Elsewhere in Europe, the Beech Marten may be an important predator of nesting Barn Owls. This mustelid will readily enter barns, outbuildings, churches and even the roof spaces of occupied dwellings, where it will take both owls and their eggs. Predation of Barn Owls by Beech Martens has been put forward as a possible reason for the decline in owl populations witnessed in some parts of Europe (Lanszki *et al.*, 2009) and may also explain why Barn Owl populations on the continent tend to nest much higher than those breeding here in Britain (Taylor, 1994).

Much has been written in the literature about interactions between Tawny Owls and Barn Owls and the possibility that Tawny Owls might occasionally take Barn Owls (e.g. Bunn *et al.*, 1982; Shawyer, 1998). While there is some circumstantial evidence for such predation within Britain, and a good number of instances of observed aggressive interactions between the two species, the handful of incidents where Barn Owls have been killed by Tawny Owls may relate more to competition for nest sites and a bird killed during such an encounter. Interestingly, Róbert Mátics investigated a series of cases where Tawny Owl chicks had been killed in the nest (Mátics, 2008). Although he did not see any direct interaction, the instances of killing only began after Barn Owls began to use the same nest boxes sequentially and the available evidence suggested that it was the Barn Owls that were responsible. The two species may, however, breed in close proximity to one another without incident where nesting opportunities are less limited; one of the first Barn Owl sites that I worked (in a hollow oak)

FIG 100. Barn Owls may sometimes be attacked and robbed of their prey by Kestrels. (Mark Hancox)

was just 22 feet away from an active Tawny Owl nest in the neighbouring tree. Both pairs successfully fledged young. Reports of intra-specific killing are also rare, although the increasing popularity of nest box cameras may lead to more incidents coming to light. Matthew Twigs of the Barn Owl Trust received a reliable report from a landowner using a camera at a Barn Owl box where what appeared to be an intruding male was killed by the resident bird.

Unsurprisingly, given its small size, the Little Owl features as an occasional prey item in the diets of more than a dozen different owl and raptor species, including: Eagle Owl, Tawny Owl, Barn Owl and Long-eared Owl (Glue, 1972). Among the diurnal avian predators are: Goshawk, Red Kite, Buzzard and Sparrowhawk, although, interestingly, there is a record of a Little Owl eating a freshly dead immature Sparrowhawk and two British records of the species raiding Kestrel nests to take the young (Mikkola, 1983).

Interactions with predators may not always be straightforward. A long-term study of Dutch Tawny Owls, Jackdaws (a nest competitor) and Goshawk (a predator of the other two species) found that Goshawks limited Jackdaw numbers, which led to an improvement in Tawny Owl breeding success. However, Tawny Owl recruitment was reduced because Goshawk predation during the post-fledging period also proved to be significant (Koning et al., 2009).

As we have seen, predation may not always be about securing food. Intraguild predation (predation within birds of prey and owls) may free up breeding territories, remove competition and reduce the risk of chick predation by other species. Fabrizio Sergio and Fernando Hiraldo, in their review of intraguild predation in owl and raptor assemblages, suggested that this is a widespread, predominantly sized-based phenomenon (Sergio & Hiraldo, 2008). They also highlighted the complexities surrounding such predation, additionally noting that predation events may differ in their ultimate cause because of varying external circumstances. For example, a decline in the abundance of favoured prey may see an increase in the number of instances of intraguild predation, but whether these are a response to the need to reduce competition for a declining resource or an attempt to secure a meal remains unclear.

POLLUTION

Owls, like other birds of prey, may be exposed to high levels of pollutants because of their position at the top of the food chain. Organochlorine pesticides, polychlorinated biphenyls (PCBs) and mercury are among a number of persistent lipophilic compounds that may 'bioaccumulate' or 'biomagnify' as they are passed up the food chain from one trophic level to another. Concentrations of these compounds tend to be low in herbivores, intermediate in insectivores and mesopredators (e.g. Little Owl) and high in top carnivores (e.g. Eagle Owl). Such compounds have been linked to reduced breeding success, increased levels of mortality and population decline (Newton et al., 1993). Levels vary with exposure and may also differ between individuals living within the same relatively small area. It has been shown that mercury levels in the feathers of Spanish Eagle Owls, which range from very low (0.03 mg/kg) to relatively high (12.80 mg/kg), are linked to diet, being greater in individuals involved in the predation of other top predators – a process known as superpredation – than in those feeding predominantly on favoured herbivores like Rabbit and Red-legged Partridge Alectoris rufa. Since Eagle Owls may switch to superpredation when the availability of favoured prey species is low, there is a potential increased risk from pollutants at a time when the population is already under stress (Lourenço et al., 2011).

Organochlorines and other pesticides

The impact of Dichlor-diphenyl-trichlor-ethane (DDT) on wildlife has been well documented (for a review see Newton, 1979). Like other organochlorine compounds, DDT was found to accumulate as you moved up the food chain. DDT was widely used as an insecticide following the end of the Second World War and it was soon joined by other compounds, such as the cyclodiene dieldrin, which was used as a seed dressing. As well as the evidence of direct mortality that was appearing in some species, many of these compounds also produced sub-lethal effects, the most famous of which is the eggshell-thinning associated with DDE, the metabolite of DDT (Ratcliffe, 1967). DDE has been shown to inhibit carbonic anhydrase, an enzyme required for normal shell formation.

Organochlorine residues have been found in various British owls, including Barn Owl, Tawny Owl, Long-eared Owl and Little Owl (Cramp, 1963; Cooke *et al.*, 1982; Newton *et al.*, 1991). They have also been found in these (and related) species elsewhere in the world. Klaas *et al.* (1988), for example, found DDE residues in all of the 18 clutches of American Barn Owl eggs collected at Chesapeake Bay in the early 1970s. Additionally, dieldrin was found in 78 per cent of the clutches and PCBs in 89 per cent. Klaas and colleagues also found that the eggshells were, on average, some 5 per cent thinner than those of eggs from collections unaffected by DDT. Experimental evidence for the effects of DDE on Barn Owl eggshells comes from the work of Vivian Mendenhall and colleagues, who fed a number of captive Barn Owls on both DDE and dieldrin (Mendenhall *et al.*, 1983). DDE was found to be associated with significant eggshell thinning, egg breakage

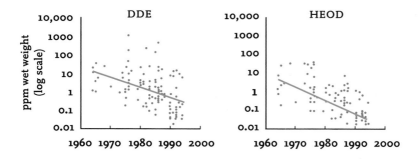

FIG 101. Trends in the residues of DDE (the main metabolite of the insecticide DDT) and HEOD (the active ingredient of dieldrin and aldrin) in Long-eared Owls found dead in Britain, 1963–95. (Redrawn from Wyllie *et al.*, 1996, with permission)

and embryo death, leading to reduced productivity, while dieldrin was linked with moderate eggshell thinning but no associated decline in productivity. The degree of eggshell thinning has been shown to vary between species, and across populations, but general patterns seem to suggest that species/populations in which thinning of 16–18 per cent occurs are likely to have shown a population decline (Newton, 1979).

Aldrin and dieldrin appear to have been a particular problem for Barn Owls in the arable regions of Britain over a period of several decades. In a study of Barn Owl mortality, using birds submitted for post-mortem examination over the period 1963–89, Ian Newton and his co-workers found nearly one in ten birds had died as a result of poisoning (Newton *et al.*, 1991). Every bird tested for the presence of organochlorines was found to have residues present, though mostly at sub-lethal levels. Most worryingly, pesticide victims made up nearly 40 per cent of all dead Barn Owls submitted from some eastern arable counties during the period 1963–77. Prey choice probably explains much of the regional differences in records of poisoned owls. Owls living within arable areas take a greater proportion of Wood Mice in their diet than those living in pastoral

FIG 102. Small mammals associated with stored seed, such as this House Mouse, may have provided a pathway for toxic chemicals to reach those Barn Owls living within arable landscapes. (Amy Lewis)

areas and with access to Field Voles. The Wood Mice, which will feed on drilled seed, provide a pathway from the toxic seed dressing to the owl that is absent in the herbivorous Field Voles. The absence of Field Voles from the Isle of Man and, again, a correspondingly greater reliance on Wood Mouse and Common Rat, could also explain the number of Barn Owl casualties linked to aldrin and dieldrin poisoning on the island (Newton et al., 1991). The link from seed dressing to owls via Wood Mice was confirmed by Jefferies & French (1970), who found an average of 10.18 ppm HEOD residue in Wood Mice trapped in a field two weeks after seed drilling. Mice trapped in a different field still contained 0.74 ppm some two months after drilling.

The levels of HEOD (a metabolite of aldrin and dieldrin) from Barn Owls diagnosed as aldrin/dieldrin victims reached 44 ppm (parts per million) and averaged 14.0 ppm. Aldrin and dieldrin remained in common agricultural use through into the mid-1970s after which their use became more restricted, falling to virtually zero by the mid-1980s. Barn Owls from the eastern counties tested for the period 1987–89 produced HEOD levels of less than 1.6 ppm (Newton et al., 1991). Ian Prestt, reviewing the changing breeding status of certain birds of prey and owls, concluded that it was likely that:

> ... for a period of 20 years or more aldrin–dieldrin may have reduced the Barn Owl population in much of eastern England below the level that the contemporary landscape could support. (Prestt, 1965)

Examination of organochlorine residues in Long-eared Owls also suggests elevated exposure in eastern areas during the period when these chemicals were in widespread use. Roughly a third of the Long-eared Owls examined between 1963 and 1977 as part of the Predatory Bird Monitoring Scheme had organochlorine residues sufficiently high as to suggest they were the cause of death; a large proportion of these birds came from eastern counties where arable dominated (Wyllie et al., 1996). Examination of a further 81 birds for the period 1981–95 revealed generally much lower levels of residue, a welcome sign, although two of the birds tested were likely to have died as a consequence of the levels they carried.

Veterinary antihelminitics

Antihelminitics are in widespread use for the control of parasitic worms in livestock. One of the best known is Ivermectin, a compound that has been shown to have detrimental effects on dung beetles and the Little Owls that predate them (Lumaret, 1993; van Nieuwenhuyse et al., 2008).

FIG 103. The use of the veterinary antihelminitic Ivermectin has been shown to have detrimental impacts on Little Owls. (Mark Hancox)

Polychlorinated biphenyls and other persistent organic pollutants
Polychlorinated biphenyls (PCBs) were widely used as coolants and dielectric fluids in electric motors, transformers and other equipment. Concerns over the toxicity of these compounds, including evidence that showed them to cause cancer in animals and humans, saw them banned in 2001 by the Stockholm Convention on Persistent Organic Pollutants. However, the persistence of these compounds in the environment, coupled with bioaccumulation, still finds them at detectable levels in birds of prey, including owls. It is known, for example, that PCBs constitute the main organohalogenated pollutants in the eggs of Little Owls in parts of continental Europe (Jaspers *et al.*, 2005). PCBs have been shown to pass from the soil into earthworms and, from these, reach the Little Owls that feed on them (van den Brinck *et al.*, 2003), something that has alarmed conservationists working on the species in the Rhine floodplain, an area where the legacy of industrial pollution may be a particular problem. Other compounds, such as dioxins, may also pose a risk to owls breeding in this area. Work in Belgium (Jaspers *et al.*, 2005), which looked at PCB levels in a sample of 40 deserted or addled Little Owl eggs, found concentrations that ranged from 786–23,204 ng/g lipid. Levels of pollutants were significantly higher in deserted eggs than those

that were addled. This may seem somewhat counter-intuitive at first glance, since you might predict that high concentrations would contribute to the failed development of an individual egg rather than to the chances of a parent bird deserting an entire clutch. Alarmingly, it is just possible that high levels of PCBs may increase the chances of a bird deserting a clutch, since work on Glaucous Gulls *Larus hyperboreus* (Bustnes *et al.*, 2011) has linked increased parental absence from the nest site with high levels of persistent organic pollutants in the blood.

Heavy metals
The widespread industrial use of compounds like lead and cadmium, coupled with their relatively low chemical reactivity, has seen heavy metal contamination of the environment and the organisms living within it. Biomagnification is, again, responsible for the accumulation of such compounds in owls and other top predators. Various studies, carried out across Europe, have revealed the presence of heavy metals in owls at levels that are typically well below the toxic thresholds that have been defined for each compound (e.g. Esselink *et al.*, 1995; Génot *et al.*,1995; Zaccaroni *et al.*, 2003). What remains unclear, however, are potential sub-lethal effects. Levels are often, but not always, greater in older individuals, suggesting accumulation with age (Zaccaroni *et al.*, 2003), and tend to be higher in areas of human activity. Larger owls, like Eagle Owl, have been found to contain higher mean concentrations than small owls, like Little Owl (Garcia-Fernández *et al.*, 1997). It has been suggested that Little Owls might be particularly susceptible to cadmium, which can reach them through contaminated earthworms. At the population level, work in the Netherlands found that the productivity of a Little Owl population living within an area contaminated by heavy metals was dramatically lower than a population from an uncontaminated area (Groen *et al.*, 2000).

Other pollutants
Many other pollutants are known to be present within the wider environment and some may affect owls. A few may be responsible for the death of the owl itself, perhaps a bird whose plumage has become coated in tar or a similar substance, while others occur at low levels within the body tissue. Environmentally derived fluoride, for example, has been detected in the bones of five owl species from birds collected in Britain and Ireland over the period 1976–82, but at lower concentrations than seen in diurnal birds of prey (Seel & Thomson, 1984). Variations in fluoride levels occurred between both species and individuals, suggesting that exposure is influenced by location and diet. Many pollutants are persistent in the environment and may pose a risk to owls over long periods of

time. Traces of the Chernobyl fallout occur at the measurable level in Barn Owls, Tawny Owls and Long-eared Owls found dead in eastern Poland more than two decades after the original release of radionuclides from the damaged reactor (Kitowski *et al.*, 2008; Mietelski *et al.*, 2008). The longevity of owls and their position at the top of the food chain allows them to be used as biomonitors for the impacts of pollutants within a wider ecosystem, something that can be seen through the Predatory Birds Monitoring Scheme already mentioned.

RODENTICIDES

For as long as humans have grown and harvested crops we have been faced with the problem of how to control the rodents that are attracted by piles of stored grain and the easy feeding opportunities that they offer. Although attempts to control troublesome rodents through the use of traps can be dated back to 3000 BC, widespread use of chemical rodent control is a modern phenomenon. Strychnine, first 'discovered' in 1818, appears to have been used in preparations used to kill birds and mammals since the 1600s in Europe and was followed by the introduction of thallium salts in the 1920s and, soon after, by zinc phosphide.

The 'First Generation' anticoagulant rodenticides
Following the Second World War and efforts to increase food production, we saw the development of new and more effective rodenticides. One of these was warfarin, a compound that inhibits the process by which blood clots form,

FIG 104. Resistance to warfarin in Common Rats led to the introduction of Second Generation anticoagulant rodenticides. (John Harding)

through disruption of certain vitamin K enzymes. Warfarin had the potential to be an effective rodenticide because it could be used safely (as far as humans were concerned) with a known antidote (vitamin K) and because it exhibited a chronic mode of action. This latter point was particularly important because it meant that symptoms would only become apparent several days after the ingestion of a lethal dose. Rats and mice are wary of new foods and will avoid returning to a food source that makes them feel unwell. By delaying noticeable symptoms the use of warfarin gets around this problem, the rodents returning to feed over several days before building up a lethal dose. Warfarin quickly became the rodenticide of choice. However, by 1958, reports of genetically acquired resistance within rats and mice were being received from across Britain (Hadler & Buckle, 1992).

The 'Second Generation' anticoagulant rodenticides
The spread of warfarin resistance prompted the development of new compounds, increasingly potent and, therefore, less likely to bring about resistance. The year 1975 saw the registration and introduction of difenacoum in the UK, the compound a thousand times more potent than warfarin and only requiring two days of feeding before a lethal load was ingested. This was followed by the UK registration of brodifacoum in 1978 and the French introduction of bromadiolone in the same year, the latter compound the result of a different area of research interest. Brodifacoum proved to be more potent than difenacoum, delivering a lethal dose through just a tiny fraction of a rat's daily food intake. Hadler & Buckle (1992) demonstrated that a 0.005 per cent brodifacoum bait would deliver an LD50 dose – the dose that will kill 50 per cent of the population to which the dose is applied – in only 1.3 g of bait (an adult Common Rat will typically consume 20–30 g of food each day). Importantly, these new compounds still demonstrated a delayed onset of action although this raised additional concerns over the possibility that they might enter the wider food chain and prove detrimental to owls and other wildlife. Concerns over overspill into non-target wildlife prompted experimentation and monitoring to establish potential risks.

A sub-lethal dose of warfarin is thought to be metabolised and excreted relatively quickly within the body, something that is supported by work carried out at the MAFF Tolworth Laboratory in the late 1970s (Townsend et al., 1981). Michael Townsend and his co-workers fed warfarin-treated mice to captive Tawny Owls, using a series of different treatments and residue levels. None of the owls died from warfarin poisoning but changes in the levels of plasma prothrombin underlined that the birds had undergone some form of biochemical response. Whether or not this response suggested any sub-lethal consequences was unclear but it could, potentially, have increased the risk to wild birds, which are more active. It is known, for example, that the susceptibility to anticoagulants can be exacerbated by changes in diet, increased activity, minor injury and stress (Mendenhall & Park, 1980).

Newton *et al.* (1990) carried out an experimental study to look at the effects of difenacoum and brodifacoum ingestion by Barn Owls. A number of owls were fed on mice that had been dosed with one or other of the two rodenticides, the owls receiving one-day, three-day or six-day treatments and regular monitoring. All of the owls that had been fed difenacoum-treated mice survived and none showed any signs of external bleeding. Only two of the six owls fed on brodifacoum-treated mice survived and even these suffered from prolonged periods of bleeding. Post-mortem examination of those birds that died revealed a high degree of internal bleeding, centred around key organs like the brain, heart or lungs. The toxicity of difenacoum on Tawny Owls has been examined by the now-defunct Agriculture Science Service (Anon, 1982) which found that all four of the owls fed difenacoum-contaminated mice died some 8–41 days after initial exposure. Residue levels in tissue taken from the birds were some 0.2 mg/kg, with somewhat higher levels in ejected pellets and significantly higher levels in the faeces. A wider suite of anticoagulant rodenticides was examined by Mendenhall & Park (1980), who tested six compounds (diphacinone, chlorophacinone, fumarin, difenacoum, bromadiolone and brodifacoum) on 36 American Barn Owls, six owls per compound. Six of the birds died – five of those fed brodifacoum and one of those fed bromadiolone – and others suffered some form of haemorrhaging. Post-mortem examination of the dead birds revealed severe internal haemorrhaging and the presence of cardiac lesions. The birds were seen to behave normally until 24 hours or so before they died, when they ceased to take food and became lethargic.

The use of anticoagulants and the occurrence in owls

Rodenticides are in widespread use on most arable farms, their use increasing from 74 per cent of farms in 1992 to 89 per cent by 2000 (Brakes & Smith, 2005). Rodenticides may also be used on game-rearing estates, sometimes for the purpose of controlling Grey Squirrel populations, where use may see compounds delivered away from buildings and, presumably, in places more accessible to Wood Mice and Bank Voles that may, in turn, be eaten by Tawny Owls. Some 91 per cent of the 215 gamekeepers questioned by Robbie McDonald and Stephen Harris reported using rodenticides on their estate. Just over half of these keepers said that they used rodenticides away from buildings and a quarter reported using them in woodland to control squirrels (McDonald & Harris, 2000). Although patterns of use were broadly similar to those seen on arable farms, keepers tended to use warfarin and chlorophacinone more commonly. It was also clear that some keepers did not follow the guidance laid down for using these compounds, with products sometimes used incorrectly, used for the wrong target species or outside of the legal season.

Incidents involving secondary poisoning are sometimes reported directly; for example, a field trial of brodifacoum, carried out in the early 1980s in southern England, resulted in the finding of several Pheasant carcasses around the trial site. This promoted a wider survey, leading to the discovery of six Magpie, two Buzzard and single Tawny Owl, Red Fox and Brown Hare carcasses containing residues of the compound (Shawyer, 1985). A more systematic approach to monitoring the potential impact of rodenticides on British owls comes from the Predatory Bird Monitoring Scheme (http://pbms.ceh.ac.uk), which includes Barn Owl among a suite of species for which regular testing of contaminant loads takes place. The presence of Second Generation anticoagulant rodenticides has been monitored in Barn Owls by the scheme since 1983, over which time more sensitive methods for detecting residues have been developed. Examination of the long-term dataset, sometimes with sensitivities adjusted downwards to allow incorporation of data from the earlier years of the scheme, can reveal patterns in changing residue levels, identify which compounds are present and the parts of the country where incidence of poisoning may be greatest (Walker et al., 2012). Since 2006, the scheme has also reported on concentrations of warfarin and the presence or absence of diphacinone and chlorophacinone. Additionally, since 2010, the scheme has sampled for difethialone, only newly licensed for indoor use as a rodenticide.

Since 1983, there has been an increase in the proportion of Barn Owls with detectable residues of difenacoum and/or bromadiolone. Both of these compounds can be bought and used by anyone and they may be used outside. Both brodifacoum and flocoumafen, which are restricted in their sale and use, have also been detected in Barn Owls sampled over the period, though their occurrence does not appear to be increasing (Walker et al., 2012). An examination of regional variation in residue levels, using data from 1990–2010, found that the proportion of owls with detectable levels of Second Generation anticoagulant rodenticides was roughly two-fold higher in England than it was in Wales or Scotland: 30 per cent of owls tested in England contained one or more Second Generation compounds, the corresponding figure in Scotland was 18 per cent and Wales 15 per cent (Walker et al., 2012). The same study, this time just looking at data from England, showed that the highest proportion of Barn Owls with residues was from eastern England, perhaps unsurprising given its largely arable landscape.

An examination of Second Generation anticoagulant rodenticides in 172 Tawny Owls, submitted through the Predatory Bird Monitoring Scheme for the periods 1990–93 and 2003–05, revealed detectable residues in roughly one in five of the birds sampled (Walker *et al.*, 2008). At 11.6 per cent, Bromadiolone was the most commonly detected, followed by difenacoum (5.8 per cent) and brodifacoum (4.7 per cent). The livers of five of the birds tested contained residues of two different rodenticides. There was no evidence of an increase in the proportion of birds with residues over the two time periods, in contrast to the increasing pattern of occurrence witnessed in the Barn Owl.

What is the impact on owl populations?

Most of the Barn Owls and Tawny Owls found to have rodenticide residues in their tissues upon post-mortem examination, seemingly died as a consequence of other mortality agents, the tissue levels well below the limits suggestive of direct mortality. We cannot, however, rule out any sub-lethal role that these compounds might play and more research into this aspect of owl mortality would be worthwhile.

Of the British owls, it would seem that the Barn Owl is the species at greatest risk from the use of rodenticides because of its association with lowland farmland and farm buildings, followed by the Little Owl and, where rodenticides are used to control Grey Squirrel populations, the Tawny Owl. Elsewhere in

FIG 105. The use of rodenticides around farm buildings places the Barn Owl at greater risk of secondary poisoning than our other owls. (Mike Toms)

Europe, anticoagulant residue levels have also been found at higher levels in Barn Owl and Tawny Owl than, for example, Long-eared Owl (Christensen *et al.*, 2012). Our other owl species are unlikely to come into contact with rodenticides as often but we should remain alert to potential problems and to the possible impact of any changes in how rodenticide use is regulated. It is also worth noting that resistance to Second Generation rodenticides has been documented in some populations of Common Rat in parts of England (Hadler & Buckle, 1992).

The impact of Second Generation anticoagulant rodenticides on wild owl populations can, it appears, be far reaching under certain circumstances. Duckett (1984), for example, attributed the collapse of his Barn Owl study population in a Malayan oil palm plantation to the use of brodifacoum and coumachlor to control a rat population on which the Barn Owls also happened to be feeding. Using data from the BTO Ringing Scheme and Nest Record Scheme, Ian Henderson and colleagues attempted to establish whether the use of rodenticides across England and Wales has had any impact on the productivity and survival rates of Barn Owls (Henderson *et al.*, 1993). Although brood size was negatively related to total Second Generation rodenticide usage, and showed a consistent negative regional and temporal association with the usage of difenacoum, no clear significant relationships could be found. A major difficulty was the small sample sizes available to the researchers, something that may have masked effects.

OTHER HUMAN-INDUCED MORTALITY

Recoveries of ringed individuals reveal occasional incidents where owls are found dead below telegraph wires or power lines, suggesting collision with a stationary object. Shawyer (1987, 1998) has published figures of 3–5 per cent for this mortality cause. Overhead wires may be difficult to spot at night, and a hunting owl that collides with the wire may fracture a wing and fall to the ground. Many of the owls found alive beneath overhead wires and taken to rehabilitation centres have wing fractures. Individuals that are not found may be taken by scavengers.

There is currently no evidence to suggest that wind turbines are having an effect on any of our owl populations. It is likely that any effect would be more pronounced for a species like Short-eared Owl or Long-eared Owl, given the habitat associations of the former and the migratory habits of both species. Barn Owls and Little Owls are unlikely to be affected by the presence of turbines; indeed, the Barn Owl Trust have records of productive Barn Owl nesting attempts made within (a) 500 m (six records) and (b) 35 m (three records) of individual turbines, together with a further six successful breeding attempts made only 750 m from a wind farm of 16 turbines (Barn Owl Trust data). Elsewhere in the World, American Barn Owl deaths have been linked to a large wind farm at the Altamont Pass Wind Resource Area in California. The American Barn Owl is a partial migrant and many of those killed appear to have been on migration through the area.

Owls may be electrocuted by alighting on uninsulated, closely spaced power cables of the type that serve many isolated rural properties or those that serve certain sections of the rail network. The number of owls killed in this manner within Britain is unknown, but probably not that high. The available evidence suggests that some owl species are at greater risk of collision and/or electrocution than others, something that is likely to be linked to behaviour and morphology. Guyonne Janns examined this possibility for a range of bird species (though sadly not owls) and found that flight behaviour was an important predictor of collision risk (Janns, 2000). More detailed work by Diego Rubolini looked at 1,300 Italian casualties associated with power lines, including 169 Eagle Owls, nine Short-eared Owls, seven Tawny Owls and single Little Owl and Ural Owl (Rubolini et al., 2005). Rubolini noted that collisions mainly affected night migrants and species with a low degree of flight manoeuvrability. Electrocution risk was found to be directly related to behaviour and size, with larger birds more often electrocuted than smaller ones, relative to their abundance. Owls and herons were the two groups most widely affected, with power lines found to be the main cause of non-natural mortality for Eagle Owls breeding in the Italian Alps. A review of 25 different studies has found electrocution frequently cited as the major cause of death in Eagle Owls; it also has revealed that its importance has progressively increased over the last 30 years (Sergio et al., 2004). Collision with power lines/electrocution is also the main cause of Eagle Owl mortality in Spain (Martínez et al., 2006).

For Europe and North America, estimates put electrocution rates at between 0.15 and 5.2 dead birds per pole per year, although this includes all species and does not allow for carcass removal by scavengers (Rubolini et al., 2005). As is the case with roads, site-specific characteristics are likely to influence the risk that a particular stretch of power line poses, something that is further modified by the nature and design of the power line itself. Electrocution of Eagle Owls in the Italian Alps, for example, usually occurs at medium voltage (15–30 kV) electricity poles (Rubolini et al., 2005). Although Sergio et al. (2004) did not find any effect on long-term breeding success, they did find that the presence of pylons within 200 m of an active Eagle Owl nest increased the chances of partial or complete brood loss during the post-fledging period, estimating that nearly one in five youngsters was lost to electrocution. At the population level, Fabrizio Sergio has also shown that territories near to power lines may be progressively abandoned, leading to the situation where Eagle Owl breeding density is negatively related to electrocution risk.

One of the five British Eagle Owl chicks to have been ringed and subsequently recovered was found dead under power cables near Church Stretton in Shropshire (Robinson & Clark, 2012). Even here, it seems, power lines may prove to be an important mortality agent should the Eagle Owl population expand. It appears that Eagle Owls may be particularly susceptible to electrocution because of their habit of favouring high perches from which to scan the surrounding landscape for potential prey.

Dead owls have also been recorded after colliding with fence wires, chicken wire or becoming entangled in netting, the latter including a case of a Barn Owl found dead in a tennis net (Shawyer, 1998). There are also a few records of owls killed when striking aircraft.

Drowning

Occasional reports of owls found dead in cattle troughs and other steep-sided containers suggest that individuals may occasionally drown when attempting to bathe. Shawyer (1987) found a surprisingly high incidence of Barn Owls that had drowned, some 6 per cent of cases, when he came to examine mortality in this species within Britain. Even higher rates have been noted for Little Owl (not in Britain but elsewhere in Europe), ranging from 2.8 per cent (Génot, 1991) up to 20 per cent (Lecomte, 1995). Shawyer noted that mortality due to drowning

FIG 106. Barn Owls may occasionally be found dead in cattle troughs, where they have become waterlogged and unable to climb out. (Mike Toms)

peaked in July, a pattern also found by the Barn Owl Trust in an examination of their mortality data. While Shawyer suggested that this was the result of nest-soiled adult females bathing, the Barn Owl Trust data for July involve only young birds, presumably inexperienced and not long independent. That a Barn Owl may quickly become waterlogged has been nicely demonstrated by David Ramsden, who showed that the weight of a 260 g Barn Owl corpse increases to 460 g when saturated in water. Dries van Nieuwenhuyse and colleagues note that Little Owl victims are a mixture of newly independent young and soiled females. Efforts have been made to tackle the problem of owls drowning in cattle troughs, most of which involve the addition of a floating tray or frame to the trough; this allows the cattle to continue to drink from the trough but provides purchase for an owl and prevents it from drowning.

Persecution

The persecution of birds of prey, including owls, is something that has a long history. In fact, raptors and owls have probably been killed ever since people started rearing livestock and managing game, with diurnal birds of prey targeted more specifically than owls. As we will see in Chapter 6, persecution of owls may sometimes also arise from fear and superstition, as well as ignorance, leading to the killing of birds that would otherwise have little or no impact upon our lives.

Owls, persecution and game-rearing interests
Much of the early persecution of owls was linked to the protection of domestic poultry and it was not until after the Great Exhibition of 1851, and the popularisation of sporting game-management, that targeted 'control' of birds of prey really took off. The efforts of gamekeepers, based largely around shooting and trapping, saw the collapse of many raptor populations and the local extinction of others. For example, five bird of prey species are believed to have been lost from Britain during the period 1851 to c. 1916: Goshawk (1889), Marsh Harrier *Circus aeruginosus* (c. 1898), Osprey *Pandion haliaetus* (1908), Honey Buzzard *Pernis apivorus* (1911) and White-tailed Eagle *Haliaeetus albicilla* (1916). Barn Owl populations appear, from a survey of county avifaunas, to have undergone a substantial decline over this period, most likely the indiscriminate victims of pole traps set for other species. John Handcock, writing in 1874, underlines this point when he says: 'There has been no discrimination used in the slaughter of so-called "vermin" – Owls too, the police of the stackyard, are sacrificed with equal disregard.' In some English counties, however, it was thought that Barn Owls did take game chicks and the species could be found on keepers' gibbets in Sussex, Bedfordshire and Wiltshire, hanging alongside

Tawny Owl, Sparrowhawk and Weasel. Tawny Owls were heavily persecuted historically, in part because of perceived threats to gamebirds but also because they would take young Rabbits and, occasionally, young hares. Henry Stevenson, in his *Birds of Norfolk*, commented on the way in which constant persecution was making the Tawny Owl extremely scarce within the county, adding a quote from a Mr Gould:

> *Were it possible for a pair of brown owls to produce a yearly record of the number of nocturnal moles, Norway rats, and destructive field mice they have destroyed, against a similar account of what has been done in this way by any five keepers, I question whether the balance would not be in favour of the owls.*

Towards the end of the 1800s attitudes began to soften as more people started to view owls as their allies rather than as foes. Barn Owls, in particular, benefited from this change but were still victim to traps set for other species. It was not until the use of pole traps was banned in 1904 that such indiscriminate slaughter started to decline. Not all our owls were viewed so favourably, since the Tawny Owl continued to be regarded as a threat to Pheasants, especially where young birds were penned prior to release. Levels of persecution dipped dramatically with the outbreak of the First World War, as keepers were called to serve their country, but it did not last and a resurgence of interest in game-rearing followed the end of the war. Concerns over the impact that the newly established Little Owl population might be having on game-rearing interests prompted the BTO's Little Owl Food Inquiry, carried out by Alice Hibbert-Ware in the 1930s (Hibbert-Ware, 1938). The findings of this work, which served to exonerate the Little Owl, found favour with a growing movement for the protection of our wild birds. Nevertheless, Little Owls continued to be shot, pole trapped and even caught in tunnel traps set at ground level

FIG 107. Now illegal, pole traps once took a heavy toll on owls and other birds of prey. Here the victim is a Little Owl. (Mike Toms)

for mammalian predators (Hewson, 1972). Perhaps the biggest leap forward in the battle against persecution came with the substantial revision made, in 1953, to the Protection of Wild Birds Bill of 1933.

Deliberate persecution did, however, continue, and even today incidents are brought to the attention of the RSPB's Wildlife Investigations Unit and the Police. Thankfully, the persecution of owls is considerably less common today, with incidents seemingly now limited to rare instances of owls (notably Tawny Owls) caught in illegal pole traps or discovered shot or poisoned. The Birdcrime report for 2010, for example, contains records of Barn Owl (Staffordshire, Wiltshire), Tawny Owl (Bedfordshire) and Short-eared Owl (North Yorkshire, South Lanarkshire) victims of shooting, trapping (Tawny Owl, Devon and North Yorkshire) and poisoning (Tawny Owl).

Elsewhere in Europe persecution is still something of a problem. Around the Mediterranean, for example, illegal and targeted persecution of owls and other birds of prey remains widespread. In Spain, for example, Inigo Fajardo (Fajardo *et al.*, 1994) found that nearly three-quarters of the dead Short-eared Owls that he studied had been shot, a figure well in excess of that noted for Barn Owl (15.5 per cent) but broadly similar to that found in Eagle Owl in the country (62.6 per cent). Another feature of the Spanish Mediterranean coast is the use of Parany traps, which catch Short-eared Owls and other migratory birds. The practice, which has been illegal since 2002, involves the establishment of stands of trees, interlaced with poles to which lime or glue-impregnated sticks are attached. The trappers sometimes use tape lures to draw in thrushes, the intended targets, but they also catch many other species, including the owls which may be attracted by the presence of ensnared songbirds. Social awareness has improved in many areas, however, resulting in changes in cultural practices formerly associated with persecution. The effectiveness of programmes to educate communities can be seen in the changing relative contributions of different human-related mortality agents to the overall pattern of mortality now seen in Spanish owls (Fajardo, 2001). It is also just worth mentioning another form of persecution that used to occur in parts of Europe, where people would raid the nests of Eagle Owls (and other raptors) to steal larger items of prey. Such items broadened the diet of those stealing the food and provided commercially valuable goods for trade.

Taxidermy and egg-collecting

During the Victorian Era in particular, owls were also persecuted to supply a market for stuffed specimens and curios. The Barn Owl, for example, was a firm favourite with taxidermists and their customers, as D'Urban and Matthew wrote:

FIG 108. Our rarer owls are still the targets of egg-collectors, whose selfish acts put the future of some species at risk. (Mike Toms)

In every little bird-stuffers shop the Barn Owl may be numbered by the half dozen distorted and caricatured, his face and wings, perhaps, converted into fire screens.

Tawny Owl, Long-eared Owl and Short-eared Owl were also targeted by Victorian taxidermists, often presented as cased exhibits, and there were many collectors who sought to obtain specimens of our less common species.

Egg-collecting was once a common practice among children but, quite rightly, it was made illegal through the 1954 Protection of Birds Act. Since then it has continued to attract the interest of a small, selfish minority, who do great damage to the populations of some of our rarest species. The eggs of owls feature in the collections that emerge when egg-collectors are caught and their collections confiscated, once again revealing the dreadful impact that their activities can have.

Other mortality

An examination of ring-recovery data and the records of rehabilitation centres underlines that owls may sometimes fall victim to other aspects of our activities. Owls may occasionally become caught in wire and netting, or become trapped within chimneys, ventilators or buildings. In parts of France there appears to be a particular problem with certain designs of metal telephone pole. These are hollow, but the entrance hole is designed in an unfortunate manner, such that once a Little Owl enters it is unable to get out again.

DISEASES AND PARASITES

Infectious diseases are thought to be common causes of disease and death in owls and other birds of prey, but there is little reliable information on their contribution to overall levels of mortality and no real understanding of what impact they might exert at the population level. Targeted research tends to be directed towards cases where disease threatens species of conservation concern or has wider health or economic implications for humans. Because of this, there has been little systematic monitoring of disease prevalence in wild owl populations and most of our understanding either comes from short-term, small-scale studies or is generated as a by-product of other work. Many studies are hampered by biases associated with the manner in which the samples are collated. For example, studies often rely on owls taken by hunters or submitted to taxidermists, individuals which may not be representative of the wider population. Similarly, examination of the owls passing through rehabilitation centres may overemphasise the importance of particular diseases because these birds may be more approachable and readily collected by members of the public. As Andrew Greenwood noted in his review of the role of disease in the ecology of British birds of prey, reported figures for deaths attributable to infectious disease or parasitism probably bear little relation to the true incidence of these mortality agents in wild populations (Greenwood, 1977).

Before turning to look at diseases and parasites of the British owls themselves, it is worth just noting the overlap between these different mortality agents. Viruses and bacteria, together with some fungi and protozoa, are increasingly regarded as being micro-parasites, organisms responsible for the majority of the epizootics – diseases that have sudden, short-term impacts on a large number of individuals – that lie behind periodic, large-scale reductions in bird numbers. Macro-parasites, such as parasitic worms (helminths) and arthropod ectoparasites, may cause large-scale reductions in bird numbers too but more usually deliver subtle effects, like reduced breeding success or lowered survival rates (Cooper, 2002). Not all parasites are associated with disease but many are. Ectoparasites feeding on blood, like ticks and fleas, may cause tissue damage or elicit an allergic reaction; they may also introduce a bacterial infection or transmit a micro-parasite.

Disease

British owls have been reported suffering from a wide range of diseases, mostly non-specific in nature and known to occur across many different bird families. The more commonly reported diseases include tuberculosis, trichomonosis and salmonellosis (Keymer, 1972; Bucke & Mawdesly-Thomas, 1974). Recoveries of ringed owls from Britain and Ireland contain very few instances where the bird was thought to have died from disease and much of our knowledge comes for birds submitted through wildlife rehabilitation centres or pollutant monitoring schemes. Some of the published findings of these studies include both captive and free-living owls so do not necessarily present a systematic assessment of disease levels within wild populations. A few studies have, however, attempted to provide such information. For example, *Salmonella* infection rates of 94 nestling American Barn Owls were examined by Kirkpatrick & Colvin (1986), who found that nearly one in ten individuals (and one in five nest sites) harboured *Salmonella* spp. *Salmonella typhimurium* has been isolated from a wild Tawny Owl found in Britain and probably occurs more frequently in our owls than is evident from the literature (Wilson & Macdonald, 1967). *Salmonella enterica* Phage Type 21b (the form often found in humans) has been isolated from a European Eagle Owl found dead in Turkey in 2005 and may also be present here (Kocabiyik *et al.*, 2006).

Owls may feature among the victims of disease outbreaks that originate in domesticated poultry and wildfowl. For example, a series of outbreaks of Newcastle Disease in Switzerland between 1994 and 1996 prompted sampling of the wider avian community, including 34 owls. Antibodies for the disease were found in Tawny Owl (85 per cent of those sampled), Eagle Owl (100 per cent of those sampled) and Barn Owl (33.3 per cent of those sampled), the authors noting that, across the whole sample, antibodies were more likely to be found in predatory species that included small birds in their diet than in species that fed on other things (Schelling *et al.*, 1999). More recent sampling, this time in Germany, did not find any antibodies to Newcastle Disease in a sample of 55 owls tested, although there was no poultry outbreak associated with the sampling period (Schettler *et al.*, 2001). The owls were also sampled for other disease agents, including Owl Herpesvirus (see below), for which a single Tawny Owl was found to have antibodies, and chlamydiosis, which was found to be ubiquitous within the sample, including in Tawny Owl (81 per cent), Long-eared Owl (86 per cent), Barn Owl (73 per cent) and Eagle Owl (25 per cent). Chlamydiosis occurs across the world and numerous strains have been identified in both birds and mammals. The strains isolated from wild birds are not normally pathogenic to them as hosts but they can be highly pathogenic to other bird species and, indeed, also to

FIG 109. Owl Herpes Virus (OHV) has been found in Short-eared Owls and other European species. (Steve Round)

humans. The *Chlamydia psittaci* discovered in these German owls was found to be linked to the age of the bird, with a greater number of positive test reactors noted with increasing age. While this could imply that the probability of an immune response increases with age, it may, more likely, reflect a higher mortality among young birds contracting the disease, something which has been noted elsewhere (Thomas *et al.*, 2007).

A number of more specific diseases are also known from owls, most notably hepatosplenitis strigis or Owl Herpesvirus (OHV). Hugo Burtscher provided the initial evidence for OHV in free-living owls from Europe, with spontaneous lethal infection noted from some Austrian Eagle Owls, Little Owls and Short-eared Owls. Burtscher & Sibalin (1975) also demonstrated the susceptibility of Little Owl and Tengmalm's Owl to OHV in the laboratory, at the same time suggesting that Barn Owl and Tawny Owl were not susceptible to experimental infection. The two researchers commented on the intriguing observation that susceptible species of owl had coloured eyes (yellow or orange) while non-susceptible species had dark eyes, though this may have been pure coincidence.

OHV is one of the most commonly diagnosed viral diseases of owls and it is often seen in captive collections. As is often the case with disease, symptoms are non-specific, infected individuals appearing lethargic and reluctant to move away when approached (Atkinson *et al.*, 2008). OHV has been put forward as the reason why initial attempts to reintroduce captive-bred Eagle Owls into parts of their former European range were unsuccessful. Once screening for OHV was introduced for those individual Eagle Owls put forward for release – with only serologically negative birds then released – reintroduction proved to be a success (Barkhoff, 1987).

West Nile Virus, a flavivirus normally transmitted by bird-feeding mosquitoes, has also been demonstrated to pose a risk to some captive owl populations. An outbreak in 2002 at a collection in Ontario, Canada, saw a 46 per cent mortality rate across 235 owls of various species. Interestingly, mortality rates were greatest among species that bred in the northern part of North America and lowest among those that bred in the south of the region, perhaps suggesting prior exposure and some degree of resistance within species whose populations occupied more southerly parts of North America (Gancz *et al.*, 2004).

Endoparasites

The parasites found within the bodies of owls are known as endoparasites and those most commonly found on owls can be grouped into single-celled organisms (Protozoa), tapeworms (Cestoda), flukes (Trematoda), roundworms (Nematoda) and spiny-headed worms (Acanthocephala).

Protozoa

Many of the parasitic protozoans are blood parasites, or 'haematozoa'. Blood parasites have been found in nearly all of the owl species so far tested, a pattern repeated within bird species more generally. Included among the blood parasites noted from British owls are those belonging to the genera *Haemoproteus*, *Leucocytozoon* and *Trypanosoma* (Baker, 1974). Our understanding of these parasites is still developing, particularly in relation to their taxonomy, and it is likely that we will see changes in their classification as our knowledge improves. Both *Haemoproteus syrnii* and *Haemoproteus noctuae* have been recorded in British Tawny Owls, the rates of occurrence ranging from one in five to one in three individuals tested (Peirce *et al.*, 1983; Appleby *et al.*, 1999b). Although the term 'avian malaria' is sometimes used to describe infection with *Haemoproteus* species it is worth noting that these parasites are different from the *Plasmodium* species that are the true malarial parasites. Both *Leucocytozoon* and *Haemoproteus* species are relatively host-specific, typically restricted to birds of the same family, with a suggestion that some may even be species-specific. In contrast, the species of *Plasmodium* appear to have a much broader host-specificity, the ability to change their character enabling them to parasitise across a number of avian families. *Haemoproteus* and *Leucocytozoon* parasites are transmitted by biting flies, like midges, black flies and hippoboscids, entering the bloodstream through the fly's saliva. Systematic information on the occurrence of blood parasites more widely within British owls is lacking, though comparable information is available from elsewhere in Europe. For instance, Krone *et al.* (2001) found blood parasites (either *Leucocytozoon* or *Haemoproteus*) in 13 per cent of the smears taken from 173 owls. Although no parasites were found in smears from 62 Barn Owls, eight Eagle Owls or single Little Owl and Short-eared Owl, *Leucocytozoon ziemanni* and *Haemoproteus syrnii* were found in Long-eared Owl and Tawny Owl. *Leucocytozoon ziemanni* is also known from the English Tawny Owl population studies carried out by Appleby *et al.* (1999b), who found it to be present in all of the Tawny Owls that they tested. A comparative central European study by Kučera found *Leucocytozoon* in 9.9 per cent of the owls examined, *Plasmodium* in 2.3 per cent of cases and *Trypanosoma* in 7 per cent of cases. Available evidence suggests that *Leucocytozoon* blood parasites are only slightly pathogenic to owls, but they have been linked to a decline in host fitness and lowered productivity (Korpimäki *et al.*, 1993). Tawny Owls appear to continue carrying these blood parasites long after the initial infection, the level of parasites maintained possibly characteristic of individual birds, a pattern likely to be repeated in other owl species.

Other protozoan parasites

Trichomonosis is one of the oldest known diseases of wild birds, with a written record extending back over many centuries. The disease, which is caused by the protozoan parasite *Trichomonas gallinae*, is sometimes referred to as 'frounce' in raptors or 'canker' in pigeons. It is primarily a disease of the upper digestive and respiratory tracts, where it can bring about tissue and organ necrosis that may result in death. The disease is cosmopolitan and has been recorded from Britain in wild Barn Owls and Tawny Owls (Hardy *et al.*, 1981). Cases from elsewhere in Europe have also involved Little Owl and Eagle Owl (Atkinson *et al.*, 2008). Owls are likely to pick up the *Trichomonas* parasite from infected avian prey. *Toxoplasma gondii*, another protozoan parasite with a wide distribution, is thought to infect virtually all warm-blooded animals. Owls may acquire the parasite through ingestion of prey containing the tissue-inhabiting stages of the parasite and it is believed that owls have a high prevalence of *Toxoplasma*, although there appears to have been little or no systematic study of the parasite in British owl populations. Its presence has been confirmed, however, in wild Little Owls and Tawny Owls from elsewhere in Europe and the Near East (Atkinson *et al.*, 2008). Firm data on the impact of the parasite on wild populations are lacking, but it has been shown to pose a significant risk to small populations of threatened species. Owls and other raptors may act as intermediate hosts for *Toxoplasma gondii* and so may also play a role in how the disease affects other organisms.

Parasitic worms

The parasitic worms represent a very diverse group of organisms, drawn from a number of different phyla. Some may be only a few millimetres in length while others can be many centimetres long; some may be found in the intestine, some in the trachea and others are to be found elsewhere. The distribution of parasitic worms between individual owls tends to be rather clumped, with a few individuals carrying very high parasite loads but most carrying very low loads.

Flukes (Trematoda)

Flukes are typically found as parasites of the intestinal tract. They are flat, leaf-like creatures with complex life cycles, often involving several hosts drawn from very different types of organism. Some are known to occur with great frequency in a wide range of avian hosts but others are specific to a small group of species or to just a single species. They tend to be most common in waterfowl but also occur in birds of prey. There appear to be few records involving owls.

Tapeworms (Cestoda)

Tapeworms are familiar parasites that are very common in the small intestine of birds and other vertebrates, occurring more frequently than other parasitic worms, from which they may be readily distinguished by their highly segmented appearance. Individual birds may be infected by more than one species of tapeworm but even in such cases, the bird frequently shows no clinical signs and the consensus is that tapeworms are rarely fatal for the host unless they occur in very large numbers. There may, however, be sub-lethal effects, mediated directly through reduced reproductive success or a general decline in fitness.

Roundworms (Nematoda)

Roundworms are most commonly found in the intestinal tract and respiratory system but they may also be found in other organs. Some of the most common are the threadworms belonging to the Capillariinae, found in the intestines of both owls and other raptors. The more widely known gapeworms (e.g. *Syngamus* spp.), which infect gamebirds and domestic poultry, have been recorded from owls on occasion. Various invertebrates may act as intermediate hosts for nematode worms and earthworms may, additionally, act as paratenic hosts – a paratenic host is similar to an intermediate host but is not essential for the parasite's development to progress. There is, therefore, a clear pathway by which nematode worms can reach species like Tawny Owl and Little Owl, for which invertebrates may be an important dietary component.

Spiny-headed worms (Acanthocephala)

Spiny-headed worms, so named because of the nature of the organ used for host attachment, are the least common of the parasitic worms to be found in owls and other birds of prey. Infection rates have been shown to vary across Europe within birds of prey in general, something that may be linked to the intermediate hosts used by the worm. The most commonly reported genus from Europe is *Centrorhynchus*, which uses grasshoppers as an intermediate host and lizards and snakes as paratenic hosts, organisms which are more abundant in southern Europe than they are in more northerly regions. Heavy infections may damage the intestinal wall, leading to peritonitis and death.

Ectoparasites

All of the parasites found living on the bodies of owls are arthropods and collectively they are known as ectoparasites. Some ectoparasites are host-specific, while others, such as the fly *Carnus haemapterus*, may be found on the nestlings of many different species. This particular species, which is just two millimetres in length and has been found on Barn Owl and Little Owl, is also known from Kestrel *Falco tinnunculus*, Great Spotted Woodpecker *Dendrocopos major*, Blackcap *Sylvia atricapilla* and Starling *Sturnus vulgaris*, among others. It is parasitic on birds during its adult stage, the adult fly feeding on the bird's blood. The eggs are laid in the nesting material and it is within this that the resulting larvae develop, feeding on organic matter before overwintering as a pupa. Infestation of a new host begins the following year – work in Germany suggesting it starts from mid-May and lasts until the end of June, repeating the process over again (Walter & Hudde, 1987). Work in Switzerland has revealed that the number of these flies on individual Barn Owl chicks is related to season, the re-use of a nest site, the age of the nestling and the degree of hatching asynchrony (see Chapter 3). The prevalence of these flies is often high, the Swiss study putting the figure at 94 per cent of the chicks examined (Roulin, 1998). A similar rate of infestation has been seen in the American Barn Owl.

Some flies may deposit eggs or larvae into flesh wounds, something that is occasionally seen in nestling owls or adult birds that have been injured during prey capture. Other flies, such as flat-flies (hippoboscids), will be familiar to nest recorders and bird ringers working on owls, often emerging from the down of a nestling owl to take up residence in your own hair or to slide up the sleeve of your jacket. A number of species are known from birds, including *Ornithomyia avicularia*, which is commonly found on British owls. Various ticks and mites are known from the British owls, including the ticks *Ixodes arboricola*, *I. frontalis*, *I. ricinus* and *I. ventalloi*, the red mite *Dermanysaus gallinae* and species of *Knemidocoptes* mite. Fleas, however, are generally rare on owls, though a number of species may be found in the nests of owls and other birds of prey. The nest debris, particularly that found in our cavity-nesting owls, may also support other invertebrate fauna. For example, a number of commensal Lepidoptera species are known from nest debris and old owl pellets, including the Skin Moth *Monopis laevigella* and the Tapestry Moth *Trichophaga tapetzella*.

Chewing lice, the Mallophaga (and part of the Phthiraptera), are represented by many dozens of different species, some of which appear to be host-specific and some which are specific to particular feather tracts (e.g. the head feathers). Of these, *Strigiphilus rostratus*, one of a number of species within a genus specific to owls, has been recorded on the Barn Owl within Britain.

The factors influencing disease risk and parasite loads

As has already been noted, the presence of parasites may have subtle, long-term consequences for an individual owl. Some researchers have found that high parasite loads lead to lower reproductive success but other researchers have failed to find any effect. This underlines the complex links that may exist between fitness, parasite load, reproductive output and external factors, such as food availability. The presence of parasites may, for example, only exert a noticeable effect when an individual owl is under stress, perhaps because the availability of prey is particularly low or because the bird is channelling a high proportion of its available resources into a breeding attempt. It is known that high reproductive output can itself lead to increased parasite burdens, suggesting that resources which may have been directed towards the immune system (and a response against parasites) were being directed elsewhere, in this case to reproductive output. Food availability may determine the overall resource available to the bird for investment in immune response or reproduction. If small mammal prey abundance limits the resources available to a breeding Tawny Owl, then we may find that years with low prey numbers lead to owls with both high parasite loads and low breeding success; in this case the low breeding success is not a direct result of parasite load, even though it might appear so in the absence of any knowledge of background food availability. The relationship between food

FIG 110. More heavily spotted female Barn Owls may be signalling their higher resistance to certain parasites, as work carried out elsewhere in Europe seems to indicate. (Mike Toms)

availability, prey abundance and parasite load is something that has been studied in a Tawny Owl population breeding in Kielder Forest in northern England (Appleby *et al.*, 1999b). The work carried out by Appleby and fellow researchers suggests that food availability during early life can have a long-term impact on the immune functioning of individual owls and their associated parasite loads. This work also showed that adult birds with access to more abundant prey populations were better at resisting parasites.

Parasite loads may show an association with particular habitat types more directly. The prevalence of *Leucocytozoon* blood parasites in European owls, which varies with habitat, has been linked to the biology of black flies (Simuliidae), the primary vectors for these parasites. Black flies are associated with freshwater streams and other waterbodies, which are home to their immature stages, so the pattern of *Leucocytozoon* occurrence in owls tends to reflect this. Owls from dry open habitats have few of these parasites, while those from moist habitats have many more (Tomé *et al.*, 2005). This pattern is also evident within individual populations; Ortego & Espada (2007), for instance, found that the number of parasite species present within Spanish Eagle Owl broods increased with the length of watercourse present within the territory. Diet is also known to influence infection risk and a broad diet may expose an owl to a wider range of host species from which parasitic worms, notably spiny-headed worms, might be contracted. Of six owl species examined for parasitic worms in Spain, Ferrer *et al.* (2004) found the Little Owl to have the highest infection rates. The generalist diet of this species was thought to be a contributory factor in the high prevalence of parasitic worms observed. Behaviour can be influential in other respects, with nest sanitation likely to be important in reducing numbers of the parasitic fly *Carnus haemapterus* in Barn Owl nests. Although they do not really build a nest, female Barn Owls have been observed to remove nest debris, such as discarded pellets, at night.

Not only may external factors influence exposure to parasites and disease but they may also determine the magnitude of an individual's immune response and the effect of infection on the bird's longer-term fitness. Mounting a response against an infection or parasite is thought to be costly, since it competes for resources with other life history components. Hardy *et al.* (1981), for example, found that several Tawny Owls showing aberrant and asymmetrical moult had advanced tuberculosis, suggesting an unresolved resource conflict between feather replacement and immune response.

Parasites may exert a selective pressure on individuals, shaping populations and their responses over time. It is unsurprising, therefore, to discover that genetic qualities also play a key role in immune response. This is something that has been investigated in several owl species, including both Barn Owl and Tawny Owl. This work has centred largely on the heritability of immune response and how individuals might advertise the presence of 'good' genes that contribute to an increased ability to fight disease or parasitism. If individuals with a lower susceptibility to disease or parasites can, as a consequence, invest more resources in the production of ornamental traits, such as the plumage spots seen in female Barn Owls, then there exists the possibility that these individuals can advertise this trait to prospective mates through an honest marker. Perhaps the best evidence for what is known as parasite-mediated sexual selection comes from work on the Barn Swallow *Hirundo rustica*, but there is also an increasing body of evidence drawn from other bird species, including the Barn Owl.

Work on the signalling associated with parasite resistance in the Barn Owl has been led by Alexandre Roulin, working on Swiss and French populations of the dark-breasted form *Tyto alba guttata*. Female Barn Owls are more heavily spotted than their mates, a feature that has been shown to be hereditable. By looking at the relationship between plumage spottiness of female Barn Owls and the parasite burdens of their chicks, Roulin and colleagues have revealed that the young of more heavily spotted females have a greater resistance to the parasitic fly *Carnus haemapterus*. Roulin used a rather ingenious experiment to determine this, cross-fostering eggs between females of known spottiness and then examining both the subsequent parasite loads of the resulting chicks and the fecundity of any parasitic flies found. Roulin had to control for the age of the mother, since older females have more spots than younger birds, and for other factors, such as whether the nest site had been used the previous year. The latter point was important because, as we have seen, the larvae of these flies feed within the nest material, emerging as adults the following breeding season around the time that the eggs hatch. As expected, Roulin *et al.* (2001) found that nestlings in boxes used the previous year carried more flies. Once this had been controlled for, however, it became clear that the chicks of females with fewer spots were more heavily parasitised by the flies. Perhaps the most interesting aspect of this work was the finding that flies collected from nests containing the young of more heavily spotted females were less fecund, suggesting that the chicks' ability to resist this particular parasite is linked to the plumage spottiness of their mother. As Alexandre put it in a different paper, 'female Barn Owls advertise their good genes' (Roulin *et al.*, 2000). There are several possible mechanisms by which favoured chicks might achieve greater resistance. They could, for instance, have skin that is either thicker or of a different composition to other chicks, but it appears more likely that they show a more efficient immune response instead. This notion is supported by other experiments carried out by Roulin where he found that the scale of the antibody response to a non-pathogenic antigen, and again observed in cross-fostered Barn Owl chicks, was positively correlated to the plumage spottiness of the genetic mother (but not the genetic father).

This aspect of the work is worthy of particular mention, since most of the earlier work carried out in this area had looked at male ornamentation – males are usually the more ornamented sex – and had found that more ornamented males had lower parasite loads (of both ecto- and endoparasites), smaller spleens and bursa of Fabricius (organs linked to immune response) and produced offspring that had lower parasite loads. A separate piece of work, looking at Barn Owls found dead on French roads, has revealed that more heavily spotted female Barn Owls have a structurally smaller bursa of Fabricius, again suggesting greater resistance to infection.

That some female Barn Owls have more and larger spots than others is a form of plumage polymorphism, something that is related to the colour polymorphism common in owls and already noted in Chapter 1. Melanin-based colour polymorphism is highly heritable and thought to be maintained through morph-specific sensitivity to different external factors, one of which might be parasitism. Work on Tawny Owls also suggests that different colour morphs may vary in their immune response. For example, Italian populations of the brown morph have been found to harbour more blood parasites than the grey morph (Galeotti & Sacchi, 2003). In a Swiss population, females of the brown morph were discovered to have a more prolonged immune response to a novel antigen than females of the grey form (Gasparini et al., 2009), again suggesting that grey morph birds have a better immune response. However, such apparent differences do require more careful scrutiny, as the work of Karell et al. (2011) demonstrates. Patrik Karell and colleagues found, from descriptive Tawny Owl data, that although both morphs had similar infection rates of blood parasites, infection was associated with decreased body mass only in brown morph birds. This appeared to suggest that grey morphs had greater resistance but the reverse was found to be the case when they used experimental medication to reduce the numbers of blood parasites and explore whether this benefited the birds in other ways during their breeding attempts. Experimental removal of the parasites saw the grey morph females significantly increase their maintenance of body mass, something not seen in treated brown phase females and suggestive of grey phase birds having to mount a more demanding immune response against parasites than was the case for brown phase birds. Collectively, these studies suggest that interactions between parasites and their owl hosts are incredibly complex, with any immune response likely to be balanced against other resource needs and varied depending upon a wide range of factors. The extent to which individual owls might then be able to 'advertise' their ability to respond to disease or parasitism will, as a consequence, remain difficult to unravel.

LONGEVITY AND SURVIVAL

An often-asked question is 'how long does a particular species live?', something that can be difficult to answer since the maximum recorded age for a wild individual may be rather different from what is typical for the species. Researchers tend to think in terms of survival rather than longevity but some indication of typical lifespan may be garnered from the recoveries of ringed birds (Table 11). This reveals, as you might expect, that larger owl species tend to be longer-lived than smaller ones, a pattern repeated in other bird families. Large size confers an increased ability to survive temporary food shortages and greater immunity from predation.

TABLE 11. Longevity records for British owls, taken from Robinson & Clark (2012). Typical lifespan is shown in brackets.

Barn Owl (4 years) 15 years 26 days

GF71020
Nestling Male – 30/05/1996 – Wick Marsh, Fingringhoe: 51°48′N 0°57′E (Essex)
Caught by ringer – 25/06/2011 – Moor Farm, Peldon: 51°48′N 0°54′E (Essex)
Distance moved 4 km

Tawny Owl (4 years) 21 years, 5 months and 13 days

AJ95106
First-year – 25/05/1967 – Malham Tarn: 54°6′N 2°10′W (North Yorkshire)
Freshly dead (natural causes) – 07/11/1988 – Maltham Tarn: 54°6′N 2°10′W (North Yorkshire)
Distance moved 0 km

Little Owl (3 years) 10 years, 11 months and 26 days

ET81575
Nestling – 13/06/1998 – South Woods Hill Farm, Pilling: 53°54′N 2°51′W (Lancashire)
Freshly dead – 08/06/2009 – Cockerham, near Lancaster: 53°58′N 2°49′W (Lancashire)
Distance moved 8 km

Long-eared Owl (4 years) 12 years, 10 months and 12 days

GP73037
Nestling – 31/05/1974 – Aberchirder: 57°34′N 2°38′W (Grampian Region)
Freshly dead (predated) – 12/4/1987 – Nordurreykir, Halsasveit, Borg: 64°42′N 20°15′W (Iceland) Distance moved 1,230 km

---

Short-eared Owl (4 years) 6 years, 7 months and 28 days

AF3938
Nestling – 08/05/1956 – Forest of Balloch, Barr: 55°13′N 4°43′W (Strathclyde)
Freshly dead (shot) – 05/01/1963 – Meelin, Newmarket: 52°16′N 9°1′W (Cork)
Distance moved 433 km

Survival rates for first-year Tawny Owls have been shown to be driven by vole abundance, being higher in those years when vole populations are at a peak. As you might expect, adult survival rates are higher than those of first-year birds, underlining greater experience and, presumably, access to a better quality territory. Estimates derived from nearly 20,000 Finnish Tawny Owls ringed between 1980 and 1999 indicate an average survival rate of 33 per cent for first-year birds, 64 per cent for second-year birds and 73 per cent in subsequent years (Francis & Saurola, 2002). Adult survival rates for Tawny Owls studied in northern England decline with age in a roughly linear fashion and show little indication of any underlying impact of prey populations (Millon *et al.*, 2011). In contrast, examination of Iain Taylor's Barn Owl data from Scotland revealed that both juvenile and adult mortality rates were correlated with vole abundance (Hone & Sibly, 2002). Adult survival rates for Little Owl may also vary over time, as suggested by an examination of ringing data collected in the Netherlands (Le Gouar *et al.*, 2011). Pascaline Le Gouar and colleagues found that adult survival rates fluctuated in a regular manner, with a year of low survival seen every fourth year or so and seemingly linked to years that were particularly dry and cold.

POPULATIONS

Changes in the size of a population over time are governed by four things: births (productivity), deaths (mortality/survival), immigration and emigration. If you can determine how each of these affects a particular population then it should be possible to predict how the population will change over time or to explain why it might already have changed in a particular way. We have already seen in Chapter 3 how productivity may change in response to changing prey abundance. We have also seen how movements, such as natal dispersal, may influence recruitment to a local breeding population. Changing levels of mortality/survival, especially those affecting first-year birds, may be particularly important in driving some of the longer-term changes seen in owl populations. However, in order to understand which of the different drivers is behind a documented change in a population it is important to have secured monitoring information over a significant period of time for each of these different demographic components. Within Britain, such information comes from the BTO's nest record (productivity) and ringing schemes (mortality/survival and movements). Information collected through these schemes can be used in integrated population models and tested against measures of population change derived from long-term monitoring programmes like the BTO/JNCC/RSPB Breeding Bird Survey. Being largely nocturnal and occurring at low densities, our owl populations are not well monitored by such schemes and information on changing populations typically comes from periodic national surveys and more detailed local studies. Examination of local studies provides the best evidence for what drives observed population changes, at least at the local level.

Iain Taylor's detailed work on Scottish Barn Owls, for example, provides good evidence that, in this population at least, the number of breeding pairs is determined by the overwinter mortality of breeding adults, the survival of first-year birds and the recruitment into the breeding population of birds of all ages. Taylor found that variations in adult mortality rates, which varied from about 20 per cent to 56 per cent between years, explained a significant component of the total variation in breeding numbers. Stability in the size of the breeding population was achieved when the mortality rate for breeding adults was roughly 35 per cent; exceed this figure and the population would decline, drop below it and the population would increase. Recruitment into the breeding population was dominated by first-year birds (roughly 63 per cent of recruits), but a substantial proportion was made up of adults that had bred before though not during the previous breeding season. Over the course of 14 years, Taylor's Barn Owl population in his core study area varied from a low of just 15 breeding pairs to a maximum of 55, the changes following the vole cycle and indicating that it was vole abundance that was influencing survival rates and recruitment.

Recruitment is also likely to be important in British Tawny Owl populations which, at 60 per cent, show a higher rate of local recruitment than seen in some of the other parts of Europe. More widely, it has been shown that fluctuations in prey abundance also influence the pattern of recruitment in Tawny Owls. When food is abundant, the proportion of young, first-time breeders increases within the population. Chicks produced during the increase phase of the vole cycle, for example, have been shown to be more likely to recruit into the breeding population the following year and it is this recruitment that comprises the main component of the population response to an abundance of food. Interestingly, however, first-time breeders are less productive and show lower levels of survival than older birds so are less important for population growth beyond that season (Karell et al., 2009).

It is also worth noting that populations in different areas may do different things. For example, Southern's study of a Tawny Owl population near Oxford showed the population (defined by the number of breeding pairs) to be roughly stable over the study period; spring numbers differed by no more than 15 per cent between years and then only when affected by a particularly hard winter. In contrast, Steve Petty's population in Kielder Forest showed annual variation of up to 24 per cent. Prey conditions between these two areas are likely to differ (the Oxford birds taking a wider range of prey and the Kielder birds taking a greater proportion of Field Voles) and this may shape the nature of the underlying demographic response.

Elsewhere in Europe, a detailed study of a declining Little Owl population in Denmark has, for example, found survival rates to have been fairly consistent over the study period, suggesting that changing mortality levels were not likely to have driven the decline. Instead it appeared that the problem was a reduction in productivity, with the parents unable to find sufficient food during the chick-rearing period. Field experiments with the population revealed that it

FIG 111. Little Owl populations in Denmark appear to be in decline because of poor productivity, but elsewhere within their European range other factors may be more important. (John Harding)

was possible to increase the proportion of hatched eggs that produced fledged young from 27 per cent to 79 per cent through the provision of supplementary food. This suggests that if the quality of the breeding habitat can be improved, providing more natural food, then the population decline might be halted (Thorup *et al.*, 2010). In contrast, long-term studies of the Little Owl in the Netherlands, where the number of breeding Little Owls has declined by more than 50 per cent since the 1970s, suggest that falling juvenile survival rates may be behind the observed decline (Le Gouar *et al.*, 2011). Local survival rates for juvenile birds also appear to be behind the declines seen in some German populations of the species (Schaub *et al.*, 2006).

Michael Schaub's work also underlines that populations don't exist in isolation. What happens to a population may also be influenced by what is happening to neighbouring populations and by the extent of movements between populations. More isolated Little Owl populations were found to have declined because of both lower survival rates of young birds and lower rates of immigration. This idea of movements between populations is key to the notion of source–sink dynamics, where a declining, poor quality population (a sink population) may only be sustained by the arrival of birds from a nearby high quality population that is producing lots of young (a source population).

Changes in the breeding populations of our owls may be determined by prey availability and survival but it is important to emphasise that these, in turn, may be shaped by other factors, such as climate, habitat and population density. If the quality of habitats, in terms of the community of prey species that they support, are altered by changes in management practices imposed by humans then we may see longer-term changes in owl populations that are determined outside of purely natural processes. Such human-mediate changes have the potential to bring about population declines, something that we will pick up again in the next two chapters.

CHAPTER 6

Owls and Humans

OUR RELATIONSHIPS WITH OWLS are many; they are often complex and sometimes contradictory. Most readers will look at these relationships with western eyes, from the viewpoint of a modern society several stages removed from its hunter-gatherer origins. Contemporary interpretations are, for this reason, likely to be somewhat different from those of our ancestors (even our relatively recent ones) and also from those peoples or cultures still in close connection with the land and the creatures with which they share it. As Jeremy Mynott notes in *Birdscapes*, owls 'present themselves to us with more associations than perhaps any other family of birds', something that appears to be 'a universal phenomenon, across time and cultures.' This chapter explores these relationships, covering not just the role of owls in our lives but also how these relationships influence the ways in which we seek to exploit, protect and conserve them. In order to fully understand our modern, western take on these relationships we first need to examine the origins of our association with owls and their changing significance in our lives.

BEGINNINGS

Owls, caves and prehistoric peoples
In the far south of Italy, where the Salento Peninsula ('the heel of Italy') pushes out into the Mediterranean, there is a cave that poses a question as to our earliest interactions with owls. Known as the Grotta Romanelli, its entrance sits on a limestone sea cliff to the south of the road that runs from Catro to Santa Cesarea Terme. This cave is one of the most important sites of the Italian Palaeolithic, yielding artefacts, rock art and other archaeological material. Some 52,000 bone remains have been excavated from the site, with the greater part of this sample (some 61 per cent) coming from at least 109 different species of bird.

The most common birds, two species of bustard (*Otis tarda* and *Tetrax tetrax*) and three of goose (*Anser fabalis*, *A. albifrons* and *Branta bernicla*), are recognisable as important prey species for the Palaeolithic hunter-gatherers who used the cave. Unsurprisingly, many of the bones show butchering marks and these are present on almost all of the bustard, goose, crane and pigeon bones, birds that we might, even today, regard as game (Cassoli & Tagliacozzo, 1997). Less expected, however, is the presence of similar butchering marks on the smaller numbers of owl, falcon and crow bones excavated from the site. Given the relatively small amount of meat carried on their carcasses, could these really have been quarry species or were they butchered for some other purpose?

A possible answer to this question comes from another cave site, this time located in western France. Situated in an area that holds a number of significant Palaeolithic sites, the Grotte de Bourrouilla, near Arancou, was occupied by late Magdalénien hunter-gatherers – one of the later cultures of the Upper Palaeolithic in Western Europe – some 13,000–12,000 years BP. Within the material excavated from the site were the remains of at least 53 Snowy Owls, many of which showed high levels of bone modification (Eastman, 1998). Agglomerations of Snowy Owl remains are a characteristic feature of late Magdalénien sites across much of France and, to a lesser extent, they have been noted elsewhere in Europe, including at the Grotta Romanelli in Italy. At some sites the Snowy Owl remains are associated with those of Eagle Owl, although it is worth noting that it can prove difficult to distinguish bone material from these two species. What is so special about these owl remains is that they appear to have been treated differently to other bird species found in the cave. While other birds showed a pattern of butchering marks indicative of the removal of flesh from the meatier parts of the carcass, the marks on the bones of the Snowy Owls suggest that these birds were skinned along the main feather tracts. Unlike the feathers of waterfowl or seabirds, those of owls are poor insulators and are easily saturated, suggesting that owl skins or individual feathers were harvested for their decorative qualities rather than for any practical purpose.

Owls as cultural characters

The use of feathers, skin or other body parts for decoration is something that has parallels in more recent hunter-gatherer societies, with the material often used as part of 'shamanic' rituals. Feathers taken from owls, for example, are known to have featured in the decorative masks and clothing of North American Indians, Inuit and certain African tribes. Could it be that the Snowy Owl and Eagle Owl remains that feature at Magdalénien sites demonstrate that these birds had an important cultural significance for Palaeolithic people?

FIG 112. Many owls carry some form of cultural significance and feature in myths, folklore and legend. (John Harding)

Much of our interpretation of the cultural significance of different creatures for our ancestors comes from the artefacts they have left behind. Rock art (also called cave art or parietal art) and carved or shaped objects (known as mobiliary art) have been the subject of detailed study. Interestingly, images of owls are rare within Palaeolithic material and there are very few examples where the material unquestionably represents an owl. One of these, and also the oldest, is an engraving carved into the wall of the Grotte Chauvet in the Ardèche region of southern France. Discovered in 1994, this cave is one of our most important sites for rock art, with many hundreds of animals depicted in black and red pigment and others engraved onto prepared surfaces. It is thought that the engravings and some of the pigment-based work date back to 32,000 BP, although a number of researchers attribute some of the images to a more recent period of history (possibly 18,000–10,000 BP).

The Chauvet owl is carved face on, the rounded head with recognisable eyes and beak and sporting a pair of ear tufts. While some researchers have suggested that the engraving represents a Long-eared Owl, it is more likely a representation of an Eagle Owl, a species that would have occupied similar sites to the hunter-gatherers who produced the carving. It has also been suggested that the owl is looking out over its back, the back denoted by the strong vertical lines that run from the head down to the bottom of the carving. While these lines could be taken to represent the individual wing feathers, they could equally be an interpretation of the vertical markings present on the chest of an Eagle Owl. One might expect a face-on image to hold more cultural significance than one viewed from behind.

The other unquestionable European image of an owl comes from another French cave, the Trois-Frères in the foothills of the Pyrenees. Although the image is crude in comparison with other rock art at the site, it appears to show a pair of Snowy Owls, with a chick positioned between them. The posture of the owls emphasises that these are ground-nesting birds and their shape strongly suggests Snowy Owl rather than Short-eared Owl, although both species may have been familiar to the artist. Other possible representations of owls are known from the region, including at Le Portel (a small cave some 30 miles east of Trois-Frères) and at Le Morin and La Marche.

Examples of mobiliary art, in the form of figurines from Dolni Vestonice in the Czech republic and a carved animal tooth from Mas D'Azil in the French Pyrenees, are equally scarce. The question of what cultural significance these owls may have had to our ancestors is a difficult one to answer, and one that might be influenced by our knowledge of more modern hunter-gatherer communities. It is not just owl images that are rare at Palaeolithic sites; bird images are equally unusual but there is one that might shed some light on the way in which birds, and in particular owls, might have been viewed by our ancestors.

In 1979, a complex of caves known as Lascaux, and located near the village of Montignac in the Dordogne, was given World Heritage Site status because of the richness and diversity of cave art contained within. Lascaux holds nearly 2,000 identifiable figures, dominated by large animals like Bison *Bison bonasus* and stag, but there are just two representations of birds. One of these appears deep in the cave, near a shaft that drops into the darkness, and is depicted alongside the representation of a human figure that lies prostrate in front of a large and virile Bison. The human hunter appears to have been killed by the Bison and this gives the bird figure a potentially shamanic meaning. The bird is simple in shape and sits on top of a single vertical line, as if topping a pole. The suggestion has been made that the image could either depict a tribal shaman in bird form or the external soul of the dead hunter. This theme has echoes within modern hunter-gatherer cultures; the bird, which is able to fly, enables the human soul to ascend into the spirit realm. It is likely that greater symbolic meaning would have been given to birds, like owls, that did not have a more practical use (*e.g.* as food) and which were associated with lonely places or the dark of the night, when human observers would have felt unsettled.

Owls appear not uncommonly on artefacts associated with cults of the European Great Goddess, appearing on burial urns, pottery, bone phalanges and amber figurines dating to the Neolithic and Early Bronze Age. Many of these show some human characteristics, including breasts, or are portrayed adorned with jewellery. More widely, early symbolic representations of owls are known from sites in places such as Guatemala, northern Australia and Inner Mongolia.

A DIVERSITY OF ATTITUDES

Owls feature in many of the major cultures that have existed down through the ages, from China's Shang Dynasty with its owl-shaped bronzes to the Greeks and their owl cups. Although there are some common themes (such as the association of owls with an approaching death) there is much variation in how they are viewed and in the role that they play in a society's beliefs. Some of these cultures, for example Australia's aborigines or Africa's bushmen, are essentially hunter-gatherer in nature and their relationships with owls may reflect most closely those of prehistoric peoples. It may be unwise, however, to make strong comparisons with such distant cultures, not least because of the sometimes contradictory attitudes seen within otherwise contemporary societies. For example, while the Native American Pawnee saw the owl as a symbol of protection, the Apache, Creek and Catawba looked upon them as an unlucky omen.

Owls and goddesses

One of the most striking images of the owl's association with the supernatural comes in the form of a Mesopotamian plaque, currently housed in the British Museum. Known as the 'Queen of the Night Relief' the plaque, modelled in high relief from baked straw-tempered clay, displays a curvaceous but thin-waisted woman, whose legs end in strongly taloned feet, mirroring those of the pair of owls that flanks her. The unnamed goddess wears an eight-horned headdress and has multi-coloured wings that hang with tips down, indicating her association with the underworld. It is thought that she was made between 1,800 and 1,750 BC and that she represents one of two Mesopotamian sister goddesses. Previous attempts to associate the figure with the demoness Lilitu (referred to in the bible as Lilith) are now thought to be a misreading of an ancient text. The figure is likely to have stood in a shrine, where her red body, set against a black background, would have made a striking feature. Interestingly, there are no other examples of owls presented within such an iconographic context within surviving Mesopotamian art, nor are there any textual references which might directly associate owls with an individual god or goddess (though see below). Do the owls of the Queen of the Night Relief invoke a supernatural significance or are they simply used to underline that this is a goddess of the night?

It is in ancient Greece that the owl holds an undisputed association with a goddess, in this case the goddess Athena. According to Greek mythology, Athena was the daughter of Zeus, a powerful goddess linked with art, wisdom, guardianship and war. Athena is frequently depicted alongside an owl, thought

FIG 113. The goddess Athena and her owl featured on Greek coins. (Mike Toms)

to be a Little Owl, and the image of the owl appears independently on many different artefacts in representation of the goddess herself. It has been suggested that the association may derive from the presence of owls in and around the Athenian temples. Alternatively, it might have been inherited from a previous culture (possibly Mesopotamian in origin and associated with the cult of the Eye Goddess). Within the poetry of Homer, Athena is often described as having bright or gleaming eyes 'γλαυκῶπις' or '*glaukopis*'. The word '*glaukopis*' is derived from '*glaukos*' (meaning gleaming) and '*ops*' (meaning eye). The Greek 'γλαύξ' or '*glaux*', which means 'owl' is derived from the same root and the gleaming eyes suggest both a bird that sees well in the dark of night and a goddess whose vision gives her wisdom.

The importance of Athena to the people of Athens saw a certain reverence of the owl itself, strengthening the association that existed between the goddess and her symbol. It also saw some of the qualities of the goddess rubbing off onto the owl and it is here that we see wisdom and the owl become synonymous. Both the goddess and 'her' owl featured on Athenian coins over several centuries, the head of the goddess on one side, the bird (usually shown in relief) on the other. Such coins became known colloquially as 'owls'. In his play *The Birds*, Aristophanes jokes:

> And first of all, what every judge is really keen to have, some owls of Laureium who'll never leave. They'll nest inside your homes, hatch in your purse, and always breed small silver change.

Laureium was the site of the silver mines from which the coins were fashioned. In the same play, Aristophanes alludes to how common owls were around Athens, or at least to the strong association of the city with owls, when he writes 'And who is it brings an owl to Athens?' in a 'taking coals to Newcastle' manner. As well as appearing on coins, the Athenian owl also appeared on various ceramic vessels, including the small measuring cups known as *glaux skyphos* (owl cups). The owl was such a central feature in Athenian daily life at this time that it is perhaps not surprising that it was viewed as a totem of good fortune. There is, for example, reference to the Athenian owl as a good omen in battle – Aristophanes again, this time in his play *The Wasps* – with the goddess sending her night bird across the host, prompting joyous omens for the Athenian armies. The Athenian proverb 'there goes an owl' was also said to indicate victory. There is even the tale of an Athenian general who, lifting the morale of his own army by releasing owls that settled on helmets and shields, routed the Carthaginians in 310 BC. The presence of the owls in this context is taken to represent the attendance of the goddess herself, standing with her loyal Athenian followers.

The owl as witch and other negative associations

The impression gained from much of the modern material dealing with the representation of the owl within Greek and Roman myth and folklore, is that the reverence afforded in Athens was particular to the Little Owl and not shared more widely (either across other owl species or across a wider geographical area). In many modern texts you will read of classical witches assuming the form of an owl and there is the general association of owls, as a group, with misfortune and evil. It is easy to assume that these modern interpretations should have their roots in well-documented classical superstition but, as we shall see, there is some debate as to the extent to which this is the case.

Antonius Liberalis, writing in the 2nd century AD, gave brief descriptions of the transformations of mythical figures into birds; his work was based on accounts that had originally been described in *Ornithogonia*, a lost manuscript written by the Greek mythographer Boios. One of these accounts concerns Polyphonte and her two sons, all transformed into birds in punishment for the sons' cannibalistic habits. Polyphonte became a 'strix' that 'cries by night, without food or drink, with head below and tips of feet above, a harbinger of war and civil strife to men'. One of her sons was turned into a vulture and the other into a 'bubo', 'a bird that is seen for no good'. As might be deduced from the name, the strix later came to be presented as an owl, yet the original description from Antonius Liberalis suggests another creature of the night, namely the bat, with its 'head below and tips of feet above'. Other early accounts, this time of Latin reference, also describe the strix with distinctly bat-like characteristics and it is not until later that we see the strix indisputably associated with the owl. The strix appears in the works of both Ovid and Horace, the latter including the creature's feathers among the ingredients for a magic charm being prepared by the witch Canidia in an attempt to secure the affections of Varus:

> *Et uncta turpis ova ranae sanguine*
> *Plumamque nocturnae strigis*

While the reference to feathers might be taken for evidence that the strix was a bird and not a bat, it is worth noting that the ancients believed the bat to be a form of bird, often ascribing it with avian properties like feathers and the production of eggs. Several authors have attempted to piece together the foundations upon which modern reference to the strix as owl is defined, with some suggesting that the only clear links come from similarities in the nature of certain superstitions. The common features link a witch, through transformation or metamorphosis, with a nocturnal bird. This nocturnal bird that was 'ill-omened' could be read as the mythical strix or a very much real owl, something that was adopted by later writers, such as Shakespeare, who borrowed heavily from the classics. Shakespeare alludes to the bird as an unlucky omen, foretelling a death:

> *And yesterday the bird of night did sit,*
> *Even at noon-day, upon the market-place,*
> *Hooting and shrieking*
>
> *(Julius Caesar*, Act I, Scene III)

While we, and possibly the author, might read this as an owl, the original source is likely to have described a strix. Whatever the true nature of the original text, it is evident from fairly early on that it was the owl that became associated with ill fortune and the supernatural. It was not just the call of the bird that was regarded as an evil omen; to see one abroad in daylight was equally unfortunate, something that Shakespeare uses to further emphasise the fate awaiting Caesar.

The legend of the strix survived into the Middle Ages and beyond, even though the notion of the witch herself was sometimes lost, leaving just the owl to be fearful of. One way to combat such misfortune was to nail the body of a dead owl to the door of a house or outbuilding, a practice that was still extant in certain European regions up until comparatively recently. Even today we see the owl linked with witchcraft through works like *Harry Potter*, where the owl remains the familiar of wizards. It is worth briefly mentioning the 'bubo' that appears in Antonius Liberalis and raising the question of whether this could be an owl and the source of apparent confusion surrounding the nature of the strix.

FIG 114. While some cultures view owls as malicious spirits, others view them as spiritual guardians. (John Harding)

The evidence underlines that the 'bubo' and the 'strix' were different creatures, so perhaps one was the owl while the other the bat. Pliny, writing in c. 77–79 AD identifies three 'birds of the night with crooked talons': the 'noctuae' (thought to be Little Owl), the 'bubo' (thought to be Eagle Owl) and the 'ululae' (thought by some to be the Tawny Owl).

BEYOND THE MEDITERRANEAN

Away from the Mediterranean Basin and its classical culture we see owls feature strongly in myth and superstition. While China's Shang Dynasty had its 'zun' wine containers, cast in bronze in the shape of owls, there was a more widespread Chinese belief that owls were harbingers of death, their calls the voices of demons crying out to their kin. There are Chinese stories that liken the call, heard when someone is about to die, to the phrase 'dig, dig', a reference to the need to prepare a fresh grave. The Chinese owl is sometimes spoken of as the 'bird which calls for the soul', alluding to the superstition that it is the owl which carries away the soul of the deceased. This association with the newly deceased is also seen in other cultures, though not always in a negative way. Some Native American tribes, for example, viewed the owl as a spiritual guide. Placing a feather taken from a live owl into the hand of a dying person would allow the owl to guide the deceased on the long journey to the afterlife. Navajo culture takes this a step further, the human soul assuming the form of an owl, and Mohave culture held the belief that departed warriors were reincarnated as owls. The strong association of the owl with human mortality has, perhaps unsurprisingly, seen the development of ambivalent or sometimes contradictory attitudes towards owls. Where, for example, one Native American tribe might see the owl as some form of spiritual guardian, a messenger acting as a conduit between the human and spirit worlds, another would see it as a malicious spirit, likely to bring about misfortune and death.

This dichotomy of associations is particularly evident in the Moche culture of northern Peru, which existed from c. 100 AD to 750 AD and produced some fine-line slip-painted ceramics. For the Moche, the owl had a dual role. On the one hand it featured as the anthropomorphic Owl Warrior in recurring dramas linked to the presentation of victims for ritual sacrifice; on the other it was the *curandera* (or healer) who, through her owl persona, assumed supernatural abilities that supported the healing ritual. The *curandera* is sometimes represented as an owl on Moche ceramics, underlining the shamanic significance attached to the character. While the Owl Warrior is often similarly presented, he is occasionally clearly portrayed as a human, wearing an owl mask and cloak. In some instances then, it is the supernatural owl being that is presented, in others it is a more truthful representation of the participant, crossing the boundary between human and supernatural through the use of a mask and cloak. Owl masks are sometimes used as part of ceremony and ritualised storytelling elsewhere. The Kuba tribe of West Africa, for example, produce highly expressive owl masks with huge eyes and short ear tufts that are used in ceremonies

FIG 115. Part of the depiction of a sacrificial ceremony from a piece of Moche pottery. The Owl Warrior is depicted centre left. (Redrawn from Donnan, 1978)

Across much of Africa the owl is still regarded with suspicion and ill omen, something that has caused difficulties with conservation efforts directed towards rare species of owl. The negative attitudes towards Africa's owls share many of the superstitions that we have already seen elsewhere, from the belief that they are witches in bird form, through to their bringing disease, foretelling death and delivering misfortune. Elsewhere, however, owls have been associated with things other than death, including birth and even the weather. Chinese children born on the day of the owl (the summer solstice) were considered likely to have a violent personality and might even murder their own mother (something which stems from the Taoist belief that young owls would pluck out their mother's eyes or even devour her)! In the south of France, however, a shrieking owl would do nothing more harmful than lead a pregnant woman to conclude that she would give birth to a girl. In Wales, a hooting owl would signal that a maiden was about to lose her virginity.

A British perspective

An understanding of the different attitudes towards owls that have existed down through history and within other cultures provides some insights into the owl's representation within British folklore and literature – the two are often intertwined. Both our written and oral traditions draw heavily upon older material, much of it imported from elsewhere. Shakespeare, for example, is believed to have used Sir Thomas North's 1579 translation of Plutarch's *Parallel Lives* as source material for many of his Roman plays and he may well have introduced references to owls from this and other Classical texts. Similarly, we see apparently local owl-based superstitions that have parallels elsewhere across Europe and beyond, with owls portrayed unfavourably as unlucky omens and harbingers of death. There is, for example, an early reference to two owls of enormous size which would appear whenever one of the members of the Wardour family (living at Arundel in West Sussex) was to depart this world. Writing in 1893, Lady Eveline Godron notes a Suffolk superstition in which the sight of an owl flying past the window of a room in which a sick person lay was taken to signify that death was approaching. On Shetland, there was the superstition that a cow would give bloody milk if frightened by a 'catyogle' (Snowy Owl). In other cases the owl was regarded as a weather prophet, as seen in the English belief that a calling owl heralded an approaching hailstorm, while in Glamorgan it was supposed to foretell snow.

The nocturnal calls of owls, in particular, could easily unsettle those unfamiliar with their true origins. In a 'letter' from July 1773, which appears in *The Natural History of Selborne*, Gilbert White noted the response of villagers to the hissing calls of nestling Barn Owls, writing how the whole village was up in arms 'imaging the church-yard to be full of goblins and spectres'. Such superstition was not solely the preserve of the uneducated. John Ruskin, in *Praeterita*, wrote 'Whatever wise people may say of them, I at least have found the owl's cry always prophetic of mischief to me.' There has been a change, however, as knowledge of owls and their behaviour has become more widely known. Beginning in the early 1900s with nature writers like Edward Thomas and the conservation efforts of the RSPB, see later in this chapter, our attitudes towards owls moved away from superstition and mistrust. It would be wrong, however, to think that the superstitious beliefs surrounding our British owls were lost many generations ago. The belief that to hear a calling owl foretold a death can still be encountered on rare occasion in certain rural parts of Britain, while persecution on the grounds of superstition was still evident during the 1940s and 1950s. Even today, the call of the Tawny Owl may be rolled out within a television or radio drama to add suspense, perpetuating the folklore around these birds.

OWLS IN ORAL TRADITION AND LITERATURE

Owls appear in the oral tradition of many cultures, where they become participants in stories and legends that are passed down through the generations. In some instances the stories take different forms across a wider area, with individual tribes relating a slightly different version. This hints at more distant origins, coupled with the adoption and development of such tales by succeeding generations and cultures. For example, a study of one particular aboriginal myth relating to an owl (Layton, 1985) highlights the extent of such variation even within a single, though extended, tribal group. Working in the Western Kimberleys, Robert Layton examined the cultural context of tribal legend and the rock art associated with it. Even though the owl features relatively little in aboriginal culture, it is a participant in some of the traditional myths and stories. In one particular legend, the heroic ancestor Wanalari takes revenge on the people for their cruel treatment of an owl but the manner of this revenge varies between tribal groups. Layton suggests that one of the reasons why he found differences in the form of the legend between different storytellers was that some of the storytellers were either not entitled to, or did not wish to, draw out the more profound implications of the legend's structure. Legends have an important place in Aboriginal culture, with its strong link to place and ancestry, and they should not be regarded as stories in the way that we might interpret them today.

Owls are part of a wider group of birds that dominate the avian references used in literature over a period of many centuries. The birds that make up this group are typically those that are either associated with a particular season (*e.g.* Cuckoo *Cuculus canorus* and Barn Swallow), are large or charismatic (*e.g.* eagles, cranes and quetzals) or are associated with particular places, times or events (*e.g.* Sacred Ibis *Threskiornis aethiopicus*, crows and owls). Owls often appear in the written word in association with wild and lonely places, with night or, as we shall see, at times considered inauspicious because of the events that subsequently unfold.

Ancient texts

Reference to owls within literature can be traced at least as far back as the ancient Indian sources that are believed to be behind Aesop's famous 'Fables'. Brought to Ceylon in the 3rd century BC, these often humorous animal stories include a tale in which the world's various creatures each elect a king to rule them. The birds initially elect an owl but the owl soon loses out to, depending on the version, either a swan, a parrot or (in a later Madagascan version of the tale) the Shrike *Dicurus forficatus*.

FIG 116. Barn Owls have featured heavily in literature over many centuries. (Steve Round)

Various owls also feature in biblical texts, most notably in the list of creatures deemed unclean and, therefore, forbidden to eat. The list appears in both Leviticus and Deuteronomy. The question of which owls appear in this list depends very much on the translation used and its date; for example, the Hebrew *Bath yaanah* has been interpreted as both Eagle Owl and Ostrich *Struthio camelus*. Perhaps one of the more reliable interpretations is that of Dr G. R. Driver, published in the *Palestine Exploration Quarterly* in 1955. Driver coupled his expert knowledge of ancient Hebrew with the ornithological knowledge of the late David Lack. Among the list of bird species identified by Driver and Lack we find:

Bath yaanah – Eagle Owl
Tachmas – Short-eared Owl
Shachaph – Long-eared Owl
Kos – Tawny Owl
Shalak – Fisher Owl
Yanshuph – Screech Owl – Barn Owl
Tishemeth – Little Owl
Qaath – Scops Owl

The English Standard version of the bible of 1990 lists just Short-eared Owl, Tawny Owl, Barn Owl and Little Owl. Owls appear elsewhere in the bible including, for example, in Isaiah where they are used to suggest the fate that awaits Babylon:

> *It shall never be inhabited … but wild beasts of the desert shall lie there, and their houses shall be full of doleful creatures; and owls shall dwell there, and satyrs shall dance there.*

Again we see the association of the owl with desolate places and misfortune.

The Middle Ages and beyond

Owls feature in many European Medieval manuscripts, covering a period from the establishment of the Saxon kingdoms (c. AD 700) to the time by which printing had radically changed the way in which manuscripts were produced (c. 1492). These manuscripts can be classified into several distinct forms, the earliest of which were copies of the gospels destined for liturgical reading in the church. From the 13th century we see the development of small, pocket-sized books for personal use. Known as psalters, these were often heavily decorated and, for a few decades around 1300 at least, we see the widespread use of birds,

FIG 117. Stained-glass quarry at St Bartholomew, Yarnton, Oxfordshire, showing an owl holding a bell. The scroll reads 'Ye schal praye for the fox'. (Gordon Plumb)

including owls, as decoration within English psalters, something that has no parallels elsewhere in Europe. In a few instances the illustration of an owl is directly relevant to the text, for example where it appears alongside other birds as part of the creation scene. In other cases it is purely symbolic, perhaps used to represent a bird of the night. It is for this reason that we see few owls in the gospel manuscripts but many more in the Apocalypses. Derived from the Book of Revelation, the Apocalypses were highly symbolic texts; roughly one in three surviving examples from England contains the image of an owl. We also see owls in bestiaries, collections of predominantly mythical information about animals, birds, plants and minerals, some of which contain an illustration showing Adam naming the birds and animals, often included among which is an owl.

None of the owls illustrated can be identified to species, with perhaps the exception of one that appears in the *Ormesby Psalter* and which, from inspection, could be taken to be a Tawny Owl. Some show ear tufts but others do not. A number of the illustrations show the owl with human characteristics, perhaps human ears or, in the case of an *English Book of Hours* illustrated by William de Drailes, human arms and hands. Elsewhere there is an illustration of an owl that appears to be tethered to a long pole held by a hunter (*De Lisle Psalter* – British Library MS Arundel 83. F. 14r). The owl is being mobbed by smaller birds, some of which are depicted stuck to the pole which, presumably covered in sticky lime, is being used to trap the songbirds. Leonardo da Vinci described how the Little Owl was used as a 'zimbello' during the hunting of thrushes and other small birds, drawing mobbing birds towards it that then became more easily captured.

Although many Medieval texts were concerned with the scholarly and spiritual life, we also find texts that deal with other matters, including romance, situation comedy and law. One particular text, *The Owl and the Nightingale* (c. 1200–15), takes the form of a debate or altercatio (a style popular on the Continent) and appears to have been written for the royal court. The owl and the Nightingale of the title are presented as two protagonists, each representing a different attitude towards life, the debate itself presented as a witty parody of legal procedures. The owl is initially portrayed as a dull, learned creature obsessed with the penitential nature of life (the church), while the Nightingale is presented as an advocate for secular pleasure, a singer of gay songs and the bringer of spring joy (the royal court). After a brief description of the two protagonists, we see the Nightingale deliver a series of charges against the owl, one of which suggests that the owl is 'unnatural' because she favours night over day. These accusations, which can be read allegorically as courtly distaste for the austerity of the church, are denied by the owl who offers to prove her innocence through trial by combat (a form of justice on the wane at the time, in which guilt or innocence was 'determined' by the intervention of God). The Nightingale manages to sidestep this offer and calls for Nicholas of Guildford (the likely author of the poem) to be appointed as judge and for the two birds to present their respective cases according to the process of law. What follows is a sophisticated debate, aimed at an aristocratic audience and centred on some of the key issues of the time, in which both birds present and counter a series of challenges upon their character. Ultimately, the owl slips up and the Nightingale and her supporters claim a victory. However, the owl demands a re-trial and, with the Nightingale agreeing to this demand, we are left in the dark as to the outcome.

In the context of our discussion on owls and our attitudes towards them, the poem's interest lies, to some degree, in the presentation of characteristics that we have already seen in earlier works. The owl is charged with being cruel, unclean and unnatural; yet she is also presented as being learned, with the scholastic gift of a perfect memory. More importantly, however, we also see a degree of original observation that is lacking in other poetry of the time (and indeed from much subsequent work prior to the 18th century). Not only is the plumage of the owl accurately described but we also see several common myths refuted; the utility of the owl, in taking mice from within farm buildings, is recognised, and the blindness of the owl by day is denied. Even the great Chaucer, in his *The Parliament of Fowls* (c. 1382), repeats the myth that owls cannot see by daylight when he writes: 'You fare with love as owls with light; the day blinds them, but they see very well in darkness' (translation by Gerard NeCastro, 2007).

Chaucer was one of a number of early writers to exploit the negative image of the owl, writing in *The Legende of Good Women*: 'The oule al nyght aboute the balkes wond, That propehte is of wo and of myschance.' This pattern was repeated by many later writers, including the likes of Michael Drayton and William Shakespeare. The use of an owl to add menace to the dark mood of a scene being acted out is typical of Shakespeare and must, it seems, draw upon a wider superstitious fear of owls among his audience. Shakespeare taps into superstition and folklore in many of his references to owls, an approach also seen in other writing of the period. Edmund Spenser, in the *Faerie Queen* writes: 'And after him the owles and night ravens flew. The hateful messengers of heavy tidings.' John Lyly, in his play *Sappho and Phaon*, alluded to the owl's shriek and night raven's croak being fatal. Shakespeare himself, famously draws on the dark superstitions associated with owls in *Macbeth* where, at the point of the brutal murder of Duncan, we read:

> Hark! Peace! It was the owl that shriek'd, the fatal bellman, which gives the stern'st good-night. He is about it.

Shortly after, Lady Macbeth adds, 'I heard the owl scream and the crickets cry.'

Other of Shakespeare's owl references are used to emphasise the sense of place. In *Titus Andronicus* we are presented with a bleak and lonely place 'Here never shines the sun; here nothing breeds, unless the nightly owl or fatal raven.' This has echoes of Farid ud-din's Persian epic *The Conference of the Birds*. Farid ud-din, perhaps better known by his other pen name of 'Attar', was a theoretician of Sufism. Here he refers to the owl as the guardian of treasure:

> I tell you, my delight
> Is in the ruin and the dead of night
> Where I was born, and where I love to wone
> All my life long, sitting on some cold stone,
> Away from all your roystering companies,
> In some dark corner where a treasure lies;
> That, buried by some miser in the dark,
> Speaks up to me at midnight like a spark;

FIG 118. 'An he that will not fight for such a hope, go home to bed, and, like the owl by day, if he arise, be mock'd and wonder'd at' – *Henry VI, Part III*. (Mark Hancox)

And o'er it like a Talisman I brood,
Companion of the serpent and the toad.

It appears that Shakespeare's owls can be tied down to two species. The
'clamorous owl, that nightly hoots and wonders at our quaint spirits' in *A
Midsummer Night's Dream* is, most likely, the Tawny Owl, while Lady Macbeth's
owl 'that shriek'd' is, perhaps, a Barn Owl. Some of the mentions use owl
behaviour as a metaphor, defining the actions or character of one of the players.
The line, spoken by the Duke of Somerset in *Henry VI, Part III* – 'An he, that
will not fight for such a hope, go home to bed, and, like the owl by day, if he
arise, be mock'd and wonder'd at' – evokes an image that even the most casual of
birdwatchers will appreciate. Elsewhere we read of an encounter between a falcon
and an owl, something which is reported from time to time in the birdwatching
literature: ''Tis unnatural, even like the deed that's done. On Tuesday last, a
falcon, towering in her pride of place, was by a mousing owl hawk'd at and kill'd.'
While I have seen a Kestrel harass a Barn Owl in this manner, I have not seen an
owl strike the first blow.

A more enlightened attitude
It is not until the 1700s that we begin to see texts that drop the superstition
and take a more realistic and appreciative approach to owls. Wordsworth seems
to have been particularly taken by owls and, aware of the superstitions still
surrounding them, defends these birds in verse on several different occasions. In
The Excursion, Book IV, we read:

Yet rather would I instantly decline
To the traditional sympathies
Of a most rustic ignorance, and take
A fearful apprehension from the owl

Elsewhere within Wordsworth's works – *Evening Voluntaries* (VII) – appears:

The Owlet ...
May the night never come, nor day be seen,
When I scorn thy voice or mock thy mien!

Percy Bysshe Shelley delivers a light account of the owl's call in his poem
'The Aziola', while Hannah Cowley writes the wonderful line: 'I wasn't born in
a wood to be scared by an owl' in her comedy *The Belles' Strategem* (1780). Not

everyone had dropped the superstitious associations, however, as we see from Sir Walter Scott, who wrote 'birds of omen, dark and foul, night-crow, raven, bat and owl', although the inclusion of 'owl' does rather help the rhythm of this line. Tennyson, in whose works the owl was the third most commonly referenced bird, occasionally draws on superstition too, but more often uses reference to owls in a more affectionate way. Interestingly, three species of owl can be identified from Tennyson's works: the Barn Owl, the Tawny Owl and the Eagle Owl. The reference to Eagle Owl is of particular interest given the history of this species within Britain. It is likely that Tennyson would have been very familiar with the species, which he uses as simile 'Round as the red eye of an eagle-owl, Under the half-dead sunset glared.' It is known that a relative of the poet, who lived not far from Tennyson at Somersby, 'kept several of these birds in a semi-wild state in an old castellated building near his house'.

Some of the writing from this period reveals authors who were equally well acquainted with owls and who could distinguish between the different species. The predominantly religious writer Thomas Gisborne, for example, wrote:

Heard ye the owl Hoot to her mate responsive? [Tawny Owl] *'Twas not she whom floating on white pinions near his barn* [Barn Owl]. *The farmer views well pleased, and bids his boy Forbear her nest.*

Perhaps some of the most honest narrative surrounding our owls can be found in the writings of John Clare (1793–1864). Clare, an agricultural labourer and poet, was a gifted observer of the wildlife and landscapes of his native Northamptonshire, publishing several volumes of verse that brought widespread, though short-lived, recognition. In 'Evening', written during a period when Clare was in an asylum, he recalls and describes a Barn Owl 'on wheaten wing, and white hood scowling o'er his eyes'. Such descriptive and accurate prose is a feature of Clare; here is a poet who has studied his subjects, rather than simply referencing them for dramatic effect.

A modern perspective

Another keen observer of the countryside, though writing much later than Clare, was the poet and writer Edward Thomas. Thomas, like Richard Jefferies before him, combined true knowledge of the countryside and its creatures with a sense of their cultural significance within our lives. This is something that we still see today, through writers like Richard Mabey and Mark Cocker. Mabey, now sharing his Norfolk borderlands with Barn Owls, is incisive when he writes: 'Few birds are so dramatically beautiful, or can bring the exquisite delicacy of flight so

FIG 119. There are few birds as strikingly powerful as an Eagle Owl. (Vincenzo Penteriani)

close to us, or can look at us so penetratingly, eye to eye.' He understands the emotional impact that the sight of a hunting Barn Owl can deliver; this is a bird that brings with it a sense of place. It is uncommon enough to be noteworthy, charismatic enough to warrant affection, but carrying with it a sense of something otherworldly and worthy of respect.

CULTURAL ATTITUDES AND CONSERVATION

Our varied and sometimes contradictory feelings towards owls, which have been shaped by our literature, beliefs and superstitions, have implications for our willingness and ability to conserve their populations in a changing world. The persecution of owls has been driven by fear, economics and ignorance. It is something that, within Britain and many other countries, has now largely been replaced by respect and the desire to conserve. The same is not true the world-over, however, and a lack of understanding continues to thwart conservation efforts directed towards some tropical owl species.

If there is one publication that can be said to represent the beginnings of owl conservation within Britain, then it is the paper by George Blaker which appeared in the autumn 1933 edition of *Bird Notes & News*, published quarterly by the RSPB. This paper, titled 'The Barn Owl in England: results of the census', was the first to draw proper attention to a decline that had been suspected for several years but never tested (Blaker, 1933). Blaker's paper provides a benchmark and, while lacking the statistical rigour of today's monitoring tools, the results have been used subsequently to determine the scale of decline over following decades. That such an investigation was launched, underlines a recognition that Barn Owl populations were in trouble – cause unknown.

Blaker's census also demonstrated that a more enlightened attitude was developing within much of the landowner and game-rearing community. Although some Barn Owls were still being shot and trapped by keepers, more and more were left untouched in recognition of the job that they did in controlling the smaller 'vermin' (see Chapter 5). The same tolerance was not afforded to all of our owls, however. Tawny Owls continued to be killed, in part because of fears that they might take Pheasant poults but also because they were blamed for the deaths of young Rabbits and hares. Suspicion that the introduced Little Owl might be taking Pheasant and partridge chicks also led to persecution and, fortunately, to the Little Owl Food Inquiry, which showed that gamebird chicks were a very minor part of the diet. Nevertheless, owls continued to fall victim to traps set for other species.

Over the following decades, and particularly from the 1970s onwards, we see the development of a wider conservation movement and the introduction of new legislation, notably the Wildlife and Countryside Act 1981, which delivered increased protection for our owls. Thanks in part to Michael Heseltine, then the newly appointed Secretary of State for the Environment, the Wildlife and Countryside Bill was steered through Parliament. In addition to pulling together and updating previous pieces of legislation, the resulting Act delivered vital new detail that sought to protect not just wild creatures but also their habitats. This was timely given the growing awareness that declines seen in some of the British owls were associated with the pressures they faced in a rapidly changing landscape. Much of the legislative focus was, however, on designated parcels of habitat found to be of 'special interest'. This meant that the wider landscape changes associated with the intensification of farming went on unchecked, something that was not good news for our owls.

FIG 120. Changes in the wider countryside are thought to be behind the declines seen in many of our bird species but are more difficult to tackle from a conservation viewpoint. (Mike Toms)

Parallel to the changes seen within nature conservation in Britain were developments in the monitoring techniques necessary to document bird populations; these would be needed to underpin conservation policy and to measure the success of resulting action. Schemes like the Common Birds Census, operated by the BTO (www.bto.org), delivered annual measures of population change across a range of species. The nocturnal habits and low population densities of our owls meant that they were poorly monitored by such schemes, prompting periodic single-species surveys like the Hawk Trust's Barn Owl Survey (Shawyer, 1987) and the follow-up Project Barn Owl, which also provided the first population estimate for the Little Owl (Toms *et al.*, 2001). Knowledge of our other owls was still lacking.

Perhaps the most important legacy of the Hawk Trust's Barn Owl Survey was the resulting public interest in owl conservation. This interest, and its associated financial support, saw the development of nest box schemes and the establishment of local owl study groups, operating in partnership with a farming and landowning community that was now more receptive and supportive. As we will see within the individual species accounts that form Chapter 7, the broad-based support for owl conservation has delivered some amazing achievements. One of the drivers behind this success has to be the regard that we now hold for our owls. Public interest has enabled the conservation community to position our owls as totems for the health of the wider environment. We have dispensed with the fear and suspicion formerly surrounding them and taken them to our hearts. As Mark Cocker and Richard Mabey recently commented in *Birds Britannica*, an owl 'somehow resembles a human, if humans ever had bird form' (Cocker & Mabey, 2005). Maybe this completes the owl's transformation from a creature of the night to one we can rightly cherish.

WHAT FUTURE FOR THE BRITISH OWLS?

The position that owls now hold within our affections, the legislation that acts to protect them and the conservation efforts being directed towards them, all suggest a positive future for British owls. There remains, however, a worrying degree of uncertainty around the scale and trajectory of current population trends for most of our breeding owls. In some instances, notably for Short-eared Owl and Long-eared Owl, there is also a surprising lack of basic knowledge about population size and breeding densities. Such information, particularly that relating to changing population trends, will be of fundamental importance in both alerting conservationists to declines and providing a benchmark against which the success of conservation actions can be assessed.

Within UK owl conservation it is the direct interactions with humans that have largely been addressed, and we have seen a marked decline in the levels of deliberate persecution, the illegal trade in wild-caught birds and the theft of eggs from nests. Some of these practices still go on, however, and will continue to do so as long as there are selfish and self-interested people around to commit such acts, but things are much better than they were just a few decades ago. They are certainly better here than is the case in many other European countries.

It is the indirect interactions with humans that continue to give greatest cause for concern, with the loss and fragmentation of favoured habitats and a changing climate the two most significant issues. As we will see in the final section of the book (the species accounts), the effects of such indirect interactions are already having a significant impact on some of our owl species. Habitat loss reduces both feeding and nesting opportunities and exacerbates other problems (such as collision with road traffic) as birds are forced to hunt or disperse over larger areas. Habitat and climate change are difficult to address, since their impacts are wide ranging and the drivers behind them complex and often driven by political or socioeconomic factors. The scales over which they operate also make it difficult to disentangle their impacts on owls from those of other factors operating over similar scales. In order to properly assess such impacts we will need to draw upon large datasets, such as the recently published *Bird Atlas 2007–11*, and support our interpretation and analyses with new information, collected from more intensive studies of our owls and their ecology.

It is within the next (final) section of the book that we will see examples of what we already know or still need to know about our individual owl species. We will see how well-studied species, like Barn Owl, have well-developed conservation strategies, based on sound science and suggestive of a more positive outlook for the future. We will also see, however, how little information we have for our two *Asio* owls and discover just how much work needs to be done as a matter of urgency. There is also the question of what to do about our two non-native owls – the Little Owl, an introduced species, and the Eagle Owl, a former native whose current population almost certainly stems entirely from aviary escapes. While the Little Owl has been here for some time, seemingly without any negative consequences, its population shows signs of decline and it could warrant conservation action. The Eagle Owl is a new arrival, at least within our current fauna, and it is unclear as to what future impacts it might have on other species should it become more widely established.

It seems unlikely that our owl community will change significantly over the coming decades, but we may see changes in the status of individual species. Sudden changes in farming policy or forest management may alter the availability of favoured habitats for owls, as they have done in the past – acting in either positive or negative ways – and we will need to draw upon our current knowledge (and fill gaps where this is lacking) in order to make predictions about the likely impacts that such changes may have.

Our knowledge of other aspects of owls' lives will also change, as increasing amounts of new research are published. As we have already seen through the course of these main chapters, new work is continually adding to what we know about owls. We will almost certainly see our understanding of the taxonomic relationships that exist between the different owl species tied down, the first step in developing a proper framework for species protection and future conservation action. We will gain new insights into how owls perceive the world around them and, in particular, we will gather new information on reproductive success and the individual, teasing out the influences of disease, genetics and territory quality. It is an interesting time to be beginning a career studying owls, whether as a paid academic or as an enthusiastic 'amateur' (and I use the term solely in the context of being 'unpaid'). As you will see from many of the examples given in the species accounts that follow, there is the potential for the amateur to make a significant contribution to our knowledge of the British owls.

CHAPTER 7

Guide to British Owls

Short-eared Owl. (Steve Round)

Common Barn Owl
Tyto alba
(SCOPOLI 1769)

FAMILY: Tytonidae

IDENTIFICATION

The Common Barn Owl is a
medium-sized owl of slender
appearance, white underneath
and washed with golden buff
above. There is a strongly defined,
heart-shaped facial disc, pale
within and with black eyes at
its centre. In the field the Barn
Owl can look particularly pale,
sometimes almost washed out
in its appearance, but when
seen close up or in the hand, an

FIG 121. Common Barn Owl. (Jill Pakenham)

intricate overlay of silvery-grey markings is revealed; these dominate the wing
coverts, the back and the head. There can be significant variation between races
and individuals but females are usually darker and more strongly marked than
males. Within Britain, particularly in study populations from northern areas,
males have white underparts with little or no speckling. Females, in contrast,
invariably have at least a wash of light ochre across their underparts, if not
something more richly *coloured*, and are strongly speckled. Iain Taylor found that
within his Scottish study population it was the degree of black speckling on the
underparts that proved to be the most reliable feature by which to determine the
sex of an individual. Almost all of the females he examined (some 98 per cent)
had at least some black speckles on the underwing coverts and on the contour
feathers covering the breast and flanks. Many females had their entire underparts
densely covered in these speckles. Most males lack any such markings on their
underparts or underwing coverts; where such markings do occur in males, they
tend to be small in number and faint in appearance. The general pattern for
females to be darker and more strongly marked than males is also repeated in
the dark-breasted race *guttata* that is occasionally recorded from Britain. Within

FIG 122. This female shows the speckling on her flanks and underwing useful for separating the two sexes. Females often show more spotting than this, males much less or none at all. (Mike Toms)

FIG 123. The pattern and width of the bars on the wing feathers may be useful to age and sex Barn Owls. (Mike Toms)

the Dutch breeding population, where both the white-breasted and dark-breasted forms occur, there is overlap in the degree of speckling between the two sexes. Dutch researchers use the pattern and width of the bars on the wing feathers as an alternative method for sexing Barn Owls, something that has yet to be properly explored as a tool within Britain (de Jong & van den Burg, 2012). As we have seen in Chapter 5, the degree of spotting on female Barn Owl appears to be a form of plumage ornamentation linked to immune function.

Studies suggest that there is little or no difference in body size between male and female Barn Owls and that, apart from during the breeding season, females are not significantly heavier than males. Male body weight appears to be fairly consistent throughout the year, at around 320 to 340 g, while that of females increases prior to egg-laying, remains high during incubation and then falls somewhat during the period when chicks are being looked after in the nest. A smaller increase in female weight during July and August may relate to birds preparing for second or replacement clutches.

Young Barn Owls are particularly unattractive during their first few days of life before the downy feathers are acquired. The first down, a short white down which is rather sparse in nature, is replaced by the mesoptile (second down), creamy in colour and dense in appearance, beginning when the bird is 10–14 days of age. Traces of the second down are still present when the chick fledges, most often around the nape,

FIG 124. A Barn Owl chick showing the characteristic down. (Mike Toms)

legs and thighs. Once this has been lost the plumage then resembles that of an adult bird and it becomes impossible to age birds in the field. In the hand, however, it is possible to use the degree of contrast between neighbouring flight feathers and the pattern of barring on both these and the tail feathers to age individuals, something that is possible because the flight feathers are moulted over a number of years, with only a few moulted each year and to a predictable pattern.

Voice

Compared to our other owls, it appears that the Barn Owl is not a particularly vocal species. The male tends to deliver his drawn-out screech, best described as 'shrrrreeee', during the period of courtship that precedes egg-laying. The screech is highly variable, sometimes sounding rather weak and somewhat hoarse but at other times strong and strident, with a clear but slightly vibrato quality. Since unmated males call more persistently than mated individuals, the call appears to serve two functions: the attraction of a mate and the advertisement of territory ownership. Observations demonstrate that the call is often given while the bird is perched on or around the nest site but it may also be given during what appears to be a ritualised display flight, the male making short circuits of the area around the nest on stiff and rather rigid wing beats. Nestling Barn Owls deliver a surprisingly loud hissing sound when disturbed, something that is equally evident when they are waiting for adults to return to the nest site with prey, underlining that this is predominantly a begging call (see Chapter 3). Often described as a 'wheezy snoring' the call can be heard over several hundred metres, making it a useful means of determining site occupancy during watches at tree cavity sites for monitoring purposes. Individual birds may bill-snap when threatened, although in my experience they do this less readily than other species, e.g. Long-eared Owl.

HISTORY

Although the Barn Owl has a long history within Britain, its fortunes have changed dramatically over this period. As we saw back in Chapter 1, Mesolithic Britain and the domination of woodland as the major habitat type would have limited opportunities for this open-country owl. Despite the popular notion that the whole of Britain was wooded at this time, it is worth noting that both the pollen record and the archaeological avifauna indicate the presence of some open country. Even so, the Barn Owl population would have been much smaller at that time than it is today, perhaps numbering fewer than 1,000 pairs, a figure that is based on the current densities seen in remaining 'wildwood' habitats like Białowieża, Poland. It is only with the clearance of woodland, associated with the switch from a hunter-gatherer to farmer lifestyle, that the opportunities available to the Barn Owl really increased. During this period of transition we start to see Barn Owl remains associated with human sites, notably Neolithic sites from south-east and south-west England, and the suspicion is that Barn Owl populations responded quickly to the increasing amounts of land being opened up to agriculture.

Remains continue to appear from archaeological sites as we move forwards in time with, for example, the species represented at more than a dozen Roman sites, extending as far north as Catterick in Yorkshire (Yalden & Arabella, 2009). Other records, from the Middle Ages onwards, are joined by increasing reference to the species within written accounts; by the 18th century the species was regarded as being the most common owl over much of the country (Latham, 1781). Traditional agricultural systems, with their relatively inefficient methods and reliance on livestock, would have left the countryside rich in prey and the owls would have been able to hunt over extensive areas of rough and damp grassland, and to seek rats and other small mammals from around farm buildings and stackyards. The association with open habitats underlines how the Barn Owl's longer-term fortunes are likely to have been strongly linked to the nature of agricultural activities.

There came a point, however, where advances in agricultural practices no longer produced conditions so favourable to Barn Owls and it seems likely

FIG 125. Like other birds, Barn Owls preen their feathers to maintain their condition. (Mark Hancox)

that British populations started to decline from the middle of the 19th century. The decline was certainly evident by the early 1900s, prompting Blaker's first national survey and the subsequent figure of 12,000 pairs derived for the English and Welsh breeding populations (Blaker, 1933). The decline identified by Blaker seems to have continued, becoming more general from the 1950s onwards, with agricultural change thought to be behind falling numbers (Prestt, 1965). By the time of the BTO's first breeding atlas (Sharrock, 1976) it was estimated that there were some 4,500–9,000 pairs in Britain and Ireland, although this was based on an untested assumption that the species was to be found at densities of two to four pairs per occupied 10-km square. The next population estimate to be calculated came from the Hawk Trust survey that was launched in 1982. This produced an estimate of 3,778 pairs in England and Wales, with a further 640 pairs in Scotland and 33 pairs in the Channel Islands (Shawyer, 1987).

Data from the BTO's second breeding atlas (1988–91) suggested a decline of 43 per cent in the number of occupied squares since the first atlas but comparisons were hampered by uncertainties over differences in the coverage achieved by the two studies (Gibbons et al., 1993). A new national survey of breeding Barn Owls in Britain was carried out between 1995 and 1997, using intensive fieldwork methods within a sample of 1,110 survey squares. The results of this work produced a new national estimate of c. 4,000 breeding pairs, for the first time using a truly repeatable survey design (Toms et al., 2001). Since the last national survey, a good deal of conservation work has been targeted at Britain's Barn Owl population and the general feeling among conservation practitioners is that the species has increased in numbers. Data from multi-species annual monitoring programmes might suggest a significant increase in Barn Owl numbers, although such schemes are not ideal for monitoring species like Barn Owl, which occurs at low density and tends to be secretive in habits. Barn Owl numbers at the start of the 2013 breeding season were thought to be at a low ebb in northern Britain, most likely the result of two difficult winters, but buoyant in East Anglia, underlining the regional differences that exist. A repeat of the most recent survey is what is really needed.

DISTRIBUTION AND HABITAT

The Barn Owl is distributed widely across Britain and Ireland, with birds breeding as far north as Caithness and Sutherland. The bulk of the breeding population is to be found in southern Scotland and England, however, again underlining the climatic limitations shaping the breeding distribution within

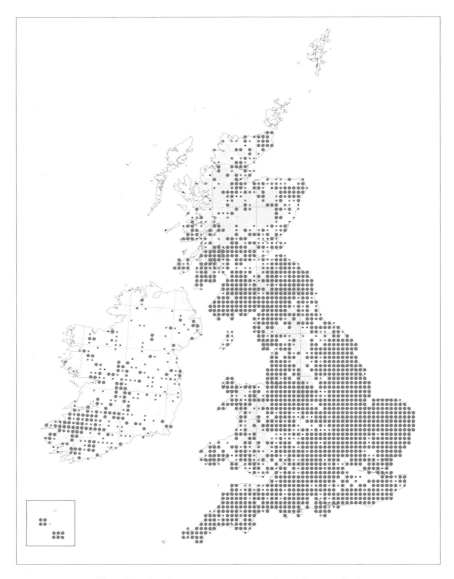

FIG 126. Barn Owl breeding distribution, 2008–11. Reproduced from *Bird Atlas 2007–11* (Balmer *et al.*, 2013), which is a joint project between BTO, BirdWatch Ireland and the Scottish Ornithologists' Club. Maps reproduced with permission from the British Trust for Ornithology.

FIG 127. A Barn Owl nest box fitted to the outside of a disused agricultural building. (Mike Toms)

Britain. Modelled abundance maps, produced for *Bird Atlas 2007–11*, suggest peak densities are to be found across large parts of East Anglia, Lincolnshire and Yorkshire, with other important populations in Kent, West Sussex, south-west England, Anglesey, Cheshire, Lancashire and south-west Scotland (Balmer *et al.*, 2013). The Barn Owl is absent as a breeding species from the Northern Isles, the Outer Hebrides and the Isles of Scilly. Within Ireland, the core breeding range is now centred on the south-west of the country, with *Bird Atlas 2007–11* revealing a substantial loss of breeding records from northern and eastern Ireland over the last 40 years. Breeding pairs have also been lost from around London, parts of the Peak District and from central Wales.

The feature common to areas occupied by breeding Barn Owls is the presence of open grassland or woodland-edge habitat, rich in small mammal prey. Rough grassland, with its populations of Field Vole, is favoured, but secondary prey species like Wood Mouse and Common Shrew become important in areas where rough grassland is less readily available. Some of the highest densities of breeding Barn Owls within Britain are to be found in the arable landscapes of the East Anglian fens. Within such intensively managed arable landscapes, small mammals are most abundant in linear strips of ditch bank, with both Wood Mouse and Field Vole important. Elsewhere, such as in the rotational plantation forests of northern England, the owls have access to Field Voles in the well-developed grassy swards that become established pre-canopy closure. As well as suitable hunting habitat, breeding Barn Owls also need access to a nesting cavity. Such sites may have been limiting in some open landscapes (e.g. fenland and the Somerset Levels) and the provision of nest boxes has almost certainly helped to increase the density of breeding pairs in such areas.

More widely, the Common Barn Owl is found breeding elsewhere across Europe, pushing east into Russia and south into Africa. The species is also found breeding on the Arabian Peninsula, mostly around the periphery, and in south-east Asia. A number of different races are recognised and it is likely that further genetic work will refine our knowledge of race limits and their associated distributions (see Chapter 1).

BREEDING ECOLOGY

For British Barn Owls the breeding season may begin as early as February, although its timing is dependent on both overwinter/early spring weather conditions and prey abundance. The average date on which the first egg is laid is earlier following a mild winter and later following a wet one, with a suggestion that (taking Britain as a whole) winter weather conditions may be more important than spring ones (Dadam et al., 2011). However, one Scottish study found mean laying date was correlated with spring temperature but not winter temperature or the degree of snow cover (Taylor, 1994), suggesting that the factors operating on the initiation of breeding activity may be rather complex, see Chapter 3. Iain Taylor's study also found that mean laying date was correlated with spring vole abundance. Daria Dadam's work, drawing on records from the national Barn Owl Monitoring Programme, revealed that the proportion of pairs initiating breeding attempts was lower following a poor winter, with the mean weight of females caught during routine monitoring visits lower than that recorded in years when overwinter conditions appeared more favourable. Clutch and brood size were also smaller following colder and wetter winters (Dadam et al., 2011). Dave Leech and his colleagues showed that, between 2002 and 2007, the average date of the first egg being laid by British Barn Owls had become progressively earlier, shifting by roughly half a day per year (Leech et al., 2008). This is a response to a changing climate, a pattern also seen in a number of other bird species (Crick et al., 1997).

During the early part of the breeding season birds increasingly concentrate their activities on the nest site, reducing the size of their hunting ranges and increasing the amount of time spent together as a pair. The two birds may fly in and out of the intended nest site, sometimes calling, and the female will often call to the male from the nest site itself, as if begging for food. On occasion the male may present his mate with a small mammal or other prey item, a behaviour that is frequently followed by copulation. When roosting together, the two birds often engage in mutual preening, behaviour that is usually delicate and sometimes accompanied by a series of soft calls. As the female begins to spend more time at the nest ahead of laying, so the male takes on the role of provider, supplying his mate with prey. Provisioning visits may provide an indication of prey availability and/or the male's abilities as a hunter; if insufficient food is provided then breeding may be delayed or not happen at all.

Favoured nest sites tend to be large cavities, often situated in mature deciduous trees or (increasingly) nest boxes sited in trees or within agricultural buildings. As we saw in Chapter 3, the type of nest site used may be more strongly influenced by its availability than any active preference on the part of the owl. I have monitored Barn Owls nesting in sites as diverse as the attic space of a ruined cottage, the ducting of an abandoned underground hospital, a disused lime-kiln tower and a

FIG 128. Disused agricultural buildings may be used by breeding Barn Owls, the birds often using the ledges present on the tops of the walls. (Mike Toms)

metal milk churn tied horizontally to the beam of a Norfolk barn. Barn Owls favour sites that are larger and less exposed than those used by Tawny Owls.

Although no nest is built, the female may form a shallow scrape within the debris that has built up from nesting attempts made in previous years, sometimes breaking up pellets with her beak. By the time that the first egg is laid the female Barn Owl is likely to have reached her peak weight (c. 410–430 g) and is significantly heavier than a non-breeding female. The eggs are laid at two- to three-day intervals, but this interval may occasionally be longer if weather conditions and/ or food availability are poor. Incubation, which begins with the first egg, lasts roughly 30–32 days and results in asynchronous hatching. Clutch size typically varies between three and seven, with a mean of 4.7 calculated during Project Barn Owl (Toms *et al.*, 2000). Incubation is the sole responsibility of the female and during this period she is entirely dependent on her mate to provide her with food. Even so, the female loses weight over the incubation period but she may still be in sufficiently good condition to initiate her annual moult. About one in four females begin their annual moult while they are incubating (Barn Owl Trust, 2012).

Upon hatching, and weighing just 12–14 g, the young Barn Owl is pink, naked and blind, completely reliant on its parent for warmth, food and protection. The eyes do not open until the chicks are just under two weeks of age. The female broods the young pretty much continuously for two to three weeks, after which time they will have developed their down and become capable of maintaining their body temperature during the brief periods when the female is off the nest. Brooding will have ceased totally by the time that the youngest chick is some 20 or so days of age. As the young get older, so they become more mobile and demanding, often coming to the nest entrance. It is at this stage that the female increasingly roosts away from the nest, though usually nearby and often elsewhere within the same building (if this is where the nest has been placed). The chicks attain their maximum weight at around 40 days of age, this weight being in excess of that at which they will ultimately fledge. The chicks remain in the nest for a few more weeks, gradually attaining the appearance of an adult as the last of the nestling down is lost, before they begin to disperse from the site to explore their local surroundings.

The Barn Owl pair may begin another nesting attempt if conditions are favourable, the female often initiating the new clutch while her mate continues to deliver food to the young of the previous attempt. These new nesting attempts may be made in a different site (or in a different part of the same building) if young are still present in the nest used originally. Barn Owls have been recorded breeding in every month of the year within Britain, although most pairs breed between April and the start of November (see Figure 58, p. 130).

FEEDING

Of all the British owls, it is the Barn Owl for which we have the most complete understanding of diet and of the range of prey species taken. The ease with which large quantities of pellets can be collected from regular sites makes it easy, though time-consuming, to study Barn Owl diet and to build up a picture of seasonal and longer-term patterns of prey use. Barn Owls hunt mainly from the wing, quartering areas of rough grassland and other suitable habitat for small mammal prey. The slow, quartering flight usually takes place at 3–4 m above the ground, allowing the owl to use both hearing and vision to identify and pinpoint potential prey. While the bird will often go straight from searching flight into a dive that sees it drop onto its prey, individuals may adjust their position, hovering briefly to get a better fix on their intended target. During the winter months in particular, Barn Owls may become perch and wait hunters, reducing their energy expenditure by using fenceposts to scan for potential prey; since small mammal prey often become concentrated in marginal habitats at this time of the year, this can prove an effective strategy for the owl (see Chapter 2).

FIG 129. Barn Owls often adjust their position before dropping down onto potential prey. (Mark Hancox)

Small mammals, notably the Field Vole, are the dominant prey taken throughout the year, although this varies with habitat. Wood Mouse and Common Shrew can be important secondary prey species, the former particularly so in the arable-dominated regions of eastern England, where the rough grassland favoured by Field Voles is limited in its availability. Field Vole populations tend to be at their low point in early spring but numbers increase through the summer as grass growth supports a boom in the vole population. This delivers a peak abundance of food at the time that the young Barn Owls leave the nest to gain independence. Bird prey are taken more in the winter months and there is a strong suggestion that some Barn Owls may make greater use of birds than others. Seasonal peaks in prey availability may also see other species, for example Common Frog and Mole, feature in individual diets for a period. Some individuals have even been noted to take advantage of bats as they leave and return to roosts. More detail on feeding habits and variations in Barn Owl diet across seasons and habitats can be seen in Chapter 2.

MOVEMENTS

Within Britain, the Barn Owl can be regarded as being sedentary in habits, with movements essentially restricted to the period of natal dispersal. Young birds begin to disperse away from their natal sites during the first few weeks after fledging, the median dispersal distance for the second month after ringing being 3 km, rising to 7.5 km and 12 km in the third and fourth months respectively. The median natal dispersal distance for British and Irish Barn Owls is just 12 km, indicating that natal dispersal movements are completed within three or four months of leaving the nest (Wernham *et al.*, 2002). Large waterbodies appear to act as a barrier to long-distance movement, although birds from Britain have been recovered on the Continent and birds from the Isle of Wight sometimes reach mainland Britain.

The foraging ranges of birds are typically 1–2 km during the breeding season, although there is an indication that some birds may forage more widely during the winter months, even though established pairs remain largely site-faithful throughout their lives. The sedentary nature of the British population differs from some continental populations, where long-distance dispersal movements of young birds are noted in some years. Such movements, termed *Wanderjahren*, take place in late summer and appear to be a response to a good breeding season followed by a crash in the vole population. It is these movements that may sometimes deliver young dark-breasted Barn Owls to our shores.

FIG 130. This Dutch-ringed Barn Owl was seen in north Norfolk one winter before being found dead. (Mike Toms)

STATUS AND CONSERVATION

Although widely distributed across much of Britain and Ireland, the Barn Owl still tends to be regarded as uncommon, a species in documented decline and the recipient of targeted conservation action and intensive monitoring work by a network of individuals, local groups and national organisations. Although Barn Owl numbers are considerably lower than they were 100 years ago, there is evidence to suggest that the conservation efforts of the last 30 years have begun to pay off. In many parts of southern Britain the Barn Owl population appears to be stable or, in some instances, increasing. This would suggest that the most recent population estimate of c. 4,000 breeding pairs (Toms et al., 2001) is now a little on the low side.

The considerable regional variation in the distribution of Barn Owls across Britain outlined earlier in this chapter, with some regions supporting breeding pairs at fairly high density and the species absent altogether from other areas, may be linked to climatic conditions. These are likely to be particularly important in northern England and Scotland, where the species occurs towards the edge of its global breeding range. The low ebb evident in current populations from the north of Britain could simply reflect a run of cold winters and/or a low point in the vole cycle, rather than something giving long-term cause for concern. Other factors, such as nest site availability, land management practices and the use of rodenticides and other chemicals, may also influence the Barn Owl's fortunes at the regional level. Similarly, much of the conservation work taking place on the ground is carried out by local Barn Owl groups and this can exert an influence on regional populations.

One of the most important outputs from the most recent national survey was the recommendation that a national monitoring scheme should be established to collect information on breeding success and productivity. Not only would such a

FIG 131. Checking a Barn Owl nest box sited in a modern barn; this contained a brood of healthy chicks. (Mike Toms)

scheme provide information on how breeding success was changing over time but it would also, given a sufficient number of contributing sites, allow for differences in breeding success between habitats to be established (Toms, 1997). The Barn Owl Monitoring Programme (BOMP), operated by the British Trust for Ornithology and funded by the Sheepdrove Trust, was launched in 2000. Barn Owl fieldworkers were asked to make regular visits to an established network of nest sites in order to assess occupancy and to collect data on breeding success. Young Barn Owls were ringed at the majority of the sites involved in BOMP, allowing valuable data to be collected on the survival and dispersal of young and, additionally, the smaller number of adult birds caught at the nest. Participants in the scheme received guidance on appropriate methods for effective monitoring and were encouraged to collect information in a standardised manner. By 2007, the number of Barn Owl nest records being submitted annually had increased four-fold.

Monitoring schemes like BOMP are about collecting information that can be used to inform and support conservation action, revealing what is happening to Barn Owl populations and identifying likely drivers for population change. Much of the conservation action itself has come from the voluntary sector, delivered through the work of national organisations like The Hawk and Owl Trust and the Barn Owl Trust. Alongside these organisations have been the efforts of a great many individuals, operating local nest box schemes and promoting appropriate habitat management. The Suffolk Community Barn Owl Project, for example, has erected more than 700 nest boxes and is involved a range of Barn Owl-related activities across the county. The Barn Owl population in Suffolk has certainly responded to these efforts and is now thought to be at a 50-year high.

Breeding and release

One aspect of the Barn Owl conservation efforts within Britain requires special mention and this is captive breeding for release. Barn Owls have been popular as caged birds, being attractive and easy to breed in captivity. Such popularity probably contributed to the idea that captive-bred Barn Owls could be released into the wild to bolster the declining wild population. During the 1980s, in particular, as many as 2,000–3,000 captive-bred Barn Owls were being released annually by up to 600 operators (Rebane & Andrews, 1995). With the notable exception of a handful of schemes operating habitat assessment and monitoring work (e.g. Meek *et al.*, 2003), most of those involved in breeding and release probably had very little understanding of what was required by Barn Owls or of the extent to which their breeding and release efforts were working or not. Owls that have been released into the wild tend to suffer from higher mortality levels, especially during the initial post-release period, than wild-born birds. Much of

FIG 132. The Barn Owl is a flagship species. (Steve Round)

this early mortality comes from starvation, suggesting that birds might be unable to hunt properly, either because they cannot find suitable prey-rich habitats or because they are naïve when it comes to prey location and capture.

A licensing scheme for Barn Owl release was introduced in January 1993, the Barn Owl's placement on Schedule 9 of the Wildlife and Countryside Act the previous year making unlicensed releases of captive-bred birds illegal. In the two years following the introduction of this legislation, some 400 Barn Owls were released under licence (Rebane & Andrews, 1995). One of the requirements of the licence was that released birds should be fitted with a BTO ring and, between April 1993 and the end of September 2000, some 1,737 rings had been issued for use on captive-bred Barn Owls (Balmer *et al.*, 2000). The number of licence applications being made declined year on year over this period, prompting a review of the licensing system itself to be launched in 2001. As a result of the review the licensing scheme was dismantled and no licences have been granted since 2002. This has put an end to the breeding and release of Barn Owls in Britain and conservation efforts are now directed towards the provision of nest boxes and the appropriate management of local habitats.

The Barn Owl also appears on Schedules 1 and 3 of the Wildlife and Countryside Act, the former making it an offence to intentionally or recklessly disturb breeding Barn Owls. If you intend to visit the nest of a Schedule 1 species, e.g. for monitoring purposes, then you must first obtain a Schedule 1 Licence. The species also appears on the Amber list of Birds of Conservation within the UK because of its placement within the SPEC 3 designation at the European level. The SPEC 3 designation includes those species which have an unfavourable conservation status in Europe but whose populations are not concentrated here. This categorisation will require some reinterpretation in view of recent taxonomic recommendations emerging from work on Barn Owl genetics (see Chapter 1). Globally, the species is categorised as being of Least Concern by BirdLife International. The Barn Owl also appears on Schedule III of the Bern Convention and on the Convention on International Trade in Endangered Species of Wild Flora and Fauna.

It is important to keep in mind that the future of the Barn Owl is not secure, and that future changes to agricultural policy and land use could see further losses. The introduction of new rodenticides could pose a serious threat, as could continued increases in the size of our road network and the volume of traffic that it transports. The Barn Owl remains a species of conservation importance, being both an important indicator of the wider health of the environment within which it lives and a flagship for conservation action.

Snowy Owl
Bubo scandiacus
(LINNAEUS 1758)

FAMILY: Strigidae

IDENTIFICATION

With a body length in excess of 50 cm and a wingspan reaching 150 cm, this very large, predominantly white owl with bright yellow eyes and black 'eyeliner', should be unmistakeable. Apart from a scattering of brown markings, an adult male Snowy Owl is almost entirely white, while an adult female shows a spread of dark scalloping across the back and wings, with narrow barring on the underparts. First-year birds

FIG 133. Snowy Owl at Malacleit, North Uist – 18 May 2005. (Steve Round)

of both sexes are more strongly marked, to the extent that first-year males show a similar extent of barring to adult females, though these are paler in colour and less distinct overall. First-year females are the most strongly marked of all. The barring of an adult female is thought to camouflage the bird as she sits on a nest, situated on rocky ground in a landscape partially covered in snow. Young Snowy Owls have white down initially but this is quickly replaced with the sooty-brown mesoptile plumage, which extends across most of the body, though not the facial disk or, when they emerge, the flight feathers.

In the field, the size and eye colouration should enable immediate separation from the much smaller, though sometimes rather pale-looking, Barn Owls and from unusually pale Short-eared Owls. Snowy Owls only rarely perch in trees and are most likely to be encountered sat on the ground in a rather upright stance, often described as being 'cat-like'. The species regularly hunts by day and, despite the illusion of bulk, is a surprisingly agile bird, capable of rapid, almost raptor-like, flight. It will also glide in a buzzard-like fashion.

Voice

Away from the nest the Snowy Owl is usually silent but a number of calls have
been documented. Bobby Tulloch, for example, noted how the resident Shetland
male uttered a rather harsh, grating bark, described as '*ergh-ergh-ergh-ergh*', lower
pitched though not dissimilar to his mate. This male was also noted to produce a
deep, rough hoot, described as '*hoorh*'. The begging call of the chicks is a whistling
squeal, high in pitch and somewhat penetrating. Newly independent young from
the breeding attempts made on Shetland were also noted to make this call.

HISTORY

The history of the Snowy Owl in Britain is very much centred on Shetland, from
where the species was added to the British List in the early 1800s on the basis
of a bird taken on Unst. There is some uncertainty over the exact date of the
first record because of a discrepancy between the account given by Laurence
Edmondston to MacGillivray – and published in 1840 – and that published in an
1822 paper on the subject by Edmondston himself. Most likely, the first record
is of an adult male, shot in spring 1812 by Edmondston, purchased by William
Bullock and put on display in a London museum. The first mainland record
came in spring 1814, a bird found dead at Felbrigg in Norfolk, the first record for
mainland Scotland not coming for another decade. Shetland is also central to the
history of the Snowy Owl as a breeding species within Britain, a pair breeding
there annually between 1967 and 1975. There is also a strong suspicion that the
species may have bred on Shetland during the early 1800s, around the time of
Edmondston's definitive report. The period between the first record and the
settlement of a confirmed breeding pair in the 1960s is characterised by a general
decline in annual records, with birds seen sporadically on the Outer Hebrides,
Shetland, Orkney and the Cairngorms.

The discovery of a breeding pair on Fetlar in June 1967 came off the back of
an obvious influx of birds during 1963 and 1964, with birds present throughout
the summer months at a number of sites. The Fetlar nest was discovered by
Bobby Tulloch (1968, 1969) and it produced five chicks from a clutch of seven
eggs, the most productive year for the pair which subsequently bred annually
until the male disappeared during the winter of 1975/76. Male chicks from
these nesting attempts were driven away by the territory-holding male and only
females remained after his disappearance, some of which laid infertile eggs in the
absence of any mates during nesting attempts made in the 1980s.

Sightings of male Snowy Owls within suitable breeding habitat in the Cairngorms during the summers of 1979–81, 1984 and 1996–98, coupled with intermittent sightings of females from 1987–93, gave hope that Snowy Owls might once again breed in Scotland. Sadly, this was not to be and the disappearance of a lone female that had been on Shetland in September 1993 left Scotland without at least one Snowy Owl present for the first time in three decades. The loss of the Fetlar's Snowy Owls is regarded by some authors as a mixed blessing. The birds had fed on the island's extensive population of Rabbits but then switched increasingly to wader chicks when myxomatosis arrived in 1970, putting breeding rarities like Whimbrel and Red-necked Phalarope *Phalaropus lobatus* at risk (Parkin & Knox, 2010).

Reports of Snowy Owls from Scotland continue to tantalise birdwatchers on an almost regular basis. Since 2002, Ireland has been the recipient of visiting Snowy Owls on an annual basis, with some birds present for extended periods and an unsuccessful breeding attempt noted in 2001. The number of individuals involved is unclear, since records may indicate individuals moving between sites or, as in the case of a female frequenting the Mullet Peninsula from 2006–10, returning in subsequent years.

FIG 134. In flight the large size of the Snowy Owl is evident. (Paul Gale)

Understandably, given the wider breeding range of the species, most British records come from the north of Scotland, the Western Isles and north-west Ireland. Reports of Snowy Owls from the southern half of Britain often turn out to be escaped falconers' birds but some, including an individual present over the winter of 1990–91, are genuine wild vagrants. The 1990–91 individual was present in Lincolnshire from December 1990 through into the following March, then reported spending a couple of days in north Norfolk before heading to Orkney, where it remained from 12 April to 5 May. This bird was last seen on Fair Isle on 11 May 1991.

DISTRIBUTION AND HABITAT

The global distribution of the Snowy Owl is essentially circumpolar, taking in Alaska, Canada, Greenland, Fennoscandia, Russia and Siberia, with birds breeding on the Arctic tundra. The species is nomadic in nature, although some populations are largely resident and remain on their breeding grounds throughout the year. Individuals and pairs may become established to the south of the core breeding range (as was the case with the birds on Shetland), where they utilise open habitats like moorland, rocky and barren island landscapes, and mountain-tops. British records have largely been restricted to the Northern Isles (notably Shetland, the Hebrides and Orkney) and the Cairngorm Plateau of the Scottish Highlands.

BREEDING ECOLOGY

Thanks to the efforts of a dedicated team of 30 observers, together with other short-term helpers, a great deal of information was collected on the breeding Snowy Owls present on Fetlar over the period 1967–75. Plumage details suggested that the same pair of birds nested on Fetlar from 1967 to 1974, with the male entering bigamous relationships with a second female in 1973 and 1974. In 1975, this second female – believed to be a younger female raised on Fetlar and probably related to the main pair – moved to the main site and raised four young with the male. Over the period, these birds fledged 23 young from 56 eggs, laid in 12 different nests (Robinson & Becker, 1986), see Table 12.

At 5.4, the mean clutch size for the nine attempts made at the main nest on Fetlar is towards the lower end of the range seen in other studies and falls within the range reported by a number of studies where food supplies were thought to

TABLE 12. Breeding records of Snowy Owl on Fetlar. (After Robinson & Becker, 1986). In addition, unmated females laid infertile eggs in 1980–83 and 1987–90.

Year	Nests	Eggs laid	Chicks fledged
1967	1	7	5
1968	1	6	3
1969	1	6	3
1970	1	5	2
1971	1	5	3
1972	1	4	0
1973	2	5 + 3	2 + 0
1974	2	5 + 1	1 + 0
1975	2	6 + 3	4 + 0

be limited. When conditions are favourable clutch sizes are more typically in the range of 7–11. However, it has been suggested that prey availability at the onset of breeding may be a poor predictor of prey availability at the chick stage in many Snowy Owl populations. This might suggest that Snowy Owls should attempt to lay as many eggs as possible, hedging their bets and accepting that younger chicks will be lost if food availability turns out to be poor (Menyushina, 1997).

The first egg of each nesting attempt on Shetland tended to be laid during mid-May, the latest being 2 June. Breeding behaviour was studied in greater detail during 1970, revealing an average interval of 50 hours between subsequent eggs and at least 200 hours between the first and last egg being laid. As is generally the case with our other owls, incubation began with the first egg and lasted for an average of 31.6 days. Four eggs disappeared from the nest at around the time that they should have hatched and at least one of these was removed by the female, who took it across the valley before breaking it open and eating the contents. Not all of the young hatched from the eggs survived; 12 died within the first 10 days of life and others before they could leave the nest. Lack of food was noted as a cause of mortality in some instances but on other occasions there seemed to be no obvious cause. The female was observed to feed a dead chick to its siblings on at least one occasion.

FIG 135. Most Snowy Owl records come from the north of Britain but some, such as this bird on the Scillies, turn up further south. (Paul Gale)

The male delivered prey (sometimes headless, a behaviour noted in other owls) to the nest, the female feeding pieces to young chicks and eating some herself. Surplus food was removed to a cache. Once the chicks were two weeks of age they would begin to wander from the nest, initially only moving a few feet and returning to the nest for food. The mean age for the oldest chick to leave the nest was at 26.2 days, the youngsters then hiding among rocks to await a delivery of food. This highlights the rapid growth rate of Snowy Owl chicks compared with many other owl species. It was at this stage that the male began to deliver prey whole to the chicks. The young owls could fly from 45 days of age, buoyantly but not necessarily gracefully, a figure a little lower than that reported from other studies. Conditions for newly fledged chicks may have been difficult in some seasons, particularly when there was poor weather. Two chicks examined in 1969, after being found dead post-fledging, were found to have died from pneumonia/ *Staphylococcus* infection and aspergillosis respectively, both suggestive of poor weather conditions. Others were seen around the island post-fledging and may have been behind the sightings of birds reported elsewhere.

FEEDING BEHAVIOUR

During the first few years, the Fetlar Snowy Owls had access to a buoyant population of Rabbits, but the introduction of myxomatosis to the island in 1970 hit the Rabbit population hard. By the 1971 breeding season Rabbits had almost disappeared from both the island and the owls' diet. The Rabbit population showed signs of recovery from 1974 onwards and clutch size increased as Rabbits again featured more strongly in the diet. The adult Snowy Owls were sit and watch predators, only rarely taking prey by quartering the ground or hovering. The male was responsible for the vast majority of the prey provided for the chicks, the female hardly providing the chicks with any food until they were more than a month old.

FIG 136. Common Gull chicks featured in the diet of the Fetlar Snowy Owls. (Dave Leech)

In addition to the Rabbits, the owls also took waders and their chicks, the
male often bringing in wader chicks one after the other once he had discovered
a brood. Included in the 20 different species of bird taken by the pair were
Oystercatcher, Whimbrel, Curlew *Numenius arquata*, Arctic Skua and Arctic Tern
Sterna paradisaea. The chicks of Common Gull and Great Black-backed Gull
were also occasionally taken. Fetlar does not have any voles but Wood Mouse,
House Mouse and Common Rat occur on the island, the former species being
an occasional prey item for the owls. Hunting activity was seen throughout the
24-hour cycle but peaked during the period of lowest illumination (2200–0300
hours). This suggests that the Fetlar owls were more nocturnal than has
been reported in other studies, perhaps reflecting the generally poor feeding
conditions and the lack of voles (which exhibit a regular cycle of activity
throughout the 24-hour period – see Chapter 1). The diet of two Snowy Owls
present on Lewis during the early 1970s also appeared to rely heavily on Rabbits,
whose bones were extracted from cast pellets and used to estimate the body
weight of the individuals taken. Estimated body weights varied between 130 and
700 g, with a mean of 320 g (Marquiss & Cunningham, 1980). Six pellets collected
from a male Snowy Owl summering on the Cairngorm Plateau in July 1980 and
24 collected from a female summering there in 1987, yielded the remains of Field

FIG 137. Red Grouse featured in the diet of Snowy Owls present on the Cairngorm Plateau.
(John Harding)

Vole, Mountain Hare, Ptarmigan, Red Grouse and Dotterel *Charadrius morinellus*, together with other unidentified grouse and wader remains (Marquiss *et al.*, 1989).

MOVEMENTS

The nomadic nature of most Snowy Owl populations appears to be driven by food supply (see Chapter 4) and individuals may cover vast distances between successive breeding attempts. Long-distance movements may be irruptive on occasion, the sudden decline in prey abundance forcing birds to move farther south. Vagrants have been reported as far south as the Azores and Bermuda. It is thought that adult females tend to winter the farthest north, with immature males wintering the farthest south. Those arriving for the first time at British sites tend to be reported during the spring (April and May). It is possible, however, that at least some individuals arrive earlier in the year but go unreported because of the low densities of observers in these more remote parts of Britain and Ireland.

The efforts of bird ringers have revealed the origins of at least one of the Snowy Owls to reach Britain; an adult female found injured on North Uist in 1992 had been ringed that spring in Hordaland, Norway. While it is likely that most British Snowy Owls originate from Arctic Eurasia, there is the possibility of birds arriving from the Nearctic. An individual found on an oil tanker in the mid-Atlantic in 1989 was subsequently released on Shetland. Just four of the 30 Snowy Owls to have been ringed in Britain have been recovered subsequently. Three of the nestlings ringed on Fetlar were recovered on the island, one of which was found there almost exactly 15 years after ringing. An adult male found dead on Lewis in 1975 had been ringed on Fair Isle in June 1972.

STATUS AND CONSERVATION

Although the Snowy Owl retains the slightest of footholds in Britain and Ireland, the longevity of individual birds suggests that a breeding pair may again establish themselves here at some point in the future. The species is listed on Schedule 1 of the Wildlife and Countryside Act 1981, as amended by the Environmental Protection Act of 1990, and it is an offence to intentionally or recklessly disturb Snowy Owls while they are at or near a nest containing eggs or young. It is also an offence to disturb the birds while they have dependent young. The Snowy Owl is also listed on Annex 1 of the EC Birds Directive and Appendix II of the Berne

FIG 138. Snowy Owls, such as this bird on North Uist, often perch on the ground, favouring an outcrop or other vantage point. (Paul Gale)

Convention. Should the species breed here again then it could be threatened by disturbance or the attentions of egg-collectors. Writing in 1980, Mick Marquiss and W. A. Cunningham commented that it was strongly rumoured that at least two of the Snowy Owls present on the Isle of Lewis between 1972–74 succumbed to human persecution, suggesting that persecution of this species may still have been a problem at that time (Marquiss & Cunningham, 1980). The conservation status of the species within Britain has not been subject to formal assessment but it does appear on SPEC 3 at the European level.

Eurasian Eagle Owl
Bubo bubo
(LINNAEUS 1758)

FAMILY: Strigidae

IDENTIFICATION

The Eurasian Eagle Owl is a very large and heavy looking owl, with bright orange eyes and powerful, heavily feathered talons. The female is the larger of the two sexes. In colour, it is strongly marked with black, dark-brown, grey and white on a wash of rusty-brown. The dark markings on the chest form broad verticals, becoming thinner on the belly and flanks.

FIG 139. Eagle Owl. (Steve Round)

The tail and flight feathers are heavily barred, the wing coverts dark-tipped, the colour extending up the shaft and bordered by grey or brown. The dark facial disk is rather indistinctly edged black (allowing useful comparison with Great Horned Owl) and short off-white eyebrows sit above the bright orange eyes, the white extending down around the bill. The strength of colour varies with race and those of Scandinavian origin are the darkest and most strongly marked. The species has prominent ear tufts, dark-tipped and somewhat pointed. The white throat patch is prominent when a bird is calling (see below).

The initial down of the chicks is off-white but this is quickly replaced by the mesoptile down, which is a pale buffish-brown. As with our other owls, the remains of this down can often be seen on recently fledged individuals. Young birds have yellow-orange irises with a 'milky' suffusion. This suffusion is lost once the young are about half-grown.

The aviary origins of most of our British Eagle Owls, coupled with knowledge that eagle owls of varying races/species have been kept in captivity here, suggests that close attention should be given to the characteristics of any birds seen in the wild. Both Rock Eagle Owl *Bubo bengalensis* and Spotted Eagle Owl *Bubo africanus* have been documented in the wild within Britain (see Escapes and Releases).

Roosting birds will utilise rock clefts, hollow trees and dense vegetative cover. They will also, sometimes, roost in more exposed locations. A perched bird will often adopt a rather upright attitude and draw itself up with plumage tightly compressed, in a manner similar to that seen in Long-eared Owl.

Voice

The territorial and advertising call of the male is a deep and highly resonant hoot, which sounds as if it is comprised of a single downward-inflected note. In fact it is comprised of two syllables, the first emphasised and the second dropping away, to produce a sound that can be described as 'HOO-o'. When heard at distance, only the first part may be evident. The call of the female is similar in structure, though somewhat higher in pitch and with the emphasis placed on the second syllable rather than the first. The pair may duet during courtship. A male may utter a series of staccato notes when advertising the nest site to his prospective mate. A number of other calls and sounds are known, including bill-snapping – which is used as an aggressive threat display – and a hoarse scream, the latter used by the female as a contact call or when demanding food from her mate. A similar call is used by the young when they are demanding food.

HISTORY

The Eurasian Eagle Owl appears on Category E of the British List, underlining that the current population is thought to be derived from aviary escapes and deliberate releases, rather than from birds that have arrived here naturally. There has, however, been some debate surrounding the status of Eagle Owls in Britain, something that prompted a review of records held by the British Ornithologists' Union (BOU) and an examination of the archaeological and fossil remains (Stewart, 2007; Melling *et al.*, 2008).

Within the archaeological and fossil record there are a number of specimens that have, at various times, been put forward as Eagle Owl remains. As we saw in Chapter 1, the identification of such remains can be tricky, making it difficult to be certain of any interpretation drawn from what are often small fragments of material. John Stewart's review, published in 2007, has helped to clarify the validity or otherwise of the Eagle Owl claims which appear in reports of archaeological excavations and similar publications. Stewart's re-examination

FIG 140. Eagle Owl chicks move away from the nest site while still dependent on their parents for food. (Vincenzo Penteriani)

reveals that many of the earlier specimens (such as those from the Pastonian Interglacial and the Late Cromerian Complex) are more likely to belong to other forms of eagle owl (Yalden & Albarella, 2008). A few of the remains do appear to match the modern European form of the Eurasian Eagle Owl and it is these which provide the best insight into the extent to which the species can be regarded as native. A right tarsometatarsus excavated from Demen's Dale in Derbyshire (Bramwell & Yalden, 1988) and two ulna fragments from the Meare Lake Village site in Somerset (Bate, 1966) are perhaps the most important in this regard. The Meare Lake Village remains are potentially the more interesting, in that they would place the species in Britain at about 2,000 years BP. However, Stewart was unable to locate these remains for his review and some uncertainty over their identification must therefore remain. This leaves the Demen's Dale tarsometatarsus, which is unquestionably Eagle Owl and which has been dated to between 5,500 and 10,000 years BP. Based on the Demen's Dale material, Stewart was able to conclude that 'the fossil and archaeological record suggest strongly that the Eagle Owl is part of the natural, native British fauna'. This, of course, says nothing about the likely origins of the current population.

In contrast to other northern European countries, there are surprisingly few references to the species within more recent history – the Eagle Owl is almost entirely absent from British literature and folklore – and this might suggest that it was lost from Britain at a very early date. The question remains, however, as to why the species, which occupied similar habitats elsewhere in Europe, should have disappeared from Britain at some point during this period. The suggestion that it was hunted to extinction by humans seems unlikely given the persistence of more conspicuous predators (e.g. Brown Bear *Ursus arctos* and Wolf *Canis lupus*), both of which survived until relatively recent times. Could it be that the owls were deliberately targeted for their feathers, reflecting a continuation of the practices seen in the late Magdalénien hunter-gatherers of continental Europe and explored in Chapter 6, or could the species have been slow to recolonise northwards after the last ice age and so failed to return before the loss of the land-bridge that had linked Britain to mainland Europe?

Regardless of the size of early Eagle Owl populations within the British Isles and the reasons for their subsequent extinction, it is evident that the present population does not result from continuous residency. Instead, it must have originated from the arrival of individuals that made their way here naturally, crossing the English Channel or the North Sea, or from birds that were deliberately released or which escaped from captivity. While the tracking studies of Adrian Aebischer and colleagues underline that juvenile Eagle Owls can disperse over very long distances, there is also evidence to suggest a reluctance to cross large bodies of water. Data from the Swedish ringing scheme and representing nearly 2,000 ring-recoveries, contain just two instances where a dispersing juvenile appears to have crossed a large waterbody (Toms, 2009). Genuine vagrants to Britain are most likely to be encountered on the east coast or reported from North Sea gas installations; however, none of the 836 records of owls logged by the North Sea Bird Club between January 1979 and February 2006 involved Eagle Owl (Melling *et al.*, 2008). Interestingly, one of the two Eagle Owl specimens used by the engraver Thomas Bewick for his illustration of the species is said to have been a badly stuffed individual taken by a Norwegian skipper while at sea off the Norwegian coast – there is no indication how far from shore the boat was when the bird was taken.

There is a suggestion from a paper by Andrew Kelly and colleagues that occasional vagrants might just reach our shores. Kelly *et al.* (2010) carried out a stable-isotope analysis of a female Eagle Owl found dead in the aircraft hanger of a former RAF base at Watton in Norfolk. The results of the analysis suggested that the two generations of feathers present in the wings of this bird had been grown in different geographical regions, but it was impossible to say for certain exactly which these regions were. While the results were consistent with an origin in north-continental Europe, Scandinavia or mid-continental Russia, the authors could not rule out the possibility that the bird had been reared in northern Britain, where the stable-isotope ratios would be similar.

There is a long history of Eagle Owls being kept in captivity within Britain, with historical accounts documenting their presence at least as far back as the mid-1600s (Ray, 1678). In fact, the presence of captive Eagle Owls in Britain may go back much further than this. Eagle Owls have a long history of being used in falconry, either trained and flown to catch prey or used, tethered, to lure other large raptors to the ground where they can be killed or captured. Because of this, there is the possibility that birds arrived here via the well-established Medieval trade routes that linked Britain to the rest of Europe and beyond into the Middle East. Trade has certainly been a feature during more recent times. J. H. Gurney, writing in 1849, described how a captive pair in the parish of Easton in Norfolk produced and reared three young in the spring of 1849. What is interesting about this report is the throwaway comment that Gurney makes about the five-week-old chicks, which he describes as being at a similar stage to 'the specimens usually imported from Norway at this time of year by London bird-dealers'. This suggests a regular trade in Eagle Owls of Norwegian origin for a domestic British market.

There is a suggestion, notably from correspondence between Lord Lilford and E.B.G. Meade-Waldo – whom we shall meet again when looking at the introduction of the Little Owl into Britain – that the release of young Eagle Owls into the wild occurred on one or more occasions during the late 1800s. Records of 'wild' Eagle Owls from this period have been reviewed by the BOU's rarities committee on several occasions, as part of work looking at the species. The majority of those records subjected to review were found to be either insufficiently documented to confirm the identification or to have been misidentified. For example, an 'Eagle Owl' shot in Shropshire in 1954 turned out to be an American Great Horned Owl, no doubt of captive origin. Even if the identification of a record was found to be correct, the presence of captive Eagle Owls meant that captive origins could not be ruled out and there were, additionally, a number of records where the release, either accidental or deliberate, of captive birds had been documented.

The species remains a popular bird with falconers today and is common in captivity. Although many of these birds are registered with an independent body in case they are lost, there is no formal requirement for licensing an Eagle Owl. A CITES (Convention on International Trade in Endangered Species) certificate is required, however, where birds are used for commercial activities such as display, importation and sale. Some 3,528 applications for CITES certificates

FIG 141. The white throat patch plays a role in Eagle Owl display. (Vincenzo Penteriani)

were made to Defra in the ten years leading up to June 2007 (Melling *et al.*, 2008), suggesting a sizeable captive population. Melling and his co-workers also examined data held by the Independent Bird Register (IBR) and were able to calculate an estimate for the number of birds being lost annually. This suggested that 60–70 registered Eagle Owls were being lost annually, nearly two-thirds of which were not recaptured. These figures did not include unregistered birds, of which 83 individuals were reported to the IBR over a 14-year period (Melling *et al.*, 2008). In addition to the uncertainty over how many captive birds are escaping annually, there is also uncertainty over the genetic origins of some of these birds. Rock Eagle Owl and Spotted Eagle Owl (Leicestershire 2003) have both been documented in the wild in Britain (Toms, 2009). Some of the individuals breeding in the wild have shown their captive origins through the presence of jesses and/or closed rings.

The first documented record of the species breeding successfully in the wild within Britain came in 1985, when a single chick was raised from a nest in Moray and Nairn. The pair involved was thought to be part of a deliberate but unofficial release, having made a failed attempt in the previous year. Since then, breeding has been attempted at several other sites (see Table 13) and has occurred annually

TABLE 13. Breeding records of Eagle Owl in Britain.

Site	Years	Outcome
Moray and Nairn	1984–85	One egg laid but found broken 1984; single chick fledged in 1985. Male killed on a road in 1985, female remained in area and continued to lay infertile eggs in at least seven years through to 1995.
Peak District	1993	Nest with four eggs which was found already deserted at Longdale.
North Yorkshire	1997–	A good number of young have been produced from the site, all of which have been ringed, and two subsequently found dead.
Hertfordshire	2002	A pair was reported to be breeding on a balcony at Hatfield Country Club. The eventual outcome of this attempt is unknown.
Harrogate	2003	Nest with three eggs on a rocky outcrop at a private site found on 21 April. The eggs were removed and incubated but proved to be infertile. The male was never seen but the female received supplementary food.
Southern England	2005	Three young raised at a site in southern England
Lancashire	2006–	2006 attempt failed at egg stage but chicks produced in 2007 (3), 2008 (2) and 2009 (1), 2010 (3), 2011 (4) and 2012 (2).
Cumbria	2009	Two young noted at a site near Geltsdale.

since 1997 (Holling *et al.*, 2007). One well-documented pair bred at a remote moorland site in Yorkshire, nesting annually from 1997 to 2005. The birds at this site were the targets of illegal persecution on a number of occasions. The nest was vandalised on at least three occasions, despite the site being under regular surveillance, and the female was found dead in December 1995, having starved to death as a result of a gunshot wound that prevented her from feeding. This female had been wearing the remains of jesses when she was first found breeding at the site, highlighting her captive origins. Some 23 chicks were fledged from the site, all ringed by BTO ringers and generating two recoveries of note. Both involved young from the same brood, ringed in April 2004. One youngster was found dead near Church Stretton (Shropshire), under powerlines, nearly 11 months later and 218 km from the natal site. The other, found freshly dead in January 2006, was 160 km from the natal site, near Peebles in the Scottish Borders. Two other nestlings

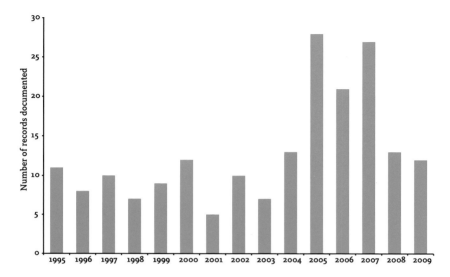

FIG 142. The number of Eagle Owl records published in county bird reports over the period 1995–2009.

have also been recovered, this time from nesting attempts made in 2007 and 2009 at a site near Dunsop Bridge in the Forest of Bowland. Both were found dead within eight months of leaving the nest (Robinson & Clark, 2012).

It is likely that other breeding attempts have been made but gone unnoticed and that our current population of these long-lived birds is sufficiently large to suggest that more will follow over the coming years. It is perhaps because of this potential that the Non-native Species Secretariat commissioned an assessment of current status and possible conservation problems were the species to become more widely established (see Figure 142). The presence of this large and enigmatic species has also prompted much discussion within the birdwatching community about its position within the British avifauna.

DISTRIBUTION AND HABITAT

The Eurasian Eagle Owl has a very wide breeding range, extending across Europe and Asia. The northern limit is formed by the open tundra landscapes favoured by the Snowy Owl, the southern bordering the Mediterranean (although a population is thought to be present in the Atlas mountains of Morocco) and across Turkey to the northern limit of the Arabian Peninsula and on to northern Pakistan and India, reaching the Pacific on the southern Chinese coast. Within this range the species is often locally rare or absent altogether, avoiding unfavourable habitats (such as dense and extensive blocks of forest).

Populations seem to do best in open country, something that is particularly evident in the southern part of their range, with scrubby habitats supporting good prey populations. The presence of rocky features, such as quarries, cliff faces and south-facing slopes, appears to be a characteristic of successful breeding territories, suggesting the importance of these in the provision of nest sites. Nest-site selection is linked to breeding success; more exposed and accessible sites suffer from lower productivity and higher failure rates, something towards which human persecution may also contribute (Olsson, 1997). Interestingly, in some areas the species has taken to nesting in working quarries, cement works and on buildings (Ristig *et al.*, 2003). The species is even known to nest within the cities of Bonn, Bratislava, Hamburg and Prague (Kelcey & Rheinwald, 2005).

Within Britain, breeding or attempted breeding records of the species have tended to be associated with moorland and moorland-edge habitats, occupying areas that include cliff faces, boulder scree and some woodland or woodland edge. Records of individual birds come from a much wider range of habitats, including urban parks and back gardens, no doubt a reflection of the captive origins of many such individuals.

BREEDING ECOLOGY

Little published information is available on the few nesting attempts to have been made by Eagle Owls breeding within Britain. The best-studied site, located in North Yorkshire, has been monitored for more than a decade, the young ringed and at least some subsequently recovered (Toms, 2009). A number of Eagle Owl nesting attempts, from across Britain more widely, are known to have failed at the egg stage, either owing to natural circumstances or deliberate persecution. Eagle Owls appear to be sensitive to disturbance at and around the nest, with several failed breeding attempts in northern England reportedly linked to human activity nearby. European researchers underline that nesting pairs are wary, often making them difficult to observe at or near the nest. Some individuals, however, are more confiding. As is the case with other wild birds, Eagle Owls may defend occupied

FIG 143. The distribution of Eagle Owl records published in county bird reports over the period 1995–2009.

nests containing unfledged chicks against would-be predators and other intruders, including humans who stray too close. Such attacks are rare, certainly much rarer than those reported for the familiar Tawny Owl, and just two substantiated cases appear in the literature. The first involved a birdwatcher attempting to approach a nest to photograph the young; the second involved a dog being walked off the leash near a nest – it was the dog that was attacked and not the dog-walker.

Eagle Owls are known to occupy their home range throughout the year. The home range may overlap with neighbouring pairs – though breeding densities are so low within Britain as to make it extremely unlikely that neighbouring pairs come into contact – and the pair only defend a smaller territory around the nest site. As we have already seen in Chapter 3, juvenile birds may even be tolerated within the breeding territory, with a suggestion that they may help provision the young. British Eagle Owls appear to begin breeding fairly early in the year, with eggs noted in nests during April.

FEEDING BEHAVIOUR

Eagle Owl diet has been well studied throughout its range and it is clear that the species is adaptable and able to exploit prey items that range in size from beetles to young deer (Mikkola, 1983). The diet is, however, dominated by small to medium-sized mammals and by medium-sized birds. The diet of British Eagle Owls reflects this. Information on the diet of Eagle Owls derived from pellets collected at sites in the Peak District and the Forest of Bowland suggests a diet dominated by Rabbit with, additionally, Mountain Hare, Pheasant, Red Grouse, Stoat, Grey Squirrel and Hedgehog (Underwood, 1995). Hedgehog also proved to be a favoured prey item for a well-watched Eagle Owl present in Hampshire during 1981. The Eagle Owls breeding in the Dunsop Valley (Forest of Bowland) were seen in 2011 to supplement their favoured prey of Rabbit with Common Rats taken from around nearby farm buildings. The addition of rat to the diet may bring with it an increased risk of rodenticide poisoning, something that should be kept in mind should any dead Eagle Owls be found.

MOVEMENTS

Eagle Owls are best regarded as sedentary birds, with little movement taking place after the initial period of dispersal undertaken by young birds leaving the nest. With so few Eagle Owls ringed or subsequently recovered in Britain, there is no reliable information on movement patterns here. However, the limited information that we do have from the relatively small number of young ringed at British nest sites does show that dispersing youngsters can move substantial distances (see History). As we have seen, there has been some debate about the dispersal capabilities of young Eagle Owls in the context of the current British population and the possibility of vagrants reaching our shores.

STATUS AND CONSERVATION

The Eagle Owl's position as a top predator could bring it into conflict with commercial game-rearing interests and, additionally, with attempts to protect species of conservation importance. Such concerns, coupled with the strong evidence of a captive origin for the current population, prompted the Non-native Species Secretariat to commission an assessment of the possible impacts of an expanding Eagle Owl population within Britain (www.nonnativespecies.org). As we have seen elsewhere in this book, the Eagle Owl is a predator of other raptor and owl species, prompting fears that an expanding population might threaten

FIG 144. Peregrines nesting within an area with a high density of Eagle Owls showed a decline in their productivity. (Edmund Fellowes)

species like Peregrine, Hen Harrier and Long-eared Owl. During the early 1990s, the presence of a female Eagle Owl in an area within the Peak District was thought to be behind the disappearance of three pairs of breeding Merlin *Falco columbarius*, one pair of Goshawk, the breeding failure of a pair of Sparrowhawk and the nest site shift of a pair of Peregrine (Underwood, 1995). However, other British raptor workers have cited examples where these species, plus Short-eared Owl and Tawny Owl, have been found to be nesting within or adjacent to established Eagle Owl territories.

Direct evidence of British Eagle Owls taking other birds of prey is lacking. However, the remains of a first-year female Hen Harrier were found near an Eagle Owl nest in the Forest of Bowland and were thought to be the result of Eagle Owl predation (Mark Grantham, pers. comm.). In June 2010, a Eurasian Eagle Owl was implicated in the failure of a nesting Hen Harrier through footage taken by a camera focussed on the nest. This footage shows the harrier leave the nest abruptly; moments later there is a movement of the heather and the appearance of the Eagle Owl – or to be more precise the legs and feet of the Eagle Owl – in the nest. Although the owl does not damage the nest contents, the Hen Harrier fails to return subsequently and the nesting attempt fails.

That newly established Eagle Owls can have an impact on their intraguild competitors, such as other owls, is suggested from work carried out elsewhere in Europe. Goshawk nesting success in northern Germany, for example, declined when Eagle Owls became established nearby, with nesting ceasing altogether when Eagle Owls moved into existing Goshawk territories. The results of the work appeared to suggest that no Goshawk could nest successfully within 500 m of an active Eagle Owl nest (Busche *et al.*, 2004). Sergio *et al.* (2007), working in the Alps, found a similar decline in nesting success within a Tawny Owl population exposed to Eagle Owls. Additional to this indirect effect, there was also evidence of direct predation of the species by its larger relative. Other work, this time in the French Jura mountains, has revealed a significant decline in the productivity of a Peregrine population when Eagle Owls were present at high densities (Brambilla *et al.*, 2006). In all three studies we are talking about Eagle Owls established at densities well above those currently seen in Britain. The fact that we have not yet seen a significant impact on other species should not be taken as evidence that such impacts might not be felt once the Eagle Owl becomes more widely established.

The Eurasian Eagle Owl has been lost from many parts of its former range as a result of persecution but efforts to reintroduce the species using captive-bred individuals have often proved successful. For example, the Swedish population declined to near extinction during the first half of the 20th century, with persecution thought to be the primary cause (Olsson, 1997). The species was given legal protection in 1950 and a national captive breeding project was launched in 1969. Some 2,759 young owls were released through this project, delivering a wild population that had topped 400 breeding territories by 1996. A reintroduction programme in Germany saw the release of some 1,500 individuals during the 1970s and 1980s and the species is now well established across many parts of its former range, additionally establishing breeding populations in Belgium and the Netherlands most likely as a direct consequence (Radler & Bergerhausen, 1988).

There have been calls from some quarters to reintroduce the species into Britain and it is possible that some of the birds at liberty in the wild here are the result of deliberate introductions rather than simply being unfortunate and accidental aviary escapes. The introduction of this top predator into our countryside is not without risks and there is also the question of the very long absence of the species from these shores. If we want to see the Eagle Owl as part of our avifauna then attempts to establish the species should follow informed discussion, weighing up the risks and the benefits before any decisions are made. The politics surrounding the presence of the species in our countryside are complex and often heated, leading to mistrust and a polarisation of views. Whatever your point of view, it is clear that we should base any judgement on the future of this magnificent bird on sound scientific evidence.

The conservation status of the Eagle Owl within Britain has not been subject to formal assessment primarily because of the perceived captive origins of the current small breeding population. As with all breeding birds within the UK, the species receives formal protection under the Wildlife and Countryside Act 1981.

Tawny Owl
Strix aluco
(LINNAEUS 1758)

FAMILY: Strigidae

IDENTIFICATION

The Tawny Owl is the typical owl, brown in colouration, with large forward-facing eyes, a rounded head and somewhat 'dumpy' appearance. Three colour forms occur within the European range, the warm chestnut brown form being by far the more common within Britain. The upperparts of British birds tend to be a rich tawny brown, mottled with both darker and lighter tones that break up the outline and help to

FIG 145. Tawny Owl. (Mark Hancox)

camouflage the bird when roosting during the daylight hours. The facial disk tends to be rather plain, outlined with darker brown or black feathering that is perhaps most evident above the eyes. Darker feathering also extends down from the forehead towards the bill, usually with patches of lighter feathering alongside this. The eyes are black. Many of the feathers that cover the base of the flight feathers are tipped with white, sometimes giving the appearance that the bird is wearing paler 'braces'. The flight feathers themselves are heavily barred, a pattern repeated on the tail though with less strength. The feathering that extends onto the legs and toes is off-white in colour and the claws are dark brown or black, often with paler bases. The bill is the colour of horn, vaguely olive-yellow in colouration.

Male and female birds are similar in appearance but can be separated in the hand on the basis of structural size and body weight. Females typically show a wing length in excess of 268 mm and a body weight in excess of 434 g, while males have a wing length of less than 255 mm and a body weight of less than

FIG 146. The length of emerging primary feathers can be used to age nestling Tawny Owls. (Paul Stancliffe)

400 g (Baker, 1993). Individuals can be aged in the hand on the basis of plumage characteristics because of the pattern of flight feather moult which occurs over a number of seasons. Young birds, showing juvenile-type flight feathers, have a thin or broken terminal band on their main flight feathers. Comparison of the flight feathers along the wing should enable contrast between moulted (adult) and unmoulted (juvenile) feathers to be established.

Young Tawny Owls are covered initially with a short, soft down, white in colour. This extends down onto the feet. The cere is pink to greyish-pink and the bill a pale bluish grey. The eyelids are edged pink (c.f. Long-eared Owl) and the eyes are blue to brown from three weeks of age. As the chicks grow so they become more off-white/grey brown in colour. Although female chicks are larger than male chicks, it is not really possible to separate the two within a brood because of the differences in age that arise from asynchronous hatching. Some indication of chick age can be determined by using the growth curves produced by Steve Percival for the British Trust for Ornithology (Percival, 1992).

Voice

The hoot of the Tawny Owl is probably the most familiar of the calls made by a British owl species. It begins with a drawn out '*hooo*' followed by a brief pause before a more subdued '*hu*' and then a resonant final phrase of '*huhuhuhooo*'. The final note, with its falling pitch, has a strong vibrato quality. The female utters a similar call, though somewhat squeaky in nature and less clearly phrased. More characteristic of the female is the '*keewik*' contact call, which may also be used by the male. The two birds may effectively 'duet', the female tagging her '*keewik*' onto the end of his territorial hoot. The nature of individual calls may vary depending on context and the degree of excitement with, for example, neighbouring males involved in a territorial dispute uttering sounds of a more discordant nature. As with other owls, Tawny Owls may bill-snap if alarmed or threatened.

HISTORY

Being a bird of woodland, the history of the Tawny Owl within Britain is probably very closely linked to the degree and type of woodland cover present. There are likely Tawny Owl remains from archaeological sites covering a range of periods, including Boxgrove in Sussex and the Devensian site of Pinhole Cave, Creswell Crags in Derbyshire (see Chapter 1). Glacial events would have pushed Tawny Owls out of Britain for long periods of time, their return only following the succession through tundra and scrub habitats back to woodland. A study of Tawny Owl genetics suggests that those present in Britain today originate from a glacial refuge located in the Balkans (Brito, 2005).

The wooded conditions of the later Mesolithic, as evidenced by remains from Demen's Dale in Derbyshire, suggest the presence of a sizeable Tawny Owl population and, additionally, a wider community of woodland birds (Yalden & Albarella, 2009). The density of Tawny Owl territories in the present day Białowieża forest of Poland, which is viewed as being similar in structure to British woodland of the Mesolithic, might suggest a British Tawny Owl population of *c.* 160,000 pairs at this time. If this is the case, then the later Mesolithic is likely to have been the period during which the British Tawny Owl population was at its peak. The transition from the Mesolithic to the Neolithic saw a switch within human society from hunter-gather to farmer and associated with this was the widespread clearance of woodland habitats in favour of open country for farming. This process will have seen the beginning of a decline in the size of the British Tawny Owl population, something likely to have continued over a very long period and almost up until the present day.

During the 19th century, when we first have good local accounts of the status of our owls, we see frequent reference to the Tawny Owl (or 'Wood Owl') as being less common than the Barn Owl and sometimes, locally, it is also described as being less common than the Long-eared Owl (Holloway, 1996). Many of these accounts also give the impression that the Tawny Owl population was in decline at the time, the blame attributed to the persecution meted out by gamekeepers and those with a sporting gun. Declining numbers were noted from Devon, Sussex, Norfolk, Shropshire and Lancashire, among others, with some of these reports extending back to the 1860s. Tawny Owls also proved popular as mounted exhibits and a good number are likely to have been killed to satisfy this particular market. Changes in the number of gamekeepers active within Britain, most notably influenced by two world wars, appears to have led to something of a recovery in the Tawny Owl population, with a number of authors suggesting that both numbers and breeding range increased during the early part of the 20th century. It is likely that the establishment of plantation forestry and other types of woodland, promoted in an attempt to make Britain less reliant on external timber sources, would also have benefited our Tawny Owls. In particular, the maturing conifer plantations enabled the Tawny Owl to colonise new areas that had been previously unsuitable. There is also a suggestion that a general amelioration of the climate over this period may have benefited British Tawny Owls; there is evidence that the species expanded its breeding range northwards more widely across Europe during the first quarter of the 20th century.

Tawny Owl numbers appear to have been largely stable across the remainder of the 20th century; Prestt (1965) and Prestt & Bell (1966) presented survey data suggesting the species was common and widespread across most of Britain, though still absent from Ireland and from most offshore islands, and Parslow (1973) suggested that the population numbered between 10,000 and 100,000 pairs. The first BTO/IWC breeding atlas, covering the period 1968–72 (Sharrock, 1976), recorded possible, probable or confirmed breeding from 2,305 of the 10-km squares within Britain and Ireland (roughly 60 per cent of those available) and placed the likely population size within a bracket of 50,000 to 100,000 pairs. Given the absence of the species from Ireland and most offshore islands, Sharrock's atlas indicated that the Tawny Owl was very widely distributed across mainland Britain. The figure produced by the second breeding atlas, covering the period 1988–91 (Gibbons et al., 1993) produced a figure of 2,054 10-km squares occupied, suggesting a slight decline which, judging from the detail on the distribution change map, may have been linked to the loss of breeding pairs

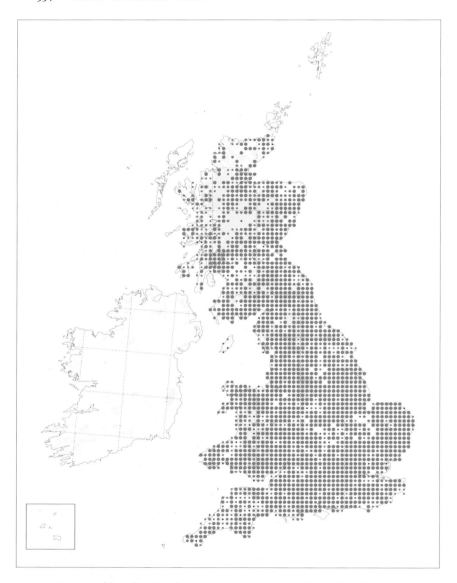

FIG 147. Tawny Owl breeding distribution, 2008–11. Reproduced from *Bird Atlas 2007–11* (Balmer *et al.*, 2013), which is a joint project between BTO, BirdWatch Ireland and the Scottish Ornithologists' Club. Map reproduced with permission from the British Trust for Ornithology.

from parts of northern Scotland. With better methods available, Gibbons and his co-authors were able to refine the population estimate to closer to 20,000 breeding pairs.

Forrester *et al.* (2007) estimated a Scottish population of fewer than 6,000 breeding pairs, based on extrapolations of known densities in particular types of breeding habitat. This figure can be broken down into: 1,800 pairs in broadleaved woodland planted before 1941; 2,230 pairs in coniferous woodland planted before 1961, and 1,858 pairs in areas of improved and neutral grassland and horticulture. Writing in 1994, Roger Lovegrove and colleagues, suggested a Welsh population numbering between 5,000 and 6,000 breeding pairs (Lovegrove *et al.*, 1994). Results from the latest breeding atlas, covering the period 2007–11 (Balmer *et al.*, 2013), report breeding pairs from 2,183 squares, a decline of 6 per cent over a 40-year period. The Tawny Owl features in the combined Common Birds Census/ Breeding Bird Survey dataset managed by BTO. Although not ideally suited to a nocturnal species like Tawny Owl, these data suggest a shallow long-term decline from 1970 to the present day, something that is worthy of further investigation through a more properly targeted survey.

DISTRIBUTION AND HABITAT

Our most familiar owl is to be found breeding across most of Britain, wherever suitable woodland habitat is available. Although primarily an owl of deciduous woodland, the species also occupies coniferous plantations, large urban parks and even mature suburban gardens, providing suitable tree cavities or nest boxes are available for breeding. More open woodland and woodland edge appear to be favoured over extensive blocks of continuous forest and it is in our lowland deciduous woodlands that the highest densities are to be found. The avoidance of closed and high density forests may be linked to the lower densities of small mammal prey species found within these habitats.

The Tawny Owl is absent from Ireland, the Isle of Wight, the Northern Isles and the Outer Hebrides, underlining its rather limited powers of dispersal and reluctance to cross large expanses of water, but it does occur on some of the Inner Hebrides and is also an occasional visitor to other islands; for example, birds are occasionally recorded from Bardsey, where they have been seen to exploit migrant songbirds attracted to the light of the island's lighthouse (Lovegrove *et al.*, 1994). The species is also absent from the highest of our uplands and the most intensive of our arable farmland habitats, presumably because of the lack of tree cover for hunting and nesting. Modelled abundance maps from *Bird Atlas 2007–11* underline these habitat preferences more clearly and also illustrate the lower densities present in our more urbanised regions. Breeding density and territory size estimates (see Table 7, p. 126) reinforce the preference for open-woodland habitats but it is worth noting that the relatively wide range of prey species taken, from small mammals to insects, earthworms and birds, has allowed the species to occupy a range of other habit types as well.

The Tawny Owl occurs as a breeding species right across Europe – it is the commonest European owl – and the breeding distribution extends south to the Mediterranean and on into parts of North Africa. It is also to be found east to northern Pakistan, although across this region the breeding distribution is best described as being discontinuous. A parallel eastern component to the breeding range, occurring at the more northerly latitudes of central Russia, is, in contrast, continuous. The breeding populations of Scotland are on the northern limit of the breeding range, although coastal populations in both Norway and Finland do extend further to the north.

BREEDING ECOLOGY

Tawny Owl pairs are resident on their breeding territories throughout the entire year and are strongly territorial in their behaviour. Territory ownership is advertised through the familiar male call, which may be heard from late autumn and throughout the winter (see Chapter 3). Defence of the territory may be backed up by visual display and, if this fails, by physical skirmishes. There are even reports of individual birds attacking mammalian intruders, including both dog and fox, the latter case involving a Tawny Owl in Yorkshire (Patterson, 1964).

The Tawny Owl is a cavity-nesting species, favouring larger cavities in hollow deciduous trees. Birds may also make use of nest boxes, the old stick nests of other species and, occasionally, sites in buildings (including chimneys). Very occasionally, Tawny Owls may nest on the ground, among rocks or between trees roots, a behaviour more commonly encountered in coniferous woodland, where natural cavities are scarce. Tawny Owls are more likely to use exposed cavity sites than Barn Owls. The female may excavate a shallow scrape within any debris present and it is into this that the eggs are laid at two to three days, often with the longest gap preceding the final egg. The first eggs are laid during February but most clutches are initiated in March. Although some Tawny Owls may begin to breed at one year of age, most probably make their first breeding attempt at two years of age.

FIG 148. Tawny Owls may utilise more open parkland habitats, breeding in the cavities that form in mature trees, such as this one. (Mike Toms)

Incubation usually begins with the first egg, leading to asynchronous hatching of the eggs several weeks later. There is some evidence that nest inspection by fieldworkers might, under certain circumstances, cause the female Tawny Owl to desert, the risk being most significant during the period of egg-laying and the initial days of incubation. This risk can be minimised by timing visits to hit the latter stages of incubation and then reducing subsequent visits by estimating predicted hatching dates from a measure of egg density. As with Barn Owl, there are published curves highlighting the changes in egg density that occur throughout incubation, allowing likely hatching dates for individual eggs to be estimated (Percival, 1992). While the female is incubating her clutch of two to three (one to five) eggs or brooding small young, she continues to receive prey from the male, who delivers small mammals, birds and other items to the nest site. If small mammal prey is scarce or if hunting activity is reduced by poor weather then the female may break from incubation to hunt herself, putting the eggs at risk of chilling.

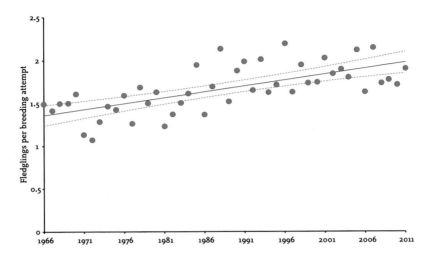

FIG 149. The productivity of British Tawny Owls, 1966–2011, as indicated by the mean number of fledglings produced per breeding attempt (FPBA). Derived from BTO Nest Record Scheme submissions. Smoothed line shows FPBA predicted from model and the confidence intervals associated with this. Redrawn from Baillie *et al.* (2012), with permission from the British Trust for Ornithology.

The female Tawny Owl broods her young for up to a fortnight after hatching, the male continuing to deliver food to the nest, and it is only after this stage that the female leaves the nest to hunt herself. Most prey is delivered at night, though some daylight deliveries have been noted, and the female may often spend the daylight hours in the nest with the chicks. Young Tawny Owls usually leave the nest ahead of fledging, moving to nearby branches at c. 25–30 days of age, where they continue to receive food from their parents. Sunde & Markussen (2005) found that the perching height of Tawny Owls immediately on leaving the nest was positively correlated with nest height. Young from nest boxes, typically placed at between 3 and 6 metres above the ground, were more likely to appear on or near the ground than those from natural sites, which were usually 10–20 m above the ground. Since Sunde also found that predation by Red Fox was a major cause of Tawny Owl mortality during the first few days of leaving the nest, the use of nest boxes could be having a detrimental impact on the Tawny Owl population under study unless they are placed at greater height.

FEEDING BEHAVIOUR

The Tawny Owl is often described as a perch and wait predator, using a suitable branch as a base from which to scan the ground below for prey, before dropping down to take its meal. This strategy suits a bird living and hunting within woodland, where movement on the wing at night is not without its perils. Tawny Owls occupying more open habitats may hunt on the wing, as revealed

FIG 150. Tawny Owls are perch and wait hunters, alert to what is going on around them. (Steve Round)

by the behaviour of two birds being radio-tracked in southern Sweden. Even within Britain the methods adopted by hunting Tawny Owls are likely to vary, as suggested by the wide range of prey species taken. Individuals feeding on earthworms will hunt on foot, moving forward and then pausing, Song Thrush-like, to cock their head and listen for the tell-tale sounds of an earthworm. Other individuals have been reported flying at bushes containing roosting birds, presumably with the intention of flushing them out into the open. The presence of fish in a few Tawny Owl diets (see Chapter 2), also serves to underline the resourceful nature of this owl when hunting.

The diet of British Tawny Owls has been less well studied than that of some of our other species, largely because Tawny Owl pellets tend not to be deposited at a single, usually enclosed, site. Instead, they are scattered in the open, often below favoured perches rather than at roosting sites; being deposited in the open also means that the pellets break down more quickly. Tawny Owl pellets have a looser structure than those of Barn Owl and tend to be paler in appearance. However, there is much variation in these features that results from the type of prey being taken. Small, hard pellets are produced when the owl has been feeding on earthworms, while those dominated by small mammal remains are grey brown in appearance and less compact. Field Vole, Bank Vole and Wood Mouse all feature commonly in British Tawny Owl diets, with the species of vole present tending to reflect the nature of the habitat over which the owls are hunting. The well-studied woodland population at Wytham in Oxfordshire was, for example, dominated by Bank Vole but the populations utilising small woodlots in a wider agricultural setting include more Field Voles. Urban birds may take more birds than their rural counterparts. Tawny Owl diet shows a strong seasonal structure, with Cockchafer and other large beetles increasingly taken during the early summer months, along with (in some populations) more birds and young Rabbits.

MOVEMENTS

The Tawny Owl is the most sedentary of our breeding owls, with few other species showing such a high degree of site-fidelity. As we saw in earlier chapters, such sedentary habits, coupled with year-round residence on a breeding territory, afford this owl a number of advantages, including familiarity with the breeding territory and the food resources that it supports. Young Tawny Owls undergo a period of rather limited natal dispersal, which sees a median distance moved of just 4 km, underlining that most youngsters establish themselves close to where they were raised. Steve Percival found that populations from the northern half of Britain tended to show longer natal dispersal movements than those from populations in the southern half of Britain (Percival, 1990). This matches the findings of work carried out elsewhere in Europe (Mikkola, 1983).

To date, there have been no overseas recoveries of British-ringed Tawny Owls and no birds from elsewhere have been reported from here. This suggests that the British population is isolated from populations elsewhere in Europe. The lack of long-distance movements also underlines why the species is absent from Ireland, the Northern Isles, the Isle of Wight and other off-shore islands.

STATUS AND CONSERVATION

The number of breeding Tawny Owls in Britain is thought to be around 20,000 breeding pairs but this estimate should be viewed as an educated 'best guess' based on a series of assumptions about likely breeding densities and habitat use. The nocturnal nature of the Tawny Owl means that it is not well-monitored through established national multi-species schemes but its sedentary habits and territorial vocalisations should allow a more robust measure of population size to be calculated from a targeted national survey. There is a suggestion from multi-species monitoring schemes that our Tawny Owl population may have undergone a period of long-term shallow decline but, being perceived as common and widespread, there have not been any calls for a more targeted study. The European Tawny Owl population is thought to number between 360,000 and 800,000 pairs and to be largely stable, although recent increases in some countries have been linked to afforestation programmes.

The Tawny Owl appears on the GREEN list of Birds of Conservation Concern, underlining a favourable conservation status. It also receives general protection within Britain through the Wildlife and Countryside Act (1981). A number of fieldworkers operate nest box schemes for Tawny Owls and there have also been several detailed studies, most notably those of Petty, Redpath and Hardy (see Chapter 3). Such studies provide both annual monitoring of breeding success and a more complete understanding of Tawny Owl ecology and habitat preferences within Britain.

Little Owl
Athene noctua
(SCOPOLI 1769)

FAMILY: Strigidae

IDENTIFICATION

This small owl, about the size of a Song Thrush, has a surprisingly chunky appearance. The head is broad and rounded with a flattened crown. Depending upon stance, the Little Owl can often appear rather long-legged and short-tailed. The upperparts are grey-brown, varying in strength of colour, and densely spotted with white. The underparts are heavily streaked

FIG 151. Little Owl. (Mark Hancox)

with longitudinal brown markings on a paler base colour. Adults and first-year birds have a lemon yellow iris which, combined with white 'eyebrows', give the owl something of a piercing stare. Nestlings have short, dense and white-coloured down initially (the neoptile or 'first down') before becoming mottled grey from their second week as the mesoptile (or 'second') down starts to grow. This is rather soft and feather-like in appearance, though clearly distinguishable from the feathers of first-year and adult birds. The neoptile down often remains attached to the tip of the mesoptile down for several weeks and is retained longest on the flanks, thighs and crown. As is the case with some of our other owls, it is possible to age nestlings by measuring the length of their growing primaries (Juillard, 1979).

First-year birds are similar in appearance to adults but can be distinguished in the hand by the more pointed feather tips shown by young birds and the larger pale spots seen on their primaries. In young birds, the tip of the outermost primary feather has white on both the inner and outer web; this is absent from the inner web in adult birds. Ageing British Little Owls in spring is more difficult, as abrasion to the primary feather tips will produce a more rounded outline, and is best based on the degree of wear on the tertial feathers. In adults these will be more heavily worn. Young birds undergo a partial post-juvenile moult soon after fledging, which is largely confined to the body and head feathers, plus the lesser and median wing-coverts. Adults undergo a complete post-breeding moult, which may start as early as June and is completed from September to early November. Little Owls may be seen during the day, perched in thin cover or on a post or branch, from which they may flush with a characteristic and often strongly undulating flight.

Female Little Owls are heavier than males, the difference being most pronounced during the breeding season. Both sexes appear to attain their maximum weight during the winter months, when birds may be a third heavier than they were at the end of the breeding season. Structurally, as evident from measurements of wing and tail length, females appear to be slightly larger than males.

Voice

The Little Owl is known to utter a wide and diverse range of calls, the most commonly heard of which is the yelping and rather shrill alarm call of 'kwiff, kwiff, kwiff, kwiff'. This has components that are reminiscent of the alarm calls of woodpecker. The song of the male is a repeated and rather nasal 'gwooooohk', which has an upward inflection. The nature of this phrase may alter as the male becomes more excited, the sound becoming more cat-like and abrupt. Both sexes use a soft contact call, perhaps best described as 'uhk' and the female may utter a rasping call at the nest, not dissimilar from the higher-pitched begging call of the young.

HISTORY

Although there is no conclusive evidence that Little Owls have ever reached Britain naturally, some early records might well refer to genuine immigrants. Any records from after 1870 should certainly be treated with caution, however, because Little Owls were first introduced successfully in 1874 – at Stonewall Park, near Edenbridge in Kent – by Mr E. G. B. Meade-Waldo. Details of this and subsequent introductions by Meade-Waldo in this area are best described in his own words:

> between that year [1874] and 1880 about 40 good birds went off. We knew of one nest in 1879. In 1896, and again in 1900, I hacked off about twenty-five. Since then they have been comparatively abundant all through our district, which is

*roughly between Tunbridge Wells and Sevenoaks. I know of generally some 40
nests in a radius of some four or five miles.*

The Stonewall Park birds spread into East Sussex and Surrey, reaching the London
suburbs by 1897. There had been at least two previous attempts at introducing
the species, the first of which saw the release of five individuals on 10 May 1842 at
Walton Hall, Yorkshire, never to be seen again. The second attempt took place in
the 1860s at a site in the New Forest but few details are available. More individuals
might have been released at Walton Hall had the rather eccentric 'Squire' Charles
Waterton not given the birds a warm bath to help them cope with the cold
conditions, following which five individuals promptly died that same night!

While some attempts at introducing the species did not fair well, including
that made by Lord Rothschild at Tring, Hertfordshire, others were more
successful. Most notable of these was Lord Lilford, who purchased Dutch-caught
Little Owls from the London markets over several years, turning them loose on his
Northamptonshire estate. Judging from the contents of a letter that Lord Lilford
sent to the Reverend Murray Matthew in 1889, it appears that a group of 40 birds
was first released into the park in July 1888. Many of these birds were recaptured

FIG 152. The bright yellow and black eyes, plus white 'eyebrows', give the Little Owl a piercing
stare. (Steve Round)

TABLE 14. First breeding records of Little Owls in selected British counties.

Year	Counties
1879	Kent
1889	Northamptonshire
1892	Bedfordshire
1894	Buckinghamshire
1897	Hertfordshire
1899	Essex
1903	East Sussex
1907	Surrey, Suffolk, Cambridgeshire, Huntingdonshire
1909	Derbyshire, Hampshire
1910	Berkshire, Norfolk
1913	Leicestershire, Nottinghamshire
1914	Monmouthshire
1915	Wiltshire
1916	Glamorganshire
1918	Isle of Wight, Dorset, Cardiganshire, Radnorshire
1919	Montgomeryshire
1920	Pembrokeshire
1921	Cheshire, Lancashire
1922	Yorkshire, Cornwall
1935	Northumberland
1958	Borders

soon after release, seemingly 'too young … to find their own food'. Others were found dead but at least some must have survived, since a pair was found with an active nest on 23 April 1889. Spurred on by this achievement, Lord Lilford released more individuals over the following years, birds seemingly responsible for the successful colonisation of much of England. By the 1920s, the Little Owl had colonised virtually every county south of the River Humber (see Table 14).

The first record from Wales was of a bird killed in Glamorgan in the 1860s. However, the Little Owl did not become established in Wales as a breeding species until 1916, when breeding occurred in Glamorgan, and it was not until the early 1960s that Little Owls had been recorded breeding in every Welsh county. The Welsh Little Owl population increased in the decade after initial establishment, reaching a peak in the 1930s. A decline was noted over the following decade, however, which was thought to be linked to a run of severe winters. The winter of 1946–47, in particular, was thought to have caused the local extinction of the species in some parts of Wales. The first Scottish record of breeding came in 1958, from Edrom in the Borders, but by the late 1970s there had still been only a few breeding records, all from the south of the country.

Parslow (1973) suggested a breeding population 1,000–10,000 pairs, a figure refined by Sharrock (1976) to 7,000–14,000 pairs based on a conservative estimate of five to ten pairs per occupied 10-km square. At the time of the first BTO/Irish Wildbird Conservancy (IWC) breeding atlas, the species had been recorded from 1,381 10-km squares, or 36 per cent of the total available across Britain and Ireland. David Glue, writing the Little Owl account for the second national atlas (Gibbons *et al.*, 1993) reported a figure of 1,381 squares occupied (11 per cent down on the previous atlas) and estimated the British population (using the same density figure adopted by Sharrock) at 6,000–12,000 pairs. Examination of the distribution change map, covering these two atlas periods, suggested the loss of breeding pairs from parts of south-west England and, additionally, much of Lincolnshire.

The Little Owl was one of the target species in Project Barn Owl, carried out by the BTO and the Hawk and Owl Trust from 1995–97 (Toms *et al.*, 2001). This study, which involved a stratified survey of randomly selected survey squares, estimated the Little Owl population to number between 4,000 and 8,500 breeding pairs, the first truly robust and repeatable measure of Little Owl population size within the UK. Evidence from the combined Common Birds Census/Breeding Bird Survey dataset suggests that the Little Owl population has undergone a moderate long-term decline, the index falling by 60 per cent over the period 1984–2009. A repeat of the 1995–97 survey would provide a more robust estimate of how the population has changed since the initial survey.

DISTRIBUTION AND HABITAT

The Little Owl breeding distribution extends across England, north to the Scottish borders and west into Wales. Although the species has established breeding populations on Anglesey and in north-west Wales, it is absent from much of the rest of the country. It is also rather scarce in many parts of south-west England, including both Cornwall and north Devon, though breeding populations in south Devon are well-established. The absence of the species from western regions is a result of range contraction over a period of 30 or so years, as revealed by the BTO-led breeding bird atlases.

Within Scotland, the Little Owl remains a scarce breeding resident, largely restricted to the southern part of the country, with a scattering of individual birds recorded up the east coast as far north as the Loch of Strathbeg, where a bird was seen in May 1991 (Forrester *et al.*, 2007). This suggests that the current breeding distribution of the species within Britain is limited at its northern edge by climatic conditions, notably the more severe winter weather experienced in this region. There have been very few records of Little Owl from Ireland, underlining the generally sedentary nature of the species and its reluctance to

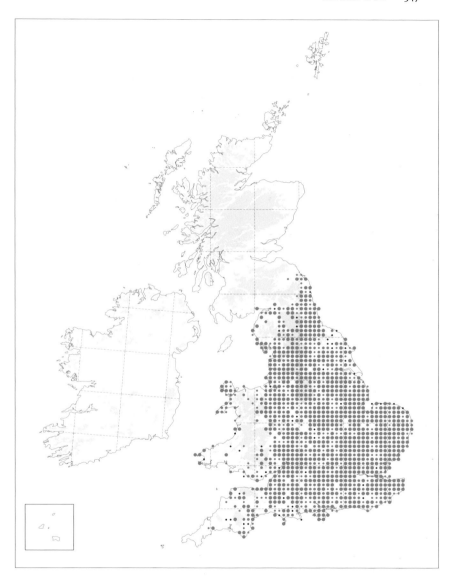

FIG 153. Little Owl breeding distribution, 2008–11. Reproduced from *Bird Atlas 2007–11* (Balmer *et al.*, 2013), which is a joint project between BTO, BirdWatch Ireland and the Scottish Ornithologists' Club. Map reproduced with permission from the British Trust for Ornithology.

FIG 154. British Little Owls do best in areas of mixed farming with well-developed hedgerows and woodland-edge habitat. (Steve Round)

cross large expanses of water. The first of these records was of a bird killed on the Kilmorony Estate in County Kildare in June 1903, the most recent a bird seen in Wicklow in December 1981. Modelled abundance maps support the avoidance of upland areas and a generally greater abundance in the east of the breeding range, with the areas of greatest modelled abundance falling within East Anglia, south-east England, the Midlands and parts of central northern England. The pattern of occurrence and its associated habitat features suggests that, as is the case elsewhere in Europe, the Little Owl is most abundant within mixed farmland landscapes, where small parcels of farmland are broken up by woodland-edge and hedgerow habitats. The presence of hedgerow trees and old farm buildings are also a key feature of the farmland landscapes used by breeding Little Owls within Britain. Most reported records of breeding Little Owls come from cavities in deciduous trees or nest boxes, and there is a clear association of natural sites with mature orchards and pollarded timber.

The Little Owl is widely distributed from northern England and Denmark south through the Mediterranean and into North Africa. The breeding range extends east across Europe and into Central Asia, extending as far east as the

Pacific coast of China. The Little Owl has also been introduced into New Zealand. Across this extensive distribution a wide range of habitats are occupied, though sharing open country with trees, bushes, hedgerows or boulders. Within Europe the breeding range typically sits below the 700 m contour, but elsewhere birds may occupy open montane regions. An examination of BTO Nest Records Scheme data (Glue & Scott, 1980) revealed that nearly two-thirds of monitored nests were located below the 61 m (200 ft) contour, while just 15 per cent were located above 122 m (400 ft).

BREEDING ECOLOGY

Little Owl pairs tend to remain on their breeding territories throughout the year, the male advertising ownership during the autumn period of juvenile dispersal and again in early spring. Calling behaviour may be noted as early as February but courtship proper is more usually a feature of March and April. Both sexes may be heard calling and, as seen in Chapter 3, courtship involves nest hole demonstrations and courtship feeding. Copulation may be frequent and much of the activity is centred on the future nest site.

The Little Owl is a cavity-nesting species, favouring a small cavity often located in a tree, building or stone wall. Tree sites are often located in hollow

FIG 155. Little Owl pairs remain on territory throughout the year. (Mark Hancox)

branches but birds also use the bole, a chamber within the roots or a vertical hole in the trunk. Pairs may also nest in Rabbit burrows, between the bales of a haystack or in a purpose-built nest box. There appears to be some reluctance to use newly erected nest boxes and pairs may roost in nest boxes over several years before eventually using them for breeding. Favoured nesting chambers tend to be dark and located at some distance from the cavity entrance; some sites may have multiple entrances. Favoured tree species include oak, Ash and various fruit trees, the nest hole typically 2–4 m above the ground. No nest as such is built, although the bird may excavate a shallow scrape within any debris present in the nesting chamber. Some sites are used over a number of years.

A clutch of three to four (two to five) white eggs is produced (almost exclusively during April or May), the eggs laid daily or, sometimes, on alternate days. Poor weather and low prey availability may also lead to an increased interval between subsequent eggs. Female Little Owls usually initiate incubation well before the clutch is complete, often starting with the first or second egg, leading to asynchronous hatching of the resulting young. While his mate is incubating, the male will often roost on an exposed perch, from which he can remain aware of potential threats to the nesting attempt; he will also provision the female. Little Owl pairs tend to become more secretive in their habits when egg-laying. Incubation averages 27–29 days, based on data submitted to the BTO Nest Records Scheme.

The young are fed by both parents, the female initially brooding the chicks and receiving prey from her mate who takes the lead role in prey provisioning for at least the first two weeks, after which the female also hunts and provides for the developing chicks. The young are usually fed after dusk, with a peak in activity through until midnight and a second from 2 am through until dawn. The chicks grow rapidly and may leave the nest for the first time at three to four weeks of age, remaining in the vicinity and continuing to receive food from their parents. Young Little Owls fledge at 30–35 days of age but remain dependent upon their parents for perhaps another month, the family sometimes remaining together through until late August. Genuine second broods are rare and replacement clutches appear to be uncommon, though this is dependent on the stage at which the first attempt has failed.

FEEDING BEHAVIOUR

As we saw in Chapter 2, Little Owls will often hunt from a perch, using this vantage point to locate potential prey before dropping onto it. Some invertebrate prey is taken on foot, the owl often gliding down to the ground and then making

FIG 156. Little Owls often hunt from a prominent perch. (Mark Hancox)

the final approach with a short series of hops. Individuals may work hedgerows, looking for the nests of other birds, or catch insects in flight. This latter behaviour may sometimes see Little Owls at street or other outdoor lighting to which moths have been attracted. Hunting behaviour tends to vary with the species being targeted and the nature of the habitat or with perch availability. Little Owls may sometimes establish larders in which surplus food is stored prior to being delivered to young or the nest site. Such behaviour may also be seen outside of the breeding season.

The diet of British Little Owls is dominated by larger insects (such as Cockchafers and other beetles), earthworms and small mammals, with small birds of secondary importance. Prey up to the size of a half-grown Rabbit may be taken and individual pairs will take advantage of locally abundant prey, as demonstrated by those breeding on Skokholm and taking large numbers of Storm Petrels (see Chapter 2). There is a suggestion that breeding success may be linked to the availability of small mammal prey, with some authors suggesting evidence of a three- to five-year cycle within British population indices derived from annual monitoring programmes (Parkin & Knox, 2010). British Little Owls appear to be unable to cope with prolonged snow cover or poor winter weather, suggesting that they may find it difficult to secure sufficient food under such conditions. This may, in part, explain the Little Owl's absence from northern and western parts of Britain and from areas of higher ground.

MOVEMENTS

Young Little Owls remain close to their natal site during the first few weeks after leaving the nest, with dispersal taking place during autumn (July to September). The median natal dispersal distance is just 7 km, larger than that seen in Tawny Owl but still indicating a species in which dispersing young settle close to their natal area. Although there is a suggestion that Little Owls from northern populations may move further than those from the south, the sample sizes involved are too small to allow true comparison. The overall impression is of a species that is generally very site-faithful as an adult, with limited dispersal of young birds away from the natal site.

STATUS AND CONSERVATION

The most recent estimate of 4,000–8,500 breeding pairs, produced from work carried out in the mid-1990s (Toms *et al.*, 2000), is now thought to be a little high, with annual monitoring through the combined Common Bird Census/Breeding Bird Survey suggesting that the British population has since declined. A decline in the annual monitoring index of a third is evident for the period 1999–2009, with a larger (54 per cent) decline since 1967 (Baillie *et al.*, 2012). While such figures suggest a moderate long-term decline, there is some uncertainty around the extent to which such multi-species annual monitoring schemes can reveal population information for species like Little Owl, which are largely inactive during the day and which occur at low densities.

Evidence of long-term declines can also be seen in many European populations and the limited information available might suggest that habitat loss and changes in farming practices are having a negative effect on Little Owls. Given these declines, the most recent estimate of 300,000 pairs for the size of the European population is almost certainly too high. Studies elsewhere in Europe (notably Letty *et al.*, 2001; and Schaub *et al.*, 2006) suggest that changing adult and first-year survival rates may exert a strong influence on population trajectory. Food availability during the breeding season may also be important for some populations (Thorup *et al.*, 2010).

FIG 157. Little Owl populations are thought to be in decline in many European countries, including Britain. (Mark Hancox)

The Little Owl receives general protection within Britain through the Wildlife and Countryside Act 1981. The loss of traditional nest sites in the form of hedgerow trees or disused farm buildings may be countered by the provision of suitable nest boxes. However, the loss of suitable hunting habitats and their populations of favoured prey species may be harder to tackle. There is also some concern over the potential effects of environmental contaminants (see Chapter 5), including pesticides and heavy metals. The collection of more information on Little Owl breeding success in relation to local habitat features, coupled with a repeat of the national survey, would provide much-needed information that could help to inform conservation policy for this species.

Long-eared Owl
Asio otus
(LINNAEUS 1758)

FAMILY: Strigidae

IDENTIFICATION

The Long-eared Owl is a medium-sized owl, slightly smaller than a Tawny Owl, with narrower wings, pale yellow-orange eyes and prominent ear tufts. Identification difficulties are more likely to be encountered in relation to Short-eared Owl than Tawny Owl (see box). The general colouration of the Long-eared Owl is a rich tawny-ochre,

FIG 158. Long-eared Owl. (Mark Hancox)

with areas of grey wash and darker streaking and spotting; these are interspersed with pale grey or white markings. The back has dark brown vermiculations, together with short brown streaks that deliver a more marbled appearance. The wings show white or off-white marbling, an effect produced by the pale fringes to the coverts. The underparts typically show a buff ground colour overlaid with darker longitudinal markings, the latter most evident on the belly and breast. The tail is closely barred dark brown on a rich ground colour. Some authors describe the face as being 'cat-like', with a somewhat angular, almost elongated appearance. The eyes, which vary from pale yellow to a more intense orange, are framed by dark patches, set within a warm-buff facial disc. The bill is dark, as are the claws, and the cere is grey. The plumage provides effective camouflage to a perched bird, and roosting birds are easily overlooked. Roosting birds usually adopt an upright posture, the body appearing rather elongated and somewhat thin. The female is the larger of the two sexes, being structurally larger in her measurements and also heavier in terms of body weight. She also tends to be darker in appearance, although neither colouration nor differences in body size are particularly useful in the field

BOX 7.1. Field identification of *Asio* owls.

When perched, and particularly when the ear tufts are visible, Long-eared Owl can be readily separated from Short-eared Owl. At other times, eye colour can prove particularly useful; the eyes of Long-eared Owl are yellow-orange, while those of Short-eared Owl are yellow. In flight the Long-eared Owl has wings that are broader and somewhat more rounded in appearance at their tips. In practice, however, this feature is difficult to apply when a bird is seen in isolation. Instead, look at the nature of the wing pattern. The general appearance of the upperside of the wing in Short-eared Owl is of sharp contrast between the dark wing tip and the extensive pale panel that sits between this and the darker carpel patch. In Long-eared Owl this panel is more richly coloured and, therefore, less obvious. Another feature of the upperwing useful for identification is the trailing edge of the secondary flight feathers (those closest to the body). In Short-eared Owl this trailing edge is pale and it contrasts strongly with the barring on the flight feathers, while in Long-eared Owl it is more richly coloured.

The darker wing tip of Short-eared Owl is also evident on the underwing, although in this instance both species show a similarly coloured pale area between the wing tip and the carpel patch, the latter being crescent-shaped in both. The underwing coverts, which extend from the carpel crescent towards the body, are more richly coloured in Long-eared Owl than they are in Short-eared Owl and they contrast with the paler ground colour of the flight feathers themselves. Another useful feature in flight is the patterning on the flank. In Long-eared Owl there is streaking from the neck along the flanks to the tail, but in Short-eared Owl the streaking is concentrated towards the front of the bird and the flanks are usually unmarked or only poorly marked.

FIG 159. When alarmed the Long-eared Owl may raise its ear tufts. (Steve Round)

Young Long-eared Owls have short soft white down, which extends down onto the feet. The cere is pink to pinkish yellow in colour, the bill pale bluish-grey. The edge of the eyelids soon turn black, a useful feature when comparing with young Tawny Owls, in which the eyelids are edged pink. The young can be aged on the basis of plumage and other features. Those four days of age or younger are small, with sparse white down; they are largely inactive, huddling together in the absence of the parent, and their eyes have yet to open. Young that are five to eight days of age will have lost their egg tooth and the eyes will have opened to reveal opaque bluish pupils and a bright yellow iris. The down that covers them will have thickened and brown flecks begun to appear on the breast and wings. The flight feathers should also start to develop at this age. As the chicks approach ten days of age they will begin to defend themselves, snapping their bills if disturbed. Dark feathers begin to develop on either side of the bill at this stage and these darken to form a 'mask'. The eyes take on a darker, more orange appearance and the ear tufts become visible. By two weeks of age the wing feathers should be well developed.

Voice

The male song or territorial call is a soft 'Hoo', reminiscent of the sound made by blowing across the top of a bottle. Although this may be far carrying, it can be difficult to pick out at distance. The 'Hoo' phrase is repeated every 2–3 seconds, beginning rather weakly but becoming stronger as the bout of calling develops. Females sometimes utter a rather weak and somewhat nasal call, best described as 'peh-ev', which may be used in a duet with their mate. As we saw in Chapter 3, another feature of courtship and territorial display is the wing-clap, which is produced irregularly during the display flight. When alarmed, birds of either sex may utter a hoarse and grating 'kvak kvak kvak' call, which has an almost bark-like character. Young Long-eared Owls beg for food by using a sharp squeaking whistle, strongly reminiscent of a squeaky gate.

HISTORY

The association with woodland that the Long-eared Owl shares with the more familiar Tawny Owl would suggest a long history within Britain, the species occupying maturing scrub and woodland habitats. However, the Long-eared Owl is poorly represented within the archaeological record for Britain and it seems likely that it would have occurred at much lower densities than the Tawny Owl, perhaps a reflection of the nature of available habitat or of competition between the two species.

Surprisingly, the Long-eared Owl was unknown as a breeding species in many counties prior to the middle of the 1800s and, additionally, it is poorly represented within literature or poetry up to this period. Occurring at low density, and being somewhat secretive in habits, it seems likely that the Long-eared Owl was widely overlooked by naturalists. It is not until the mid-1800s that we see wider acknowledgement of the species and its status. MacGillvray, writing in 1840, describes the Long-eared Owl as Scotland's commonest owl. There is a suggestion that the Long-eared Owl may have become more common during the 1800s as a consequence of the maturing plantations of both native and exotic conifers planted in earlier decades. Many of the early nesting records for counties like Norfolk, Hampshire and Kent come from these new plantations. Henry Stevenson's three-volume account of the birds of Norfolk recognises how common the Long-eared Owl had become in Norfolk by the late 1800s. This pattern of increase seems to have been short-lived here, as in certain other counties; the subsequent decline seen in Norfolk is thought to have been triggered as the numbers of Tawny Owls began to increase again, following a fall in the levels of persecution. There is reasonable evidence that the decline was taking place across much of southern England and Wales and the Long-eared Owl certainly appears to have become rather scarce in these areas by the 1930s. After this period the decline seems to have become more widespread, although populations in Scotland and Ireland – Tawny Owl is absent from the latter country – remained buoyant.

The Atlas of Breeding Birds in Britain and Ireland (Sharrock, 1976) recorded evidence of possible, probable or confirmed breeding from 942 10-km squares, roughly a quarter of those available, prompting the author to suggest a breeding population numbering at least 3,000 pairs but almost certainly less than 10,000 pairs. This estimate was refined by Gibbons et al. (1993) in the second breeding atlas, with a population estimated to be between 2,200 and 7,200 pairs. Interestingly, while it was assumed that the density of breeding pairs was similar to that used by Sharrock, there had been a 28 per cent reduction in the breeding range between the two atlas periods. This might suggest that the estimate produced by David Gibbons and his colleagues was perhaps a little high. Both sets of authors accept that there may be problems with their estimates of both distribution and population size, a consequence of the species being nocturnal and secretive in its habits and not suited to the atlas methodology. The most recent attempt to map the distribution of breeding Long-eared Owls (Balmer et al., 2013) also suffers from the same difficulties, delivering a figure of 900 occupied 10-km squares and suggesting the loss of further breeding pairs from across the British and Irish range.

DISTRIBUTION AND HABITAT

The Long-eared Owl shows a wide breeding distribution across Britain and Ireland, with many of the key breeding populations centred on areas of mature conifer plantation where, presumably, competition with the Tawny Owl is reduced. The Long-eared Owl remains a scarce breeding species in south-west England and Wales but it exhibits a fairly good breeding status within Ireland, where there has been a pronounced increase in breeding records from south-west Ireland over the last 20 or so years. This may reflect the introduction and establishment of the Bank Vole to this region but it is tempered somewhat by the apparent loss of breeding birds from the eastern part of Ireland. Losses from south-west Scotland, parts of Yorkshire, coastal Suffolk and south-east England also give cause for concern. More widely, the Long-eared Owl occurs throughout much of the Northern Hemisphere, breeding as far north as the July 15°C isotherm and south to the southern USA, North Africa and parts of India and Pakistan. Individuals from some populations winter to the south of this core range.

British Long-eared Owls are associated with coniferous woodland and scrub habitats during the breeding season, typically where dense nesting cover is bordered by more open areas that are used for hunting. The species may breed in deciduous woodland but it is thought that competition with the Tawny Owl limits its use of this habitat. Possible competition with the Tawny Owl may also explain the increased abundance of the species in Ireland and on the Isle of Wight, both being areas from which breeding Tawny Owls are absent. Pairs may also be found breeding in farmland shelterbelts and among low bushes within areas of grazing marsh or sand dune. The ability to exploit a range of different habitat types probably stems from this owl's breeding requirements, namely a suitable nest platform and some open grassland habitat with its small mammal populations. In the absence of a suitable nest platform, in the form of the old stick nest of another species, the Long-eared Owl may nest on the ground.

Bird Atlas 2007–11 indicates that wintering Long-eared Owls tend to show an easterly bias to their distribution in Britain, with a similar pattern noted in Ireland (Balmer *et al.*, 2013). While to some extent this pattern is not dissimilar to the breeding distribution (within Britain at least), it might indicate the arrival of wintering birds from further north and east, swelling the size of the population present. Birds roosting communally during the winter months often favour scrubby patches or hawthorn or other shrubs. These roosts may contain as many as 20 individuals and are best located by first finding areas where good numbers of

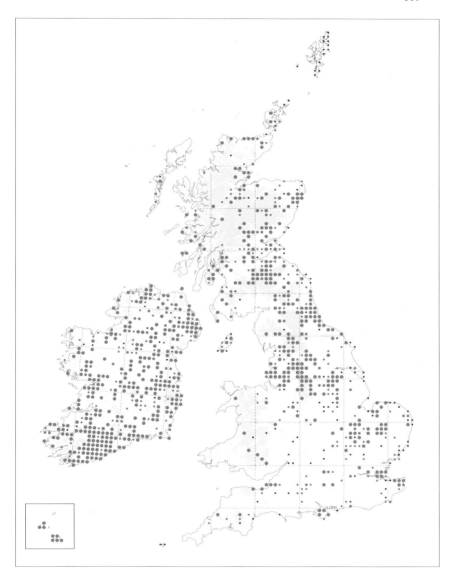

FIG 160. Long-eared Owl breeding distribution, 2008–11. Reproduced from *Bird Atlas 2007–11* (Balmer *et al.*, 2013), which is a joint project between BTO, BirdWatch Ireland and the Scottish Ornithologists' Club. Map reproduced with permission from the British Trust for Ornithology.

FIG 161. Wintering Long-eared Owls may be found at traditional sites. (Mark Hancox)

Long-eared Owls can be found hunting. Some traditional sites may be used over several winters. Downland scrub is favoured in parts of southern England, but elsewhere birds may be associated with farmland, coastal marshlands, inland bogs and heathland, or even the rough ground of extensive industrial sites.

BREEDING ECOLOGY

The Long-eared Owl usually adopts the old stick nest of another species (often a crow or Magpie) but may take to nesting baskets placed in suitable tress or even nest on the ground, at the base of a tree or under a bush. The species has, on occasion, been recorded using open-fronted Kestrel nest boxes. Breeding birds often favour small patches of woodland situated in open country, often close to damp grassland, and many nests are situated in low-lying districts below 150 m above sea level. Scottish birds tend to breed at higher altitudes, suggesting that it is the availability of suitable hunting habitat that is important rather than some climatic factor associated with altitude.

Although individual pairs defend a breeding territory, they forage over a much larger area. One study in Scotland, for example, found birds foraging at distances of over 2.5 km from the nest in years of low vole abundance (Scott, 1997). Most of the nest records for British Long-eared Owls relate to birds nesting in trees, with roughly three-quarters of these favouring conifers. Pines are the most commonly used trees, followed by spruce, fir and larch. Whether this represents selection for particular types of tree or merely reflects differences in the abundance of these trees in favoured locations is unclear. Some pairs use willow or hawthorn, the nests placed in these tending to be sited closer to the ground (averaging *c.* 5 m) compared to those in conifers (which average 7.5 m). Very occasionally, Long-eared Owls will utilise tree cavities or, as noted above, nest on the ground, the latter behaviour sometimes noted in areas that have been clear-felled. As we saw in Chapter 3, the old stick nests of other species (notably crow or Magpie) are used most often, although birds may also use the old nests of Grey Heron *Ardea cinerea* and Woodpigeon or even take over an abandoned squirrel drey. Long-eared Owls will occupy a nesting basket deliberately erected for them (Garner & Milne, 1997). Favoured sites are usually those situated below the canopy, providing some cover for the pair. Occupied nests tend to have pellets and droppings present below them.

Pairs begin to advertise their territory with male song from late January, although birds that have wintered away from their breeding territory probably start somewhat later, perhaps not until March or early April. Those that appear

FIG 162. Long-eared Owls use the old stick nests of other species. (Richard Castell)

to retain a territory throughout the year normally occupy a new nest each season, typically situated within a short distance of the one used the previous year. The male call of 'Hoo-Hoo-Hoo-Hoo' is often given from a high perch and is repeated many times over, the bird sometimes breaking off from calling to make a display flight. The display flight seems most strongly associated with the period during which the pair are selecting a suitable nest site. The amount of song declines from April onwards and may be curtailed by heavy rain or high winds (Clark & Anderson, 1997). It appears that not all pairs found on territory will make a breeding attempt in a given year; Andrew Village, for example, found that 17 per cent of the pairs in his study area did not breed in a given year (Village, 1981).

Most British clutches are laid between mid-March and the end of April, but in some years pairs may lay as early as mid-February. The clutch of three to four (range, one to six) eggs is laid on alternate days, with incubation beginning from the first egg and leading to asynchronous hatching. Females may abandon a nesting attempt if disturbed during the period of egg-laying. If a first attempt fails during the early part of the breeding season then the pair may make another attempt. Genuine second broods are very rare, being more likely only if the first attempt was made particularly early in the year. The incubation period averages 28 days, but may be as short as 25 days or as long as 30 days. During this period the female tends to sit tightly, receiving food from her mate, who typically delivers two to four prey items per night.

The chicks, which weigh c. 16 g at hatching, develop rapidly and are brooded continuously by the female for at least the first week of life, after which the female may help the male to catch and deliver prey. Even at this stage, the bulk of this responsibility continues to fall on the male. Most of the feeding visits are made at night, although the adults may occasionally be seen hunting during the hours of daylight. Young Long-eared Owls branch at 23–24 days, leaving the nest but continuing to receive food from their parents. At this stage the young may be particularly vocal, uttering their squeaky gate begging call. Adult Long-eared Owls are not normally aggressive in defence of the nest or its contents, though they may fly at an intruder or feign injury in an attempt to lure them away from the nest. Older chicks may adopt a defensive posture if disturbed, which sees them fluff up their body plumage, spread their wings and lean forward, eyes wide open.

FEEDING BEHAVIOUR

Long-eared Owls are the most nocturnal of the British owls and are seldom seen hunting during daylight hours. Field Vole appears to be the most important prey species for British Long-eared Owls, with Wood Mouse, Bank Vole and Common Rat of secondary importance. Wood Mouse and Common Rat are the most important small mammal prey species for Long-eared Owls in Ireland. Bird prey become more important outside of the breeding season in Britain but, for reasons outlined in Chapter 2, our understanding of their contribution may be incomplete (Glue & Hammond, 1974).

The hunting method most commonly observed is of a bird quartering open ground at a height of 1–3 m. While it is likely that open ground, with rough grassland and an abundant Field Vole population, is of great importance to Long-eared Owls, the presence of large numbers of Wood Mouse and Bank Vole in pellet samples would seem to suggest that hunting activity often takes place within woodland, where it easily overlooked by birdwatchers. Those observations that are available of Long-eared Owls hunting within woodland show the birds quartering at low level beneath the canopy, often breaking these flights by perching on suitable vantage points (such as a stump row or fallen tree).

Winter roost sites provide a good opportunity to collect pellets, which accumulate beneath favoured perches, but visits to collect these should be restricted to late afternoon or dusk, so that birds are not forced to leave the roost during the hours of daylight when they may be mobbed. Winter feeding ranges can be substantial, perhaps exceeding 100 ha on occasion.

MOVEMENTS

The rather limited information available on our breeding Long-eared Owls suggests that youngsters begin to disperse away from their natal sites between one and two months after leaving the nest. However, long-distance movements may not be made until later and even then it is not clear just how far our breeders

FIG 163. Long-eared Owl arrivals appear to vary between years, both in terms of the number of individuals reaching Britain and in their timing. (Hugh Harrop)

actually move. The median natal dispersal distance of 42 km is based on just a handful of recoveries of young birds recovered during a subsequent breeding season. It is thought that many of the pairs breeding in the southern half of Britain remain on or close to their summer territories throughout the year, while birds from farther north show a greater tendency to move elsewhere for the winter. Our wintering population additionally includes birds that have arrived here from Fennoscandia, Eastern Europe and Russia, with very few exchanges of birds between here and the Low Countries.

Differential migration is known to occur in the species, with male Long-eared Owls tending to remain further north than females during autumn and winter. This leads to unequal sex ratios, heavily biased towards females, in the birds caught at British bird observatories on autumn migration or found dead here during winter (see Chapter 4). Movements appear to vary between years, both in terms of the number of individuals reaching Britain and in their timing. Peak arrivals take place during October, but birds may be seen arriving as early as July and as late as December. Most of these movements take place at night and appear to involve birds moving on their own, although there is a suggestion that small flocks may move together in some years. Peak numbers have tended to arrive every two to five years, with cycles correlated between sites.

STATUS AND CONSERVATION

Our knowledge of the size of the Long-eared Owl breeding population in Britain is rather inadequate, being based on national atlas surveys rather than a targeted approach better suited to a nocturnal species which occurs at low density. The most recent estimate might suggest a breeding population numbering between 1,100 and 3,600 pairs, with perhaps a similar number of birds in Ireland and both populations probably tending towards the lower end of the estimated range. The Long-eared Owl is certainly more common elsewhere within Europe, with a population likely to be in excess of 200,000 breeding pairs. Breeding numbers appear to fluctuate in relation to vole abundance, a pattern noted widely in Europe and from a handful of studies within Britain (Roome, 1992; Williams, 1996).

The Long-eared Owl receives general protection within Britain through the Wildlife and Countryside Act 1981 and is given additional protection in Northern Ireland and on the Isle of Man through listing on Schedule 1 of the Wildlife (Northern Ireland) Order 1985 and Schedule 1 of the Wildlife Act 1990 (Isle of Man).

With a lack of systematic monitoring information, the belief that most European populations are largely stable cannot be tested. There is the suspicion, however, that the species may be in decline in some areas, including Britain, as changing habitat suitability and increased competition from Tawny Owl takes its toll. The creation of rough grassland habitats for Field Voles, even if relatively small scale, coupled with the provision of wicker nesting baskets to suitable sites, could help to support the species. More important, however, would be the introduction of a systematic monitoring scheme or periodic targeted surveys.

Short-eared Owl
Asio flammeus
(PONTOPPIDAN 1763)

Family: Strigidae

IDENTIFICATION

The Short-eared Owl is a
medium-sized owl, generally
pale in appearance with yellow
eyes and rather long and narrow
wings. The small ear tufts are only
visible when the bird is agitated
or adopts a threat display. As we
have seen in the previous species

FIG 164. Short-eared Owl. (Steve Round)

account, there is potential for confusion with the Long-eared Owl under certain
circumstances. The upperparts have a ground colour of pale buff overlaid with
a pattern of darker markings that give the bird a mottled appearance. The facial
disc is also pale buff, less warm in tone than that of Long-eared Owl, and with
dark patches surrounding the piercing yellow eyes. The feathering between and
above the eyes and around the bill is white, the bill itself the colour of dark horn
but with a paler tip. The base colour of the upperside of the flight feathers is
generally somewhat warmer in tone than the body plumage and is overlaid with
darker barring. In flight the noticeably dark wing tips can be seen, as can the pale
trailing edge to the wing, both of which characters are useful in separating this
species from Long-eared Owl. The underparts are pale buff, becoming off-white
on the belly. The darker streaking is concentrated towards the head and breast,
leaving the belly unmarked. The underside of the wings again shows the black
wing tips and, additionally, a crescent-shaped carpal patch, the latter feature
shared with Long-eared Owl. Males are generally lighter in plumage colour than
females, with paler facial discs, and show less heavy streaking (Village, 1987).
Although the heavier of the two sexes, the females are only slightly larger than
the males in structural features. Seen in the field, the Short-eared Owl appears
large-headed, with long, narrow wings and a buoyant flight, the latter sometimes
described as being rather moth-like with its bouncing wingbeats.

Short-eared Owl chicks are covered with a short, rather soft down, creamy buff above and white below. The down extends onto the feet, the cere is pink and the bill a bluish-grey in colouration. Although only limited information on ageing nestling Short-eared Owls has been published, a rough age can be determined by using the following equations, produced by Arroyo *et al.* (2000).

For chicks less than 15 days of age: age (days) = (mass (g) + 15.6)/18.2)
For males older than 15 days of age: age (days) = (wing length (mm) + 28.6/7.9)
For females older than 15 days of age: age (days) = (wing length (mm) + 42.2/7.9)

The degree of plumage development and the presence of down can also be used to estimate nestling age. From 10–15 days of age many chicks can be sexed from the patterning on the secondary feathers. Males have a paler underwing, with fewer dark transverse lines than females, and show clearer contrast between the outer and inner web colouration of the upperwing (see Arroyo *et al.*, 2000).

Voice
The Short-eared Owl has a rather limited repertoire of calls and, apart from the alarm calls uttered near the nest, is not particularly vocal. The rarely heard male territorial call is comprised of low-pitched, repeated phrases which deliver a somewhat soft and hollow-sounding '*boo-boo-boo-boo-boo*'. There is little gap

FIG 165. Short-eared Owls may display their small ear tufts when agitated. (Mark Hancox)

between the individual 'boo' components, bringing to mind the sound of a distant steam train. Each phrase typically consists of six to 20 notes, with perhaps two delivered per second. The alarm call, usually heard near the nest but sometimes uttered after an encounter with another owl or bird of prey, is a rather sharp-sounding 'chef-chef-chef', the individual phrases of which may be more drawn out on occasion. The female has a hoarse sounding call of 'cheh-ef' which may be extended to 'cheeeef' when begging. The begging call of the young is a long wheezing 'pssssh-sip'. Adult birds wing-clap as part of their courtship display, often using a series of two to six claps, and these may, additionally, sometimes be directed towards an intruder.

HISTORY

The presence of breeding Short-eared Owls at latitudes bordering the Arctic Circle, coupled with its nomadic habits, suggests that this would have been one of the first owl species to colonise Britain following the retreat of the glaciers. Short-eared Owl remains from Pin Hole Cave in Derbyshire support this assertion, the deposits at this cave dated to a period of warming that occurred within the Devensian Glaciation. Contemporary to this fauna are remains of Snowy Owl, two species of lemming and two species of northern vole, all from Kent's Cavern in Devon and suggestive of a tundra-dominated landscape. The Short-eared Owl is also well-represented from other Late Glacial sites and from sites associated with the Neolithic, including both Ibister and the Links of Notland in Orkney (Yalden & Albarella, 2009). Records also come from later sites, extending through the Roman period to the Middle Ages and beyond.

By the late 1800s there is good local evidence of breeding Short-eared Owl populations centred on the uplands of northern England and Scotland, together with a population utilising the fenland and coastal marshes of East Anglia. A decline in the lowland population was noted during this period, as efforts to drain and reclaim these lowland wetlands for agriculture reduced hunting and nesting opportunities for the owls. Occasional breeding records from more southerly locations appear to be linked to the occasional vole plagues that were a feature of the time. Populations from northern England and across Scotland were more regular in their occurrence, though again breeding numbers appear to be strongly linked to the state of the vole cycle. Orkney and the Outer Hebrides were strongholds for the species, with smaller numbers of Short-eared Owls breeding on the Inner Hebrides and the Scottish mainland. Shetland supported sporadic nesting during the 1800s.

During the early 1900s, breeding became more regular in some upland areas within England and Wales, seemingly linked to the programme of afforestation that was delivering extensive areas of rough grassland, packed with Field Voles, during the early phase of plantation establishment. Lockie, writing in 1955, documented just how productive the Short-eared Owls using these habitats could be. High densities, small hunting ranges and large clutch and brood sizes all pointed to an abundance of small mammal prey. The numbers breeding in East Anglia also showed an upturn, as pairs exploited the coastal grazing marshes now established on reclaimed saltmarsh (Holloway, 1996). The general pattern throughout the 20th century appears to have been one of increase as more plantations were established, but the estimate of 1,000–10,000 breeding pairs adopted by Parslow (1973) is probably rather optimistic. Sharrock (1976) provides a more believable estimate of c. 1,000 pairs, based on the 550 10-km squares in which probable or confirmed breeding was noted by atlas fieldworkers during the first breeding atlas, and Gibbons et al. (1993) suggested that the population at the time of the second breeding atlas, could have numbered as many as 3,500 pairs. At the time of the second breeding atlas regular breeding of the Short-eared Owl in Ireland had still not been established.

The most recent breeding atlas (Balmer et al., 2013) recorded 245 10-km squares in which probable or confirmed breeding had been noted. Just four confirmed nesting attempts and one probable nesting attempt were recorded from Ireland, the four confirmed breeding attempts all coming from the extreme north-east of the region. The three breeding atlases suggest the loss of breeding Short-eared Owls over the last 40 years from the East Anglian coastal fringe, from Breckland, the Wash, the uplands of central Wales, much of southern and south-west Scotland and from large parts of north-east Scotland. Does this provide evidence of a population now breeding further north in response to a warming climate or has the quality of the habitats in these areas simply become unsuitable for the required densities of favoured prey? This is something to which we will return later in this chapter.

DISTRIBUTION AND HABITAT

The breeding distribution of the Short-eared Owl within Britain underlines that this is a bird of upland moorland and other open habitats, with the bulk of the breeding population largely restricted to the Pennines of northern England and the uplands of central and southern Scotland (see Figure 166). The species is absent from the highest uplands of northern Scotland, from most of Ireland

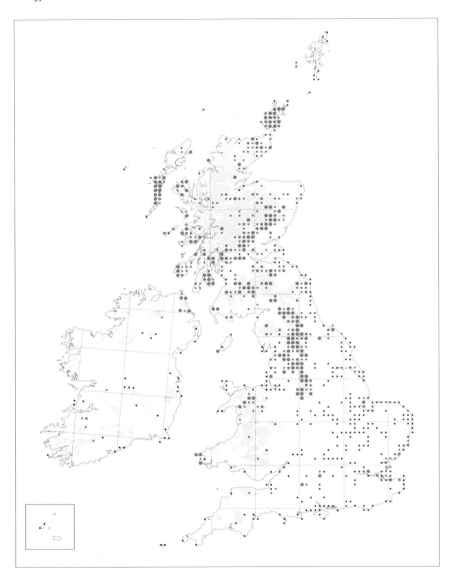

FIG 166. Short-eared Owl breeding distribution, 2008–11. Reproduced from *Bird Atlas 2007–11* (Balmer *et al.*, 2013), which is a joint project between BTO, BirdWatch Ireland and the Scottish Ornithologists' Club. Map reproduced with permission from the British Trust for Ornithology.

FIG 167. Short-eared Owls occupy coastal grasslands during the winter months. (Amy Lewis)

and from Shetland, although it is a common breeding species on Orkney and some of the Outer Hebrides. Occasional breeding pairs are to be found on the coastal marshes of East Anglia and in north and west Wales. As we have just seen, examination of data collected through the BTO-led bird atlases suggests recent breeding losses from many former haunts. Beyond our shores the Short-eared Owl is to be found breeding across most of the Northern Hemisphere, within suitable sub-Arctic and temperate regions. The species is absent from the northernmost regions fringing the Arctic Ocean but occurs south to the Mediterranean and the deserts of Central Asia. In America the distribution is discontinuous, with birds found breeding in both North America and the southern part of South America, the latter including a breeding population on the Falkland Islands.

Breeding sites tend to be located within areas of upland grassland, open moorland or within young conifer plantations, the birds moving into lowland grassland habitats, fens and coastal grazing marshes during the winter months. The small numbers of pairs that breed within lowland coastal sites tend to do so erratically, perhaps suggesting opportunistic use by birds unable to secure more traditional sites elsewhere.

BREEDING ECOLOGY

British Short-eared Owls are strongly territorial during the breeding season, with pairs on territory by March or early April, and territory holders respond aggressively to trespassing owls. Breeding territories can be as small as 16 ha when vole numbers are very high, but territories are more usually in the range of 100–140 ha (Village, 1987). The open-country habitats used for breeding favour visual displays of territorial ownership and Lockie (1955) noted three different types of display used for this purpose. The first involves the use of exaggerated wing beats, the wings brought much higher over the back than seen in normal flight; the second involves bringing the wings together below the body to produce an audible wing-clap. The third form of display, termed a 'skirmish', involves the territory-holding bird hovering in front of the trespasser and presenting its talons.

Display is also used in courtship, as we saw in Chapter 3, with wing-clapping a key feature used by the male. This usually involves the male gaining height in a steep climb before bringing his wings together, a process that may be repeated a dozen or more times. Copulation is often preceded by the presentation of prey by the male to his mate and is followed by the female flying to the nest scrape. The Short-eared Owl nests on the ground, usually selecting a site that is hidden in tall heather, bracken or grasses. The female typically excavates a shallow scrape and it is into this that she lays her clutch of four to eight (3–14) eggs; the pair spends a lot of time near the nest site before laying begins. Females may line the scrape with short (3–6 cm) pieces of vegetation (see Figure 65). The eggs are laid at intervals of one to two days, with incubation beginning as soon as the first egg has been laid. This results in asynchronous hatching and the youngest chicks may die or be eaten by siblings if food is in short supply (see Chapter 3). Normal clutch

FIG 168. This decapitated chick may have been killed by a predator or, conceivably, by a sibling or parent. (James Bray)

FIG 169. Short-eared Owl breeding success has been linked to the availability of voles. (Michael Demain)

sizes are four to eight eggs but can number 14 in years of peak vole abundance. While incubating eggs or brooding young, the female owl will often half close her eyes, seemingly to hide the glaring yellow iris and to make the sitting bird less conspicuous. The male will often favour a perch within 30 m of the nest and invariably positions himself so that he can see the nest, spending the rest of his time patrolling the territory or hunting for food. The male provides his mate with prey, with feeding visits most likely during early morning or early evening.

Once the eggs have hatched and the young are a few days old, both adults will hunt for food. Breeding Short-eared Owls are often vigorous in their defence of the nest, attacking intruders, potential predators and human observers. A male with a sitting female or young in the nest may deploy a distraction display, initially circling around the intruder and uttering the alarm call. If the intruder approaches to within a few metres of the nest then the male may dive into the ground with a surprising amount of force, rolling over with wings outstretched and giving the appearance of being injured. Pairs nesting in close proximity may, on occasion, participate in group defence. Short-eared Owls may sometimes strike at a human observer. Nests may be lost to predation, with Carrion Crow, Hooded Crow and Red

Fox all documented predators of British Short-eared Owl nests. The risks associated with ground nesting are likely to be one of the reasons for the rapid growth and development seen in young Short-eared Owls. The chicks may increase their body weight by 300 per cent over the first five days post-hatching, with a similar increase also noted over the next five days. Predation risk may also explain why young Short-eared Owls leave the nest at between 12 and 17 days of age, unfledged and reliant on the food that continues to be delivered by the parent birds. The young beg for food from their parents with a hissing call and quivering display. The urge to feed begging chicks may be further stimulated by the conspicuous white feathering on either side of the chick's bill, although this has yet to be tested experimentally. The chicks are usually sufficiently well developed to be able to take to the wing from about 24 days of age. Genuine second broods may be produced in years with an abundance of prey and an early start to the nesting season, though the species is generally single brooded in Britain. Early failures may result in a replacement attempt, the birds relaying as late as June (Hardey *et al.*, 2006).

FEEDING BEHAVIOUR

The Short-eared Owl is, as we have seen, a small mammal specialist. Here in Britain, Field Vole is the principal prey item, forming 83 per cent of the 1,857 prey items collected from the 11 breeding sites analysed by David Glue. The remaining 17 per cent was comprised of Wood Mouse, Common Shrew, various birds and other items. A Short-eared Owl diet from Rhum, where Field Vole is absent, was dominated by Wood Mouse, Common Rat and Pygmy Shrew (Glue, 1977a). The diets of five pairs breeding on Skomer were dominated by Bank Vole and Rabbit, together accounting for 86 per cent of the items, with Wood Mouse, Rock Pipit *Anthus petrosus* and Storm Petrel of secondary importance. During winter the Field Vole remains the favoured prey species but there is good evidence that small birds become more important, their contribution to winter diet being 14 per cent (compared with *c.* 4 per cent in summer).

Hunting birds locate small mammal prey through the use of a quartering flight, usually between 30–200 cm above the ground and involving a mix of flapping and gliding flight. On occasion the owl may switch mid-flight to a hover, staring at the ground intently before dropping onto the prey. Individuals may also hunt from a perch, a behaviour that is more common when the weather conditions turn unfavourable. Having caught a prey item, the owl often retires to a favoured perch to eat its prize, unless the prey is to be delivered to the nest or a dependent youngster.

During winter, Short-eared Owls typically roost close to the areas over which they are hunting. Roosting sites are usually on the ground, typically among some taller cover, and are often located on a bank or area of higher ground with a good field of view. Although birds often roost singly, several individuals may roost together. Roosts do not usually exceed half a dozen birds and gatherings in excess of a dozen are unusual. However, particularly large roosts have been documented in the past. For example, a roost of 46 birds was noted in the Halvergate area of Norfolk in the winter of 1964/65 and 116 were found in the same area on Christmas Eve 1972 (Allard, 1998).

MOVEMENTS

As we discovered in Chapter 4, the Short-eared Owl is regarded as a nomadic species, whose populations wander in search of areas with an abundance of favoured vole prey. Some populations, however, appear to live a more settled existence. British populations show a high degree of natal dispersal, the median natal dispersal distance rising from 9 km in the second month after ringing to 61 km, 228 km, 418 km and 449 km in subsequent monthly periods (Wernham *et al.*, 2002). A recent review of Short-eared Owl movements across Europe has found a general trend for decreasing distances between ringing and recovery locations

FIG 170. A quartering Short-eared Owl. (Steve Round)

since at least the 1970s (Calladine *et al.*, 2012). This might suggest that the birds are responding to a general dampening of the vole cycles that underpin such movements and, potentially, a gradual amelioration in winter weather conditions, allowing the birds to winter further north than they used to. Continental populations are most strongly migratory in the north of the breeding range, with populations from further south better described as partial migrants. Other birds may be nomadic in habits, responding to changing prey availability.

During the winter most upland haunts are abandoned and the owls become more widely distributed across lowland sites. Wintering Short-eared Owls are probably most numerous in the coastal lowlands of northern England and southern Scotland, with other sites in the coastal margins of Lincolnshire, Norfolk, Suffolk and Kent. Some of these wintering birds originate from Scandinavia, Iceland and other parts of northern Europe.

STATUS AND CONSERVATION

It seems likely that the British breeding population lies within the range of 750 to 3,500 pairs, with perhaps 300–3,000 of these in Scotland and 300–1,000 in England. There may be significant variation between years as birds respond to changing prey abundance over large areas. The European population is estimated to be in the range 9,000–35,000 pairs, with a further 10,000–100,000 pairs in Russia.

The Short-eared Owl receives general protection within Britain through the Wildlife and Countryside Act 1981 but receives additional protection in Northern Ireland and on the Isle of Man through listing on Schedule 1 of the Wildlife (Northern Ireland) Order 1985 and Schedule 1 of the Wildlife Act 1990 (Isle of Man). Additionally, the species appears on Schedule II of the Wildlife Act 1976 in Ireland. The species is regarded as being of conservation concern more widely within Europe, largely because of the declines seen in populations in Eastern Europe and Russia, where agricultural intensification and the drainage of wetlands has reduced breeding opportunities. The Short-eared Owl appears on the Amber list of birds of conservation concern within Britain because of the declines seen elsewhere within its European range. More work is required to refine our knowledge of the size of the British breeding population, its distribution and the extent of movements made by birds both wintering and breeding here. Grassland improvement, increased grazing pressure and disturbance at breeding sites are all potential threats to the species within Britain. Additionally, deliberate persecution and egg-collecting also pose a threat at some sites.

Other Owls

Just three other species of owl appear on the British list. These owls – Common Scops Owl *Otus scops*, Northern Hawk Owl and Tengmalm's Owl – are vagrants whose rare appearances attract the interest of birders and the wider birdwatching community. Common Scops Owl is the most frequent of the three to visit our shores and is typically reported during the spring migration period, while the other two arrive as a consequence of occasional eruptive movements from breeding grounds located well to the north-east of Britain. Aviary escapes are behind occasional records of other, more exotic owl species.

Common Scops Owl
Otus scops
(LINNAEUS 1758)

Family: Strigidae

Records of Common Scops Owl are to be found in many county bird reports and individuals are reported on an almost annual basis. The species was added to the British List thanks to a bird shot at Wetherby (West Yorkshire) in the spring of 1805. Few details remain for this bird, which subsequently entered the collection of Charles Fothergill. The impression from the

FIG 171. Common Scops Owl. (Hugh Harrop)

literature is that the number of individuals reaching Britain has declined over the longer term, probably reflecting a range contraction and the loss of populations from the northern edge of the breeding range.

The majority of the 37 British records catalogued by the British Birds Rarities Committee (BBRC) since 1950 involve individuals that were either trapped or found dead or injured. Some individuals have also been found exhausted on fishing vessels and oil platforms in the North Sea. Even within its breeding range, the Scops Owl is a difficult bird to see and its presence is often best confirmed from its distinctive call – a rather monotonous low whistle. There have been occasions where a vagrant male, arriving in Britain, has established a territory and begun to call. In June 2006, for example, a calling male established itself near the quiet riverside village of Thrupp in Oxfordshire, fooling the villagers into thinking its calls were those of a faulty alarm on a local canal boat. Fortunately, one of the villagers was put in touch with the County Bird Recorder, triggering a major twitch. Scops Owls reaching the north of Britain tend to be found on offshore islands with little cover, making viewing easier.

Common Scops Owl favours open woodland habitats where thick cover for roosting and nesting are close to more open areas which are used for foraging. They have, however, taken to farmland and orchards, even nesting in larger urban parks and gardens within some parts of their breeding range. This range itself extends from Portugal and Morocco in the west to central Asia in the east, and from Central France in the north to Morocco and Pakistan in the south, with a European breeding population estimated at 77,000–96,000 pairs (Hagemeijer & Blair, 1997). While the more southerly populations are resident in nature, northern populations are migratory, wintering to the south of the Sahara. It is these birds that are occasional vagrants to Britain, with the peak in springtime records (April to June) underlining that individuals may sometimes overshoot their destination during migration. Most spring records involve birds either making first landfall near the south coast or, possibly, last landfall in the Northern Isles. There is a question, however, of whether the birds appearing in the north of Scotland might originate from more easterly populations than those arriving in the south of England. The species has been recorded in every month except February and there is a small cluster of records that matches the autumn migration period. There have been 14 records of the species from Ireland, the only one of these three vagrant species to have been reported from there.

This is a small owl, about the size of a Blackbird and, therefore, smaller and slimmer in appearance than our own Little Owl. The grey and brown plumage, marked with black and white, is highly cryptic and has been likened to the bark of an old and gnarled tree. The eyes are yellow and the species has ear tufts which, when raised, give the appearance of a diminutive Long-eared Owl. The voice, mentioned above, consists of a series of single flute-like notes, each lasting less than a second and repeated at intervals of 2–3 seconds. The alarm call, a sharp 'kweeoh', is similar to that of Little Owl and is one of a number of other calls made by the species.

Northern Hawk Owl
Surnia ulula
(LINNAEUS 1758)

FAMILY: Strigidae

FIG 172. Northern Hawk Owl. (Hugh Harrop)

The Northern Hawk Owl is a very scarce vagrant to our shores, with just a handful of accepted records from Britain (Parkin & Knox, 2010, give nine) and none from Ireland. The species has an extensive circumpolar distribution, associated with the vast tracts of boreal taiga and forest tundra and extending from Norway east across Europe and Asia, into Alaska and then east again across North America to coastal Labrador. The Northern Hawk Owl is nomadic in habits and may make substantial irruptive movements if rodent populations crash. It is these movements that sometimes bring these owls into Central Europe and, very occasionally, into Britain. The first record, a bird of the North American race caparoch, came from a collier vessel operating off Looe (Cornwall) in 1830. Of the subsequent records, a number were also thought to involve birds of the North American race, the remainder either being attributed to one of the two Eurasian races ulula and tianschanica or remaining unidentified. Records predominantly come from the last third of the year (August to December), as was typified by the most recent record of the species (within the period covered by this book), an individual found roosting in a garden at Frakkafield near Lerwick (Shetland mainland) on 12–13 September 1983 and relocated at Gorie (Bressay) a week later (Rogers et al., 1984). This individual was believed to be of the race ulula and its arrival followed a huge influx of Northern Hawk Owls into southern Sweden, where at least 1,000 birds were believed to be present. The influx also saw birds reported from Norway and Denmark, together with a single individual from Germany. None reached Belgium or the Netherlands despite the numbers involved farther north and east.

Northern Hawk Owl is a bold and striking bird, active by both day and night, often perching in a conspicuous position and seemingly fearless of humans. The flight, which is usually direct and made with rapid wing beats, interspersed with open-winged glides, is reminiscent of Sparrowhawk, perhaps because of the long tail and short, somewhat pointed wings. It may, however, hover in a Kestrel-like fashion when hunting. The underparts are strongly barred, the back a mix of dark brown, black and white. Perhaps the most striking feature is the face; the eyes are piercing yellow and the off-white facial disk strongly outlined with black. Birds of the North American race *caparoch* are darker and more strongly marked than their Eurasian counterparts *ulula* and *tianschanica*. The male call, which has a bubbling quality, starts softly before increasing to a vibrating trill that ends abruptly. Both sexes give a kestrel-like call when excited.

Our understanding of population trends and status of Eurasian populations is hindered by the large fluctuations in breeding numbers from year to year. Such changes are linked to the abundance of favoured small rodent prey, populations of which typically cycle with a three- to five-year periodicity. In North America, cyclical populations of Snowshoe Hare *Lepus americanus*, whose youngsters are an important item in the breeding season diet, may exert a similar influence.

Tengmalm's Owl
Aegolius funereus
(LINNAEUS 1758)

Family Strigidae

In common with the Northern Hawk Owl, records of Tengmalm's Owl from Britain seemingly owe their origins to irruptive movements, prompted by a crash in favoured prey populations and delivering birds from breeding populations present in the boreal and

FIG 173. Tengmalm's Owl. (Hugh Harrop)

montane forests of Eurasia. The origins of one bird are known for certain, an individual ringed as a nestling at Greften, Norway, on 10 June 1980 and recovered at Fishburn, Durham, the following January, having covered a distance of 1,013 km. The wider breeding range is not dissimilar to that of Northern Hawk Owl either, but with the addition of smaller and rather local breeding populations in the Pyrenees, the lowland forests of northern Germany and more mountainous forests in southern Germany, northern Italy, the Balkans and Greece. Birds favour boreal and subalpine forests, where mature trees provide the natural cavity sites and old woodpecker nest holes (Black Woodpecker *Dryocopus martius* is favoured in Europe and Pileated Woodpecker *Dryocopus pileatus* in North America) used as nest sites. In some areas, forest management practices have reduced the availability of natural sites and the species now relies on the provision of nest boxes.

Northern populations tend to be more migratory in habits than those from farther south, although this tendency is seemingly restricted to adult females and young birds of both sexes, the adult males generally being sedentary in their habits across all populations. Where the sex of individuals has been determined, the British records are dominated by female birds.

The species was added to the British List on the basis of a specimen killed at Widdrington, near Morpeth (Northumberland), in January 1812. The first Scottish record came nearly 50 years later, a bird caught in a deserted stable on Cramond Island by a visiting wildfowler during a severe snowstorm in December 1860. It was kept alive for a few days but then killed and mounted. BBRC records contain just seven individuals since 1950, the most recent of which involved a bird found at Egilsay, Orkney, in early summer 1986 (Rogers *et al.*, 1987). Most records, however, come from the winter months (November to February).

Tengmalm's Owl is similar in size to Little Owl but with a proportionally larger and more rounded head and a strong, somewhat square, facial disk, which is off-white in colour and bordered by dark brown or black, with white eyebrows. The creamy-white underparts are streaked with brown, while the upperparts are a soft grey brown and marked with white spots of varying size. The different races vary in colour, with the North American race *richardsoni* being the most strongly coloured of those recognised. The tail is short, the wings relatively long and the legs and tarsi covered in dense feathering. Strictly nocturnal in habitats, Tengmalm's Owl lacks the Little Owl's undulating flight. The most familiar call is the series of four to nine staccato '*oo*' notes, used by the male as a territorial call, but other calls are also made (see König & Wieck, 2008, for a complete description of these).

Escapes and Releases

A search through county bird reports reveals occasional reports of other owl species from across Britain. These typically involve individuals that have either escaped from private collections or, in some instances, have been deliberately released by owners no longer able or willing to look after them. A large proportion of these reports refer to Eurasian Eagle Owl, a species already covered in this chapter and which has been subject to some discussion as to whether or not

FIG 174. Rock Eagle Owl is one of a number of species known to have escaped from aviary collections within Britain. (Steve Round)

the individuals present in Britain today can be considered as being native. In fact, examination of 70 county or regional bird reports for the period 1995–2008 reveals 222 records of 'non-native' owls, 87 per cent of which are of Eagle Owl. The other owls reported include Spotted Eagle Owl (1), Rock Eagle Owl (2), Great Horned Owl (11), Megallan Horned Owl *Bubo megallanicus* (1), Snowy Owl (3), Barn Owl (4) and Rufous-legged Owl *Strix rufipes* (1). The Snowy Owl and Barn Owl records refer to birds of known captive origin. Other odd records emerge from time to time; once, for example, I received photographs of one of the African white-faced owls *Ptilopsis* sp., reputedly taken in the wild in Norfolk. Some of these owls may remain at liberty for long periods of time. One Great Horned Owl appears to have been present at Graffham, Cambridgeshire, from 2003 to at least 2009. It is important to collate and monitor records of non-native owls at liberty within Britain, not least because there is the potential for these introduced species to become established, with unknown consequences for our native owl species.

References

Adair, P. (1892) The Short-eared Owl (*Asio accipitrinus*, Pallas) and the Kestrel (*Falco tinnunculus*) in the vole plague districts. *Annals of Scottish Natural History* 1892: 219–231.

Aebischer, A., Nyffeler, P. & Arlettaz, R. (2010) Wide-range dispersal in juvenile Eagle Owls (*Bubo bubo*) across the European Alps calls for transnational conservation programmes. *Journal of Ornithology* 151: 1–9.

Allard, P. (1998) Memories of Short-eared Owls on Halvergate Marshes. *Norfolk Bird Club Bulletin* 30: 8–10.

Altwegg, R., Roulin, A., Kestenholz, M. & Jeni, L. (2003) Variation and covariation in survival, dispersal and population size in barn owls *Tyto alba*. *Journal of Animal Ecology* 72: 391–399.

Altwegg, R., Roulin, A., Kestenholz, M. & Jeni, L. (2006) Demographic effects of extreme weather in the Barn Owl. *Oecologia* 149: 44–51.

Altwegg, R., Schaub, M, & Roulin, A. (2007) Age-specific fitness components and their temporal variation in the Barn Owl. *The American Naturalist* 169: 47–61.

Andrews, P. (1990). *Owls, Caves and Fossils*. The University of Chicago Press, Chicago.

Anon (1982) Secondary toxicity hazard to owls from difenacoum. *Pesticide Science* 1981: 36–37.

Appleby, B.M., Anwar, M.A. & Petty, S.J. (1999b) Short-term and long-term effects of food supply on parasite burdens in Tawny Owls *Strix aluco*. *Functional Ecology* 13: 315–321.

Appleby, B.M., Petty, S.J., Blakey, J.K. & Macdonald, D.W. (1997) Does variation of sex ratio enhance reproductive success of offspring in Tawny Owls (*Strix aluco*)? *Proceedings of the Royal Society, London B* 264: 1111–1116.

Appleby, B.M. & Redpath, S.M. (1997) Variation in the male territorial hoot of the Tawny Owl *Strix aluco* in three English populations. *Ibis* 139: 152–158.

Appleby, B.M., Yamaguchi, N., Johnson, P.J. & Macdonald, D.W. (1999a) Sex-specific territorial responses in Tawny Owl *Strix aluco*. *Ibis* 141: 91–99.

Arroyo, B.E., DeCornulier, T. & Bretagnolle, V. (2000) Sex and age determination of Short-eared Owl nestlings. *Condor* 102: 216–219.

Askew, N.P., Searle, J.B. & Moore, N.P. (2007) Agri-environment schemes and foraging of Barn Owls *Tyto alba*. *Agriculture, Ecosystems & Environment* 118: 109–114.

Atkinson, C.T., Thomas, N.J. & Hunter, D.B. (2008) *Parasitic diseases of wild birds*. Wiley-Blackwell, Ames, Iowa.

Bachmann, T., Klän, S., Baumgartner, W., Klaas, M., Schröder, W. & Wagner, H. (2007) Morphometric characterisation of wing feathers of the Barn Owl *Tyto alba pratincola* and the pigeon *Columba livia*. *Frontiers in Zoology* 4:23 doi:10.1186/1742–9994–4–23.

Bachmann, T. & Wagner, H. (2011) The three-dimensional shape of serrations on Barn Owl wings: towards a typical natural serration as a role model for biomimetic applications. *Journal of Anatomy* 219 : 192–202.

Bagnoli, P., Fontanesi, G., Casini, G. & Porciattti, V. (1990) Binocularity in the Little Owl, *Athene noctua* 1: anatomical investigation of the Thalamo Wulst Pathway. *Brain Behaviour and Evolution* 35: 31–39.

Baillie, S.R., Marchant, J.H., Leech, D.I., Renwick, A.R., Eglington, S.M., Joys, A.C., Noble, D.G., Barimore, C., Conway, G.J., Downie, I.S., Risely, K. & Robinson, R.A. (2012). *BirdTrends 2011*. BTO Research Report 609. British Trust for Ornithology, Thetford.

Baker, K. (1993) *Identification Guide to European Non-passerines*. British Trust for Ornithology, Thetford.

Baker, J.R. (1974) Protozoan parasites of the blood of British wild birds and mammals. *Journal of Zoology, London* 172: 169–190.

Balmer, D.E., Adams, S.Y. & Crick, H.Q.P. (2000) *Report on Barn Owl Release Scheme Monitoring Project Phase II*. BTO Research Report 250. British Trust for Ornithology, Thetford.

Balmer, D.E., Gillings, S., Caffrey, B.J., Swann, R.L., Downie, I.S. & Fuller, R.J. (2013) *Bird Atlas 2007–11: the breeding and wintering birds of Britain and Ireland*. BTO Books, Thetford.

Barkhoff, M. (1987) *Die Krankheiten de Uhus* (Bubo bubo) *und ihre Bedeutung für die Wiedereinbürgerung in die Bundesrepublik Deutschland*. Veterinary Medical Dissertation, Gissen, Germany.

Barn Owl Trust (2012). *Barn Owl Conservation Handbook*. Pelagic Publishing, Exeter.

Barthelemy, E. & Bertrand, P. (1997) Recensement de la Chevêche d'Athéne *Athene noctua* dans le massif du Garlaban (Bouches-duRhône). *Faune de Provence* 18: 61–66.

Bate, D.A. (1966) Bird bones. pp. 408–410 in Gray, H.S.H. *The Meare Lake Village*. Vol 3. Taunton Castle, Taunton.

Baudvin, H. (1978) Les causes d'échec des nichées de chouette effraie (*Tyto alba*). *Le Jean le Blanc* 14: 1–51.

Baudvin, H. (1980) Les surplus de proies au site de nid chez la Chouette effraie, *Tyto alba*. *Nos Oiseaux* 35: 232–238.

Baudvin, H. (1997) Barn Owl (*Tyto alba*) and Long-eared Owl (*Asio otus*) mortality along motorways in Bourgogne-Champagne: report and suggestions. pp. 58–61 *in* Duncan, J.R., Johnson, D.H. & Nicholls, T.H. (Eds) *Proceedings of the 2nd Owl Symposium: Biology and Conservation of Owls of the Northern Hemisphere*. United States Department of Agriculture Forest Servive. General Technical Report NC-190.

Bavoux, C., Mimauld, L. & Seguin, N. (2001) Barn Owl (*Tyto alba*) capturing Red Swamp Crayfish *Procambarus clarkii* in Charente-Maritime (Western France). *Alauda* 69: 323–324.

Baxter, E.V. & Rintoul, L.J. (1953) *The Birds of Scotland*. Oliver & Boyd, Edinburgh & London.

Bendel, P.R. & Therres, G.D. (1993) Differential mortality of Barn Owls during fledging from marsh and off-shore nest sites. *Journal of Field Ornithology* 64: 326–330.

Benton, M.J. (1999) Early origins of modern birds and mammals: molecules versus morphology. *BioEssays* 21: 1043–1051.

Bettega, C., Delgardo, M.M., Campioni, L., Pedrini, P. & Penteriani, V. (2011). The quality of chicks and breeding output do not differ between first and replacement clutches in the Eagle Owl *Bubo bubo*. *Ornis Fennica* 88: 217–225.

Beven, G. (1965) The food of Tawny Owls in London. *London Bird Report* 29: 56–62.

Beven, G. (1979) Little Owl's method of catching Cockchafers. *British Birds* 72: 594.

Birrer, S. (2009) A synthesis of 312 studies of the diet of the Long-eared Owl *Asio otus*. *Ardea* 97: 615–624.

Blanc, T. (1958) Au garde-manger hivernal de la Chevêche. *Nos Oiseaux* 24: 321.

Blaker, G. (1933) The Barn Owl in England: results of the census. *Bird Notes & News* 15: 169–172.

Bochénski, Z.M. & Tomek, T. (1994) Patterns of bone fragmentation in pellets of the Long-eared Owl (*Asio otus*) and its taphonomic implications. *Acta Zoologica Cracoviensia* 37: 177–190.

Bochénski, Z.M., Tomek, T., Boev, Z. & Mitev, I. (1993) Patterns of bone fragmentation in pellets of the Tawny Owl (*Strix aluco*) and the Eagle Owl (*Bubo bubo*) and their taphonomic implications. *Acta Zoologica Cracoviensia* 36: 313–328.

Bond, G., Burnside, N.G., Metcalfe, D.J., Scott, D.M. & Blamire, J. (2004) The effects of land-use and landscape structure on Barn Owl (*Tyto alba*) breeding success in southern England, U.K. *Landscape Ecology* 20: 555–566.

Bourqin, J.-D. (1983) Mortalité des rapaces le long de l'autoroute Genève-Lausanne. *Nos Oiseaux* 37: 149–169.

Brakes, C.R. & Smith, R.H. (2005) Exposure of non-target small mammals to rodenticides: short-term effects, recovery and implications for secondary poisoning. *Journal of Applied Ecology* 42: 118–128.

Brambilla, M., Rubolini, D. & Guidali, F. (2006) Eagle Owl *Bubo bubo* proximity can lower productivity of cliff-nesting Peregrines *Falco peregrinus*. *Ornis Fennica* 83: 20–26.

Bramwell, D. & Yalden, D.W. (1988) Birds from the Mesolithic of Demen's Dale, Derbyshire. *Naturalist* 113: 141–147.

van den Brinck, N.W., Groen, N.M., de Jonge, J. & Bosveld, A.T.C. (2003) Ecotoxicological suitability of floodplain habitats in the Netherlands for the Little Owl (*Athene noctua vidalli*). *Environmental Pollution* 122: 127–134.

Brito, P.H. (2005) The influence of Pleistocene glacial refugia on Tawny Owl genetic diversity and phylogeography in western Europe. *Molecular Ecology* 14: 3,077–3,094.

Brommer, J.E., Ahola, K. & Karstinen, T. (2005) The colour of fitness: plumage coloration and lifetime reproductive success in the Tawny Owl. *Proceedings of the Royal Society* (B) 272: 935–940.

Bruderer, C. & Denys, C. (1999) Inventaire taxonomique et taphonomique d'un assemblage de pelotes d'un site de nidification de *Tyto alba* de Mauritanie. *Bönner Zoologische Betreitung* 48: 245–257.

Bucke, D. & Mawdesly-Thomas, L.E. (1974) Tuberculosis in a Barn Owl. *Veterinary Record* 19: 373.

Bultot, J., Márie, P. & Van Nieuwenhuyse, D. (2001) Population dynamics of Little Owl *Athene noctua* in Wallonia and its driving forces. Evidence for density dependence. *Oriolus* 67: 110–125.

Bunn, D.S. (1972) Regular daylight hunting by Barn Owls. *British Birds* 65: 26–30.

Bunn, D.S. (1974) The voice of the Barn Owl. *British Birds* 67: 493–501.

Bunn, D.S. & Warbuton, A.B. (1977) Observations on breeding Barn Owls. *British Birds* 70: 246–256.

Bunn, D.S., Warburton, A.B. & Wilson, R.D.S. (1982) *The Barn Owl*. T & A D Poyser, Calton.

van den Burg, A.B. (2002) A comparison of nutrient allocation in eggs of Barn Owls *Tyto alba* and Eurasian Sparrowhawks *Accipiter nisus*. *Ardea* 90: 269–274.

Burtscher, H. & Sibalin, M. (1975) Herpesvirus strigis: host spectrum and distribution in infected owls. *Journal of Wildlife Disease* 11: 164–169.

Busche, G., Jurgen, H. & Kostrzewa, A. (2004) Preliminary results on competition of nest-sites and predation between Eurasian Goshawk (*Accipiter gentilis*) and Eagle Owls (*Bubo bubo*) in northern Germany. *Die Vogelwarte* 42: 169–177.

Bush, S.E., Villa, S.M., Boves, T.J., Brewer, D. & Belthoff, J.R. (2012) Influence of bill and foot morphology on the ectoparasites of Barn Owls. *Journal of Parasitology* 98: 256–261.

Bustnes, J.O., Bakken, V., Erikstad, K.E., Mehlum, F. & Skaare, J.U. (2001) Patterns of incubation and nest-site attentiveness in relation to organochlorine (PCB) contamination in Glaucous Gulls. *Journal of Applied Ecology* 38: 791–801.

Buxton, E.J.M. (1947) Little Owl taking Grass-snake. *British Birds* 40: 55.

Cairns, J. (1915) Breeding-habits of the Long-eared Owl in Scotland. *British Birds* 9: 124–125.

Calladine, J., Garner, G., Wernham, C. & Buxton, N. (2010) Variation in the diurnal activity of breeding Short-eared Owls *Asio flammeus*: implications for their survey and monitoring. *Bird Study* 57: 89–99.

Calladine, J., du Feu, C. & Du Feu, R. (2012) Changing migration patterns of the Short-eared Owl *Asio flammeus* in Europe: an analysis of ringing recoveries. *Journal of Ornithology* 153: 691–698.

Campioni, L., Delgado, M.D.M. & Penteriani, V. (2010) Social status influences microhabitat selection: breeder and floater Eagle Owls *Bubo bubo* use different post sites. *Ibis* 152: 569–579.

Cassoli, P.F. & Tagliacozzo, A. (1997) Butchering and cooking of birds in the palaeolithic site of Grotta Romanelli (Italy). *International Journal of Osteoarchaeology* 7: 303–320.

Cayford, J. (1992) Barn Owl ecology on East Anglian farmland. *RSPB Conservation Review* 6: 45–50.

Chitty, D. (1938) A laboratory study of pellet formation in the Short-eared Owl (*Asio flammeus*). *Proceedings of the Zoological Society, London* 108: 267–287.

Christensen, T., Lassen, P. & Elmeros, M. (2012) High exposure rates of anticoagulant rodenticides in predatory birds species in intensively managed landscapes in Denmark. *Archives of Environmental Contamination and Toxicology* 63: 437–444.

Churchfield, S. (1982) The influence of temperature on the activity and food consumption of the Common Shrew. *Acta Theriologica* 27: 295–304.

Clark, R. (1975) A field study of the Short-eared Owl, *Asio flammeus* (Pontoppidan) in North America. *Wildlife Monographs* 47: 1–67.

Clark, K.A. & Anderson, S.H. (1997) Temporal, climatic and lunar factors affecting owl vocalizations of western Wyoming. *Journal of Raptor Research* 31: 358–363.

Clarke, J.A. (1983) Moonlight's influence on predator/prey interactions between Short-eared Owls (*Asio flammeus*) and deermice (*Peromyscus maniculatus*). *Behavioural Ecology and Sociobiology* 13: 205–209.

Clevedon Brown, J. & Twigg, G.I. (1969) Studies on the pelvis in British Muridae and Cricetidae (Rodentia). *Journal of Zoology, London* 158: 81–132.

Clevedon Brown, J. & Twigg, G.I. (1971) Mammalian prey of the Barn Owl (*Tyto alba*) on Skomer Island, Pembrokeshire. *Journal of Zoology, London* 165: 527–530.

Cocker, M. & Mabey, R. (2005) *Birds Britannica*. Chatto & Windus, London.

Coles, C.F. & Petty, S.J. (1997) Dispersal behaviour and survival of juvenile Tawny Owls (*Strix aluco*) during the low point in a vole cycle. pp 111–118 *in* Duncan, J.R., Johnson, D.H. & Nicholls, T.H.

[eds] *Biology and Conservation of Owls of the Northern Hemisphere*. United States Department of Agriculture, Forest Service Technical Report NC-190.

Coles, C.F., Petty, S.J., Mackinnon, J.L. & Thomas, C.J. (2003) The role of food supply in the dispersal behaviour of juvenile Tawny Owls *Strix aluco*. *Ibis* 145: E59–68.

Collett, R. (1871) On the asymmetry of the skull in *Strix tengmalmi*. 1871: 739–743.

Cooke, A.S., Bell, A.A. & Haas, M.B. (1982) *Predatory birds, pesticides and pollution*. ITE, Cambridgeshire.

Cooper, J.E. (2002) *Birds of prey: health and disease*. 3rd Edition. Blackwell Science Ltd, Oxford.

Cott, H.B. (1921) Tawny owl nesting in a rookery. *British Birds* 14: 234.

Cramp, S. (1963) Toxic chemicals and birds of prey. *British Birds* 56: 124–138.

Crick, H.Q.P., Dudley, C., Glue, D.E. & Thomson, D.L. (1997) UK birds are laying eggs earlier. *Nature* 388: 526.

Crease, A.J. (1992) Barn Owls and Jackdaws sharing nest site. *British Birds* 85: 378–379.

Dadam, D., Barimore, C.J., Shawyer, C.R. & Leech, D.I. (2011) *The BTO Barn Owl Monitoring Programme: Final report 2000–2009*. BTO Research Report 577. British Trust for Ornithology, Thetford.

Dalbeck, L. & Heg, D. (2006) Reproductive success of a reintroduced population of Eagle Owls *Bubo bubo* in relation to habitat characteristics in the Eifel, Germany. *Ardea* 94: 3–21.

Davenport, D.L. (1982) Influxes into Britain of Hen Harriers, Long-eared Owls and Short-eared Owls in winter 1978/79. *British Birds* 75: 309–316.

Davis, A.H. & Prytherch, R. (1976) Field identification of Long-eared and Short-eared Owls. *British Birds* 69: 281–287.

Dawson, M.J. (1997) Cannibalism by Tawny Owl. *British Birds* 90: 576

Delgado, M.d.M., Penteriani, V., Revilla, E. & Nams, V.O. (2010) The effect of phenotypic traits and external cues on natal dispersal movements. *Journal of Animal Ecology* 79: 620–632.

Derting, T.L. & Cranford, J.A. (1989) Physical and behavioural correlates of prey vulnerability to Barn Owl (*Tyto alba*) predation. *American Midland Naturalist* 121: 11–20.

Dobinson, H.M. & Richards, A.J. (1964) The effects of the severe winter of 1962/63 on birds in Britain. *British Birds* 57: 373–434.

Donázar, J.A. (1988) Seleccion del habitat de nidificacion por el Buho Real (*Bubo bubo*) en Navarra. *Ardeola* 35: 233–245.

Donnan, C.B. (1978) *Moche Art of Peru: Pre-Columbian symbolic communication*. UCLA Fowler Museum of Cultural History, University of California.

Duckett, J.E. (1984) Barn Owls (*Tyto alba*) and the 'second generation' rat-baits used in oil palm plantations in Peninsular Malaysia. *Planter, Kuala Lumpar* 60: 3–11.

Duffy, K. & Kerlinger, P. (1992) Autumn owl migration at Cape May Point, New Jersey. *Wilson Bulletin* 104: 312–320.

Dufty, A.M. & Belthoff, J.R. (2001) Proximate mechanisms of natal dispersal: the role of body condition and hormones. pp. 217–229 in Clobert, J., Danchin, E., Dhondt, A.A. & Nichols, J.D. [eds] *Dispersal*. Oxford University Press, Oxford.

Duke, G.E. (1997) Gastrointestinal physiology and nutrition in wild birds. *Proceedings of the Nutrition Society*. 56: 1049–1056.

Duke, G.E., Jegers, A.A., Loff, G. & Evanson, O.A. (1975) Gastric digestion in some raptors. *Comparative Biochemistry and Physiology* 50: 649–656.

Dunthorn, A.A. & Errington, F.P. (1964) Casualties among birds along a selected road in Wiltshire. *Bird Study* 11: 168–182.

Durant, J.M., Gendner, J.-P. & Handrich, Y. (2004a) Should I brood or should I hunt: a female Barn Owl's dilemma. *Canadian Journal of Zoology* 82: 1011–1016.

Durant, J.M., Gendner, J.-P. & Handrich, Y. (2010) Behavioural and body mass changes before egg laying in the Barn Owl: cues for clutch size determination? *Journal of Ornithology* 151: 11–17.

Durant, J.M. & Handrich, Y. (1998) Growth and food requirement flexibility in captive chicks of the European Barn Owl (*Tyto alba*). *Journal of Zoology, London* 245: 137–145.

Durant, J.M., Massemin, S. & Handrich, Y. (2004b) More eggs the better: egg formation in captive Barn Owls (*Tyto alba*) *The Auk* 121: 103–109.

Dyson, M.L., Klump, G.M. & Gauger, B. (1998) Absolute hearing thresholds and critical masking ratios in the European Barn Owl: a comparison with other owls. *Journal of Comparative Physiology* 182: 695–702.

Earhart, C.M. & Johnson, N.K. (1970) Size dimorphism and food habits of North American owls. *Condor* 72: 251–264.

Eastman, A. (1998) Magdalénians and Snowy Owls; bones recovered at the grotte de Bourrouilla (Arancou, Pyrénées Atlantiques). *Paléo* 10: 95–107.

Eick, M. (2003) Habitatnutzung und dismigration des Steinkauzes *Athene noctua*. Eine telemetriestudie in Zusammenarbeit mit der forschungsgemeinschaft zur erhaltung einheimischer eulen e.V. (FOGE), dem Staatlichen Museum für Naturkunde Stuttgart und der Max-Planck Forschungsstelle für Ornithologie, Vogelwarte Radolfzell. Diplomarbeit. Universität Hohenheim.

Ellsworth, E.A. & Belthoff, J.R. (1999) Effects of social status on the dispersal behaviour of juvenile Western Screech Owls. *Animal Behaviour* 57: 833–892.

Epple, W. & Bühler, P. (1981) Eiwenden, eirollen und positionswechsel der brütenden schleier-eule *Tyto alba*. *Okologie der Vogel* 3: 203–211.

Ericson, P.G.P., Anderson, C.L., Britton, T., Elzanowski, A., Johansson, U.S., Källersjö, M., Ohlson, J.I., Parsons, T.J., Zuccon, D. & Mayr, G. (2006). Diversification of Neoaves: integration of molecular sequence data and fossils. *Biology Letters* 2: 543–547.

Errington, P.L. (1932) Technique of raptor food habits study. *Condor* 34: 73–86.

Erritzøe, J. (1999) Causes of mortality in the Long-eared Owl *Asio otus*. *Dansk Ornitologisk Forening Tidsskrift* 93: 162–164.

Erritzøe, J. & Fuller, R. (1999) Sex differences in winter distribution of Long-eared Owls (*Asio otus*) in Denmark and neighbouring countries. *Die Vogelwarte* 40: 80–87.

Esselink, H., van der Geld, F.M., Jager, L.P., Posthuma-Trumpie, G.A., Zoun, P.E.F. & Baars, A.J. (1995) Biomonitoring heavy metals using the Barn Owl (*Tyto alba guttata*): source of variation especially relating to body condition. *Archives of Environmental Contamination and Toxicology* 28: 471–486.

Everett, M.J. (1968) Kestrel taking prey from Barn Owl. *British Birds* 61: 264.

Exo, K.-M. (1982) Habitatstruktur, brutbiologie und bestandsentwicklung einer Steinkauzpopulation. *Journal of Ornithology* 123: 346.

Exo, K.-M. (1983) Habitat, siedlungsdichte und brutbiologie einer niederrheinischen Steinkauzpopulation (*Athene noctua*). *Okologie Vögel* 5: 1–40.

Exo, K.-M. (1989) Tagesperiodische aktivitätsmuster des steinkauzes (*Athene noctua*). *Vogelwarte* 35: 94–114.

Exo, K.-M. (1992) Population ecology of Little Owls *Athene noctua*, in Central Europe, a review. pp 64–75 in Galbraith, C.A., Taylor, I.R. & Percival, S. (Eds) *The ecology and conservation of European owls*. JNCC, Peterborough.

Exo, K.-M. & Hennes, R. (1980) Beitrag zur populationsökologie des Steinkauzes (*Athene noctua*) – eine Analyse deutscher und niederländischer ringfunde. *Die Vogelwarte* 30: 162–179.

Fain, M.G. & Houde, P. (2004) Parallel radiations in the primary clades of birds. *Evolution* 58: 2558–2573.

Fairley, J.S. (1967) Food of Long-eared Owls in north-east Ireland. *British Birds* 60: 130–135.

Fairley, J.S. & Clark, F.L. (1972) Food of Barn Owls, *Tyto alba*, over one year at a roost in Co. Galway. *Irish Naturalists Journal* 17: 219–222.

Fairley, J.S. & Smal, C.M. (1988) Correction factors in the analysis of the pellets of the Barn Owl *Tyto alba* in Ireland. *Proceedings of the Royal Irish Academy B* 88: 119–133.

Fajardo, I. (2001) Monitoring non-natural mortality in the Barn Owl (*Tyto alba*), as an indicator of land use and social awareness in Spain. *Biological Conservation* 97: 143–149.

Fajardo, I., Babiloni, G. & Miranda, Y. (2000) rehabilitated and wild Barn Owls (*Tyto alba*): dispersal, life expectancy and mortality in Spain. *Biological Conservation* 94: 287–295.

Fajardo, I., Pividal, V. & Cebellos, W. (1994) Causes of mortality of the Short-eared Owl (*Asio flammeus*) in Spain. *Ardeola* 41: 129–135.

Fajardo, I., Pividal, V., Trigo, M. & Jiménez, M. (1998) Habitat selection, activity peaks and strategies to avoid road mortality by the Little Owl *Athene noctua*. *Alauda* 66: 49–60.

Fernandez, J.M. & Pinedo, X. (1996) A case of the Eagle Owl (*Bubo bubo*) preying on a Louisiana Red Crayfish (*Procambarus clarkii* (Crustacea. Decapoda). *Alauda* 64: 396.

Ferrer, D., Molina, R., Castekka, J. & Kinsella, J.M. (2004) Parasitic helminths in the digestive tract of six species of owls (Strigiformes) in Spain. *The Veterinary Journal* 167: 181–185.

Flegg, J.J.M. & Cox, C.J. (1968) Winter food of Long-eared Owls in Kent. *Bird Study* 15: 163–164.

Forman, R.T.T. (2000) Estimate of the area affected ecologically by the road system in the United States. *Conservation Biology* 14: 31–35.

Forrester, R., Andrews, I.J., McInerny, C.J., Murray, R.D., McGowan, R.Y., Zonfrillo, B., Betts, M.W., Jardine, D.C. & Grundy, D.S. (2007) *Birds in Scotland*, The Scottish Ornithologists' Club, Aberlady.

Francis, C.M. & Saurola, P. (2002) Estimating age-specific survival rates of Tawny Owls recaptures versus recoveries. *Journal of Applied Statistics* 29: 637–647.

Francis, C.M. & Saurola, P. (2004) Estimating components of variance in demographic parameters of Tawny Owls, *Strix aluco*. *Animal Biodiversity & Conservation* 27: 489–502.

Frylestam, B. (1972) Über Wanderungen und Sterblichkeit beringter skandinavischer Schleiereulen *Tyto alba*. *Ornis Scandinavica* 3: 45–54.

Fuller, M., Holt, D. & Schueck, L. (2003) Snowy Owl movements: variation on the migration theme. pp. 359–366. *in* Berthold, P., Gwinner, E. & Sonnenschein, E. (eds.) *Avian Migration*. Springer Verlag, Berlin.

Fux, M. & Eilam, D. (2009) How Barn Owls (*Tyto alba*) visually following moving voles (*Microtus socialis*) before attacking them. *Physiology & Behaviour* 98: 359–366.

Galeotti, P. (1990) Territorial behaviour and habitat selection in an urban population of the Tawny Owl *Strix aluco* L. *Bollettino di Zoologia* 57: 59–66.

Galeotti, P. (1998) Correlates of hoot rate and structure in male Tawny Owl *Strix aluco*: implications for male rivalry and female mate choice. *Journal of Avian Biology* 29: 25–32.

Galeotti, P. & Rubolini, R.D. (2007) Head ornaments in owls: what are their functions? *Journal of Avian Biology* 38: 731–736.

Galeotti, P. & Sacchi, R. (2003) Differential parasitaemia in the Tawny Owl (*Strix aluco*): effects of colour morph and habitat. *Journal of Zoology* 261: 91–99.

Galeotti, P., Tavecchia, G. & Bonetti, A. (2000) Parental defence in Long-eared Owls *Asio otus*: effects of breeding stage, parent sex and human persecution. *Journal of Avian Biology* 31: 431–440.

Gancz, A.Y., Barker, I.K., Lindsay, R., Dibernardo, A., McKeever, K. & Hunter, B. (2004) West Nile Virus outbreak in North American owls, Ontario 2002. *Emerging Infectious Diseases* 10: 2135–2142.

Garcia-Fernández, A.J., Motas-Guzmán, M., Navas, I., Maria-Mojica, P., Luna, A. & Sánchez-Garcia, J.A. (1997) Environmental exposure and distribution of lead in four species of raptors in southeastern Spain. *Archives of Environmental Contamination and Toxicology* 33: 76–82.

Garner, D.J. & Milne, B.S. (1997) A study of the Long-eared Owl *Asio otus* using wicker nesting baskets. *Bird Study* 45: 62–67.

Gasparini, J., Bize, P., Piault, R., Wakamatsu, K., Blount, J.D., Ducrest, A.-L. (2009) Strength and cost of an induced immune response are associated with a heritable melanin-based colour trait in female Tawny Owls. *Journal of Animal Ecology* 78: 608–616.

Gassmann, H. & Bäumer, B. (1993) Zur populationsökologie des Steinkauzes (*Athene noctua*) in der westlichen Jülicher Börde. Erste ergebnisse einer 15 jährigen studie. *Vogelwarte* 37: 130–143.

Génot, J.-C. (1991) Mortalité de la Chouette chevêche, *Athene noctua*, en France. *Nos Oiseaux* 38: 139–148.

Génot, J.-C., Lecci, D., Bonnet, J., Keck, G. & Venant, A. (1995) Quelques données sur la contamination chimique de la Chouette chevêche, *Athene noctua*, et de ses oeufs en France. *Alauda* 63: 105–110.

Géroudet, P. (1965) *Les Rapaces Diurnes et Nocturnes d'Europe*. Delachaux & Niestlé, Neuchâtel.

Gibbons, D.W., Ried, J.B. & Chapman, R.A. (1993) *The New Atlas of Breeding Birds in Britain and Ireland: 1988–1991*. T & A D Poyser, London.

Gilbert, H.A. (1947) Water-Rail as prey of Short-eared Owl. *British Birds* 40: 160.

Gloyn, J.C. (1990) Movement of Barn Owl nestlings ringed on the Isle of Wight. *Isle of Wight Bird Report 1990*: 95–97.

Glue, D.E. (1970a) Avian predator pellet analysis and the mammalogist. *Mammal Review* 1: 53–62.

Glue, D.E. (1970b) Prey taken by Short-eared Owls at British breeding sites and winter quarters. *Bird Study* 17: 39–42.

Glue, D.E. (1971) Ringing recovery circumstances of small birds of prey. *Bird Study* 18: 137–146.

Glue, D.E. (1972) Bird prey taken by British owls. *Bird Study* 19: 91–95.

Glue, D.E. (1973a) Edible Dormouse and Grey Squirrel as Tawny Owl prey. *Quarterly Journal of Forestry* 67: 248–249.

Glue, D. (1973b) Seasonal mortality in four small birds of prey. *Ornis Scandinavica* 4: 97–102.

Glue, D.E. (1974) Food of the Barn Owl in Britain and Ireland. *Bird Study* 21: 200–210.

Glue, D.E. (1976) Long-eared Owl invasion. *BTO News* 78: 5.

Glue, D.E. (1977a) Feeding ecology of the Short-eared Owl in Britain and Ireland. *Bird Study* 24: 70–78.

Glue, D.E. (1977b) Breeding biology of Long-eared Owl. *British Birds* 70: 318–331.

Glue, D.E. & Hammond, G.J. (1974) Feeding ecology of the Long-eared Owl in Britain and Ireland. *British Birds* 67: 361–369.

Glue, D. & Jordan, R. (1989) Early 20th Century Barn Owl *Tyto alba* diet in Hampshire. *Hampshire Bird Report for 1988* : 79–83.

Glue, D. & Langley, B. (1993) Tawny Owl systematically taking fantail pigeons from a Cornish dovecote during springs 1990–1992. *Birds in Cornwall 1992*: 163–164.

Glue, D.E. & Nuttall, J. (1971) Adverse climatic conditions affecting the diet of a Barn Owl in Lancashire. *Bird Study* 18: 33–34.

Glue, D.E. & Scott, D. (1980) Breeding biology of the Little Owl. *British Birds* 73: 167–180.

Goddard, T.R. (1935) A census of Short-eared Owls in Newcastleton, Roxburghshire. *Journal of Animal Ecology* 4: 113–118.

Gomes, L., Grilo, C., Silva, C. & Mira, A. (2009) Identification methods and deterministic factors of owl roadkill hotspot locations in Mediterranean landscapes. *Ecological Research* 24: 355–370.

Goodman, S.M. & Glynn, C. (1988) Comparative rates of natural osteological disorders in a collection of Paraguayan birds. *Journal of Zoology*, London 214: 167–177.

Le Gouar, P.J., Schekkerman, H., van der Jeugd, H.P., Boele, A., van Harxen, R., Fuchs, P., Stroeken, P. & Van Noordwijk, A.J. (2011) Long-term trends in survival of a declining population: the case of the Little Owl (*Athene noctua*) in the Netherlands. *Oecologia* 166: 369–379.

Grainger, J.P. & Fairley, J.S. (1978) Studies on the biology of the Pygmy Shrew *Sorex minutus* in the west of Ireland. *Journal of Zoology*, London 186: 109–141.

Greenwood, A. (1977) The role of disease in the ecology of British raptors. *Bird Study* 24: 259–265.

Groen, N.M., Boudewijn, T.J. & De Jonge, J. (2000) De effecten van overstroming van de uiterwaarden op de Steenuil. *De Levende Natuur* 5: 143–148.

Grzywaczewski, G. (2009) Home range size and habitat use of the Little Owl *Athene noctua* in East Poland. *Ardea* 97: 541–545.

Gunson, K.E., Mountrakis, G. & Quackenbush, L.J. (2010) Spatial wildlife-vehicle collision models: a review of current work and its application to transportation mitigation projects. *Journal of Environmental Management* 92:1074–1082.

Gurney, J.H. (1849) The Eagle Owl (*Strix Bubo*) breeding in confinement. *The Zoologist* 7: 2566–2567.

Gurney, J.H. & Turner, E.L. (1915) Notes on a Long-eared Owl nesting on the ground in Norfolk. *British Birds* 9: 58–67.

Hadler, M.R. & Buckle, A.P. (1992) Forty-five years of anticoagulant rodenticides – past, present and future trends. pp 149–155 *in* Borrecco, J.E. & Marsh, R.E. *Proceedings of the Fifteenth Vertebrate Pest Conference 1992*, University of Nebraska, Lincoln.

Hagemeijer, W.J.M. & Blair, M.J. (1997) *The EBCC Atlas of European Breeding Birds: their Distribution and Abundance*. T & A D Poyser, London.

Handrich, Y., Nicolas, L. & Le Maho, Y. (1993) Winter starvation in captive Common Barn-Owls: physiological states and reversible limits. *The Auk* 110: 458–469.

Hansen, L. (1952) The diurnal and annual rhythm of the Tawny Owl. *Dansk Ornithologisk Forenings Tidsskrift* 46: 158–172.

Hanson, D.E. (1973) X-ray photographs of Little Owl pellets. *British Birds* 66: 32–33.

Hardey, J., Crick, H.Q.P., Wernham, C.V., Riley, H.T., Etheridge, B. & Thompson, D.B.A. (2006) *Raptors: a field guide to survey and monitoring*. The Stationary Office Ltd, Edinburgh.

Harding, B.D. (1986) Short-eared Owl mortality on roads. *British Birds* 79: 403–404.

Hardouin, L.A., Tabel, P. & Bretagnolle, V. (2006) Neighbour-stranger discrimination in the Little Owl *Athena noctua*. *Animal Behaviour* 72: 105–112.

Hardy, A.R. (1977) *Hunting ranges and feeding ecology of owls in farmland*. PhD Thesis, University of Aberdeen, Aberdeen.

Hardy, A.R. (1992) Habitat use by farmland Tawny Owls, *Strix aluco*. pp 55–63 *in* C.A. Galbraith, I.R. Taylor and S. Percival (eds.) *In 'The Ecology and Conservation of European Owls'*. JNCC, Peterborough.

Hardy, A.R., Hirons, G.J.M. & Stanley, P.I. (1981) The relationship of body weight, fat deposit and moult to the reproductive cycles in wild Tawny Owls and Barn Owls. pp. 159–163 *in* Cooper, J.E. & Greenwood, A.G. (Eds) *Recent Advances in the Study of Raptor Diseases*. Chiron Publications, Keighly.

Harmening, W.M. & Wagner, H. (2011) From optics to attention: visual perception in barn owls. *Journal of Comparative Physiology A* 197: 1031–1042.

Harris, S., Morris, P., Wray, S. & Yalden, D. (1995) *A Review of British Mammals: population estimates and conservation status of British mammals other than cetaceans.* JNCC, Peterborough.

Harris, S. & Yalden, D.W. (2008) *Mammals of the British Isles: Handbook – 4th Edition.* Mammal Society, Southampton.

Harrison, C.J.O. (1960) The food of some urban Tawny Owls. *Bird Study* 7: 236–240.

Harrison, C.J.O. (1987) Pleistocene and Prehistoric birds of south-west Britain. *Proceedings of the University of Bristol Spelaeological Society* 18: 81–104.

Harvey, P.V. & Riddiford, N. (1990) An uneven sex ratio of migrant Long-eared Owls. *Ringing & Migration* 11: 132–135.

Haverschmidt, F. (1946) Observations on the breeding habits of the Little Owl. *Ardea* 34: 214–246.

Heaver, D.J. (1987) The diet of Little Owls on Ynys Enlli. *Bardsey Bird Observatory Report for 1986* : 81–95.

Henderson, I.G., McCulloch, M.N. & Crick, H.Q.P. (1993) *Barn Owl productivity and survival in relation to the use of second generation rodenticides in 1988–1990.* BTO Research Report 106. British Trust for Ornithology, Thetford.

Hendrichsen, D.K., Christiansen, P., Nielsen, E.K., Dabelstreen, T. & Sunde, P. (2006) Exposure affects the risk of an owl being mobbed – experimental evidence. *Journal of Avian Biology* 37: 13–18.

Hernandez, M. (1988) Road mortality of the Little Owl (*Athene noctua*) in Spain. *Journal of Raptor Research* 22: 81–84.

Hewson, R. (1972) Changes in the number of Stoats, rats and Little Owl in Yorkshire as shown by tunnel trapping. *Journal of Zoology, London* 168: 427–429.

Hibbert-Ware, A. (1938) *Report of the Little Owl Food Inquiry 1936–37.* British Trust for Ornithology, H F & G Witherby, London.

Hillis, P., Fairley, J.S., Smal, C.M. & Archer, P. (1988) The diet of the Long-eared Owl in Ireland. *Irish Birds* 3: 581–588.

Hindmarch, S., Krebs, E.A., Elliott, J.E. & Green, D.J. (2012) Do landscape features predict the presence of Barn Owls in a changing agricultural landscape? *Landscape and Urban Planning* 107: 255–262.

Hirons, G.J.M. (1976) *A population study of the Tawny Owl Strix aluco and its main prey species in woodland.* D.Phil Thesis, Univ. of Oxford.

Hirons, G.J.M. (1985) The effects of territorial behaviour on the stability and dispersion of Tawny Owls (*Strix aluco*) populations. *Journal of Zoology, London* 1: 21–48.

Hirons, G.J.M., Hardy, A.R. & Stanley, P.I. (1979) Starvation in young Tawny Owls. *Bird Study* 26: 59–63.

Hirons, G.J.M., Hardy, A.R. & Stanley, P.I. (1984) Body weight, gonad development and moult in the Tawny Owl (*Strix aluco*). *Journal of Zoology, London* 202: 145–164.

Holling, M. & The Rare Breeding Birds Panel. (2007). Non-native breeding birds in the United Kingdom in 2003, 2004 and 2005. *British Birds* 100: 638–649.

Holloway, S. (1996). *The Historical Atlas of Breeding Birds in Britain and Ireland 1875–1900.* T & A D Poyser, London.

Holroyd, G.L. & Trefry, H.E. (2011) Tracking movements of *Athene* owls: the application of North American experiences to Europe. *Animal Biodiversity and Conservation* 32: 379–387.

Holsegård-Rasmussen, M.H., Sunde, P., Thorup, K., Jacobsen, L.B., Ottesen, N., Svenne, S. & Rahbek, C. (2009) Variation in working effort in Danish Little Owls *Athene noctua.* *Ardea* 97: 547–554.

Holt, D.W., Maples, M.T., Petersen-Parret, J.L., Korti, M., Seidensticker, M. & Gray, K. (2009) Characteristics of nest mounds used by Snowy Owls in Barrow, Alaska, with conservation and management implications. *Ardea* 97: 555–561.

Hone, J. & Sibly, R.M. (2002) Demographic, mechanistic and density-dependent determinants of population growth rate: a case study in an avian predator. *Philosophical Transactions of the Royal Society, London* B 357: 1171–1177.

Hosking, E.J. & Newberry, C.W. (1945) *Birds of the Night*. Collins, London.

Hosking, E.J. & Smith, S. (1943) Display in the Barn Owl. *British Birds* 37: 55–56.

Housome, T., O'Mahony, D. & Delahay, R. (2004) The diet of Little Owls *Athene noctua* in Gloucestershire, England. *Bird Study* 51: 282–284.

Howland, H.C., Merola, S., Basarab, J.R. (2004) The allometry and scaling of the size of vertebrate eyes. *Vision Research* 44: 2043–2065.

Huffeldt, N.P., Aggerholm, I.N., Brandtberg, N.H., Jørgensen, J.H., Dichmann, K. & Sunde, P. (2012) Compounding effects on nest-site dispersal of Barn Owls *Tyto alba*. *Bird Study* 59: 175–181.

Illner, H. (1991a) Influence d'un apport de nourriture supplémentaire sur la biologie reproduction de la Chouette chevêche, *Athene noctua*. *Nos Oiseaux* 40:153–177.

Illner, H. (1991b) Road deaths of Westphalian owls: methodological problems; influence of road type and possible effects on population levels. pp 94–100 in Galbraith, C.A., Taylor, I.R. & Percival, S. *The Ecology and Conservation of European Owls*. JNCC, Peterborough.

Janns, G.F.E. (2000) Avian mortality from power lines: a morphologic approach of a species specific mortality. *Biological Conservation* 95: 353–359.

Jaspers, V., Covaci, A., Maervoet, J., Dauwe, T., Schepens, P. & Eens, M. (2005) Brominated flame retardants and organochlorine pollutants in eggs of Little Owl (*Athene noctua*) from Belgium. *Environmental Pollution* 136: 81–88.

Jeal, P.E.C. (1976) Prey of Short-eared Owls in breeding quarters in the Outer Hebrides. *Bird Study* 23: 56–57.

Jefferies, D.J. & French, M.C. (1970) Mercury, cadmium, zinc, copper and organochlorine insecticide levels in small mammals trapped in a wheat field. *Environmental Pollution* 10: 175–182.

Johnson, P.N. (1991) Development of talon flange and serrations in the Barn Owl *Tyto alba*: a guide to ageing. *Ringing and Migration* 12: 126–127.

Johnson, P.N. (1994) Selection and use of nest sites by Barn Owls in Norfolk, England. *Journal of Raptor Research* 28: 149–153.

De Jong, J. & Van den Burg, A. (2012) A new method to sex Barn Owls *Tyto alba*. *Ardea* 100: 95–97.

Juillard, M. (1979) La croissance des jeunes Chouettes Chevêches, *Athene noctua*, pendant leur séjour au nid. *Nos Oiseaux* 35: 113–124.

Karell, P., Ahola, K., Karstinen, T., Kolunen, H., Siitari, H. & Brommer, J.E. (2011) Blood parasites mediate morph-specific maintenance costs in a colour polymorphic wild bird. *Journal of Evolutionary Biology* 24: 1783–1792

Karell, P., Ahola, K., Karstinen, T., Zolei, A. & Brommer, J.E. (2009) Population dynamics in a cyclic environment: consequences of cyclic food abundance on Tawny Owl reproduction and survival. *Journal of Animal Ecology* 78: 1050–1062.

Kekkonen, J., Kolunen, H., Pietiäinen, H., Karell, P. & Brommer, J.E. (2008) Tawny Owl reproduction and offspring sex ratios under variable food conditions. *Journal of Ornithology* 149: 59–66.

Kelcey, J.G. & Rheinwald, G. (2005) *Birds in European Cities*. Ginster Verlag, Germany.

Kelly, A., Leighton, K. & Newton, J. (2010) Using stable isotopes to investigate the provenance of an Eagle Owl found in Norfolk. *British Birds* 103: 213–222.

Kemp, J. (1981) Breeding Long-eared Owls in West Norfolk. *Norfolk Bird Report 1980:* 262–264.

Keymer, I.F. (1972) Diseases of birds of prey. *The Veterinary Record,* May 20th, 1972: 579–594.

Kirkpatrick, C.E. & Colvin, B.A. (1986) *Salmonella* spp. in nestling Common Barn Owls (*Tyto alba*) from southwestern New Jersey. *Journal of Wildlife Diseases* 22: 340–343.

Kitowski, I., Mietelski, J.W., Gaca, P. & Grzywaczewski, G. (2008) 90Sr, 241Am and Plutonium in skeletons of Barn Owl (*Tyto alba* Scop.) from southeast Poland. *Polish Journal of Environmental Studies* 17: 243–246.

Klaas, E.E., Wiemeyer, S.N., Ohlendorf, H.M. & Swineford, D. (1988) Organochlorine residues, eggshell thickness and nest success in Barn Owls from Chesapeake Bay. *Estuaries* 1: 46–53.

Klein, Á., Nacy, T., Csörgő, T. & Mátics, R. (2007) Exterior nest-boxes may negatively affect Barn Owl *Tyto alba* survival: an ecological trap. *Bird Conservation International* 17: 263–271.

Knudsen, E.I. (1988) Early blindness results in a degraded auditory map of space in the optic tectum of the Barn Owl. *Proceedings of the National Academy of Science* B: 6211–6214.

Knudsen, E.I. & Konishi, M. (1979) Mechanisms of sound localization in the Barn Owl (*Tyto alba*). *Journal of Comparative Physiology* 133: 13–21.

Kocabiyik, A.L., Cangul, I.T., Alasonyalilar, A., Dedicova, D. & Karpiskova, R. (2006) Isolation of *Salmonella enterica* Phage Type 21b from a Eurasian Eagle Owl (*Bubo bubo*). *Journal of Wildlife Diseases* 42: 696–689.

König, C. & Weick, F. (2008). *Owls of the World,* 2nd Edition. Christopher Helm, London.

Koning, F.J., Koning, H.J. & Baeyens, G. (2009) Long-term study on interactions between Tawny Owls *Strix aluco,* Jackdaws *Corvus monedula* and Northern Goshawks *Accipiter gentilis. Ardea* 97: 453–456.

Konishi, M. (1973) Locatable and non-locatable acoustic signals for Barn Owls. *American Naturalist* 107: 775–785.

Korpimäki, E. (1987) Prey caching of breeding Tengmalm's Owls *Aegolius funereus* as a buffer against temporary food shortage. *Ibis* 129: 499–510.

Korpimäki, E., Hakkarainen, H. & Bennett, G.F. (1993) Blood parasites and reproductive success of Tengmalm's owls: detrimental effects on females but not on males? *Functional Ecology* 7: 420–426.

Korpimäki, E. & Norrdahl, K. (1991) Numerical and functional responses of Kestrels, Short-eared Owls and Long-eared Owls to vole densities. *Ecology* 72: 814–826.

Krone, O., Priemer, J., Streich, J., Sömmer, P., Langgemach, T. & Lessow, O. (2001) Haemosporida of birds of prey and owls from Germany. *Acta Protozoologica* 40: 281–289.

Laaksonen, T., Korpimäki, E. & Hakkarainen, H. (2002) Interactive effects of parental age and environmental variation on the breeding performance of Tengmalm's Owls. *Journal of Animal Ecology* 71: 23–31.

Du Lac, S. & Knudsen, E.I. (1991) Early visual deprivation results in a degraded motor map in the optic tectum of Barn Owls. *Proceedings of the National Academy of Science, USA.* 88: 3426–3430.

Lambrechts, M.M., Wiebe, K.L., Sunde, P., Solonen, T., Sergio, F., Roulin, A., Møller, A.P., López, B.C., Fargallo, J.A., Exo, K-M., Dell'Omo, G., Constantini, D., Charter, M., Butler, M.W., Bortolotti, G.R., Arlettaz, R. & Korpimäki, E. (2012) Nest box design for the study of diurnal raptors and owls is still an overlooked point in ecological, evolutionary and conservation studies: a review. *Journal of Ornithology* 153: 23–34.

Langford, I.K. & Taylor, I.R. (1992) Rates of prey delivery to the nest and chick growth patterns of Barn Owls *Tyto alba.* pp 101–104 *in* Galbraith, C.A., Taylor, I.R. and Percival, S. *The Ecology and Conservation of European Owls*. JNCC, Peterborough.

Lanszki, J., Sàrdi, B. & Széles, G.L. (2009) Feeding habits of the Stone Marten (*Martes foina*) in villages and farms in Hungary. *Natura Somogyiensis* 15: 231–246.

Latham, J. (1781) *General Synopsis of Birds, Volume 1*. White, London.

Laursen, J.T. (1997) Irruption of Barn Owl *Tyto alba* in Denmark in 1990–91. *Dansk Ornitologisk Forenings Tidsskrift* 91: 59–62.

Layton, R. (1985) The cultural context of hunter-gatherer rock art. *Man*, New Series 20: 434–453.

Lecomte, P. (1995) Le statut de la Chouette chevêche *Athene noctua* en Ile-de-France. Evolution et perspectives. *Alauda* 63: 43–50.

Lederer, W. & Kämpfer-Lauenstein, A. (1996) Einfluss der witterung auf die brutbiologie einer Steinkauzpopulation (*Athene noctua*) in Mittelwestphalen. *Populationsökologie Greifvögel und Eulenarten* 3: 353–360.

Leech, D.I., Barimore, C.J. & Shawyer, C.R. (2008) *The Barn Owl Monitoring Programme 2002–2007*. BTO Research Report 523. British Trust for Ornithology, Thetford.

Leech, D.I., Shawyer, C.R., Barimore, C.J. & Crick, H.Q.P. (2009) The Barn Owl Monitoring Programme: establishing a protocol to assess temporal and spatial variation in productivity at a national scale. *Ardea* 97: 421–428.

Leigh, R. (2001) The breeding dynamics of Little Owls in North West England. pp 67–76 *in* Génot, J.-C., Lapios, J.-M., Lecomte, P. & Leigh, R (eds). *Chouette chevêche et territoires*. Actes du Colloque International de Champ-sur-Marne, November 25–26, 2000. ILOWG.

Lenton, G.M. (1984) The feeding and breeding ecology of Barn Owls *Tyto alba* in Peninsular Malaysia. *Ibis* 126: 551–575.

Leslie, R.H., Venables, U.M. & Venables, L.S.V. (1952) The fertility and population

structure of the Brown Rat (*Rattus norvegicus*) in cornricks and some other habitats. *Proceedings of the Zoological Society, London* 122: 187–238.

Letty, J., Génot, J.-C. & Sarrazin, F. (2001) Analysis of population viability of Little Owl (*Athene noctua*) in the northern Vosges natural park (North-Eastern France). *Alauda* 69: 359–372.

Lisney, T.J., Iwaniuk, A.N., Bandet, M.V. & Wylie, D.R. (2012) Eye shape and retinal topography in owls (Aves: Strigiforms). *Brain, Behaviour and Evolution* Online early DOI: 10.1159/000337760.

Lockie, J.D. (1955) The breeding habits and food of Short-eared Owls after a vole plague. *Bird Study* 2: 53–69.

Lockley, R.M. (1938) The Little Owl Inquiry and the Skokholm Storm-Petrels. *British Birds* 31: 278–279.

Lourenço, R. Tavares, P.C., del Mar Delgado, M., Rabaça, J.E. & Penteriani, V. (2011) Superpredation increases mercury levels in a generalist top predator, the Eagle Owl. *Ecotoxicology* 20: 635–642.

Love, R., Webbon, C., Glue, D.E. & Harris, S. (2000) Changes in the food of British Barn Owls (*Tyto alba*) between 1974 and 1997. *Mammal Review* 30: 107–129.

Lovegrove, R., Williams, G. & Williams, I. (1994) *Birds in Wales*. T & A D Poyser, London.

Lowe, V.P.W. (1980) Variation in digestion of prey by the Tawny Owl (*Strix aluco*). *Journal of Zoology, London* 192: 283–293.

Luder, R. & Stange, C. (2001) Entwicklung einer population des Steinkauzes *Athene noctua* bei Basel 1978–1993. *Der Ornithologische Beobacter* 98: 237–248.

Lumaret, J.P. (1993) Insectes coprophages et médicaments vétérinaires: une menace à prendre au sérieux. *Insectes* 91: 2–3.

Luniak, M. (1996) Inventory of the avifauna of Warsaw – species composition, abundance and habitat distribution. *Acta Ornithologica* 31: 67–80.

Lyman, R.L., Power, E. & Lyman, R.J. (2003) Quantification and sampling of faunal remains in owl pellets. *Journal of Taphonomy* 1: 3–14.

Macdonald, D.W. (1976) Nocturnal observations of Tawny Owls *Strix aluco* preying on earthworms. *Ibis* 118: 579–580.

MacDonald, M.A. & McDougall, P.A. (1972) Crop contents of a Tawny Owl. *Scottish Birds* 6: 175–176.

Marchesi, L., Pedrini, P. & Sergio, F. (2002) Biases associated with diet study methods in the Eurasian Eagle-Owl. *Journal of Raptor Research* 36: 11–16.

Marks, J.S. (1985) Yearling male Long-eared Owls breed near natal nest. *Journal of Field Ornithology* 56: 181–182.

Marks, J.S., Dickinson, J.L. & Haydock, J. (1999) Genetic monogamy in Long-eared Owls. *The Condor* 101: 854–859.

Marks, J.S., Dickinson, J.L. & Haydock, J. (2002) Serial polyandry and alloparenting in Long-eared Owls. *The Condor* 104: 202–204.

Marquiss, M. & Cunningham, W.A.J. (1980) Food of Snowy Owls in Outer Hebrides. *Scottish Birds* 11: 56–57.

Marquiss, M., Smith, R. & Galbraith, H. (1989) Diet of Snowy Owls on Cairn Gorm plateau in 1980 and 1987. *Scottish Birds* 15: 180–181.

Marti, C.D. (1973) Food consumption and pellet formation rates in four owl species. *Wilson Bulletin* 85: 178–181.

Marti, C.D. (1974) Feeding ecology of four sympatric owls. *The Condor* 76: 45–61.

Marti, C.D. (1999) Natal and breeding dispersal in Barn Owls. *Journal of Raptor Research* 33: 181–189.

Marti, C.D. & Wagner, P.W. (1985) Winter mortality in Common Barn-Owls and its effect on population density and reproduction. *The Condor* 87: 111–115.

Martin, G.R. (1977) Absolute visual threshold and scotopic spectral sensitivity in the Tawny Owl, *Strix aluco*. *Nature* 268: 636–638.

Martin, G.R. (1982) An owl's eye: schematic optics and visual performance in the Tawny Owl *Strix aluco* L. *Journal of Comparative Physiology* 145: 341–349.

Martin, G.R. (1986) Sensory capacities and the nocturnal habit in owls. *Ibis* 128: 266–277.

Martin, G.R. (1990) *Birds by night.* T & A D Poyser Ltd, London.

Martínez, J., Gil, F., Zuberogoitia, I., Martinez, J.A. & Calvo, J.F. (2005) First record of cooperative nesting in the Eagle Owl *Bubo bubo*. *Ardeola* 52: 351–353.

Martínez, J.A., Martínez, J.E., Mañosa, S., Zuberogoitia, I. & Calvo, J.F. (2006) How to manage human-induced mortality in the Eagle Owl *Bubo bubo*. *Bird Conservation International* 16: 265–278.

Martínez, J. & Zuberogoitia, I. (2001) The response of the Eagle Owl (*Bubo bubo*) to an outbreak of the rabbit haemorrhagic disease. *Journal für Ornithologie* 142: 204–211.

Mascha, E. (1904) Uber die Schwungfedern. *Zeitschrift für wissenschaftliche Zoologie* 77: 606–651.

Masefield, J.R.B. (1928) Little Owl nesting in railway point box. *British Birds* 21: 95–96.

Massemin, S. & Handrich, Y. (1997) Higher winter mortality of the Barn Owl compared to the Long-eared Owl and the Tawny Owl: influence of lipid reserves and insulation. *The Condor* 99: 969–971.

Massemin, S., Le Maho, Y. & Handrich, Y. (1998) Seasonal pattern in age, sex and body condition of Barn Owls *Tyto alba* killed on motorways. *Ibis* 140: 70–75.

Massemin, S. & Zorn, T. (1998) Highway mortality of Barn Owls in northeastern France. *Journal of Raptor Research* 32: 229–232.

Mátics, R. (2003) Direction of movements in Hungarian Barn Owls (*Tyto alba*): gene flow and barriers. *Diversity & Distributions* 9: 261–268.

Mátics, R. (2008) Interspecific offspring killing in owls. *Biological Journal of the Linnaean Society* 95: 488–494.

Mayhew, D.F. (1977) Avian predators as accumulators of fossil mammal material. *Boreas* 6: 25–31.

McDonald, R. & Harris, S. (2000) The use of fumigants and anticoagulant rodenticides on game estates in Great Britain. *Mammal Review* 30: 57–64.

Meade-Waldo, E.G.B. (1912) The food of the Little Owl. *British Birds* 6: 64–65.

Meek, W.R., Burman, P.J., Nowakowski, M., Sparks, T.H. & Burman, N.J. (2003) Barn Owl release in lowland southern England – a twenty-one year study. *Biological Conservation* 109: 271–282.

Meek, W.R., Burman, P.J., Nowakowski, M., Sparks, T.H., Hill, R.A., Swetnam, R.D. & Burman, N.J. (2009) Habitat does not influence breeding performance in a long-term Barn Owl *Tyto alba* study. *Bird Study* 56: 369–380.

Melling, T., Sudley, S. & Doherty, P. (2008) The Eagle Owl in Britain. *British Birds* 101: 478–490.

Mendenhall, V.M., Klaas, E.E. & McLane, A.R. (1983) Breeding success of Barn Owls (*Tyto alba*) fed low levels of DDE and dieldrin. *Archives of Environmental Contamination and Toxicology* 12: 235–240.

Mendenhall, V.M. & Park, L.F. (1980) Secondary poisoning by anticoagulant rodenticides. *Wildlife Society Bulletin* 8: 311–315.

Menyushina, I. (1997) Snowy Owl (*Nyctea scandiaca*) reproduction in relation to lemming population cycles on Wrangel Island. pp. 572–582 *in* Duncan, J.R., Johnson, D.H. & Nicholls, T.H. (Eds) *Proceedings of the 2nd Owl Symposium: Biology and Conservation of Owls of the Northern Hemisphere*. United States Department of Agriculture Forest Service. General Technical Report NC-190.

Meunier, F.D., Verheyden, C. & Jouventin, P. (2000) Use of roadsides by diurnal raptors in agricultural landscapes. *Biological Conservation* 92: 291–298.

Meyrom, K., Motro, Y., Leshem, Y., Aviel, S., Izhaki, I., Argyle, F. & Charter, M. (2009) Nest-box use by the Barn Owl *Tyto alba* in a biological pest control program in the Beit She'an valeey, Israel. *Ardea* 97: 463–467.

Mietelski, J.W., Kitowski, I., Gaca, P., Frankowska, P., Tomankiewicz, E., Błażej, S. & Kierepko, R. (2008) Radionuclides in bones of diurnal birds of prey and owls from the Eastern Poland. *Chem. Anal.* (Warsaw) 53: 821–834.

Mikkola, H. (1976) Owls killing and killed by other owls and raptors in Europe. *British Birds* 69: 144–154.

Mikkola, H. (1983) *Owls of Europe*. T & A D Poyser, Calton, England.

Mikkola, H. (2012) *Owls of the World. A photographic guide*. Helm, London.

Millon, A., Petty, S.J., Little, B. & Lambin, X. (2011) Natal conditions alter-age specific reproduction but not survival or senescene in a long-lived bird of prey. *Journal of Animal Ecology* 80: 968–975.

Mitchell, D. (1994) Observations on the breeding hunting behaviour of Little Owls near and east Hampshire village. *Hampshire Bird Report for 1992*: 75–78.

Mitford, R. (1876) Barn Owl and its castings. *The Zoologist, London* 11: 4832.

Mlíkovský, J. (1998) A new barn owl (Aves: Strigidae) from the early Miocene of Germany, with comments on the fossil history of the Tytoninae. *Journal fur Ornithologie* 139: 247–261.

Moore, T.G. & Mangel, M. (1996) Traffic related mortality and the effects on local populations of Barn Owls (*Tyto alba*). pp 125–140 *in* Evink, G., Ziegler, D, Garrett, P. & Berry, J. *Transportation and wildlife: reducing wildlife mortality and improving wildlife passageways across transportation corridors*. Conference Proceedings, Florida Department of Transportation, Tallahassee.

Morris, P.A. (1979) Rats in the diet of the Barn Owl (*Tyto alba*). *Journal of Zoology, London* 189: 540–545.

Morris, P.A. & Burgis, M.J. (1988) A method for estimating total body weight of avian prey items in the diet of owls. *Bird Study* 35: 147–152.

Mourer-Chauviré, C. (1987) Les Strigiformes (Aves) des Phosporites du Quercy (France): Systématique, Biostratigraphie et Paléobiogéographie. Documents des Laboratoires de Géologie de Lyon 99: 89–135.

Muir, R.C. (1954) Calling and feeding rates of fledged Tawny Owls. *Bird Study* 1: 111–117.

Müller, W., Epplen, J.T. & Lubjuhn, T. (2001) Genetic paternity analyses in Little Owls (*Athene noctua*): does the high rate of parental care select against extra-pair young? *Journal für Ornithologie* 142: 195–203.

Newton, I. (1979) *Population ecology of raptors*. T & A D Poyser, Berkhamstead.

Newton, I. (2002) Population limitation in holarctic owls: pp 3–29 in Newton, I., Havanagh, R, Olsen, J. & Taylor I.R. *Ecology and Conservation of Owls*. CSIRO Publishing, Collingwood, Australia.

Newton, I. (2008) *The Migration Ecology of Birds*. Academic Press, London.

Newton, I., Wyllie, I. & Asher, A. (1991) Mortality causes in British Barn Owls *Tyto alba*, with a discussion of aldrin-dieldrin poisoning. *Ibis* 133: 162–169.

Newton, I., Wyllie, I. & Asher, A. (1993) Long-term trends in organochlorine and mercury residues in some predatory birds in Britain. *Environmental Pollution* 79: 143–151.

Newton, I., Wyllie, I. & Freestone, P. (1990) Rodenticides in British Barn Owls. *Environmental Pollution* 68: 101–117.

van Nieuwenhuyse, D., Génot, J.-C. & Johnson, D.H. (2008). *The Little Owl. Conservation, Ecology and Behaviour of* Athene noctua. Cambridge University Press, Cambridge.

Nilsson, I.N. (1978) Hunting in flight by Tawny Owl (*Strix aluco*). *Ibis* 120: 528–531.

Norberg, A. (1968) Physical factors in directional hearing in *Aegolius funereus* (Linne) (Strigiformes), with special reference to the significance of the asymmetry of the external ears. *Arkiv for Zoologi* 20: 181–204.

Ohayon, S., van der Willigen, R.F., Wagner, H., Katsman, I. & Rivlin, E. (2006) On the Barn Owl's visual pre-attack behaviour: I. Structure of head movements and motion patterns. *Journal of Comparative Physiology* A 192: 927–940.

Ohayon, S., Marmening, W., Wagner, H. & Rivlin, E. (2008) Through a Barn Owl's eyes: interactions between scene content and visual attention. *Biological Cybernetics* 98: 115–132.

Okill, J.D. & Ewins, P.J. (1978) The food of Long-eared Owls in winter. *Shetland Bird Report* 1977: 48–50.

Olsson, V. (1997) Breeding success, dispersal and long-term changes in a population of Eagle Owls *Bubo bubo* in southeastern Sweden. *Ornis Svecica* 7: 49–60.

Ortego, J. & Espada, F. (2007). Ecological factors influencing disease risk in Eagle Owls *Bubo bubo*. *Ibis* 149: 386–395.

Overskaug, K. & Bølstad, J. (1998) Geographical variation in female mass and reproductive effort in the Tawny Owl in Europe. *Fauna Norvegica Ser. C. Cinclus*: 21: 1–6.

Overskaug, K., Bølstad, J., Sunde, P. & Øien, I. (1999) Fledging behaviour and survival in northern Tawny Owls. *The Condor* 101: 169–174.

Overskaug, K. & Kristiansen, E. (1994) Sex ratio of accidentally killed Long-eared Owls *Asio otus* in Norway. *Ringing & Migration* 15: 104–106.

Parejo, D. & Avilés, J.M. (2010) Predation risk determines breeding territory choice in a Mediterranean cavity-nesting bird community. *Oecologia* 165: 185–191.

Parkin, D. T. & Knox, A.G. (2010) *The Status of Birds in Britain & Ireland*. Christopher Helm, London.

Parslow, J.(1973) *Breeding Birds of Britain and Ireland*. **Berkhamsted.**

Patterson, A. (1964) Tawny Owl attacking fox in winter. *British Birds* 57: 202–203.

Payne, R.S. (1971) Acoustic location of prey by Barn Owls (*Tyto alba*). *Journal of Experimental Biology* 54: 535–573.

Pearce, G. (1986) Barn Owl laying three clutches in five months. *Devon Birds* 39: 93.

Peirce, M.A., Greenwood, A.G. & Cooper, J.E. (1983) Haematozoa of raptors and other birds from Britain, Spain and the United Arab Emirates. *Avian Pathology* 12: 447–459.

Penteriani, V. (2002) Variation in the function of Eagle Owl vocal behaviour: territorial defence and intra-pair communication. *Ethology, Ecology and Evolution* 14: 275–281.

Penteriani, V. (2003) Breeding density affects the honesty of bird vocal displays as possible indicators of male/territory quality. *Ibis* 145: e127–135.

Penteriani, V. & Delgado, M.D.M. (2008) Brood-switching in Eagle Owl *Bubo bubo* fledglings. *Ibis* 150: 816–819.

Penteriani, V., Delgado, M.D.M., Alonso-Álvarez, C., Pina, N.V., Sergio, F., Bartolommei, P. & Thompson, L.J. (2007b) The importance of visual cues for nocturnal species: Eagle Owl fledglings signal with white mouth feathers. *Ethology* 113: 934–943.

Penteriani, V., Delgado, M.D.M., Alonso-Alvarez, C. & Sergio, F. (2007a) The importance of visual cues for nocturnal species: Eagle Owls signal by badge brightness. *Behavioural Ecology* 18: 143–147.

Peneteriani, V., Delgado, M.D.M., Campioni, L. & Lourenço, R. (2010) Moonlight makes owls more chatty. *PLoS One* 5 (1) e8696.

Penteriani, V., Delgado, M.D.M., Maggio, C., Aradis, A. & Sergio, F. (2005) Development of chicks and pre-dispersal behaviour of young in the Eagle Owl *Bubo bubo*. *Ibis* 147: 155–168.

Penteriani, V., Gallardo, M. & Roche, P. (2002) Landscape structure and food supply affect Eagle Owl (*Bubo bubo*) density and breeding performance: a case of intra-population heterogeneity. *Journal of Zoology, London* 257: 365–372.

Percival, S.M. (1990) *Population trends in British Barn Owls* Tyto alba *and Tawny Owls* Strix aluco *in relation to environmental change*. BTO Research Report 57. British Trust for Ornithology, Thetford.

Percival, S. (1992) Methods of studying the long-term dynamics of owl populations in Britain. pp. 55–63 *in* Galbraith, C.A., Taylor, I.R. & Percival, S. (Eds) *The ecology and conservation of European owls*. JNCC, Peterborough.

Pereira, M., Lourenço, R. & Mira, A. (2011) The role of habitat connectivity on road mortality of Tawny Owls. *GeoFocus* (Articulos) 11: 70–90.

Peters, D.S. (1992) A new species of owl (Aves: Strigiformes) from the Middle Eocene Messel Oil Shale. *Natural History Museum of Los Angeles County Science Series* 36: 161–169.

Petty, S.J. (1992) *Ecology of the Tawny Owl* Strix aluco *in the spruce forests of Northumberland and Argyll*. Ph.D. Thesis. Open University, Milton Keynes.

Petty, S.J., Anderson, D.I.K., Davidson, M., Little, B., Sherratt, T.N., Thomas, C.J. & Lambin, X. (2003) The decline of Common Kestrels *Falco tinnunculus* in a forested area of northern England: the role of predation by Northern Goshawks *Accipiter gentilis*. *Ibis* 145: 472–483.

Petty, S.J., Little, B. & Anderson, D. (1986) Incestuous breeding and abnormal movement by a female Barn Owl *Tyto alba*. *Ringing and Migration* 7: 23–24.

Petty, S.J. & Pearce, A.J. (1992) Productivity and density of Tawny Owls *Strix aluco* in relation to the structure of a spruce forest in Britain. pp 76–83 *in* Galbraith, C.A., Taylor, I.R. and Percival, S. (eds) '*The Ecology and Conservation of European Owls*'. JNCC, Peterborough.

Petty, S.J., Shaw, G. & Anderson, D.I.K. (1994) Value of nest boxes for population studies and conservation of owls in coniferous forests in Britain. *Journal of Raptor Research* 28: 134–142.

Petty, S.J. & Thirgood, S.J. (1989) A radio-tracking study of post-fledging mortality and movements of Tawny Owls in Argyll. *Ringing and Migration* 10: 75–82.

Piechocki, R. (1960) Über die winterverluste der Schleiereule (*Tyto alba*). *Vogelwarte* 20: 274–280.

Plant, C.W. (1976) Some observations on the winter diet of the Barn Owl (*Tyto alba*) on Skomer Island, Dyfed, Wales. *Nature in Wales* 15: 54–59.

Poganiatz, I. & Wagner, H. (2001) Sound-localization experiments with Barn Owls in virtual space: influence of broadband interaural level differences on head-turning behaviour. *Journal of Comparative Phsyiology* A 187: 225–232.

Pons, P. (2000) Height of the road embankment affects probability of traffic collision by birds. *Bird Study* 47: 122–125.

Poulakakis, N., Lymberakis, P., Paragamian, K. & Mylonas, M. (2005) Isolation and amplification of shrew DNA from Barn Owl pellets. *Biological Journal of the Linnaean Society* 85: 331–340.

Prestt, I. (1965) An enquiry into the recent breeding status of some of the smaller birds of prey and crows in Britain. *Bird Study* 12: 196–221.

Prestt, I. & Bell, A.A. (1966) An objective method of recording breeding distribution of common birds of prey in Britain. *Bird Study* 13: 277–283.

Raczyński, J. & Ruprecht, A. (1974) The effect of digestion on the osteological composition of owl pellets. *Acta Theriologica* 14: 25–38.

Radler, K. & Bergerhausen, W. (1988) On the life history of a reintroduced population of Eagle Owls (*Bubo bubo*). pp 83–94 *in* Garcelon, D.K. & Roemer, G.W. (Eds) *Proceedings of the International Symposium on Raptor Reintroductions*. Institute of Wildlife Studies, Arcata, USA.

Ramsden, D.J. (2003) *Barn Owls and major roads: results and recommendations from a 15-year research project.* Barn Owl Trust, Ashburton.

Ranazzi, L., Manganaro, A., Ranazzi, R. & Salvati, L. (2000) Woodland cover and Tawny Owl *Strix aluco* density in a Mediterranean urban area. *Biota* 1: 27–34.

Ratcliffe, D.A. (1967) Decrease in eggshell weight in certain birds of prey. *Nature* 215: 208–210.

Ratcliffe, D. (1993) *The Peregrine.* T & A D Poyser, London.

Ray, J. (1678) *The Ornithology of Francis Willughby.* John Martyn, London.

Rebane, M. & Andrews, J. (1995) *An evaluation of Barn Owl Re-introduction in Great Britain and the effectiveness of Schedule 9 licensing.* Report to the Department of the Environment. Andrews Ward Associates, Huntingdon, Cambridge.

Redpath, S.M. (1995) Habitat fragmentation and the individual: Tawny Owls *Strix aluco* in woodland patches. *Journal of Animal Ecology* 64: 652–661.

Redpath, S.M., Appleby, B.M. & Petty, S.J. (2000) Do male hoots betray parasite loads in Tawny Owl? *Journal of Avian Biology* 31: 457–462.

Reynolds, P. & Gorman, M.L. (1999) The timing of hunting in Short-eared Owls (*Asio flammeus*) in relation to the activity patterns of Orkney Voles (*Microtus arvalis orcademsis*). *Journal of Zoology* 247: 371–379.

Rich, P.V. & Bohaska, D.J. (1976) The World's oldest owl: a new strigiform from the Paleocene of southwest Colorado. *Smithsonian Contributions to Paleobiology* 27: 87–93.

Ristig, Ü., Wadewitz, M. & Zang, H. (2003) Der Uhu *Bubo bubo* im nördlichen Harzvorland. *Vogelwelt* 124: 249–253.

Robinson, M. & Becker, C.D. (1986) Snowy Owls on Fetlar. *British Birds* 79: 228–242.

Robinson, R.A. & Clark, J.A. (2012) The Online Ringing Report: Bird ringing in Britain & Ireland in 2011. BTO, Thetford. (http://www.bto.org/ringing-report)

Rodríguez, A., Garcia, A.M., Cervera, F. & Palacios, V. (2006) Landscape and anti-predation determinants of nest site selection, nest distribution and productivity in a Mediterranean population of Long-eared Owls *Asio otus*. *Ibis* 148: 133–145.

Rogers, B. & Graham, M. (1979) Motion parallax as an independent cue for depth perception. *Perception* 8: 125–134.

Roome, M. (1992). The Long-eared Owl in Derbyshire. *Derbyshire Bird Report* 1991: 90–95.

Rogers, L.M. & Gorman, M.L. (1995) The diet of the Wood Mouse *Apodemus sylvaticus* on set-aside land. *Journal of Zoology, London* 235: 77–83.

Rogers, M.J. & the Rarities Committee. (1984) Report on rare birds in Great Britain in 1983. *British Birds* 77: 506–562.

Rogers, M.J. & the Rarities Committee. (1987) Report on rare birds in Great Britain in 1986. *British Birds* 80: 516–571.

Rosenberg, K.V. & Cooper, R.J. (1990) Approaches to avian diet analysis. *Studies in Avian Biology* 13: 80–90.

Roulin, A. (1998) Cycle de reproduction et abondance du diptère parasite *Carnus hemapterus* dans les nichées de chouettes effraies *Tyto alba*. *Alauda* 66: 265–272.

Roulin, A. (2001) Food supply differentially affects sibling negotiation and competition in the Barn Owl (*Tyto alba*). *Behavioural Ecology and Sociobiology* 49: 514–519.

Roulin, A. (2002a) Offspring desertion by double-brooded female Barn Owls (*Tyto alba*). *The Auk* 119: 515–519.

Roulin, A. (2002b) Short- and long-term fitness correlates of rearing conditions in Barn Owls *Tyto alba*. *Ardea* 90: 259–267.

Roulin, A. (2004a) Covariation between plumage colour polymorphism and diet in the Barn Owl *Tyto alba*. *Ibis* 146: 509–517.

Roulin, A. (2004b) Effects of hatching asynchrony on sibling negotiation, begging, jostling for position and within-brood food allocation in the Barn Owl *Tyto alba*. *Evolutionary Ecology Research* 6: 1083–1098.

Roulin, A. & Bersier, L.F. (2007) Nestling Barn Owls beg more intensely in the presence of their mother than in the presence of their father. *Animal Behaviour* 74: 1099–1106.

Roulin, A., Colliard, C., Russier, F., Fleury, M. & Grandjean, V. (2008) Sib-sib communication and the risk of prey theft in the Barn Owl *Tyto alba*. *Journal of Avian Biology* 39: 593–598.

Roulin, A., Dreiss, A., Fioravanti, C. & Bize, P. (2009) Vocal sib-sib interactions: how siblings adjust signalling level to each other. *Animal Behaviour* 77: 717–725.

Roulin, A., Ducrest, A.L. & Dijkstra, C. (1999) Effects of brood size manipulations on parents and offspring in the Barn Owl *Tyto alba*. *Ardea* 87: 91–100.

Roulin, A., Jungi, T.W., Pfister, H. & Dijkstra, C. (2000) Female Barn Owls (*Tyto alba*) advertise good genes. *Proceedings of the Royal Society, London* B 267: 937–941.

Roulin, A. Riols, C., Dijkstra, C. & Ducrest, A-L. (2001) Female plumage spottiness signals parasite resistance in the Barn Owl (*Tyto alba*). *Behavioural Ecology* 12: 103–110.

Rubolini, D., Gustin, M., Bogliani, G. & Garavaglia, R. (2005) Birds and powerlines in Italy: an assessment. *Bird Conservation International* 15: 131–145.

Ruprecht, A. (1979) Bats as constituents of the food of Barn Owls (*Tyto alba*) in Poland. *Ibis* 121: 489–494.

Sacchi, R., Galeotti, P., Boccola, S. & Baccalini, F. (2004) Occupancy rate and habitat variables influencing nest-box use by Tawny Owls *Strix aluco*. *Avocetta* 28: 25–30.

Saint Girons, M.-C. (1973) L'age des micromammiferes dans le regime de deux rapaces nocturnes, *Tyto alba* et *Asio otus*. *Mammalia* 37: 409–456.

Šálek, M. & Lövy, M. (2012) Spatial ecology and habitat selection of Little Owl *Athene noctua* during the breeding season in Central European farmland. *Bird Conservation International* 22: 328–338.

Sangster, G., Collinson, J.M., Knox, A.G., Parkin, D.T. & Svensson, L. (2004). Taxonomic recommendations for British birds: second report. *Ibis* 146: 153–157.

Sarradj, E., Fritzsche, C. & Geyer, T. (2010) Silent owl flight: bird flyover noise measurements. *Proceedings of the 16th AIAA/ CEAS Aerocoustics Conference*. American Institute of Aeronautics and Astronautics. doi: 10.2514/6.2010–3991

Sasvári, L. & Hegyi, Z. (2010a) Feeding effort of male Tawny Owls *Strix aluco* follows a fixed schedule: a field experiment in the early nestling period. *Acta Ornithologica* 45: 181–188.

Sasvári, L. & Hegyi, Z. (2010b) Parents raise higher proportion of high quality recruits from low fledgling production in the local population of Tawny Owls, *Strix aluco*. *Folia Zoologica* 59: 206–214.

Sasvári, L., Hegyi, Z., Csörgő, T. & Hahn, I. (2000) Age-dependent diet change, parental care and reproductive cost in Tawny Owls *Strix aluco*. *Acta Oecologica* 21: 267–275.

Sasvári, L., Nishiumi, I., Péczely, P. & Hegyi, Z. (2010) Post-hatching testosterone concentration reflects nestling survival and pre-fledging offspring condition in the Tawny Owl *Strix aluco*. *Ornis Fennica* 87: 26–34.

Sasvári, L., Péczely, P. & Hegyi, Z. (2009) Plasma testosterone profile of male Tawny Owls *Strix aluco* in relation to breeding density, breeding experience, and offspring provision. *Acta Ornithologica* 44: 59–68.

Saunders, D.R. (1962) Owls feeding on young seabirds. *British Birds* 55: 591.

von Sauter, U. (1956) Beiträge zur Ökologie der Schleiereule (*Tyto alba*) nach den Ringfunden. *Vogelwarte* 18: 109–151.

Saxby, H.L. (1862) Barn Owl preying on fish. *The Zoologist*, London 20: 8281.

Schaefell, F & Wagner, H. (1996) Emmetropization and optical development of the eye of the Barn Owl (*Tyto alba*). *Journal of Comparative Physiology A* 178: 491–498.

Schaub, M., Ullrich, B., Knötzsch, G., Albrecht, P. & Meisser, C. (2006) Local population dynamics and the impact of scale and isolation: a study on different Little Owl populations. *Oikos* 115: 389–400.

Schelling, E., Thür, B., Griot, C. & Audigé, L. (1999) Epidemiological study of Newcastle Disease in backyard poultry and wild bird populations in Switzerland. *Avian Pathology* 28: 263–272.

Schettler, E., Langgemach, T., Sömmer, P., Streich, J. & Frölich, K. (2001). Seroepizootiology of selected infectious disease agents in free-living birds of prey in Germany. *Journal of Wildlife Diseases* 37: 145–152.

Schifferli, von A. (1949) Schwankungen des Schleiereulenbestandes *Tyto alba* (Scoppoli). *Der Ornithologische Beobacter* 46: 61–75.

Schmidt, N.M., Olsena, H., Bildsøeb, M., Sluydtsc, V. & Leirsb, H. (2005) Effects of grazing intensity on small mammal population ecology in wet meadows. *Basic & Applied Ecology* 6: 57–66.

Schmidt, K.-H. & Vauk, G. (1981) Zug, rast, ringfunde auf Helgoland durchziehender Wald und Sumpfohreulen (*Asio otus* und *Asio flammeus*). *Die Vogelwelt* 102: 180–189.

Schönfeld, M., Girbig, G. & Sturm, H. (1977) Beitrage zur populations-dynamik der Schleiereule *Tyto alba*. *Hercynia* 14: 303–351.

Schönn, S, Scherzinger, W., Exo, K.-M. & Ille, R. (1991) *Der Steinkauz*. Die Neue Brehm-Bücherei. Wittenberg Lutherstadt: A. Ziemsen Verlag.

Scott, D. (1979) Long-eared Owls and other owls taking Moorhens. *British Birds* 72: 436.

Scott, D. (1997) *The Long-eared Owl*. The Hawk and Owl Trust, London.

Seel, D.C. & Thomson, A.G. (1984) Bone flouride in predatory birds in the British Isles. *Environmental Pollution* (Series A) 36: 367–374.

Seel, D.C., Thomson, A.G. & Turner, J.C.E. (1983) Distribution and breeding of the Barn Owl (*Tyto alba*) on Anglesey, North Wales. *Bangor Occasional Paper No. 16*. ITE, Bangor.

Seidensticker, M.T., Flockhart, D.T.T., Holt, D.W. & Gray, K. (2006) Growth and plumage development of nestling Long-eared Owls. *The Condor* 108: 981–985.

Sergio, F. & Hiraldo, F. (2008) Intraguild predation in raptor assemblages: a review. *Ibis* 150 (Supplement 1): 132–145.

Sergio, F., Marchesi, L., Pedrini, P., Ferrer, M. & Penteriani, V. (2004) Electrocution alters the distribution and density of a top predator, the Eagle Owl *Bubo bubo*. *Journal of Applied Ecology* 41: 836–845.

Sergio, F., Marchesi, L., Pedrini, P. & Penteriani, V. (2007) Co-existence of a generalist owl with its intraguild predator: distance-sensitive or habitat-mediated avoidance? *Animal Behaviour* 74: 1607–1616.

Sharrock, J.T.R. (1976) *The Atlas of Breeding Birds in Britain and Ireland*. T & A D Poyser, Calton.

Shaw, G. (1995) Habitat selection by Short-eared Owls *Asio flammeus* in young coniferous forests. *Bird Study* 42: 158–164.

Shaw, G. & Dowell, A. (1989) Breeding by closely-related Barn Owls. *Ringing & Migration* 10: 98.

Shawyer, C.R. (1987) *The Barn Owl in the British Isles: Its Past, Present and Future*. The Hawk Trust, London.

Shawyer, C.R. (1998) *The Barn Owl*. Arlequin Press, Chelmsford.

Shawyer, C.R. & Dixon, N. (1999) *Impact of roads on Barn Owl Tyto alba populations*. Unpublished Report to the Highways Agency, London.

Shawyer, C.R. & Shawyer, V.M. (1995) *An investigation of the Barn Owl population within the Avon and Western Rother catchments*. The Hawk and Owl Trust Report, London.

Singheiser, M., Plachta, D.T.T., Brill, S., Bremen, P., van der Willigen, R.F. & Wagner, H. (2010) Target-approaching behaviour of Barn Owls (*Tyto alba*): influence of sound frequency. *Journal of Comparative Physiology* A 196: 227–240.

Smal, C.M. (1987) The diet of the Barn Owl (*Tyto alba*) in southern Ireland, with reference to a recently introduced prey species the Bank Vole (*Clethrionomys glareolus*). *Bird Study* 34: 113–125.

Smith, C.R. & Richmond, M.E. (1972) Factors influencing pellet egestion and gastric pH in the Barn Owl. *Wilson Bulletin* 84: 179–186.

Smith, T.L. (1925) Tawny Owl hatching fowl's eggs. *British Birds* 18: 80–81.

Sommer, R.S., Niederle, M., Labes, R. & Zoller, H. (2009) Bat predation by the Barn Owl *Tyto alba* in a hibernation site of bats. *Folia Zoologica* 58: 98–103.

Sonerud, G.A., Steen, R., Løw, L.M., Røed, L.T., Skar, K., Selås, V. & Slagsvold, T. (2012) Sex-biased allocation of prey from male to offspring via female: family conflicts, prey selection, and evolution of sexual size dimorphism in raptors. *Oecologia* online early.

Southern, H.N. (1954) Tawny Owls and their prey. *Ibis* 96: 384–410.

Southerm H.N. (1970) The natural control of a population of Tawny Owls (*Strix aluco*). *Journal of Zoology, London* 162: 197–285.

Southern, H.N., Vaughan, R. & Muir, R.C. (1954) The behaviour of young Tawny Owls after fledging. *Bird Study* 1: 101–110.

Speakman, J.R. (1991) The impact of predation by birds on bat populations in the British Isles. *Mammal Review* 21: 123–142.

Spencer, K.G. (1965) Avian casualties on railways. *Bird Study* 12: 257.

Starley, B. (1912) Long-eared Owl laying in a tenanted nest of Magpie. *British Birds* 6: 66–67.

Steinbach, M.J. & Money, K.E. (1973) Eye-movements of the owl. *Vision Research* 13: 889–891.

Stewart, J.S. (2007) The fossil and archaeological record of the Eagle Owl in Britain. *British Birds* 100: 481–486.

Sunde, P. (2008) Parent-offspring conflict over duration of parental care and its consequences in Tawny Owls *Strix aluco*. *Journal of Avian Biology* 39: 242–246.

Sunde, P., Bølstad, M.S. & Desfor, K.B. (2003a) Diurnal exposure as a risk sensitive behaviour in Tawny Owls *Strix aluco*? *Journal of Avian Biology* 34: 409–418.

Sunde, P., Bølstad, M.S. & Møller, J.D. (2003b) Reversed sexual dimorphism in Tawny Owls, *Strix aluco*, correlates with duty division in breeding effort. *Oikos* 101: 265–278.

Sunde, P. & Markussen, B.E.N. (2005) Using counts of begging young to estimate post-fledging survival in Tawny Owls *Strix aluco*. *Bird Study* 52: 343–345.

Sutcliffe, S. (1990) The food of the Little Owls on Skomer Island. *Pembrokeshire Bird Report* 1989: 24–26.

Tattersall, F.H., Macdonald, D.W., Hart, B.J., Manley, W.J. & Feber, R.E. (2001) Habitat use by Wood Mice (*Apodemus sylvaticus*) in a changeable arable landscape. *Journal of Zoology, London* 255: 487–494.

Taylor, I. (1991) The dynamics of a cyclic predator-prey system: the Barn Owl *Tyto alba* and the Field Vole *Microtus agrestis*. *Ibis* 133: 134–135.

Taylor, I. (1994) *Barn Owls: predator-prey relationships and conservation*. Cambridge University Press, Cambridge.

Taylor, I.R. (2002). Occupancy in relation to site quality in Barn Owls (*Tyto alba*) in south Scotland. pp. 28–39 *in* Newton, I., Kavanagh, R., Olsen, J. & Taylor, I. (2002). *Ecology and Conservation of Owls*. Proceeedings of the Owls 2000 Conference. CSIRO Publishing, Collingwood, Australia.

Thomas, N.J., Hunter, D.B. & Atkinson, C.T. (2007) *Infectious diseases of wild birds*. Blackwell Publishing, Oxford.

Thorpe, W.H. & Griffin, D.R. (1962) The lack of ultrasonic components in the flight noise of owls compared with other birds. *Ibis* 104: 256–257.

Thorup, K., Sunde, P., Jacobsen, L.B. & Rahbek, C. (2010) Breeding season food limitation drives population decline of the Little Owl *Athene noctua* in Denmark. *Ibis* 152: 803–814.

Ticehurst, C.B. (1939) On the food and feeding habits of the Long-eared Owl (*Asio otus otus*). *Ibis* 17: 512–520.

Ticehurst, N.F. & Hartley, P.H.T. (1948) Report on the effect of the severe winter of 1946–7 on birds. *British Birds* 41: 322–334.

Tome, D. (2000) Estimating individual weight of prey items for calculation of the biomass in the diet of Long-eared Owl (*Asio otus*): is it worth the extra efforts. *Folia Zoologica* 49: 205–210.

Tome, D. (2003) Nest site selection and predation driven despotic distribution of breeding Long-eared Owls *Asio otus*. *Journal of Avian Biology* 34: 150–154.

Tome, D. (2011) Post-fledging survival and dynamics of dispersal in Long-eared Owls *Asio otus*. *Bird Study* 58: 193–199.

Tomé, R., Santos, N., Cardia, P., Ferrand, N. & Korpimäki, E. (2005) Factors affecting the prevalence of blood parasites of Little Owls *Athene noctua* in southern Portugal. *Ornis Fennica* 82: 63–72.

Toms, M.P. (1994) Small mammals in agricultural landscapes. *The Raptor* 21: 57–59.

Toms, M.P. (1997) *Project Barn Owl – evaluation of an annual monitoring programme.* BTO Research Report 177, British Trust for Ornithology, Thetford.

Toms, M.P., Crick, H.Q.P. & Shawyer, C.R. (2000) *Project Barn Owl Final Report.* BTO Research Report 197. British Trust for Ornithology, Thetford.

Toms, M.P., Crick, H.Q.P. & Shawyer, C.R. (2001) The status of breeding Barn Owls *Tyto alba* in the UK, 1995–97. *Bird Study* 48: 23–37.

Toms, M.P. (2002). Barn Owl. pp. 426–428 *in* Wernham, C., Toms, M., Marchant, J., Clark, J., Siriwardena, G. & Baillie, S. (2002). *The Migration Atlas: Movements of the Birds of Britain and Ireland.* Poyser, London.

Toms, M.P. (2009) Eagle Owls in Britain: origins and conservation implications. *British Wildlife* 20: 405–412.

Townsend, M.G., Fletcher, M.R., Odam, E.M. & Stanley, P.I. (1981) An assessment of the secondary poisoning of Warfarin to Tawny Owls. *Journal of Wildlife Management* 45: 242–248.

Trimnell, H.C. (1945) Little Owls feeding young on newts. *British Birds* 38: 174–175.

Tryon, C.A. (1943) The Great Grey Owl as a predator on pocket gophers. *The Wilson Bulletin* 55: 130–131.

Tubbs, C.R. (1974) *The Buzzard.* David & Charles, Newton Abbot.

Tulloch, R.J. (1968) Snowy Owls breeding in Shetland in 1967. *British Birds* 61: 119–132.

Tulloch, R.J. (1969) Snowy Owls breeding in Shetland. *British Birds* 62: 33–36.

Ullrich, B. (1980) Zur populationsdynamik des Steinkauzes (*Athene noctua*). *Vogelwarte* 30: 179–198.

Underwood, B. (1995) Escaped or released Eagle Owls? *Yorkshire Birding* 4: 60–61.

Vickers, H.S. (1935) Little Owl's nest under railway. *British Birds* 28: 84–85.

Viitala, J., Korpimäki, E., Palokangas, P. & Koivula, M. (1995) Attraction of kestrels to vole scent marks visible in ultraviolet light. *Nature* 373: 425–427.

Village, A. (1981) The diet and breeding of Long-eared Owls in relation to vole numbers. *Bird Study* 28: 215–224.

Village, A. (1987) Numbers, territory size and turnover of Short-eared Owls, *Asio flammeus*, in relation to vole abundance. *Ornis Scandinavica* 18: 198–204.

Wagner, H. & Schaeffel, F. (1991) Barn Owls (*Tyto alba*) use accommodation as a distance cue. *Journal of Comparative Physiology* 169: 515–521.

Walker, L.A., Llewellyn, N.R., Pereira, M.G., Potter, E.D., Sainsbury, A.W. & Shore, R.F. (2012) *Anticoagulant rodenticides in predatory birds 2010: a Predatory Bird Monitoring Scheme (PBMS) report.* Centre for Ecology and Hydrology, Lancaster.

Walker, L.A., Turk, A., Long, S.M., Wienburg, C.L., Best, J. & Shore, R.F. (2008) Second generation anticoagulant rodenticides in Tawny Owls (*Strix aluco*) from Great Britain. *Science of the Total Environment* 392: 93–98.

Walsh, P.M. (1984) Diet of Barn Owls at an urban Waterford roost. *Irish Birds* 2: 437–444.

Walsh, P.M. & Sleeman, D.P. (1988) Avian prey of a wintering Short-eared Owl population in south-west Ireland. *Irish Birds* 3: 589–591.

Walter, G. & Hudde, H. (1987) Die Gefiederfliege *Carnus hemapterus* (Milichiidae, Diptera) ein Ektoparasit der Nestlinge. *Journal für Ornithologie* 128: 251–255.

Watson, D. (1977). *The Hen Harrier.* T & A D Poyser, Berkhamstead, Hertfordshire.

Watson, J. (1997) *The Golden Eagle.* T & A D Poyser, London.

Webster, J.A. (1973) Seasonal variation in mammal content of Barn Owl castings. *Bird Study* 20: 185–196.

Wernham, C., Toms, M., Marchant, J., Clarke, J., Siriwardena, G. & Baillie, S. (2002). *The Migration Atlas: movements of the birds of Britain and Ireland.* Poyser, London.

Wijnandts, H. (1984) Ecological energetics of the Long-eared Owl. *Ardea*, 72: 1–92.

Williams, K. (1964) Tawny Owls feeding young on fish. *British Birds* 57: 202.

Williams, R.S.R. (1996) *Ecology and population dynamics of the Long-eared Owl Asio otus.* PhD Thesis, University of East Anglia.

van der Willigen, R.F. (2011) Owls see in stereo much like humans do. *Journal of Vision* 11: 1–27.

van der Willigen, R.F., Frost, B.J. & Wagner, H. (2002) Depth generalization from stereo to motion parallax in the owl. *Journal of Comparative Physiology* A 187: 997–1007.

Wilson, J.E. & MacDonald, J.W. (1967) *Salmonella* infection in wild birds. *Veterinary Journal* 123: 212–219.

Wink, M., Heidrich, P., Sauer-Gürth, H., Elsayed, A-A. & Gonzalez, J. (2008) Molecular phylogeny and systematics of owls (Strigiformes). pp 42–63 in König, C. & Weick, F. (2008). *Owls of the World,* 2nd Edition. Christopher Helm, London.

Witherby, H.F., Jourdain, F.C.R., Ticehurst, N.F. & Tucker, B.W. (1938) *The Handbook of British Birds.* Volume 2. H F & G Witherby, London.

Wroot, A.J. (1985) A quantitative method for estimating the amount of earthworm (*Lumbricus terrestris*) in animal diets. *Oikos* 44: 239–242.

Wyllie, I., Dale, L. & Newton, I. (1996) Uneven sex-ratio, mortality causes and pollutant residues in Long-eared Owls in Britain. *British Birds* 89: 429–436.

Yalden, D.W. (1977) *The identification of remains of owl pellets.* Mammal Society, Reading.

Yalden, D.W. (1985) Dietary separation of owls in the Peak District. *Bird Study* 32: 122–181.

Yalden, D.W. & Albarella, A. (2009). *The History of British Birds.* Oxford University Press, Oxford.

Yalden, D.W. & Warburton, A.B. (1979) The diet of the Kestrel in the Lake District. *Bird Study* 26: 163–170.

Yom-Tov, Y. & Wool, D. (1997) Do the contents of Barn Owl pellets accurately represent the proportion of prey species in the field? *The Condor* 99: 972–976.

Zaccaroni, A., Amorena, M., Naso, B., Castellani, G., Lucisano, A. & Stracciari, G.L. (2003) Cadmium, chromium and lead contamination of *Athene noctua*, the Little Owl, of Bologna and Parma, Italy. *Chemosphere* 52: 1251–1258.

Zens, K.-W. (2005) *Langstudie (1987–1997) zur Biologie, Ökologie und Dynamik einer Steinkauzpopulation* (Athene noctua Scoploi 1769) *im Lebensraum der Mechenicher Vpreifel.* Dissertation zur Erlangung des Doktorgrades der Mathematisch-Naturwissenschaftlichen Fakultätc der Rheinischen Friedrich-Wilhelm-Universität Bonn.

Zhou, Z. & Zhang, F. (2002) A long-tailed, seed-eating bird from the Early Cretaceous. *Nature* 418: 405–409.

Zuberogoitia, I., Zabala, J., Martínez, J.A., Hildago, S., Martínez, J.E., Azkona, A. & Castillo, I. (2007) Seasonal dynamics in social behaviour and spacing patterns of the Little Owl *athene noctua. Ornis Fennica* 84: 173–180.

Index

The New Naturalist Library